PIETY AND REBELLION

Essays in Ḥasidism

New Perspectives in Post-Rabbinic Judaism

Series Editor: Shaul Magid (Indiana University, Bloomington)

PIETY AND REBELLION

Essays in Ḥasidism

SHAUL MAGID

Boston
2019

Library of Congress Cataloging-in-Publication Data

Names: Magid, Shaul, 1958- author.
Title: Piety and rebellion : essays in Hasidism / Shaul Magid.
Description: Boston : Academic Studies Press, 2019. | Series: New perspectives in post-Rabbinic Judaism
Identifiers: LCCN 2018057559 (print) | LCCN 2018058640 (ebook) | ISBN 9781618117526 (ebook) | ISBN 9781618117519 (hardcover)
Subjects: LCSH: Hasidism–History.
Classification: LCC BM198.3 (ebook) | LCC BM198.3 .M34 2019 (print) | DDC 296.8/332–dc23
LC record available at https://lccn.loc.gov/2018057559

ISBN 978-1-64469-115-1
ISBN 978-1-61811-752-6 (electronic)

Design and Typeset by Lapiz Digital Services
On the cover: Salvador Dalí,
"For That Is Thy Life," 1968, lithograph.
Reproduced by permission.

Published by Academic Studies Press
28 Montfern Avenue
Brighton, MA 02135,
USA
P: (617)782-6290
F: (857)241-8936
press@academicstudiespress.com
www.academicstudiespress.com

For Kinneret,

on her eighteenth birthday

may you find both piety and rebellion in everything you do

Contents

Acknowledgments

Most of the essays in this volume were written over the course of about twenty years. At Brandeis University, where I completed my doctorate, I was privileged to study with Michael Fishbane who taught us how to read canonical texts both creatively and subversively in a way that made these essays possible. During that time, I was privileged to teach at three institutions of higher education; Rice University, the Jewish Theological Seminary of America, and Indiana University/Bloomington. Each institution gave me distinctive perspectives on the nature of scholarship more generally and on the work included in this volume. Those I would like to thank at these three institutions, colleagues and students, are too numerous to list. I do want to acknowledge Martin Kavka, Steven Hood, and Adam Black who attended my first on-going seminar in Nahman of Bratslav during my tenure at Rice from 1994–1996, each offering insight into their own thinking about this Ḥasidic master. I would also like to mention Talya Fishman and David Nirenberg, colleagues at Rice who welcomed me into academia and whose insights still resonate with me more than twenty years later. At JTS I greatly benefitted from many of my colleagues including Neil Gilman and Seth Schwartz who were constant conversation partners in the cafeteria and beyond. To the many rabbinical students who attended my seminars in Kabbalah and Ḥasidism at JTS, you have taught me much that I retain to this day and your work continues to inspire me as I follow your careers. Thanks to Aubrey Glazer who has always offered his unique perspective and caused me to re-think mine. At Indiana I have greatly benefited from many of my colleagues and students, including Steven Weitzman, Jeffrey Veidlinger, Mark Roseman, Michael Morgan, Constance Furey, Winnifred Sullivan, Sarah Imhoff, Barbara Krawcowicz, Jessica Carr, and Brian Hillman. I want to thank Menachem Butler for his encouragement and to Daniel Reiser and Don Seeman for inviting me to a conference in Warsaw on R. Kalonymous Kalman of Piasczeno that I could not attend but inspired me to write an essay on his wartime Torah. Elliot Wolfson continues to be a friend, an inspiration, and a source of support. To Aryeh Cohen, a constant *havruta* in all manner of work and life, and to Pinhas Giller, Eric Jacobson, and Eliyahu Stern for their sharp insight and enduring wit. To Eden Pearlstein for his poetry and passion, and to Basya Schechter for the soundtrack. I want to thank Nathaniel Berman for the years of learning on Fire Island including the pre-dawn study of the works of Nathan of Gaza. Thanks to Susannah Heschel for inviting me to teach at Dartmouth as the Brownstone Visiting Professor of Jewish Stusies and for all her support. I want to acknowledge Nancy Levene for the years together when some of these essays took shape. Her critical eye is on many of these pages.

The prehistory of these essays takes me back to my years as a *ḥaredi* Jew in Boro Park, Brooklyn, and Jerusalem where I was fortunate to learn from both teachers and friends. First of all, Dovid Din, my first teacher in Ḥasidism who I followed into the labyrinthine world of his own imagination, Moshe Mykoff, Baruch Gartner, today both great teachers of Ḥasidism, and master of Kabbalah, R. Mordechai Attiah with whom I studied Lurianic Kabbalah for three years in Jerusalem. And to R. Chaim Brovinder for his guidance and wisdom and for never letting us take ourselves too seriously.

Most of these essays have appeared in scholarly journals or collections and I want to thank each one for giving me permission to re-print these essays in this volume. They include NYU Press, Eerdman's Press, Indiana University Press, Harvard University Press, Ben Gurion University Press, and the Jewish Quarterly Review.

Thanks go to Igor Nemirovsky and Alessandra Anzani of Academic Studies Press for their undying support and special thanks to Hila Ratzabi for her keen editorial insight and poetic hand.

To my mother, who is always there for us, in all ways, my children Yehuda, Chisda, Miriam, Kinneret, Danielle and Galil, you are the true source of blessing. To Annette Yoshiko Reed, whose encouragement knows no bounds, and whose love exceeds all limits. This book would not have existed without her.

This book is dedicated to my daughter Kinneret for her eighteenth birthday. As you go out into the world I hope you find your passion, and may the words on these pages find some small place in your heart and in your life. May you always travel this world with both piety and rebellion.

September 17, 2018
Erev Yom Kippur
Lebanon, New Hampshire

Introduction

My Way to (Neo) Ḥasidism[1]

I

Alterity

Alterity. For me, as a young secular Jew from the flesh-pots of the New York suburbs, from Jewish Workman Circle summer camp and a mixed-race public school where popular culture was all that was sacred, that is what Ḥasidism and ḥasidic life represented: the promise of alterity. Of course, I had never even heard the word "Ḥasidism" until I was at least ten or eleven and, even then, only in books. The word was never uttered at home. Perhaps it is more accurate to say, then, that as long as I can remember, alterity more generally was something that intrigued me, the notion of living or being "otherwise," as Levinas taught me many years later. I saw myself as different, but not different enough to feel alienated, just different enough to feel like the suburban life I was experiencing was not all there was, and also was not enough. But being alienated was part of the counterculture I was reared in, so that alienation was itself that which produced cohesiveness.

It was in my teens when I first read Jack Kerouac's *On the Road* and came to realize alterity was something people actually embodied. It was a

1 I am intentionally not discussing my personal life in this introduction, including marriage and children, as I want to focus on the trajectory that brought me to Ḥasidism, led me away from it, and then brought me back again. This introduction seeks to frame the trajectory that led to the essays in this volume that were written over the course of the past twenty years or so.

short time between that first reading of Kerouac and when I drove off in my 1972 Volkswagen minibus on New Year's Eve 1977 that took me literally "on the road" to the mountains of New Mexico with no purpose other than to experience the feeling of being unbound, what I later came to know as the notion of "*lishma*": that wonderful experience where there is no place of arrival other than where you happen to stop at the end of the day. Of course, such freedom, even the possibility of such experiential liberation, is a privilege of a middle-class life with a safety net that was not fool-proof but strong enough so that you needn't worry that you would end up homeless and destitute with no one to call—the way Neal Cassidy ends up in flop houses on the Bowery or on the streets of Denver in *On the Road*. I did not have the courage to take it to that extreme but I played around the edges. Not exactly a hitchhiker with a credit card (there were plenty of those too) but certainly one with a phone number where people who loved you would likely answer, scold you, and then wire the necessary money to get you out of a jam. I remember some of those calls with both trepidation and gratitude. For some reason when I left home all my father gave me was a gas credit card, hoping, I assume, I would not run out of gas on some abandoned road on the fruited plain.

But the road to Jewish alterity for me began even earlier in my childhood, if only in my imagination. My paternal grandmother, an immigrant from the Pale of Settlement, used to take me on annual trips to places outside the bubble of New York. One year we visited what was then called "Amish country" in Pennsylvania. What struck me a child of the gilded suburbs was the simplicity—what the Amish call "plainness"—of their lives. It was perhaps my first real experience that it was possible to live "otherwise." The smell of hay, the rural rolling green hills, shoofly pie (an Amish delicacy made of molasses and pie crust), and the horse-drawn carts offered a world I hadn't known existed. The second memory was during trips to visit relatives in Brooklyn. We would often take the Brooklyn-Queens Expressway which runs right under the ḥasidic enclave of Williamsburg. As a child I recall getting glimpses of *ḥasidim* stroll on the overpass as we sped by underneath wondering who they were and how they lived. I knew I was a Jew and they were Jews but I could not understand what tied us together. The connection between *ḥasidim* and the Amish, and Christianity, remained strong throughout my childhood and even into adulthood, when I discovered Thomas Merton and became enthralled with monastic Christianity, or when I published an essay on the Mennonite theologian John Howard Yoder.

The door to Jewish alterity may have first appeared to me explicitly as a child of about ten or eleven when I read Chaim Potok's *My Name is Asher*

Lev at the behest of my mother, whose suggestion was based on artistic talents that I exhibited as a burgeoning adolescent. At that time, and perhaps until about 16, if I seriously thought about my future it was likely as a painter. Inadvertently, *Asher Lev* also introduced me to the strange and compelling world of Ḥasidism. But also, Ḥasidism as rebellion, not against the world but against itself. The final scene in the book, the ultimate moment of ḥasidic rebellion, was when Asher Lev, having already left his ḥasidic world for the art world in Greenwich Village, paints a large crucifixion. And the man hanging on the cross is none other than his ḥasidic father. Many years later I would publish a book, *Ḥasidism Incarnate*, and use Marc Chagall's "Yellow Crucifix" as the cover, having no recollection of that final scene in *Asher Lev* that was so arresting to me as a young boy.

This sense of Ḥasidism as alterity occurred to me, decades later, soon after I moved to Boro Park, Brooklyn, to study in *yeshivah* and begin my life as a *ḥaredi* Jew. I was walking down a side street one evening in autumn and happened upon one of the many ḥasidic synagogues in the neighborhood. On the outside wall there was a sign announcing a *shi'ur* (Torah class) by a well-known rabbi. In English and Yiddish the sign read: "Come hear this great sage, Mozei Shabbos, parshat Noah." What struck me was not the rabbi, who I had never heard of, or even "Mozei Shabbos" which in Boro Park is simply Saturday night. What struck me was there was no date given except "parshat Noah." I realized that in this world, time was marked not by the English calendar and not even by the Jewish calendar but by the Torah reading that will be read in synagogue that week. All the Jews in Boro Park knew the date by the *parashah* of the week. A non-Jew passing by, or even a secular Jew from the outside, would not know the date of this lecture. There was an experience of alterity in that moment that was exhilarating. Time marked only by Torah—in the middle of New York City.

II

Macrobiotic New Mexico, the Holy Land, and the Holy

After a brief stint living in Albuquerque after dropping out of college in 1977, I moved north near Santa Fe, and I found myself living in a macrobiotic impromptu commune of sorts in the small hamlet called Galisteo, populated mostly by Native Americans, Mexicans, a few old-timers, and hippies. It was in Santa Fe where I came to know Bill Rosenberg, a New York Jew who was a practicing acupuncturist and macrobiotic healer who had lived for a short time in Denver, where he came across Rabbi Shlomo Twersky, an iconoclastic ḥasidic rabbi who had attracted many *ba'alei teshuvah* to his small circle. The Twersky family rose to notoriety in Chernobyl in the late eighteenth century with a ḥasidic master Menahem Nahum Twersky. The dynasty then migrated to Tolne, Skvere, and other locales before settling in America and Palestine/Israel. In America one branch of the family settled in Milwaukee and then moved to cities like Pittsburgh and Boston. Rosenberg had touched Judaism lightly in those days, and being the only two Jews in our small circle we bonded and remain in touch to this day. Bill is now Ze'ev Rosenberg, an Orthodox Jew who teaches Eastern medicine at the Pacific College of Oriental Medicine in San Diego. Rosenberg played an important role for me because he gave me what was perhaps my first Jewish book in about 1977, a copy of the recently published *Fragments of a Future Scroll* by a rabbi named Zalman Schachter (later Schachter-Shalomi). A meandering hodgepodge of reflections, translations, and inspirational writing, *Fragments* was my first entry into the literary world of Ḥasidism , admittedly through a neo-ḥasidic lens. Studying macrobiotics and oriental medicine had primed me for what was to come, but it was *Fragments* that made me decide to take my minibus back east and make some money to visit the strange country called Israel that I knew nothing about.

I returned to Manhattan some time that spring. Working as a street messenger by day and a dishwasher in a macrobiotic restaurant by night and sleeping on a futon on the floor in my parents' modest Manhattan apartment, I soon saved enough to buy a one-way ticket to Israel with no definite plan to return. As a child I knew nothing about Israel. My family were Workman Circle people and much of what I knew about being Jewish came from attending the Workman Circle Camp Kinder Ring on Sylvan Lake, near Hopewell Junction, NY. We rarely if ever spoke about Israel, learned Yiddish and not Hebrew, and knew more about socialism than Zionism. So when I boarded the plane to Israel I carried no ideological baggage at all, something friends later have attributed to the ease with which I was able to adopt a leftist political stand on matters of Israeli politics and policies.

Over the course of a few months travelling alone and with some people I met on the way, I came upon a small group of young *yeshivah* students very much like myself, who happened to also be macrobiotic. On their prodding I attended a few classes in a run-down yet charming building that housed the Beit Joseph Novordok *yeshivah* on Shmuel ha-Navi Street in Jerusalem. The *yeshivah* where I was attending—known as "Brovinders," led by an American rabbi, Chaim Brovinder—was renting space from the Novordok *yeshivah* which consisted of a few dozen seemingly ill-adjusted pale-skinned students who seemed to come straight out of a Roman Vishniac photograph. The founder of this group was an ascetic man in Russia named R. Yosef Yuzel of Novordok (1847–1919), a by-product of the Mussar movement of R. Israel Salanter. Known for their ascetic practices and introverted piety, Novordokers were strange birds even in a fairly strange world. My most vivid memory of them was that fifteen minutes before *minḥah* (the afternoon prayer recited at 1pm in many *yeshivot* before lunch) they would close their *gemaras* (talmudic tractates), gather in the front of the cavernous sanctuary, and engage in an act of collective crying. It was actually quite startling to witness a group of young men crying together, bemoaning their unworthiness and blemished selves, imperfect servants of God trying to stay away from the temptations that swarmed all around them. Many of us Americans smirked at such overt piety but I secretly admired it.

I began to attend classes in the *yeshivah* more frequently until I enrolled full-time and moved in with the group of friends living in a small apartment in new *ḥaredi* neighborhood, Sanhedria Murkhevet, about a 20-minute walk from the *yeshivah*. Without realizing it I had become a *yeshivah* student, cut my hair, removed my earring, and delved into the bizarre and fascinating world of the Mishnah and Talmud. I came with no background in Hebrew and thus struggled massively during that period, but those around me were kind, helpful, and compassionate. In particular, Rabbi Brovinder become a mentor for me; his intellectual rigor and biting sense of humor kept us sane in a world that otherwise appeared like a parallel universe to many of us. He taught us how to "learn," how to think inside a talmudic *sugya*, and also how to not take ourselves too seriously, the last being the most challenging for many of us. In those years (the late 1970s) the *ba'al teshuvah* movement was still in its heyday, Jerusalem was an open city (walking through east Jerusalem at night was not something we worried about), Israel was cheap (it had not yet moved from the Lira to the Shekel), and private telephones were rare. We had no televisions, and radio was useless since we were not yet fluent in modern Hebrew. We felt blessedly cut off from our American roots and lived a kind of reflexive orientalist existence in a world that resembled that of our great-grandparents and not our parents. I smelled the fragrance of alterity in the multi-ethnic Jerusalem neighborhood of Bukharim where we hung around after classes ended, a neighborhood that housed both the austere Novordok *yeshivah* and the hedonistic Turkish baths.

The four or five people I lived with became close friends. They were all students of some enigmatic and mysterious ḥasidic rabbi who lived in

America named Dovid Din. They spoke of "Dovid" with a rare combination of intimacy and reverence, telling stories about his intense pious behaviors, such as praying the morning service for three hours or his long daily immersions on the mikveh, and about his bad teeth. Tales of his brilliant Torah discourses that spanned the spectrum from the sixteenth-century kabbalistic teaching of Isaac Luria to the poetry of William Blake or the Sufi poet Rumi. He was also a strict macrobiotic. He had sent his "boys" (as he called them) to Jerusalem to become literate in Talmud and codes. Intrigued by these stories I became a kind of vicarious student to this unknown teacher, and after some time I realized I needed to meet him.

There were a variety of reasons I first left Jerusalem that spring but meeting Dovid was certainly one of them. Returning to Manhattan I had no immediate plans and spent some time studying shiatsu massage at the Shiatsu Center in Manhattan. I was also able to get the address of a place where Dovid was teaching in Brooklyn and made my way there to meet what for me had already become a mythic figure. My first memory of him is a bit vague. He was giving a class in an unaesthetic study house in Flatbush with oil-cloth tablecloths and fluorescent lights. He was indeed an ethereal figure, almost transparent, dressed in Satmar-style ḥasidic garb (including stockings and knee-length pants) and wearing a scarf in the early summer. After the class I went to introduce myself. He seemed to recognize my name as my Jerusalem friends must have mentioned me, but he made no indication of any interest in who I was. Just another traveler passing through, he assumed. "Ah yes, I heard about you," he almost whispered. "*Shalom aleikhem*," he said, and put out his white, bony, and very feminine hand.

I was resolute to make myself known to him and began attending meetings more frequently, befriending some of the misfits and vagabonds who often frequented his classes. It was a ḥasidic underworld of sorts, lost souls wandering the streets of lower Manhattan looking for some Jewish satori. Then there were a few middle-aged female university professors who saw something in Dovid that we didn't. A few of them became his benefactors. There were also some "normal" ḥasidic Jews who came as well, but they showed little interest in us and we had nothing really to say to them. In their world we were interlopers, Dovid serving as the bridge that each crossed with caution to meet the other. Even then those ḥasidic enclaves had an underbelly, those who occupied the margins, looking for something more than what their communities could offer.

After a month or two I realized I had to make a decision. I was still living with my parents in Manhattan and spending more and more time in Brooklyn. I had been toying with religious observance but wasn't sure it was something I could maintain. It was ḥol *ha-mo'ed* (the intermediate days) of Sukkot, 1979. I woke up in a sweat with a high fever. Sitting up suddenly in bed it hit me. My time here was over. I needed to move to Brooklyn and immerse myself in the world of Torah.

III

The Ḥasidic Underground and Yeshivah Life

Life in Boro Park, Brooklyn, was a macabre experience of living in an alternative universe that was a subway ride away from a city that offered everything. I lived in a dilapidated house in a mixed ḥasidic and Hispanic neighborhood on the outskirts of Boro Park that Dovid had one lived in with his family before moving to the other side of Boro Park. They may have been evicted. One was never quite sure who was actually living in that house. Some of those I knew from Jerusalem had returned and then a variety of other stragglers, vagrants, hangers-on, or those simply travelling through inhabited that house at various times. If there was space on the floor we could accommodate one more. Both the ḥasidic and Hispanic neighbors were equally baffled as to who we were and what we were doing there. We were robbed many times, but the intruders eventually gave up because we had nothing worth stealing. One of the most memorable robberies happened while we were eating the third meal on Shabbat, singing ḥasidic *niggunim* together as the sky darkened. Little did we know that as we were singing, burglars had broken into a back room and stolen the backpack of someone who had just arrived from Jerusalem. The only thing of value, or that which we most lamented, were some tabs of LSD that were lost forever. I hope our Hispanic brothers and sisters had a nice trip.

I first began studying in a small study house in Crown Heights with a young Lubavitcher *ḥasid* named Baruch Wertzburger. I was contemplating moving to Crown Heights to attend Yeshivat Hadar Torah. Ḥabad seemed liked a logical choice as it was much more structured than the more diffuse world of Boro Park, mirroring the more disciplined and conformist world of Ḥabad and the more free-flowing world of Polish Ḥasidism. I even packed all my things in my small Mazda to move into the dorms in Crown Heights. I arrived late at night, parked my car on Eastern Parkway and spent the night in the *yeshivah* without unpacking. In the morning I walked around and decided it wasn't for me. So instead of unpacking my car I just pulled away and drove back to Boro Park. Ḥabad Ḥasidism was compelling and uplifting, but there was something about the rebbe worship in Ḥabad that turned me off. I attended numerous Farbrengens with the Lubavitcher rebbe and the intensity was enormous as he carried the room with his charisma, but day-to-day Crown Heights just seemed too cultish for me. Boro Park was more eclectic and more dysfunctional. I liked that. I continued coming to Crown Heights daily to Wertzburger's small classes in Ḥabad Ḥasidism, beginning with *Sefer ha-Tanya* and then reading through some of the present rebbe's *siḥot*. My Hebrew was getting much better and I began to get the map of the terrain of ḥasidic texts.

Eventually I needed a bigger *yeshivah* with more subjects of study. I stumbled upon a new *yeshivah* in Flatbush run by two *roshei yeshivah*, one a Lakewood-trained *rosh yeshivah* named R. Chaim Friedman, proficient in the Lithuanian style of learning, and the second a Satmar *ḥasid* named R. Yizhak Ashkenazi. Here I spent a little more than two years really honing my skills in Gemara and *halakhah* and continued studying Ḥasidism and Kabbalah with Dovid and his circle (of which I had become by that time an inside member). Learning the Lithuanian method of Talmud by Rabbi Friedman and the broader rather than deep method popular among *ḥasidim* was illuminating. Rabbi Ashkenazi was perhaps the first person I met who really knew the entire Talmud by heart. He was from the Aleksander ḥasidic dynasty—people referred to him as the Alekser Rebbe—and he set up a small ḥasidic shul in the basement of his house. The Alekser dynasty was founded by R. Shraga Feivel of Gritsa, who was student of R. Yizhak Worka, a contemporary of R. Menahem Mendel of Kotzk. R. Ashkenazi's family had drifted to Satmar in America, but he retained the stature of ḥasidic aristocracy and was viewed by others with reverence. *Ḥasidim* often wandering in the *yeshivah* to ask him questions or ask for money. He took a special liking to a few of us, especially me, perhaps because he knew Dovid and also saw I was heading in the ḥasidic direction, whereas most of my classmates were not. My clothing had become more and more ḥasidic in style, I wore a black hat and suit and white shirt all the time, and unlike many others in the *yeshivah* I was interested in Ḥasidism. I was appointed his driver, mostly because I was the one who had a car and had the proper dress for the occasion. We spent many evenings traveling around Brooklyn and sometimes to New Jersey and Monsey, New York, a religious town in Rockland Country, to raise money (what is called *schnorring*). R. Ashkenazi was a master. On one occasion we sat at an ornate dining room table of a rich Jew in Monsey. Conversation ensued but the topic of money was never mentioned. Then at one point, the man took out a checkbook, wrote a check, and slid it across the table. Without a break in the conversation R. Ashkenazi looked at the check and with no expression, slid it back to the gentlemen. The conversation continued. This went on two or three times until R. Ashkenazi put the check with the "right" amount into his pocket. Then we got up, shook hands, and left. That is how it is done.

One other person worth mentioning from that *yeshivah* was a rabbi named Yona Frankel, probably in his thirties, a modern Orthodox rabbi who lived in Long Beach, Long Island, but traveled every day to Boro Park to teach *ba'alei teshuvah*. He viewed it as something wondrous, and I felt this was his kind of *pro bono* for the cause of Torah. I studied Mishnah and Talmud with him for about a year, and his patience still remains with me. My most vivid memory of him was the time he asked me to drive him to deliver a *hespid* (eulogy) for an elderly woman who had died. We entered the chapel in the funeral home and I took a seat in the front and began reciting psalms, which is the custom. R. Frankel began delivering a long and impassioned eulogy for this woman. At some point I turned my head to the audience behind me. There was only one woman sitting there, the dead woman's caretaker. The rest of the chapel was empty. R. Frankel had been delivering this passionate eulogy for this one woman, or maybe not even for her. I had never encountered such a person growing up.

At this time, my relationship with Dovid was deepening and I become one of his close disciples. I use the term "disciple" carefully, as that is what we were. He served as a rebbe and spiritual guide and we treated him as such. We did constitute a "family" of sorts and, in retrospect, we probably would have met the bar of being considered a cult, but we were so integrated into the *ḥaredi* community around us no one really noticed. Except one person.

In those days (the late 1970s) Aryeh Kaplan, who was already well known an Orthodox writer, lived on the outskirts of Boro Park. His books on Kabbalah had been published by Samuel Weiser, who owned a New Age press from Maine. This bothered some of the more conformist *ḥaredim* in Boro Park, and thus I think Kaplan's decision to live on the margins of Boro Park was more than symbolic. An ultra-Orthodox Jew of Sephardic descent, who was a *ba'al teshuvah* himself, and once served as a rabbi in a Conservative synagogue (which in Boro Park is basically the same as a church), Kaplan decided to stay on the margins of that world. A deeply pious man, he would have an open house after Friday night dinner, and we sometimes walked there to listen to him. The neighborhood was not safe at night, and thus going to Kaplan's home itself required a modicum of *emunah* (faith). His dining room was adorned with a series of bizarre oil paintings. At some point, with no training as an artist, Kaplan decided to refrain from study for a year and devote himself to painting. After the year he stopped and never painted again. Those paintings were the product of his experiment.

He would gesture to someone to ask him a question about the weekly Torah portion and then he would just spin off of that for what seemed like hours (it probably wasn't). In any event, Kaplan emphatically did not like Dovid. It was a kind of fissure in the scene because there was a lot of overlap in those years between Dovid and Kaplan. Kaplan saw something in Dovid he didn't trust, but he didn't know what. We just never mentioned Dovid in Kaplan's presence. Many years later Kaplan's intuitions about Dovid turned out to be right. He was hiding something.

During this time, I began to integrate more into the *ḥaredi* world even as we were always looked upon as different. But we were "walking the walk" so intensely, and seeing us at the mikveh at 5:30am on a freezing January morning before *davenning* made them respect us even as they probably would not allow us to marry their daughters. The quasi-monastic life we led was very conducive to me, and I began to feel like I was living like those Amish in Pennsylvania and the *ḥasidim* walking over the Brooklyn-Queens Expressway I had seen as a child. I felt like I had found some alterity. I was living "otherwise." I once got a phone call from a high school girlfriend. It happened to be Thanksgiving and she asked where I was eating Thanksgiving dinner. "Thanksgiving?" I responded. "Oh, I didn't know that." I smiled at that remark. I had found a way off the grid. She later told me she thought I was living in a crack house in south Brooklyn. Who in America doesn't know it's Thanksgiving? Welcome to ḥasidic Boro Park.

Ḥasidism opened itself to me as a textual tradition and a lived life simultaneously. I studied the texts and tried to live the life they professed, or expected. In the classic Augustinian sense, I took my return too far. I did not have the slight cynical edge many have who grow up in that world. Texts became an appendage: we carried them around (one always had a *sefer* with them in case they had a few minutes to open it), we read them on the subway, we spoke of them to friends in the street, at airports, on lines in supermarkets, at Shabbos tables. In those years I felt that studying Torah wasn't something we did, it was part of who we were. The line separating work from leisure did not exist. That itself was a kind of alterity. And yet we also lived it in subversive, countercultural ways. We allowed our past "hippie" lives a place at the table, as long as it played by the new rules. In that sense we had a secret from those around us. They had a right not to trust us. We were also interlopers, perhaps the worst kind, because we were offering a different rendering of their world, which seemed like a previous rendering of their world in terms of piety but a strange fruit culturally. Some of it came to the surface in culinary matters. We would bake whole wheat challah and rush it to our guests for Shabbos late Friday afternoon because we didn't eat processed flour. We introduced many *ḥasidim* to tofu, ginseng, vegetarianism, yoga, shiatsu, and health food. There were not many ḥasidic Jews in Boro Park who had tasted vegetarian *cholent* (a traditional hot Shabbat dish made of beans, potatoes, and meat) until we came around.

One of the great spaces of cultural syncretism in those years was a kosher macrobiotic restaurant on 6th street between 1st and 2nd avenue in Manhattan called Caldron's Well. It also had a small health food store right next door. These were the late 1970s when punk was widespread. On a given night at the Caldron one could find a table of *ḥasidim* talking Torah, a table of punks with pink mohawks and safety pins through their cheeks talking music, hippies with small disheveled kids, a *shidduch* date of straight-looking Orthodox Jews who had chosen the wrong kosher restaurant, a table of Hari Krishna folks, and next to them, black jazz musicians on a break from a gig a few blocks away talking Coltrane. The founder of the restaurant was Moshe Schlass, an ex-biker hippie who had become a Lubavitcher *ḥasid*, who was a kind of master of ceremonies of the bizarre syncretism he loved. He eventually moved to the Old City of Jerusalem, where he lives today, and left the restaurant to his first wife, who ran it for another decade until she had a child late in life and sold it. The Caldron was the main hangout for many of us in those years. We would sit there drinking bancha tea for hours and talk, learn, just breathe in the vibe of the East Village. We felt part of the counterculture and we secretly liked that. It was there I first met Yossi Klein Halevi, who was a one-time member of Meir Kahane's Jewish Defense League and also part of the wider circle of Dovid's "boys," who had started a hip newspaper called *The New Jewish Times*. The front page of the inaugural edition in the late 1970s had a split screen photo of people at a raucous punk rock show and Friday night *davenning* at the Bobov ḥasidic synagogue in Boro park—a study in comparative contrast. We felt like we were making a mark.

When I think about my exposure to ḥasidic texts, I realize the very notion of critical study of these texts was so foreign, so utterly odd in those days, that I never thought much about it. I suppose we had the typical insider's critique that those "scholars" could not really understand these texts, because a full understanding would require living the life, being "on the path," as they say. Decades later, as I have spent a good part of my academic career doing just that, I can still sense the difference, and there is still some small voice in me that says, "If you hadn't been *there* in some fashion, something would be missed here." I don't know if I believe it, and I also think those *there* miss something precisely because of that "thereness." In any case, I can, and do, study these texts in a variety of often contradictory ways. My own academic approach does not eschew the traditional approach in principle. In fact, in my work on Ḥasidism I try to show that, in many cases, the texts lend themselves to the undoing of the traditional ways of reading them. This is not to suggest I have unearthed any esoteric meaning or have disclosed any essential nature of Ḥasidism. Rather, it is to suggest that the texts themselves contain multivalent layers and the lens one chooses to use as a reader can yield a variety of results that the texts themselves can sustain, even though in some cases those readings may stand in contradiction to one another. Here deconstruction has served me as a useful tool. My own allergy to normative readings of these texts comes in part because at a certain time in my life I was convinced that was the only way to read them. In that sense, my readings are products of my own internal battle with normativity and innovation.

Even during my years in Boro Park and *ḥaredi* Jerusalem these texts we studied often seemed to some of us to rub against the grain of the world that used them as a template for life and practice. Perhaps that is because some of our teachers, like Dovid and Aryeh Kaplan, were teaching these texts in quite iconoclastic ways, not necessary by choice but by design. Neither had received the tradition from the inside alone, each came to it from the outside and then, gaining literacy in the tradition, began to teach themselves. Kaplan was much more adept textually and also more conservative, albeit not as pious, as Dovid. But in general, what was happening among the sub-cultural Boro Park *ba'alei teshvah ḥasidim* was a syncretistic exercise under the auspices of haredism. We were living the life, in many ways more fully than our ḥasidic neighbors, and we were spending the thousands of hours in study required to get our credentials. But we were a subculture. And although we would have denied it then, we were forming a new kind of neo-Ḥasidism.

This "movement" was being fed by Zalman Schachter, Shlomo Carlebach, the Diaspora Yeshiva Band, Ḥabad, Bratslav, and the orientalist veneration of Eastern Europe. We knew about Buber, Heschel, Gershom Scholem, and even Joseph Soloveitchik—but they didn't interest us that much. We felt we were in the belly of the beast, and their writings were for outsiders: they were modern, they were not countercultural enough. We would rather just study the ḥasidic texts they were studying and skip the scholars as intermediaries. We had no idea that they had value as more than interpreters of Ḥasidism. Years later, I learned how wrong I was.

IV

The Enigma of Over-Belief

Life with Dovid was hard. Besides being obstinate and stubborn, he moved very slowly and deliberately, and he demanded others do so as well. Thus being with him meant slowing down your body clock. He also had a bizarre lack of fear. I recall walking or driving with him on Houston Street in Manhattan late at night after classes he gave at the Charles Street Synagogue in the West Village in the early 1980s. Dovid would often ask me to pull over and wait for him as he got out of the car to give a wino or a junkie on the street all the money he had. Or being stopped at a red light by a panhandler and Dovid rolling down the window and handing him a $20 bill he got for his class as a donation. In those downtown neighborhoods, where we would go late at night to vegetable stands in Little Italy, Dovid was known by the winos and junkies as the "The Rabbi" because he would always give them money. Dovid was always on welfare, food stamps, etc.; he was real mendicant Jew, claiming his work was serving God. He wore black stockings and a long coat in the style of some ḥasidic Jews, and once when waiting on line at the Welfare Office, two black women on line ahead of him saw him, and one said to the other, "Girl, let that dude ahead of you in line. Look, the dude is so poor he ain't even got no pants!"

Davenning with Dovid could be uplifting and it could be maddening. He had a monastic cadence and took hours. Literally. And we all recited everything together in a kind of Tibetan or maybe closer to a Gregorian chant. Dovid had an amazing capacity for concentration and focus. Maybe more than I have ever witnessed. If you were able to tune into that wavelength it was exhilarating. If you were in a hurry, you felt like jumping out of the window.

We were once travelling together back from Israel to New York. We had an early morning flight and thus had to *daven* at Ben Gurion airport. Dovid refused to quicken his pace at all. It turned out the flight had almost completed boarding and he was still ending his *davenning.* I urged him to take off his tefillin and finish on the plane. He refused. By the time we arrived at the gate the attendant told us the gate was closed. I pleaded, and the woman finally agreed and let us go to the tarmac. A bus came to pick us up to bring us to the plane. When we arrived, security was standing in front of the steps to the plane and directed the driver not to open the door. On our way down I heard the woman upstairs complain to security that two ḥasidic Jews refused to finish their prayers and thus held up the flight. The plane door closed and we were driven back to the gate. I was furious. Dovid had no emotion whatsoever. He looked incredulous when I began to complain to him. "For something like this you are losing your temper?" Either the world conformed to his dictates or he gladly suffered the consequences.

We were redirected to a flight through Paris. When we arrived in Paris we found out there was an airport strike and no planes were departing. We had little money. We spent two days and two nights in the Paris airport drinking only water and eating only the peanuts that we had with us. Dovid refused to eat anything else because of *kashrut*. I was his disciple and I went along with his requests. But I was not happy about it. In those moments I felt like I had entered into the ḥasidic tales we read. Texts and life merged into one annoying mix. I learned that alterity has another side, that the extremism I romanticized often didn't take others into account, that piety too often trumped others who got in the way. It was an important lesson.

Learning with Dovid was both arduous and exhilarating. And here I think my initial understanding of Ḥasidism becomes apparent. The texts were not to be read, but one had to *make* Ḥasidism out of the Ḥasidism (and here I think Dovid was a master, even as he often read the texts wrong). That is, the texts were portals of ideas that one could read and explain and then do to them what they have just done to the tradition. I think Buber understood that better than Scholem. Scholem wanted to know what the texts said; Buber was interested in how they provide a template for how to think about serving God. Buber was not compelling for me at this early stage, because he was so intent on finding the essence he let external acts of piety through devotion dissipate. Buber wanted to create something really new. We were deeply enmeshed in the romanticism of the old. It was only years later that I began to see how deeply Buber understood this material. But secretly we too did not accept the old readings, and Dovid was offering something new—except his resistance to the tradition didn't go left but right. It was not that traditional norms demanded too much; it was that they did not demand enough. The kind of antinomianism of Buber became for Dovid a hypernomianism. *Halakhah* was just the beginning. He essentially became a Jewish monk (he was married and had a family but his devotional life was monastic). He answered Buber's move outward by a move inward to achieve a similar end, in my view. Buber would have understood Dovid more than Scholem would have.

Dovid didn't know Hebrew nearly as well as he thought he did. He knew it well enough; he could read Hebrew texts and explain them (often mispronouncing words but getting the meaning right). Many people who came from a traditional upbringing used to complain about Dovid's mispronunciations but were compelled enough by the content of what he said to return again and again. In any case, what the text was, or what the text said, took on more meaning once he began to expound on them. At that point the text became superfluous. In retrospect, some of it was second-rate New Ageism, but Dovid was really a poet by nature, and his use of language and imagery and his general education in the Humanities (he dropped out of college his senior year but had a Dylanesque ear for the poetic) enabled him to bring Nahman of Bratslav to life as if he was in conversation with Walt Whitman. Or Isaac Luria as if he were sitting with Rumi or Ibn Arabi. It was an interesting exercise. It's not that he actually quoted any of these non-Jewish sources very often. It is, rather, that his rendering of the texts we were reading were given a universal spiritualist appeal that spoke beyond the confines of their world. It was this unspoken synthesis that I think drew many of us to him; it enabled us to retain a part of the world we came from and not become swallowed up into a *ḥaredi* world that was often not very pious. And not very interesting, and certainly did not have the aesthetic ear many of us thought, or hoped, Judaism possessed. Most of the *ḥasidim* we lived amongst were just ordinary people who happen to be born into a particular community. Some of them were indeed true gems of piety and devotion but they were the exceptions. And we knew that.

We envisioned Dovid as a leader of a kind of New Age ḥasidic syncretistic Judaism that could be both ultra-Orthodox and spiritually open. Rav Abraham Isaac ha-Kohen Kook coined the phrase "behaviorally constricted and thoughtfully expansive." We never studied Kook, because Kook was a Zionist and Dovid identified more with the anti-Zionist Neturei Karta or Satmar types. Had Dovid read Rav Kook, stripped of his Zionism, he would have liked him.

Dovid attended many ecumenical retreats and spoke as easily with a Buddhist monk as with a Trappist novice. His justification was always that it is "*kiruv*," finding wayward Jews to bring them back to Judaism. But in retrospect, I think he needed to get out of the *ḥaredi* world he inhabited. He was far more critical of that world than he let us believe, but because they were largely clueless of what he was up to, and they provided a perfect place to hide, he remained part of that community. Looking back, I think my interest in comparative readings of ḥasidic texts with Christianity probably came from Dovid's spiritual ecumenicism that he got, in part, from Zalman Schachter years before. Dovid had worked for Zalman as a personal secretary when Zalman taught at the university in Winnipeg in the mid-1960s. After many of us left him in the mid-1980s Dovid began studying Christian theology with Ewert Cousins at Fordham University. Many years after Dovid died I inherited a few boxes of books on early Christianity and Gnosticism from the Fordham University library that were decades overdue. I still have some of them.

In those years a group of about eight of us lived in either Boro Park or Jerusalem. We usually had apartments in both places, and different combinations lived in either place. We were constantly going back and forth. One of the Boro Park houses was an old decrepit house on 42nd street off 10th avenue, on the outskirts of Boro Park in a mostly Latino neighborhood. Besides those of us who were permanent residents, that is, our names were on the lease, the house was consistently inhabited by a variety of vagrants, misfits, and all manner of *ḥaredi* and quasi-*ḥaredi* riffraff. One guy who looked a like one of Fagan's boys from *Oliver Twist* always rode around in a wheelchair (that he did not need), wearing fingerless gloves, terrorizing ḥasidic locals. Another was so OCD that we found him late at night one Friday night in the middle of a side street in Boro Park. He would not move because he noticed a piece of lint of his coat and, since one is not permitted to carry on Shabbat (Boro Park has no *eruv* that would permit carrying), he thought he could not continue walking without "carrying" the piece of lint. And he could not brush it off because it was "*muksa*" (something that one cannot touch on Shabbat because it has no use). He was determined to stand there until Shabbat ended twenty hours later! It took us a full 30 minutes to convince him he was permitted to walk home with the lint on his coat. There are many other such bizarre incidents, but this suffices to give you a sense of the world I'd entered into.

V

Aliyah and Kabbalah

I finally moved to Jerusalem permanently in 1981. In part it was to break from Dovid and in part to settle into a more conventional *ḥaredi* life in the Holy Land. I had no Zionist affiliations or aspirations whatsoever. I lived in a small apartment in the Old City of Jerusalem with a close friend without any electricity or hot water. We didn't pay the bill and they shut off the utilities, and we realized we didn't really need them. We went to sleep when it got dark and awoke around 4am to go to the mikveh and then *daven* with the sunrise (*vatikin*) at the kotel every morning. We lived downstairs from a kabbalist named R. Mordecai Sheinberger who had a kabbalistic *yeshivah*, Kol Yehuda, in the Old City. R. Sheinberger was from the Ashlag school of Kabbalah. Yehuda Ashlag (1885–1954) was a Polish kabbalist who moved to Jerusalem in 1922. He was somewhat of an iconoclast and is mostly well known for his commentary to the Zohar entitled *Ha-Sulam* (The Ladder). He also published a popular book called *Talmud Eser Sefirot* (*On the Ten Sefirot*) that became popular among Phillip Berg and The Kabbalah Centre people (Berg was a student of R. Yehuda Zvi Brandwein, a student of Ashlag). Dovid often used that book in some of his classes. We used to eat Shabbat dinner at the Sheinberger's every Shabbat, a beautiful but very poor family with many children. My roommate Baruch Gartner, now a well-known teacher of Ḥasidism in Jerusalem, and I asked R. Sheinberger to teach us. He said his schedule was very busy but if we woke him up at 2am he would study with us until it was time for the morning *davenning*. So about four nights a week we would walk up one flight of stairs and lightly knock on his door at 2am and he would answer in a bathrobe and we would sit and study Zohar and Ashlag for a few hours. We did this through one entire winter.

I later studied Lurianic Kabbalah with R. Mordecai Attiah, a Syrian kabbalist from the Shalom Sharabi tradition who was very antagonistic toward Sheinberger and the Ashlag school. The original Sharabi (1720–1777) was a Yemenite kabbalist who immigrated to Palestine, where he founded the Beit El *yeshivah* in the Old City. The *yeshivah* building still stands, but the *yeshivah* moved to the Zikhron Moshe neighborhood at some point. He was one of the most celebrated kabbalists of the Lurianic school and composed the first comprehensive *siddur* with mystical intentions according to Lurianic teaching. His tradition lives on today in Nahar Shalom *yeshivah* in the Nahla'ot neighborhood on Jerusalem that was led, when I was there in the 1980s, by R. Mordecai Sharabi (no relation to Shalom Sharabi). R Attiah's grandfather, also named Mordecai Attiah, who was a study-partner with Rav Kook, came from the Sharabi tradition, and so the younger R. Mordecai Attiah who I studied with was a part of that tradition. They did not look kindly upon the Ashlageans, thinking them a diluted and mistaken interpretation of Luria. When I began studying with R. Attiah my relationship with R. Sheinberger ended. They often sparred over publishing rights to various editions of kabbalistic texts and could barely hear the other's name mentioned.

I studied with R. Attiah for about three years. I entered the *yeshivah* wanting to study Lurianic Kabbalah. I asked him if I could enter his closed *shi'ur* every afternoon from 4pm to 6pm. He assigned me texts to prepare for the *shi'ur* with his father R. Eliyahu Attiah, a sweet and learned man who knew the entire *Tanakh* by heart. Recite the first words of any verse and he could finish it without a mistake. We sat for a few hours and prepared the material. I recall we were studying a book called *Da'at Tevunot* of the Ben Ish Hai, R. Yosef Hayyim (1835–1909), a late nineteenth-century Baghdadi kabbalist. At 3pm I dutifully entered the room, which consisted of tables set up in a big square, each person taking his appointed seat. It was a mix of people from the *yeshivah* and various students of the grandfather for years, who worked in menial jobs. One was a bank clerk, and one was an old Jew with a long white beard named Yehezkel who was an exterminator. He arrived every afternoon with this grey exterminating uniform and equipment. When there was a particularly difficult question in the text R. Attiah always deferred to Yehezkel, who had studied for many years with R. Attiah's grandfather and was a master of this material, but always very humble. I felt it was a slice of old Jerusalem that few outsiders witnessed.

R. Attiah entered the room, shut the door, sat down, opened his book, looked at me and pointed toward the door. "Please leave," he said. Confused, and disappointed, I took my book and left. I told his father, who never attended the *shi'ur*, what had happened. He said, "Don't worry, we'll try again tomorrow." I repeated the same thing for over a week. I sat in my seat; he entered the room and summarily told me to leave. I was frustrated, but I really wanted to be part of the group. After about ten days or so, same story, he came in, sat down, opened the book, and looked at me. This time he smiled, stroked his beard, and then asked someone to read. I was in.

My time with R. Attiah was quite intense. I became very close with him and he rewarded my diligence with attention. He was not particularly enamored by Ḥasidism in general, and over time I began to alter my dress to be less ḥasidic. I retained my long *payot* but began to wear short coats and a more modern hat. I had become more immersed in Lurianic Kabbalah than Ḥasidism. Even after I left the *yeshivah* and then the Orthodox world, I still periodically go to visit him. On one visit I gave him a copy of my book on Lurianic Kabbalah, *From Metaphysics to Midrash*. He smiled and hugged me when I gave it to him, but I am quite certain he never read it. His spoken English was fine, but I cannot imagine he would have made the effort to read it. I hope it is still sitting somewhere on a shelf in his library. My understanding of ḥasidic texts was greatly enhanced by the years I studied with him. Since much of ḥasidic literature is based on the Lurianic system, knowing it as intimately as I did though his tutelage made me better prepared when ḥasidic literature became an academic profession.

During some of those years I would divide my time between Yeshivat ha-Mivtar, also known as "Brovinders," and R. Attiah's Yeshivat ha-Hayyim ve-ha-Shalom. I would study Gemara in the morning at Brovinders and Kabbalah in the afternoon with R. Attiah. R. Brovinder had a profound impact on me. In those years I was deeply invested in the *ḥaredi* life. And yet there was something about me that still felt outside. R. Brovinder was born and raised in Brooklyn in the heart of postwar Modern Orthodoxy. He studied with Rav Soloveitchik at Yeshiva University and immigrated to Israel with many from his world in the years following the Six-Day War. A brilliant talmudist and gifted teacher, he also received his PhD in Semitic languages at the Hebrew University, studying with the philologist Moshe Goshen-Gottstein. Although modern in every sense, he was a deep believer in the *yeshivah* as an institution and the world of the *yeshivah* as a place where true innovative scholarship could take place. He knew Dovid Din from those of us who attended his *yeshivah* and, while skeptical, he enjoyed the quirkiness and also the diligence that many of us exhibited inside the walls of his institution. If you studied hard and asked good questions, you won his respect.

At a certain point, intrigued by those of us who were devotees of ḥasidic texts, R. Brovinder decided to try his hand at it. Friday mornings in *yeshivah* are usually left for individual or elective study, as life turned to Shabbat by early afternoon. R. Brovinder established a Friday morning class in Nahman of Bratslav's *Likkutei MoHaRan*, one of the classic texts of early Ḥasidism. We thought it was a victory of sorts, getting this Litvak *rosh yeshivah* to study *Likkutei MoHaRan* with us. The *shi'ur* continued for a few years, and, looking back, it was pivotal for me as a student of Ḥasidism. It was the first time I had studied ḥasidic literature with someone who was outside the world of Ḥasidism. R. Brovinder read it as he would read any Jewish text, and one saw the joy he felt at realizing the interpretive genius of Nahman. While we felt we had some impact on him, it was really his approach that had a big impact on me. I learned what it was like to read a text outside its context, and not as a purely devotional act but as a critic as well. He later tried the same thing with Luria's *Eiẓ Ḥayyim*, but it was not successful. *Eiẓ Ḥayyim* requires a different set of skills and knowledge base than Ḥasidism. A *yeshivah*-trained *rosh yeshivah* with no real kabbalistic training could not easily crack the Lurianic nut. That itself was an interesting lesson for me as I moved forward.

For three years, from 1986–1989 we lived on Moshav Me'or Modi'im, a small communal town (*moshav*) near Lod founded in the late 1970s by disciples of Shlomo Carlebach. I think of it as there where I really began to understand how Carlebach's countercultural reading of ḥasidic texts served as the foundation for a certain kind of religiosity. And in some way I felt I had a window into seeing how ḥasidic communities are born years before they began to take shape. At that time, most of the members of the *moshav* were connected in some way Carlebach, who also had a house there and spent most of his summers using the *moshav* as his base of operations. There is much to write about life there and the people we lived with in close proximity, many of whom were and remain wonderful souls. But for my limited purpose here I learned to see how Ḥasidism in a "neo" register actually "worked" outside the normative framework of ḥasidic communities elsewhere.

It was there I experienced a different kind of ḥasidic focus on experience (*deveikut*), on camaraderie, on the shared sense of purpose that evolves from intense focus on one individual's view of the world, then the one I experienced in Boro Park or Me'ah She'arim. It was more close-knit, more countercultural, more confused in many ways, than traditional ḥasidic communities, and yet it contained an energy that was palpable and fructifying. Modi'im was also far less misogynist and paranoid than conventional ḥasidic communities. And I also experienced the way the focus on one charismatic leader creates all kinds of destructive elements and internal dissent. Yet at that time I remember thinking that in some way, that is the price, that the intensity and focus simply could not be generated and certainly not sustained without charisma. I learned many years later from Zalman Schachter-Shalomi that such charisma could transfer among various individuals within a community, that is, that the rebbe could be a function and not a person, what he called "rebbitude."

Modi'im differed from ḥasidic communities in other ways I found refreshing. Established ḥasidic courts read ḥasidic literature devotionally and try to emulate its values, but they are also very entrenched in habits and traditions developed long ago, and the communal structure is very invested in keeping them intact. This is part of what one could call ḥasidic conservatism. Neo-ḥasidic life at Modi'im in the mid- to late-1980s did not have the trappings or the weight of a tradition to maintain. Its members were creating their devotional life on the fly, as it were, many coming from the American counterculture with progressive values that were then recalibrated to conform to some manner of traditional ḥasidic life and contemporary Israeli society. This resulted in a variety of apparently contradictory values, for example, a broad and sincere openness to the world and a strident right-wing political stance on the question of Palestinians. A belief in the holiness of the land that often easily elided to the holiness of the state by some who in the U.S. protested the state, patriotism, and its warring policies. As one friend from Modi'im, who tragically died quite young, wrote on her Facebook profile regarding her political views, "Right on Israel, left on everything else." Modi'im was a study in contrasts, with Carlebach's vision of Ḥasidism its driving engine.

VI

Ordination as an Exit Strategy

It was at Brovinders that I received rabbinical ordination with a group led by R. Yaakov Warhaftig of Mechon Harry Fischel. After being examined orally and in writing by both Warhaftig and Brovinder, we were taken to an examination by R. Zalman Nechemia Goldberg who led a *kollel* in the Geulah neighborhood of Jerusalem where we also received a separate ordination. He was an intensely impressive man, then probably in his 60s, gentle, learned, and deeply pious. I did not know then that this ordination was, in a way, my diploma from Orthodoxy and would also enable me to make extra money when I became a graduate student in the U.S.

As time went on I began to feel more alienated from the *ḥaredi* world. I felt questions I was asking were not being engaged, and the romantic world of Ḥasidism that Dovid introduced me to was really the creation of his own imagination. With him in Brooklyn and me in Jerusalem, the connection seemed more and more tenuous. And the more I knew, the more I saw that his textual prowess was indeed wanting. He knew that, and his stubbornness and stridency could not adjust. One could not move from being a student to a friend; his vision of himself and the world he wanted to create could not allow that. My relationship with him was ending and so was my infatuation with haredism. I walked into a barber shop on Me'ah She'arim Street in Jerusalem one Friday morning and asked the non-*ḥaredi* Mizrahi barber to cut my long *payot*. He initially refused. I guess he didn't want to take the responsibility. I persisted. Finally, he obliged. I was looking for a way out. It seemed to me a physical change was the easiest place to begin.

It was at this time that I began to think about life outside the *ḥaredi* world. I decided to apply to be a candidate fellow at the Shalom Hartman Institute in Jerusalem. I also applied to the MA program in Jewish thought at the Hebrew University. I spent two years at Hartman where I was first exposed to scholarship on the texts I studied only in *yeshivah*. And it was there I came under the influence of David Hartman, a fascinating, if difficult, man whose erratic behavior one needed to suffer to understand his larger project of Judaism and modernity (he could treat you as a son one day and then act as if he didn't know you the next). I learned a great deal from him during those years, and in many ways in conjunction with Brovinder (they both studied with Soloveitchik in the 1960s) it turned me further away from the *ḥaredi* world and toward academia. After two years at Hartman I moved to the rabbinic program at the Seminary of Jewish Studies, the academic arm of the Masorti (Conservative) Movement in Jerusalem. It was a very intense atmosphere, the learning was high quality, and I made close friends forged through the study and analysis of the textual tradition. It was there I studied with the renowned Bible scholar Moshe Greenberg, the talmudists Shamma Friedman and his brother Mordecai Akiva Friedman, and many other Hebrew University professors who taught there. At that point I had no intention of becoming a Conservative rabbi, I already had Orthodox ordination, but I was interested in critical Talmud study and that was the only way to get into Professor Friedman's Talmud class.

At the Hebrew University between 1984 and 1988 I was fortunate to have studied with some of the luminaries in the post-Scholem, Shlomo Pines, Natan Rotenstreich generation. I studied with David Flusser, Aviezer Ravitzsky, Marcel Dubois, Adi Zemah, Yermiyahu Yovel, and Paul Mendel-Flohr, among others. And in particular Eliezer Schweid. It was Schweid who would have the most lasting influence on me from the Hebrew University. I attended his seminar almost every semester I was there. One of the most lasting things about Schweid was the way he was able to embody the thinkers he was teaching or reading such that he channeled them in a way that seemed totally uncritical. Yet just as he drew you into the thought processes of a thinker, whether it was Maimonides, A. D. Gordon, Hermann Cohen, Nahman Krochmal, Hayyim Bialik, or Uri Zvi Greenberg, he began to offer his critique. It showed me that moving to the critical phase of analysis of any text before one enters deeply into it on its own terms weakens one's ability to be critical. I found this as a flaw in some scholarship I subsequently read, and this influenced my method of teaching as well. Before one criticizes a text one needs to understand it on its own terms. This at times requires a "suspension of disbelief" and at times setting aside one's own initial reasons for engaging the text, although, as Max Weber taught, one must also come back to those initial reasons later on. For those of us, and there were many, who moved from *yeshivah*-style learning, where critique was not part of the ethos, to academia, where criticism stands at the center of the scholarly enterprise, Schweid's method was both comforting and compelling. It has stayed with me throughout my career. Moreover, some of us who took the path from devotion to critique were never quite comfortable with the way those categories were viewed from both sides as contradictory. For me, the subjective and objective always lived in tension, and my academic scholarship and my sermons were different but also sometimes fed off one another in what I found to be interesting, and surprising, ways.

During those three years at the Hebrew University I never took a course in Kabbalah or Ḥasidism. I had studied those materials quite intensively in *ḥaredi* circles and with R. Attiah, and when I entered the secular university I was more interested in philosophy and Jewish thought, something I had much less exposure to in *yeshivah*. When I decided to continue for a doctorate, Ḥasidism was not a subject that particularly interested me. I wanted to study the philosophy of history of Nahman Krochmal. When I arrived at Brandeis University in 1989 to study for my doctorate under the tutelage of the Maimonides scholar Marvin Fox, I took a required course in Jewish Bibliography taught by the Judaica librarian Charles Cutter (this was just on the cusp of computer technology and we did not utilize computers at all in this course). As a final paper we had to prepare an exhaustive bibliography of any subject and I chose early to mid-nineteenth-century Polish Ḥasidism for reasons that I have since forgotten. During my years in Boro Park and Israel I was often part of a circle that hung around Shlomo Carlebach, who often cited the Polish ḥasidic tradition, in particular R. Mordecai Joseph of Izbica, known as the Izbicher. So I complied a bibliography of the disciples of R. Simha Bunim of Pryzsucha (of whom Mordecai Joseph was one).

Through that exercise I once again became drawn to Ḥasidism, now as an academic subject. I felt I now had the critical tools to examine this material anew and the textual skills in both classical and ḥasidic Judaism to write an academic study. A book on the Izbicher had recently been published by a historian of Eastern European Jewry, Morris Faierstein, called *All is in the Hands of Heaven*, and since the Izbicher only published one book, *Mei ha-Shiloaḥ*, I felt here was not enough room for another book on this enigmatic thinker. On the advice of a friend I began to explore the work of his grandson, R. Gershon Henokh of Radzin, a voluminous writer and editor of his grandfather's *Mei ha-Shiloaḥ*. I had known about R. Gershon Henokh and even read some of his work but had never explored it in great detail. Upon examination I discovered a large trove of material, including a book entitled *Ha-Hakdamah ve-ha-Petiḥah*, a kind of historical prolegomenon to Ḥasidism, tracing its roots through the medieval philosophical and kabbalistic tradition. This brought together my interest in medieval Jewish philosophy, the philosophy of history, and Ḥasidism in a way that offered me a frame to think about the theological issues in the Izbica/Radzin tradition in a fresh way. I had found my subject which, in some way, is half the challenge.

With the years of study in *ḥaredi* and traditional circles, which I had done without any pretense of a career, certainly not in academia, I entered the academic guild in the early 1990s. I felt somewhat of an outlier even as my *yeshivah* background, long beard, and large kippah gave me insider's privilege in those days. Many of my colleagues in graduate school had come from Ivy League universities, some from classical rabbinical seminaries. I came from a tiny experimental liberal arts college, Goddard College in Plainfield, Vermont, and years in the *ḥaredi* world as a *ba'al teshuvah*. I had entered through the portal of an enigmatic ḥasidic teacher, Dovid Din, lived the life of a Bratslaver *ḥasid*, moved to the hippie/*ḥaredi* Moshav Modi'im and the world of Shlomo Carlebach and Zalman Schachter, and had three small children and little money. I was far from the polished, button-down student that was more common in Jewish Studies graduate programs. But because of my time in *yeshivah*, and my "story," I was able to enter the guild through a side door.

Marvin Fox, an old-school Maimonides scholar and devout Orthodox Jew, for some unknown reason took a liking to me, appreciated the textual skills I came with, and supported my studies. One memory stands out. After I had submitted a chapter of my dissertation, he invited me to his home to talk about it. I nervously entered his home with a massive library. He told me to have a seat at the dining room table and he would join me in a moment. When I reached the table I saw the copy of the chapter I gave him, marked extensively with red ink and beside it a stack of about nine or ten ḥasidic books from the library. The books were the ḥasidic texts I was writing about. He obviously did not own them and had taken them out of the library to look up all the sources I cited. What struck me was both the seriousness with which he took the project and also how he viewed it as a learning opportunity to read ḥasidic works that he had never read throughout his long career. Fox was a proud man who took himself very seriously (we used to refer to him as F-x), but he could also be quite humble. He knew what he didn't know and was never too proud to learn something new. Michael Zank, now a professor at Boston University, and I were his last two students. He retired in the spring of 1994, the semester we both defended, and tragically died of non-smokers' lung cancer about a year later. I could not have asked for a more learned, honest, and generous man to launch my career.

A second faculty member with whom I had close contact at Brandeis was Michael Fishbane. Fishbane gave a graduate seminar every semester, an ongoing study of midrashic texts, that most of my cohort attended regularly. Trained as a Bible scholar, Fishbane was then making the transition to rabbinic literature and the study of myth, and we were, to some extent, his Guinea pigs. It was an exhilarating seminar, and although I can't recall quite how, I think I absorbed a lot of how he read texts—a rare combination of rigor and creativity—that I incorporated into my work on Ḥasidism.

The other person from that period with whom I had close contact was Professor Isadore Twersky of Harvard, who also served as a ḥasidic rebbe from the lineage of Talne. I was a regular at his small synagogue in Brighton, Massachusetts, and often attended his *shi'urim* in the early 1990s. One afternoon the phone rang, and when I picked up a voice said, "Hello, this is Yitzhak Twersky, can I please speak to Shaul." I was so taken by the informality—Yitzhak—I didn't know who it was at first. He called to ask if I would serve as a Teaching Fellow for a course he gave at Harvard on Aristotle, Aquinas, and Maimonides. Of course I agreed and spent the semester with three other graduate students at Harvard working for him. I never studied with Twersky formally but he readily read some of my work and offered many good suggestions. He was an exemplar of a scholar with integrity and honesty. I personally wished he would have been more outspoken and critical on some of the issues in the Orthodox community we inhabited but his reserved personality and extreme caution prevented him from doing so. When he died, the night before the funeral we all spent hours in his home with his body covered on the floor reciting Psalms, as is the custom. I remember walking up close to the body and expressing anger that he had left the world with so much left unsaid. As I saw it then, it was a missed opportunity.

VII

Academia and Discovering Alterity Anew

Scholars often claim they think "out of the box," but in reality academia is often a profession of boxes, and one's dissertation serves as a label. You are marked by that first work and it can take some time to erase that mark to pursue other scholarly interests. So I emerged in the academic world as a scholar of Ḥasidism. This always seemed strange to me because my interests were always much broader and because at the Hebrew University those labels do not quite fit. Many of those I studied with there, Eliezer Schweid for example, were quite eclectic in their interests. While in the U.S. they might be considered dilettantish, in Israel where the study of Judaism was part of the culture of the society, they were simply scholars of Judaica. Whether by inclination or training I saw myself similarly, or at least aspired toward that goal, yet I realized that I first had to make my mark from the box I created through my dissertation.

For the next decade or so I concentrated on carving a space for myself in the guild of academia. First at Rice University and then at the Jewish Theological Seminary I published academic articles in journals, revised my dissertation for publication, and played the role of a Jewish Studies academic. My interests were somewhat eclectic, including Jewish mysticism and Ḥasidism and medieval and modern Jewish thought. Rice was a great place to start and I made friends and learned much from my colleagues. My tenure at JTS from 1997–2004 was quite wonderful in many ways. I made relationships I keep to this day and I felt a part of a religious movement that, while not my own, was something I felt I could contribute to. It was here that I began to consider what it meant to be a Jewish public intellectual and hone the skills of functioning in the academy and outside it.

It was during those years, that I also felt I lost some of the alterity that drove me to Ḥasidism since I was a child, the sense of otherness and living otherwise that first attracted me to these texts and this world. The Conservative Movement stands very much in the mainstream of American Jewish life, and while the seminary offered me the opportunity to speak to a broader audience and to have a role in training Conservative rabbis for their lives in the pulpit, it also seemed a bit of an unnatural fit when some of my views became more eclectic and less conventional.

Once I became adept enough at academic parlance I began thinking about how the ḥasidic and kabbalistic texts I was reading could be used to make another kind of intervention, how can they be used against themselves as a template to describe a world other than their own. I was not drawn by any essentialist argument. By that time, I had been sufficiently influenced and convinced of post-structuralism and post-modernism such that I could not believe there was any essence to be discovered. But I still believed the texts were electric and were generative, even as I was often and increasingly critical of their assumptions and conclusions.

The critical approach thus was not fully satisfying for me. I felt I needed a constructive component, and the question for me became how I could explore that, to express it, within the confines of academic discourse, or perhaps beside academic discourse. The academy is understandably very wary of such endeavors and thus the proper path of exploration was not simple. I did not want to abandon my perch in the academy. In some way this became one of the most challenging aspects of my intellectual career and spiritual life in those years. My station in history helped. I was living at a time when various critiques of modernity, broadly conceived, were growing roots in academia and particular in religious studies. The work of people such as J. Z. Smith and others in his wake opened up the possibility of thinking critically about religion without a sharp historical, or historicist, knife. The works of scholars such as Daniel Boyarin and Elliot Wolfson, the latter of whom was on my dissertation committee and remained an important colleague, mentor, and friend, enabled many of us to break free from the confines of how scholarship was previously defined. My desire was not to develop any confessional approach; rather it was to explore my material outside its own claims, enabling it to speak to contemporary issues and concerns.

In some way this was more natural, even expected, in the Israeli academic system where I began. Under the influence of Eliezer Schweid, Aviezer Ravitzky, David Hartman, among others, applied scholarship was if not a given then certainly accepted. Schweid in particular was interested in applied scholarship as it related to the culture of Zionism and collective existence in Israel more generally. Schweid viewed scholarship as generating culture as much as critiquing it.

But the early 1990s I had already decided to make my home in America and thus my interests turned more toward the American Jewish experience, initially in regard to religiosity and later culture more generally. By the time I arrived at JTS in 1997 I had all but left Orthodoxy. While still mostly observant, I became fully committed to egalitarianism and, more importantly, no longer identified with the Orthodox community. And yet my *ḥaredi* past stayed with me internally, and my own religious life was lived largely refracted through the texts I read and the friends I read them with. For example, with a student and friend David Seidenberg, we began what David labeled the Ḥasidic Egalitarian Minyan, first at Anshei Hesed, a Conservative synagogue in Manhattan, and then in the basement of JTS. It lasted for three or four years, our attempt to draw together disparate but somehow also congenial approaches to Jewish life and practice.

Whereas Ḥasidism for me was once the counterculture I sought to embody, now it served a kind of *ad hoc* and under-theorized neo-Ḥasidism, which was intentionally misappropriating ḥasidic ideas and even behaviors. In the beginning this move to the margins of academia, where normative scholarly attention meets personal aspiration and inclination, was largely intuitive rather than reasoned, as I had no real sense of what to do with it or even whether to share it publicly in writing. I published a few small topical essays that experimented with these ideas but I had no real direction or even goal. I just knew, or hoped, that Ḥasidism and Kabbalah could be more than academically interesting and that I could somehow find a voice to express that in an academically responsible way.

In *Ḥasidism on the Margin* (2004) I tried to thread the needle of a serious academic study that would resonate with non-academics. One critical review claimed I was too inside the texts and too constructive in my interpretation. Perhaps in retrospect the critic was correct. I was not adept enough at the task. The problem was that I had no theoretical frame, no broader vision of what I wanted to do or what I wanted to say. In 2005 I was working on a book on Lurianic Kabbalah using a New Historicist lens to look at Lurianic metaphysics and the question of cultural production, that is, how the metaphysics creates history and does not record or respond to it. The book was later published as *From Metaphysics to Midrash*. During that time, I received a request from Jo Ellen Kaiser who was then an editor at *Tikkun Magazine* where I had published a few essays over the years. She asked if I would write an essay for *Tikkun* on contemporary Jewish Renewal. I received the invitation while I was living on Fire Island where I had a summer pulpit at the Fire Island Synagogue, an egalitarian synagogue in Ocean Beach, New York, where I have served as the rabbi since 1997. I had never really thought about Jewish Renewal as a subject of scholarly inquiry but something about it piqued my interest. Accepting the task, I had no idea it would provide for me the frame I lacked. And it would also serve for me as a new kind of alterity, in some way a looping back to a much earlier time in my life, an alternative to a purely scholarly life (not that anyone has one anyway) or at least an outlet for my scholarship that I found refreshing. With the salty air of the sea in my lungs, I began to think more seriously about Jewish Renewal.

VIII

Jewish Renewal, Neo-Ḥasidism, and American Post-Judaism

The essay I submitted on Jewish Renewal was far too long for a publication like *Tikkun*. Jo Ellen asked if I would be willing to divide and publish it serially, to which I agreed. It was published in three installments in 2005 and 2006. Only after delving into the thought of Renewal and its founder Zalman Schachter-Shalomi did I think about writing a book-length study of the topic. But I still felt the issue needed a broader frame. From this came *American Post-Judaism*. But more than that, through this project I became reacquainted with Schachter-Shalomi, whom I had met in the late 1970s at a wild Renewal Shabbat at the Freedom Farm outside Philadelphia. I am quite sure he did not recall meeting me, but we crossed paths numerous times after that when he used to visit his daughter and her family in Moshav Modi'im, where I had lived from 1986 to 1989.

During my research and writing of *American Post-Judaism*, which was not a book about Ḥasidism but was certainly a book that, in part, attempted to reimagine neo-Ḥasidism in a cultural and not only a religious register, I became quite close to Schachter-Shalomi and in some way again found the alterity I was seeking. This project also brought me back to where things all began for me. Dovid Din had been Schachter-Shalomi's secretary when he was the Hillel director at the University of Winnipeg in the mid-1960s, when Dovid showed up in a converted school bus with a group of hippies looking to buy land for their commune. The others went on their way and Dovid stayed behind to work for Schachter-Shalomi. Dovid's Jewish journey thus began with Schachter-Shalomi, and even as he went deep into the *ḥaredi* world while Schachter-Shalomi took haredism and crafted it in his own image, there was something about Dovid, and the things I learned from him, that remained quite close to Schachter-Shalomi. And there was something about Dovid, a kind of wayward son, that Schachter-Shalomi never gave up on. Years after Dovid died tragically of complications from anorexia at the age of 46 in 1987, Schachter-Shalomi would ask me about his wife and children when we spoke on the phone. It seemed to me a combination of genuine care combined with a small dose of guilt.

As close as I felt to Schachter-Shalomi, I could not enter the Renewal world he created. I always remained on the margins, both because that is where I felt most comfortable and because many in that community did not quite trust my "academic" and "critical" assessment of their rebbe. Externally I had moved further away in terms of religious practice, and yet my *ḥaredi* past was too embedded in my psyche to allow me to take the New Age as seriously as is required in order to enter that world fully.

In any case, after *American Post-Judaism* I returned to the study of Ḥasidism with new energy. I now felt free to look at these texts I loved with new eyes. Having moved to the Department of Religious Studies at Indiana University in 2004 I was now surrounded by other scholars of religion the way I had not been at JTS. And living in Indiana made me feel for the first time I was living in the kind of America that did not exist in New York City. *American Post-Judaism* was fully a product of that "American" experience, and my subsequent book, *Ḥasidism Incarnate: Ḥasidism, Christianity, and the Making of Modern Judaism*, was also a product of living in a multidimensional and multivalent academic community. I felt a kind of ownership of those texts in ways I had not before, a confidence that I had something to contribute to their continued relevance. Rather than viewing them solely within the orbit of Jewish life and practice, I argued that given the focus on the experience and proximity of God to the *ḥasid*, and given the notion of the ḥasidic *ẓaddik* as *axis mundi* (to borrow a locution form Art Green's popular and important essay) the parallels to Christianity were more than occasional, and worth tracing. The point was not to make direct connections, something that would be difficult if not impossible to do. Rather, I offered a phenomenological claim of similitude as a response to similar spiritual orientations and concerns coupled with the Zohar's polemic against Christianity by adopting Christian motifs that Ḥasidism absorbed without knowing of their polemical roots.

IX

Coming Back to Ḥasidism Once Again

The present volume collects a series of reflections on Ḥasidism that spans about twenty years. Most of the essays appeared elsewhere in scholarly journals or volumes; a few are new. They illustrate my struggle with ḥasidic texts, my closeness to them, and my distance from them. In retrospect perhaps they reflect more about me than about them, but all scholarship is, or should be, autobiographical. Academics in the humanities have the blessed opportunity to contemplate the world through a particular lens that both reflects and teaches them about the texts they read and the worlds they come from, and about themselves and why they find these texts so compelling, even, or precisely, when they disagree with them.

In any case, I hope to convey in these essays how the texts were a product of their time and remain alive, at least for me, not as exemplars of any lifestyle or practice, although they are certainly also that for some, but as exempla of the pursuits of consciousness and meaning, often through the creative misappropriation of traditional motifs to serve a different end. In this way, I suppose I return to Buber, albeit with a different focus. Unlike

Buber I am not looking for a ḥasidic essence. That was for a different time. In these essays I am looking, perhaps, for an alterity that could open the texts to the world and shine light on the possible global implicactions at work in the recesses of a highly parochial tradition. In this sense I am taking Dovid Din's transnational monastic piety and Schachter-Shalomi's rendering of Renewal as the "fourth turning of Ḥasidism" to a new place. While Jewish collective existence remains important to me as a Jew, as a scholar of Ḥasidism and as one who hopes my work extends beyond those parochial parameters, I do not place Jewish "continuity" at the center of my intellectual and spiritual project. Although, as Hannah Arendt replied when asked about her being a Jew, "I can't quite think of being anything else."

Over the course of the years when these essays were written, I explored a variety of other subjects in my academic work and in topical writing. A book on Lurianic Kabbalah, on American Judaism, on the little-known Elijah Zvi Soloveitchik's Hebrew commentary to the New Testament, and many essays on modern Jewish thought, Mussar, Judaism and Christianity, and Zionism. A friend once noted laconically that I had "left Jewish mysticism behind." But that is not quite true. My interests have always been eclectic as far back as my adolescence, and my training at the Hebrew University mitigated *against* the American academic doctrine of focused expertise. Eliezer Schweid wrote on everything from the Hebrew Bible to globalization; my doctoral advisor at Brandeis, Marvin Fox, wrote on everything from rabbinic literature to Kant, even though he was primarily a Maimonides scholar.

But wherever my restless mind and heart may have led me, I always seem to come back to Ḥasidism. There is something in its mix of metaphysical speculation and its messy depiction of the human condition that never grows old for me. To me, ḥasidic literature feels like an old friend who knows you well and who has been with you on a long journey, and in and with whom you always find something new. Like an old friend, it is in relation, what Buber liked to call the "in-between" where real insight occurs. These essays are an example of that "in-between." Not always loving, not always joyous, not always satisfying. I am not sure the ḥasidic texts I examine here are, as one scholar described Ḥasidism, "words of fire." But they are certainly words that breathe life into this Jew trying to find his way in the world. Thus far I have come. *Ashreinu mah tov ḥelkeynu* ("oh to be happy with one's lot").

Shaul Magid
Fire Island 2018/5778

Early Ḥasidism

Chapter 1

"What happened, happened": R. Ya'akov Yosef of Polonnoye on Ḥasidic Interpretation

The history and literature of Ḥasidism are two of the most extensively researched areas of Jewish mysticism. Historians, sociologists, anthropologists, psychologists of religion, ethnographers, and theologians have examined Ḥasidism as a Marxist critique of rabbinic culture; a rereading of classical Kabbalah; a form of Jewish revivalism; a conservative response to, and extension and normalization of, Sabbateanism; a mystical psychology; and a source for modern existential philosophy.[1]

From the beginning, scholarship on Ḥasidism has been divided into two basic camps. Gershom Scholem examined Ḥasidism as a branch of Jewish mysticism even as Martin Buber, one of the most prominent earlier examiners of Ḥasidism in the first decades of the twentieth century, tried to downplay the mystical elements in Ḥasidism by suggesting that it is better described as a form of religious existentialism. Scholem's chapter on Ḥasidism in his seminal *Major Trends in Jewish Mysticism* ("The Latest Phase") is indicative of his general approach. Calling Ḥasidism a "mystical psychology," Scholem claimed that although it is based on the Jewish mystical tradition it did not add anything new to the history of Kabbalah. Other scholars have weighed in, all claiming in one way or

---

I dedicate this chapter to Rabbi Chaim Brovinder, with unending gratitude.

1 For classic studies in these areas, see Immanuel Etkes, "The Study of Ḥasidism: Past Trends and New Directions," in *Ḥasidism Reappraised*, ed. Ada Rapoport-Albert (London: Littman Library of Jewish Civilization, 1997), 447–64; Rachel Elior, *The Mystical Origins of Ḥasidism* (Portland, OR: Littman Library of Jewish Civilization, 2006), 195–205; and Zeev Gries, "Ḥasidism: The Present State of Research and Some Desirable Priorities," *Numen* 34, no. 1 (1987): 97–108; 34, no. 2 (1987): 179–213.

another (mostly contra Buber) that Ḥasidism does constitute a form of Jewish mysticism although its relationship to classical Kabbalah is a more vexing problem.[2]

In a recent work that offers a schematic view of the mystical origins of Ḥasidism as well as Ḥasidism as a field of research, Rachel Elior illustrates the complex relationship between Ḥasidism and the mystical traditions upon which it is based. She writes, "These mystical innovators set out to contribute something new to the mystical outlook and its implications on earth. The novelty of the Ba'al Shem Tov's approach was that it replaced the dualistic mystical perception of good and evil, exile and redemption, with a new holistic perception based on three essential theological elements: the entirety of the divine presence everywhere; the accessibility of the hidden divine realm to every member of the community; and the essential equality of all modes of divine worship."[3] Although such declarative statements may not fully encapsulate a tradition that is quite variegated and multivalent, her point is well taken and largely correct; that is, Ḥasidism is surely a link in the chain of the Jewish mystical tradition but one that in some ways undermines or revises the basic metaphysical framework of previous Kabbalah.

The other camp was initiated largely by Ben Zion Dinur and Simon Dubnow. These scholars, among many others that followed, examined Ḥasidism as a social phenomenon and maintained that the only way to understand it as a movement was to view it in its historical, social, and socio-economic context, using external Polish, Russian, Ukrainian, and Galician sources to verify the claims that the *ḥasidim* made about themselves. In a recent essay reviewing what can be called the new phase of the controversy, Yohanan Petrovsky-Shtern called these two camps *Ḥasidei de'kokhvaya* (star-struck Ḥasidism) and *Ḥasidei de'ar'a* (earth-bound Ḥasidism).[4]

---

2 This is the topic of Moshe Idel's *Ḥasidism: Between Ecstasy and Magic* (Albany: SUNY Press, 1995), esp. 31–146. One salient response to Buber's view of Ḥasidism can be found in Rivka Shatz-Uffenheimer's essay, "Man's Relation to God and World in Buber's Rendering of the Ḥasidic Teaching," in *The Philosophy of Martin Buber*, ed. Paul Arthur Schilpp and Maurice Friedman (La Salle, IL: Open Court, 1967), 403–34. For an examination of this debate, see Jerome Gellman, "Buber's Blunder: Buber Replies to Scholem and Shatz-Uffenheimer," *Modern Judaism* 20 (2000): 20–40. Scholem's essays on Ḥasidism have recently been collected in one volume and published as *The Latest Phase: Essays on Ḥasidism by Gershom Scholem* [Hebrew], ed. David Assaf and Esther Liebes (Jerusalem: Am Oved, Magnes Press, 2008).

3 Elior, *Mystical Origins*, 37.

4 See Yohanan Petrovsky-Shtern, "Review Essay: *Ḥasidei de'ar'a* and *Ḥasidei dekokhvaya*: Two Trends in Modern Jewish Historiography," *AJS Review* 32 (2008): 141–67.

Both groups function within the discipline of history. The first group is devoted to the internal sources of Ḥasidism, largely viewing them diachronically as carriers of an age-old tradition of Jewish mysticism. *Ḥasidei de'kokhvaya* scholars are interested in terms such as *deveikut* and concepts such as the *ẓaddik* and how *ḥasidim* adapted or revised classical kabbalistic metaphysics. Though interested in the historical and cultural context in which these changes emerged, they are generally less skeptical of internal sources. The *Ḥasidei de'ar'a* scholars take a synchronic view and are less interested in the "ideas" as abstract entities, maintaining that all ideas must be viewed as emerging from particular social and cultural contexts.

Though sympathetic to both, I find myself generally inclined toward the *Ḥasidei de'kokhvaya* approach, largely as a consequence of my interests and training. While it is certainly true that Ḥasidism is deeply influenced and connected to the Jewish mystical tradition (even the *Ḥasidei de'ar'a* scholars acknowledge that) and can be examined in that light, Ḥasidism is also a modern example of a new traditional way of reading the Bible that has received little attention. For example, while Zev Gries has offered important insights into the structure of ḥasidic publishing, specifically its choice of organizing ḥasidic homilies according to the weekly Torah portion, scholars have paid less attention to the way Ḥasidism contributes to and perhaps even spearheads a traditionalist revival of the Hebrew Bible. In this sense Ḥasidism may be viewed as a response (whether conscious or not is hard to determine) not only to religious modernity in general but also to the critique of Scripture that serves as one of modern religion's ideational foundations.

Below I will argue that R. Ya'akov Yosef Katz of Polonnoye (d. 1792), one of the most influential masters of the first generation of *ḥasidim*, had a particular understanding of Ḥasidism's relation to Scripture that in subsequent generations became the unspoken frame of much of ḥasidic literature. His approach stands in direct opposition, both structurally and substantively, to Moses Mendelssohn's Bible project and to later biblical criticism.[5] The extent to which he was aware of either of these is unknown to me. Yet, in another sense, both the progressive modern reformers and the ḥasidic masters—separated by both ideology and geography—are engaged in a similar project of reinserting the Bible into the center of Jewish intellectual life.[6]

5 For a useful and general introduction to the critical study of the Hebrew Bible, see Jacob Weingreen, *Introduction to the Critical Study of the Text of the Hebrew Bible* (New York: Clarendon, 1982), esp. 1–10, 25–37.

6 Although the Bible serves as the template for the classical mystical text the Zohar, it does so in a different way than in Ḥasidism. In brief, the Zohar uses the narrative of Scripture

It is also significant to note here that Ya'akov Yosef, one of the most celebrated disciples of the Ba'al Shem Tov, was not a noted Kabbalist before "converting" to Ḥasidism, as was, for example, his contemporary Dov Baer (the Maggid) of Mezritch. He was a noted pietist and ascetic, as well as a respected halakhic jurist, and was intimately familiar with the corpus of kabbalistic writing, but he was not known to be mystically inclined.

Whereas most early modern and modern meta-halakhic literature is based on, or interprets, Scripture, the centrality of Scripture that dominated the medieval and early modern world of biblical exegesis (Sa'adia Ga'on, Rashi, Rashbam, Ibn Ezra, Nahmanides, Gersonides, Bahya ibn Asher, Seforno, and others) gave way to the dominance of Talmud, responsa literature, Kabbalah, pietism, and Mussar for many learned Jews living deep inside the Jewish textual tradition. In most traditional Jewish institutes of higher learning in the modern period, at least until the second half of the twentieth century, the Hebrew Bible, or *Ḥumash*, was not studied systematically. It was assumed that one knew (often by memory) his Scripture (until recently these institutes of higher learning were exclusively for boys) and that one had looked through the classical medieval commentators (largely on one's own), but a careful analysis of Bible was not the concern of traditional Jewish education until very recently.[7] Enlightenment works such as Moses Mendelssohn's German translation of the Hebrew Bible and its accompanying commentary (*Bi'ur*) and the rise of biblical criticism (beginning, perhaps, with Spinoza and then extending through modernity among Protestants and later Catholics and Jews) brought the Bible back into focus for progressive Jews in the modern period (including, of course, Zionists), and we can safely say that the Hebrew Bible plays a prominent role in the

---

to describe its metaphysical system. On medieval Kabbalah more generally, Gershom Scholem writes, "In conclusion it should be said that the conception of the Torah as a fabric woven of names provided no concrete contribution to concrete exegesis. It was, rather, a purely mystical principle and tended to remove Torah from all human insight into its specific meanings, which are, after all, the sole concern of exegesis. But this did not trouble the kabbalists. To them the fact that God expressed Himself, even if His utterance is far beyond human insight, is far more important than any specific 'meaning' that might be conveyed" (Scholem, "The Meaning of Torah in Jewish Mysticism," in Scholem, *On the Kabbalah and Its Symbolism* [New York: Schocken, 1969], 43).

7 An exception to this can be found in many Modern Orthodox and *ba'alei teshuvah yeshivot*, where medieval Bible commentaries are studied seriously and systematically. I had the privilege of studying in Yeshivat ha-Mivtar in Jerusalem for more than four years with Rabbi Chaim Brovinder (among others), where scriptural exegesis was taken as a serious course of study.

construction of these modern Judaisms.[8] Of course, these movements are shunned by ḥasidic leaders and their communities as heretical.[9] And yet Ḥasidism is engaged in its own Bible revolution, framing its unique perspective through creative and often daring readings of the scriptural narrative. I use Ya'akov Yosef of Polonnoye not only because he is one of the most celebrated of the early ḥasidic masters but also because I believe he inaugurates a particular revolution in reading the Hebrew Bible that has become standardized in subsequent ḥasidic literature.

Ya'akov Yosef Katz of Polonnoye's *Toldot Ya'akov Yosef* and the Return to Scripture

Ya'akov Yosef Katz of Polonnoye is considered one of the most important disciples of the Ba'al Shem Tov, or Besht, and a major architect of early Ḥasidism. A well-known and respected rabbinic scholar, jurist (*av beit din*), and ascetic pietist, he "converted" to Ḥasidism after an encounter with the Besht.[10] His commentary on the Book of Exodus (*Ben Porat Yosef*, 1781) contains one of the earliest versions of the famous letter of the Besht that arguably served as the touchstone of the ḥasidic movement. Unlike his contemporary, the younger Dov Baer (the Maggid) of Mezritch, Ya'akov Yosef did not attract a large circle of followers, and it was Dov Baer and not Ya'akov Yosef who was chosen as the Besht's successor. Yet Ya'akov Yosef is widely known as the most important ideological architect of early Ḥasidism

8 See, for example, Eliezer Schweid, *Filosophia shel ha-TANAKH ki-Yesod Turbut Yisrael*, published in English as *The Philosophy of the Bible as a Foundation of Jewish Culture*, trans. Leonard Levin (Brighton, MA: Academic Studies Press, 2008).

9 On Ḥasidism and the influence of modernity through the Jewish Enlightenment, see Raphael Mahler, *Ḥasidism and the Jewish Enlightenment* (Philadelphia: Jewish Publication Society of America, 1985); and Marcin Wadzinski, *Haskala and Ḥasidism in the Kingdom of Poland* (Portland, OR: Littman Library of Jewish Civilization, 2005). On a ḥasidic polemic that directly addresses Mendelssohn, see the anonymous Bratslav treatise *Kinat ha-Shem Ẓeva'ot* (Lemberg, ca. 1870–85). For a brief discussion of this text, see Mendel Piekarz, *Studies in Braslav Ḥasidism* (Jerusalem: Mosad Bialik, 1972), 197–202.

10 For one such tradition, see Abraham Kahana, *Sefer ha-Ḥasidut* (Warsaw: Levin-Epstein, 1922), 105; cited in Samuel H. Dresner, *The Zaddik* (New York: Abelard-Schuman, 1960), 38–40. Most of the material on Ya'akov Yosef's relationship to the Besht is taken from *Shivḥei ha-Besht*, ed. Avraham Rubenstein (Jerusalem: Reuven Mass, 1991), 99–110. *Shivḥei ha-Besht* was first published in 1814, and its historicity regarding the biographical figure of the Besht has been the subject of scholarly scrutiny; see, for example, Moshe Rosman, *The Founder of Ḥasidism: A Quest for the Historical Baal Shem Tov* (Berkeley: University of California Press, 1996).

through his widely read Torah commentary *Toldot Ya'akov Yosef* (1780).[11] His ḥasidic commentaries are uncharacteristically replete with complex and sometimes lengthy digressions on talmudic passages (*sugyot*) both halakhic and aggadic, medieval talmudic commentaries, Kabbalah, and the entire body of medieval and early modern pietistic literature.[12] It is also a book with a very definite agenda, responding to traditional critics of the nascent ḥasidic movement by defending Ḥasidism as the necessary corrective to the wayward state of Jewish spiritual life.[13]

Ya'akov Yosef was particularly fond of two works of Torah homilies that are consistently cited throughout his work: the sixteenth-century pietist and mystic Moshe Alsheikh's *Sefer Alsheikh* and the Torah commentaries of Ephraim of Lunshitz, who lived and preached in Poland in the late sixteenth century.[14] He also often refers to the Torah commentary of Isaac Abarbanel, a fifteenth-century leader of Iberian Jewry. In fact, it appears that Ya'akov Yosef modeled his commentary on Abarbanel, who characteristically begins his exegesis in the medieval scholastic mode by posing a series of questions, which he proceeds to answer in his homily (more on this below).

Although Ya'akov Yosef cites kabbalistic works such as the Zohar and Lurianic Kabbalah quite frequently, one would be hard-pressed to call his work kabbalistic or mystical in any conventional sense. Mystical literature, though cited frequently, is often not central but is usually engaged as

---

11 The standard edition of the *Toldot Ya'akov Yosef* is printed in two volumes; all references here come from the 1973 Jerusalem edition (ed. Gedalyali Nigal and Mosad Harav Kook). Newer annotated editions have appeared in the past decade. The *Toldot* is divided into three distinct but linked parts. The introduction is more than a short précis of the book; it is, in fact, a small book unto itself. It seems to have been constructed as a prolegomenon to Ḥasidism more generally, touching on many themes that became popular in ḥasidic writing. In this regard, the introduction resembles the introduction to the *Sefer ha-Zohar*, which doesn't introduce a book as much as a spiritual movement. The second part of the book contains homilies according to the weekly Torah portion. The third section is a collection of teachings that Ya'akov Yosef heard from his master, the Besht. His other works include *Ẓofnat Pa'aneaḥ* (1782) and *Ketonet Pasim* (1866). On various, significant dimensions of the editorial process of the *Toldot Ya'akov Yosef*, see Zeev Gries, "The Ḥasidic Managing Editor as an Agent of Culture," in Rapoport-Albert, *Ḥasidism Reappraised*, 149, 150.

12 See Mendel Piekarz, *Be-Yemei Ẓemikhat ha-Ḥasidut* (Jerusalem: Bialik Institute, 1978), 15–16.

13 See Gedalyah Nigal, *Manhig ve-Edah* (Israel: Yehuda, 1962), 19. *Toldot Ya'akov Yosef* was printed in two locales, Karetz and Miedzyboz, in the same year (1780); both editions were initially printed without approbations.

14 For some examples of Ya'akov Yosef's citations of Alsheikh, see *Toldot Ya'akov Yosef*, 9b, 55a, 116a, 142a, 234b, 267b, 268b, 307a, 661a. For Lunshitz, see *Toldot Ya'akov Yosef*, 90a, 102b, 443a, 724a. This is not an exhaustive accounting.

part of the larger body of classical Jewish literature.[15] For example, a comment by the medieval Tosafists (a group of twelfth-century French sages who glossed the Babylonian Talmud) can just as easily warrant his sustained attention as a mystical or esoteric idea from the Zohar. Whereas his contemporary, Dov Baer, was a much more mystical and charismatic personality, whose works are replete with mystical and ecstatic observations, Ya'akov Yosef is more grounded and his work more focused on what he considered the two essential challenges of *ḥasidim*: first, to gain legitimacy from the rabbinic elite—of which he was a part before his conversion to Ḥasidism—without which Ya'akov Yosef thought Ḥasidism had no chance of success. This may, in part, be behind his long and learned digressions on rabbinic sources. Though he likely wrote that way before converting to Ḥasidism, maintaining that style in light of his ostensible commitment to the masses after becoming a disciple of the Besht seems curious. It also may inform the way he tries to situate Ḥasidism in the trajectory of the classical pietism of Alsheikh and Lunshitz, both of whom were well respected and widely read in his period. Second, he believed that a firm commitment to the unlearned masses was an essential core of his master's innovative project and one to which he was ideologically committed. One way he addresses this is to develop a form of zaddikism (worship of the righteous one, or *ẓaddik*) that views Jewish society as comprising two distinct groups: the elite and the masses, both of whom need each other. The former he calls "men of form" (*anshei ẓura*) and the latter "men of matter" (*anshei ḥomer*).[16] The Aristotelian form/matter dichotomy, which he likely gleaned from Maimonides and other medieval sources, is deployed to both describe and construct his historical and geographical context. He lived in a world where the rabbinic elite dominated the intellectual discourse and the masses were largely ignored. On the one hand, he had to convince the elite that reaching out to the masses was not simply an act of kindness but an essential part of their own identity, a central tenet of their vocation, and crucial for the welfare of Israel.[17]

15 In general, see Zeev Gries, "Kabbalistic Literature and Its Role in Ḥasidism," in Gries, *The Book in the Jewish World, 1700–1900* (Portland, OR: Littman Library of Jewish Civilization, 2007), 69–90. Moshe Idel similarly suggests that, aside from kabbalistic ḥasidic circles such as Zhidatchov-Komarno, early ḥasidic masters "understood this classic [the Zohar] of Jewish mysticism the same way they approached other books of Judaism, namely as pointing to the values of devotion, ecstasy, and exaltation" ("Abraham Joshua Heschel on Mysticism and Ḥasidism," *Modern Judaism* 29 [2009]: 92).

16 See Dresner, *The Zaddik*, 113–40.

17 Dresner, *The Zaddik*, 148–72.

And he wanted to curb the growing hatred among the masses (including the wealthy) for the learned rabbis.[18]

The most serious challenge to Ḥasidism in its early period was its rejection by the rabbinic elite, perhaps most forcefully illustrated in the Gaʾon of Vilna's 1777 letter against Ḥasidism and various other anti-ḥasidic edicts that followed in its wake.[19] Yaʿakov Yosef knew he had to quell the emerging antagonism among many of the unlearned Jews against the rabbinic elite by viewing them as providing an essential function in the Jewish community. Given his status as a well-respected rabbinic leader and a member of that elite class (unlike his master the Besht, who was not well regarded in those circles) he was well situated for such a task.[20] One could posit that these two challenges, both of which have been noticed by scholars, serve as the pillars of his theological and sociological project.

Most ḥasidic literature is printed as abbreviated or extended homilies on the weekly Torah portion. While this may be partially due to printers' decisions (most ḥasidic masters did not publish their own work and much of it was published posthumously and in limited editions), the appearance of ḥasidic literature, beginning in 1780 with *Toldot Yaʿakov Yosef* on the Pentateuch, gave the educated Jewish public an entire literature devoted to spiritualistic commentaries and meditations on the Bible.[21] Biblical characters were brought to life and constructed as models of piety from this new ḥasidic perspective. Rabbinic literature (Talmud and Midrash) was freely deployed alongside kabbalistic ideas to present this new way of Ḥasidism which, though pietistic in nature, departed significantly from the ascetic pietism of the past and offered its readers a way of serving God joyously. This is not to say that Ḥasidism invented this genre. Collections of learned homilies and extended commentaries on the Bible surely existed between the end of the classical period of medieval biblical exegesis and the emer-

18 See, for example, Yaʿakov Yosef, *Ben Porat Yosef* (Lemberg, n.d.), 106a.

19 For this and many other documents against the Ḥasidim, see Mordecai Wilensky, *Ḥasidim u-Mitnaggedim* [Hebrew] (Jerusalem: Bialik Institute, 1970). On Yaʿakov Yosef's attack against the "learned community" focused on the method of casuistry (*pilpul*), see, for example, *Toldot Yaʿakov Yosef*, 141b, 163b; and *Ben Porat Yosef*, 91a.

20 Yet it seems that Yaʿakov Yosef's previous reputation did not protect him from vehement attack. Soon after its appearance, *Toldot Yaʿakov Yosef* was the victim of sharp criticism by the anti-ḥasidic forces, perhaps most forcefully by the anti-ḥasidic polemic *Zemir Ariẓim*; see Mordecai Wilensky, "Criticism on the Book *Toldot*" [Hebrew], The Joshua Starr Memorial Volume (New York, 1953), 183–89; and Dresner, *The Zaddik*, 66–68. More strongly, scholarship reveals that it was likely burned in Vilna, Krakow, and Brody.

21 On the relationship between ḥasidic literature and printing, see Zeev Gries, *The Book in Early Ḥasidism* [Hebrew] (Israel: Hakibbutz Hameuchad, 1992), esp. 17–68.

gence of Ḥasidism. Ḥasidism's innovation here is the way it made these homilies on the Bible the very foundation of its intellectual focus and the centerpiece of its spirituality.

This new orientation is carefully constructed, and even spearheaded, by Ya'akov Yosef in his various works, particularly in his *Toldot Ya'akov Yosef.* In fact, as I demonstrate below, Ya'akov Yosef spends much time in this work building his ḥasidic perspective by questioning the continued relevance of the Bible and presenting the approach of his master as the solution that will save the Bible from obsolescence, obscurity, and even heresy.

It is unclear how much of this focus on the Bible is driven by the fact that the two dominant sources of Jewish spiritual life—Talmud and Kabbalah—were largely inaccessible to the unlearned masses he wanted to reach. The Bible, on the other hand, was something most moderately educated Jews knew—not deeply and often not very well—but they had enough familiarity with the narrative to be drawn in. And such a book could be studied alongside the weekly Torah portion read in synagogues on Shabbat. Although it is true that one who is not well versed in the entire body of Jewish meta-halakhic literature will often have difficulty deciphering some of Ya'akov Yosef's terse and referential writing, his work is also interspersed with more palatable and tangible explanations and teachings that he heard directly from his master, the Besht, which often become touchstones for his more learned explanations directed, perhaps, toward his rabbinic audience.[22]

His work thus exhibits the complexity of writing *for* two very disparate communities *about* very disparate communities: the rabbinic elite and the masses. On the one hand, he wanted to introduce the Besht and his way to the rabbinic elite whose exposure to Ḥasidism was largely through the sometimes bizarre and often uninformed behavior of some young followers in their towns and cities. Yet he also wanted to give the unlearned public a text that would affirm their role and introduce them to the Besht's ideas in a more nuanced way than they may have heard orally in stories or parables.

Biblical Relevance: "What was, was! Why do we need to know this?"

There is an oft-cited passage from the Zohar that if the narrative of the Bible is merely a collection of "stories," that is, if the Bible is "merely" literature in the colloquial way in which we understand that term, there are other

---

22 He is often quite open about his method; see, for example, *Toldot Ya'akov Yosef*, 86b, 103a, 131b; and Nigal, *Manhig ve-Edah*, 92, 93.

literatures more compelling and more interesting (Zohar 3:152a). In short, the Zohar contests what became a more modern description of the Bible as "the greatest story ever told": As a "story," the Zohar suggests, it is far from the "greatest story ever told"; moreover, even if it is a great story, it is not told particularly well. The Zohar presents this as a justification of its own esoteric project: that each story, each character that the Zohar describes, each episode, passage, even each word in Scripture, points to a higher spiritual reality.[23] In short, the Bible is holy to the extent to which it can be unlocked by the esoteric teachings in the Zohar. This self-justificatory approach had a deep impact on the history of Kabbalah; it is used in a slightly different way and to different ends by Ya'akov Yosef in his *Toldot Ya'akov Yosef*. As mentioned above, Ya'akov Yosef adopted the late medieval model of scriptural exegesis by beginning his commentary on any weekly portion with a series of questions which then become the template of his homily (*drash*). But the similarity to medieval exegesis ends there.

Unlike most late medieval commentaries, the question that appears most often in the *Toldot* is why, in fact, this particular episode is written in the Torah at all! This takes numerous forms. Sometimes Ya'akov Yosef begins, as in the story about Sarah's postmenopausal pregnancy (Gen. 18:9–15), by saying, "These are just stories [*sipurei devarim be-alma*]; what happened, happened [*mah de-havei havei*]!"[24] On Jacob loving Joseph more than his other sons, he asks, "Why mention these stories in the Torah? What happened, happened."[25] These kinds of statements, and there are many, are almost always followed by, "If the Torah is eternal [*niẓḥi*], how is this relevant for all times [*be-khol et u-ve-khol zeman*]?" This is not only used when discussing biblical stories, but also in reference to the description of commandments (*miẓvot*).[26] For example, regarding the sabbatical year (*shemittah*), he notes,

23 This is aptly stated by Abraham bar Hiyya in his *Megillat ha-Megalleh* (Berlin, 1924), 75: "Every letter and every word in every section of the Torah have a deep root in wisdom and contain a mystery from among the mysteries of [divine] understanding, the depths of which we cannot penetrate"; cf. Scholem, "The Meaning of Torah in Jewish Mysticism," 63.

24 *Toldot Ya'akov Yosef*, 59b.

25 *Toldot Ya'akov Yosef*, 102b.

26 See, for example, *Toldot Ya'akov Yosef*, 3b, 4a, 70b, 111b. Cf. Nigal, *Manhig ve-Edah*, 19–20. Nigal spends considerable time on the question of relevance regarding the *miẓvot* but almost ignores the fact that these kind of statements in *Toldot Ya'akov Yosef* are made more frequently regarding the narrative of Scripture.

> There are many problems to address [*ve-ha-sefakot rabo*] [in the Torah's description of the sabbatical year]. Regarding the question, "What is the difference between the sabbatical year [*shemittah*] and Sinai?" (b. Zevahim 115b) we [already] know Rashi's explanation.[27] Second, since the sabbatical year is one of the 613 *mizvot*, how is it relevant in our time [which it must be] given that the Torah and its *mizvot* are eternal?"[28]

This is a particularly interesting case, as it may be an example where Ya'akov Yosef's question of scriptural relevance ("Why is this written? What happened, happened.") may challenge the question asked by the Midrash and cited by Rashi (discussed below). Although it is arguably the case that all classical biblical exegesis tries to make Scripture cohere, I argue that Ya'akov Yosef—illustrated in his uncharacteristic question—is making a stronger claim. His concern is not about scriptural coherence but about its relevance to any reader at any time in history.[29]

The question of textual relevance may be moot for medieval exegetes. Given the assumption of the divine origin of the Torah, relevance is precisely about understanding the text. But although Ya'akov Yosef and much of subsequent Ḥasidism accepted the divine origin as true, that was a necessary but not sufficient condition for the relevance of the text—to understand the text is to understand divine will. If we accept that piety and devotion stand at the center of ḥasidic spirituality, the text must serve those human needs. While contextual interpretation (*peshat*) might provide sense to a particular biblical episode, it does not by definition make the episode relevant to the life of the reader. If relevance, as opposed to sense, cannot be provided, it is not clear to Ya'akov Yosef why it needs to be part of a divine and eternal document. Hence the question, "Why is this written in the Torah?" What seems different here than in classical midrash or medieval exegesis (*parshanut*) is not the desire for relevance *per se*; that exists in both midrash and *parshanut*. Rather, it is the exclusivity of relevance such that if a text cannot be made to speak to the reader it has no purpose whatsoever. Hence, "Why is this written in the Torah?" In the *Toldot*, and I would argue

27 Rashi asks, "'What is [the connection] between *shemittah* and Mount Sinai?' Behold, all the *mizvot* were given at Mount Sinai. Rather, just as with *shemittah* all the details were given at Sinai, so, too, all the details of all the *mizvot* were given at Sinai." See also the *Sifra* to Lev. 1:1 and Rashi on Lev. 25:1.

28 *Toldot Ya'akov Yosef*, 414a.

29 Daniel Boyarin discusses the idea that one of the goals of midrash is about "filling in the gaps" of the biblical narrative and, in doing so, making the narrative more coherent (*Intertextuality and the Reading of Midrash* [Bloomington: University of Indiana Press, 1994], 1–20).

in Ḥasidism more generally, the interpreter of the biblical text serves as a bridge—not between the text as such and the reader but between the text and the one who reads it in order to know how to serve God. Beyond the first-tier dimension of *knowing* what the text says or knowing *what* to do, Ḥasidism is focused on a second tier question: *how* to do what one is commanded to do.

The midrash on the sabbatical year cited by Rashi asks why the laws of *shemittah* immediately follow a description of the theophany at Sinai. The midrashic answer cited by Rashi is to teach us that just as all the details of the laws of *shemittah* were given at Sinai, so, too, were all the laws of the Torah given at Sinai in all their details, even though the Torah is often circumspect about many of the details of these commandments. This addresses two distinct, and distinctly rabbinic, issues. First, it resolves a seemingly unclear, and jarring, transition in Scripture from the laws of *shemittah* to the mention of Sinai. Second, it bolsters rabbinic legislation (the details of *miẓvot*) by rooting the entire rabbinic project in the theophany at Sinai, something the rabbis obliquely proclaim in the first chapter of *Pirkei Avot*. The rabbinic sages use Scripture's ostensible disjuncture between Sinai and *shemittah* as an occasion to champion their own project. Ya'akov Yosef surely agrees with this project, and yet here he appears somewhat dissatisfied with the rabbinic answer and follows his citation of the midrash by asking about the general relevance of *shemittah*, regardless of where it is situated in the scriptural narrative or what it tells us about rabbinic legislation. In other words, according to Ya'akov Yosef, the rabbinic explanation may be a necessary condition, though an insufficient one, to explain why these two factors (*shemittah* and Sinai) are juxtaposed.

One reason for what I take to be the intentional juxtaposition of these questions—why not ask the more general question first, as is Ya'akov Yosef's custom, and then cite the midrashic question?—would be that Ya'akov Yosef wanted to suggest that Rashi's reading is inadequate here. Although it resolves a textual anomaly and supports the rootedness of rabbinic legislation under the aegis of Scripture, it misses the more fundamental point of why we need to read the Torah in the first place; that is, it does not explain what *shemittah* might *mean* to a reader for whom its original or literal meaning is irrelevant. Because *shemittah* is a commandment limited to the territory of the Land of Israel (*Ereẓ Yisrael*), Rashi's approach fails to integrate *shemittah* as a source for Jewish devotion in a non-territorialized Judaism. Ya'akov Yosef may be suggesting that without an answer to *this* question Scripture cannot serve as a template for devotion and (here I admittedly speculate) cannot, therefore, survive the weight of modern (heretical) critique. He then goes on to ask a series of additional textual questions, but the question of relevance remains at the center. Ya'akov Yosef subsequently brings to bear a series of rabbinic texts to answer this question, suggesting that his question is already implied in classical literature if one reads it with this query in mind. It is this question as an interpretive lens that he claims is the ḥasidic innovation. And the application of this innovation inaugurates a fundamentally new reading of Scripture.

Ya'akov Yosef's concern with biblical relevance is not rhetorical; it holds what I take to be his main interpretive and theological concern. In many cases the question of relevance is followed by a variation of the theme "this can be explained in two ways [*bi-shnei panim*]." Sometimes, albeit not always, this is followed by a citation from Maimonides, juxtaposed with an oral tradition from the Besht (*shamati mi-mori*). This technique suggests that Ya'akov Yosef may be trying to situate the Besht as an alternative to a more conventional approach to Torah (the citations from Maimonides are almost always from his legal code and not his philosophical works). Maimonides is often set up as the standard and then (re)read to conform to the Besht's understanding. Here is one example of his use of a classic Maimonidean principle.

> *Now when Pharaoh let the people go* (Exod. 13:17). The questions [*sefekot*] here are self-evident along with the obvious question [*safek yadua*] "Why are these stories written and how do they relate to every individual and at all times?" I can explain this in two ways, as Maimonides writes, "The middle path is the straight path. If one leans to one extreme one must go to the other extreme and remain there for some time until he uproots his first [extreme] trait after which he can return to the middle path."[30]

Ya'akov Yosef then goes on to apply this Maimonidean (really, Aristotelian) principle of the "golden mean" to explain why God has to send Israel in a roundabout way in order to get to where it needed to be. But perhaps we can also find a subtler message here about "two ways" to serve God. The conventional model until Ḥasidism was one of pious asceticism and the division of society between the elites and the masses. (As an Aristotelian, Maimonides supported such a position.) Ḥasidism suggests (at least in the Besht's portrayal imagined by his early disciples) a non- or even anti-ascetic pietism and supports a more integrative relationship between the elite and

30 *Toldot Ya'akov Yosef*, 164a.

the masses.[31] The *Toldot Ya'akov Yosef* works with this notion of "two ways" in at least two, perhaps three, directions: first, the explicit notion of "two forms of worship"; second, the division of two communities (the elite and the masses); and, perhaps third, the notion of two ways of reading (for textual clarity and for devotional guidance).

The notion of two different forms of worship (although these are never defined as conventional and ḥasidic, that seems implied) looms large in the *Toldot Ya'akov Yosef* and is often introduced by asking about the relevance of a biblical episode. Commenting on the verse describing Lot in Sodom, "But they said, 'Come close, and go!' They said, '[he, Lot] came here as an alien'" (Gen. 19:9). Ya'akov Yosef asks, "Why write the story of the Sodomites in the Torah at all and how is this relevant to every person at all times?" He then explains this "in two ways," offering two interpretations of how proximity—to God or to one's neighbor—can be dangerous. In the first way, he cites from what he only calls *ketavim* (writings) about the recitation of the bedtime *Shema*. His second way is based on a Tosafot from the talmudic tractate Shabbat.

From his ensuing discussion, the reference to the anonymous *ketavim* is clearly a kabbalistic source, likely from the Lurianic Kabbalah (Lurianic literature has numerous lengthy homilies on the bedtime Shema) about two types of fear of God.[32] The point here is that one should be aware that if one comes too close (whether to God or to a friend) that proximity can often result in distance. (He cites the phrase *raẓo va-shov*—"running toward and retreating"—from Ezekiel's vision of the angels [Ezek. 1:14].) Hence one needs to be cautious as one approaches spiritual or relational intimacy. In the second way, he uses the Tosafot's suggestion that God had to "hang the mountain over Israel's heads" (at Sinai) because even though they had already said, "We will do and we will understand" (Exod. 24:7), the theophany might be so traumatic that they would recant their initial commitment. He continues:

> So it is with the Exodus from Egypt that resulted in extreme intimacy [*kiruv gadol*]. Afterward, things returned to their natural course. So, too, with a person's worship of God. First it is "come close" and then "go" from a distance . . . as I once heard a parable of a father and son: When he teaches his son to walk, he first holds his hand and afterward, when he becomes accustomed

---

31 The conventional wisdom about ḥasidic populism has been challenged in Ada Rapoport-Albert, "God and the Tzadik as the Two Focal points of Ḥasidic Worship," *History of Religions* 18 (1979): 296–324.

32 See, for example, Meir Poppers, *Pri Eiẓ Ḥayyim* (Jerusalem, 1988), 319–44.

to walking, the father removes his hand. So, too, the son "comes close" and then "goes."[33]

In this "first way" one has to exhibit caution so as not to undermine one's desire for God by always keeping a safe distance. Intense proximity is discouraged. In the "second way" one throws caution to the wind in order to achieve an experience of extreme intimacy that is then followed by a natural separation and stabilization even as that separation, following the father and son analogy, retains a sense of intimacy, albeit from some distance. His example is Israel's intense (ecstatic?) experience of the Exodus and then the retreating process of forty-nine days between that event and the theophany at Sinai, which corresponds to the forty-nine days of the *Omer* as an organic progression from Passover to Pentecost (*Shavu'ot*).

Notably, here, the way of caution is exhibited through a kabbalistic text, and the way of experimentation and religious enthusiasm is exhibited through the classic talmudic commentary of the French Tosafists. The first may describe the non-ḥasidic elite who were critical, or at least wary, of nascent Ḥasidism's ecstatic expression of spiritual intimacy, while the second "way"—the Beshtian or ḥasidic way—is illustrated through a reading of traditional talmudic commentary. It seems that here Ya'akov Yosef, almost always addressing two distinct audiences in his work, curiously justifies the ḥasidic way through the texts of the non-ḥasidic community and justifies the non-ḥasidic way by using a kabbalistic text more commonly deployed for the purposes of conveying the ḥasidic message.[34]

If this reading is plausible, it would support my claim that Ya'akov Yosef structured his homilies and took considerable care in choosing which literary genre to use to make his views known. Here we see his two principles at work. First, this is all prefaced by the fundamental question of his exegetical enterprise (two ways of reading Scripture), that is, "why do we need these [biblical] stories anyway?" The stories in the Torah are only justified when they can serve as templates to describe some element of human devotion. Second, he describes two modes of devotion, the ḥasidic way and the nonḥasidic way. Here, unpredictably, he uses the Tosafists to exemplify the ḥasidic form of worship and the Kabbalists to describe the non-ḥasidic form of devotion. We do not know whether this is an intentional reversal. If it is (and it surely could be), it may be how he illustrates the third manifestation of "two ways," that is, toward two distinct communities. By exemplifying

33 *Toldot Ya'akov Yosef*, 61a.

34 On the dual nature of Torah, speaking to two distinct audiences, see *Toldot Ya'akov Yosef*, 57b.

the ḥasidic way of devotion through a comment by the Tosafists, he may be communicating to his non- or anti-ḥasidic rabbinic readers that the Besht's approach is rooted in the very rabbinic tradition they hold dear.

One final example explores a well-known disagreement between ḥasidic and non-ḥasidic Judaism on the relationship between one's thoughts and actions in regard to divine worship. The standard formula has it that the non-ḥasidic pietists argue that one should empty one's distracting thoughts (sometimes defined as the "evil inclination" or *yeẓer ha-ra*) before undertaking the performance of a *miẓvah*. The Besht counters this by arguing that one should engage in acts of divine worship even (or precisely) with these distracting thoughts and that the power of one's worship will elevate these thoughts to their (holy) root above. Commenting on the verse, "So on that day [*ba-yom ha-hu*] Esau started back that day on his way to Se'ir. But Jacob journeyed on to Sukkot and built a house there" (Gen. 33:16, 17), Ya'akov Yosef writes: "One could ask, why does it say 'on that day'; second, what do we learn from this; third, how is this relevant to every individual at all times?"[35] The first question is the classic medieval question about seemingly extraneous words or phrases. The second question is transitional, serving as a bridge to the third question that takes us beyond the medieval exegetical agenda and into the realm of ḥasidic reading. The questions are immediately followed with, "I heard from my master [the Besht]" about a passage from the Zohar stating that Israel was only being exiled after they disbelieved in God and David.[36] Ya'akov Yosef then continues with a drawn-out kabbalistic interpretation of this passage that is not directly relevant to our limited concerns but returns to his initial question later in the homily. I pick up the text on the following page where he returns to his initial question, why write "on that day," implying, I assume, that Esau and Jacob went their separate ways "on the [very] same day."

> I can now explain my question "what was, was." There are two types of divine worship which constitutes a fundamental principle [*klal gadol*] . . . One is that a person must purify one's thoughts first and then perform the *miẓvah*, in action or words, in order to be pure without any extraneous distractions. We see this in the verse, "And Isaac went out walking [i.e., to pray] in the field close toward evening [*lifnot erev*] (Gen. 24:63). When Isaac went out to pray he was careful to remove and to turn away [from all distractions] as

35 *Toldot Ya'akov Yosef*, 97a.

36 Zohar 2:175b.

> it is said, *lifnot erev*. This [the verb *lifnot* literally means "to turn"] refers to all his evil and extraneous thoughts in order that his prayer may be pure . . .
>
> The second way, which is deeper [*penimi'ut yoter*], is illustrated in the Mishnah, *Pirkei Avot*, "Do not say 'when I have time I will study'; perhaps you won't have time..." (m. Avot 2:4). The simple meaning suffices. "When I will push away my extraneous thoughts I will organize my study schedule but now I am busy." Do not say this, perhaps you will never have time and thus never study. The same is true for prayer . . . I heard from my master [the Besht] on the verse, "I have considered my ways and I have turned back to your decrees" (Ps. 119:59). That is, one should commence with Torah and prayer *with* the evil inclination, that is, "not for the sake of heaven," and, in this way, the evil inclination will not protest against you [on high] and you will conclude "for the sake of heaven." This is the meaning of the verse, "I have considered my ways and I have turned back to your decrees . . ." What comes from this [interpretation] is that one must trick [*lignov da'at*] one's evil inclination into joining him at first and then afterward one must be strident and make it all "for the sake of heaven" . . . Even though this is dangerous, as one enters into the exilic state of the evil inclination by joining forces with him... Nevertheless be scrupulous so that you can develop [*la'alot*] and pray to God that He should aid you against this evil inclination. In that case, this way is superior to the first way.[37]

This well-known teaching of the Besht has been examined by many. I wish to draw attention to the way it is born from a rereading of the verse in Genesis 33. Going back to the Besht's question on the words in Genesis 13:16 "on that day [*ba-yom ha-hu*]" citing the Zohar (3:77b), the Besht (as conveyed by Ya'akov Yosef) suggests that this locution ("on that day") refers to the day of redemption.[38] In other words, at the time of redemption Esau and Jacob will go their separate ways *but not before*. Hence the first way of serving God by waiting to deflect all distractions before enacting a *mizvah* is futile because it is impossible (and hence inappropriate) in this exilic existence. Trying to separate one's extraneous thoughts before engaging in devotional acts is not a product of appropriate caution but the opposite, an act of hubris.[39] Here he deploys the mishnah in Avot 2:4 about waiting

37 *Toldot Ya'akov Yosef*, 98d, 99a.

38 *Toldot Ya'akov Yosef*, 97b.

39 A very different reading, albeit one that makes similar moves can be found in Nathan of Gaza, "*Drush ha-Menorah*," published in *Be-Ikvot Mashiaḥ*, ed. Gershom Scholem (Jerusalem: Tarshish Books, 1944), 97–99.

until one has time before undertaking a regime of study. In this homily, he illustrates this point with the reference to the biblical passage of Jacob "journeying on to Sukkot to build a house there" to refer to the Temple in Jerusalem or the period of redemption. What may be implied here is that the exile continues precisely when one does *not* engage with the evil inclination in order to uplift it, since nonengagement with one's evil inclination will result in delinquency in one's devotional life.

This may also apply to Jacob's commitment to have a reunion with Esau, which frames the biblical episode in question. One must engage the evil inclination in order to separate from it. This comes across even more strongly in his reading of another mishnah from *Pirkei Avot*, "Who is a wise man? One who learns from everyone" (m. Avot 4:1). Ya'akov Yosef writes, "From 'everyone' includes learning from one's evil inclination [*yeẓer ha-ra*]."[40] To offer a reading that would situate "on this day" solely within the context of the biblical story (this is common in medieval exegesis) is the old paradigm that Ya'akov Yosef is contesting, not because it is false *per se* but because in his mind it does not, and cannot, bring Scripture (back) to life. This, according to Ya'akov Yosef, is precisely what the Besht, and *ḥasidim* more generally, were coming to remedy.

Ḥasidism's whole new approach to worship, what Abraham Joshua Heschel referred to more broadly as "a new approach to Torah,"[41] is founded on the seemingly extraneous words "on this day" in what appears to be a story that, in Ya'akov Yosef's rendering, is not on its face necessary to the biblical narrative. I read Heschel's locution "a new approach to Torah" in a hyperliteral rather than colloquial way—a new approach to *reading* Torah, a new approach to the Bible.

The innovative nature of Ḥasidism (or lack thereof) has been discussed by many scholars. Most of these discussions revolve around concepts such as the role of the *ẓaddik*, the centrality of prayer over study, or the anti-ascetic nature of ḥasidic worship. What has not received adequate treatment is the way Ḥasidism, in developing its approach to worship, is also offering a new way to read Scripture. My suggestion here is not simply to note that ḥasidic ideology is born from its reading of Scripture. That is obvious. By prefacing so many of his observations with "Why do we need this at all?" Ya'akov Yosef is *reintroducing* the Bible as the primary template for Jewish spirituality and, in doing so, is reinserting the Bible into a

40 *Toldot Ya'akov Yosef*, 99a.

41 See Abraham Joshua Heschel, "Ḥasidism as a New Approach to Torah," in *Moral Grandeur and Spiritual Audacity*, ed. Susannah Heschel (New York: Farrar, Straus & Giroux, 1996), 33–39.

traditional Jewish world that was dominated by the study of Talmud and codes. The Zohar turned to the Bible as a way to found its esotericism and cosmology. Ya'akov Yosef does so to teach his readers a new way to serve God, a new way to be human, not simply by using biblical archetypes as exemplars but by suggesting that without the Besht's new way of creating biblical relevance by making the Bible about human devotion ("for all individuals, at all times") the eternal nature of the Bible is threatened—that is, without reading it primarily for its devotional import, the Bible could not withstand its modern critique.

Although biblical criticism had not yet reached maturity in the latter part of the eighteenth century, and the Jewish Enlightenment was still some decades away where Ya'akov Yosef lived, that he stressed the need to confirm the Bible's eternal nature (*niẓḥi'ut*) by reading it as pointing outside its own narrative marks an important and underexamined dimension of Ḥasidism's innovative spirit.[42] Whether this was a direct response to Bible criticism or perhaps a more unconscious move generated by a sense of modernity's looming challenge is not known. But given that the *Toldot Ya'akov Yosef* is a work explicitly written for more than one audience, we should not discount the possibility that its polemical tone extended beyond the topical debate between the rabbinic elite and nascent Ḥasidism. There may be a veiled triangulation here. Without explicitly acknowledging this, most ḥasidic literature subsequent to the *Toldot* adopts this practice, although the foundational question—"Why is this relevant?"—is rarely rehearsed. It is simply taken for granted.

Conclusion

My argument here is that we need to examine Ḥasidism through a wider lens than just as another manifestation of the Jewish mystical tradition. The hermeneutical contribution of Ḥasidism, while surely deeply informed by Kabbalah and pietism, largely lies in its focus on the Bible as the template of ḥasidic spirituality. This "innovation" is cultivated by Ya'akov Yosef in his *Toldot Ya'akov Yosef*. Ya'akov Yosef does more than simply base his ḥasidic ideology on Scripture. He begins his exegetical enterprise by marking a flaw, if you will, in the very nature of how Jews read their Bible. The Bible had become disconnected from the lives of its readers because the exegetical frame that surrounded it did not present the Holy Writ as a template

42 See Wodzinski, *Haskala and Ḥasidism*, 9–33.

for devotion but rather as a divine text whose internal fissures and ambiguities required clarification and whose narrative (sometimes) needed to be justified. These concerns are shared by classical biblical exegesis (and its subsequent consumers) and modern Bible critics, using different methods and yielding different—often opposite—results. By the late eighteenth century, traditional readers of the Hebrew Bible were often, consciously or not, responding defensively to the accusation of the Bible critics against the divine origin of the Pentateuch. Early ḥasidic masters are not often counted among these defenders. I argue here that Ya'akov Yosef may be doing so not by openly engaging Bible criticism—of which he likely knew almost nothing—but by criticizing the traditional approach of biblical exegesis that he believed undermined the argument of the Bible's eternality.

By consistently asking—and in a loud voice—"Why is this written?" Ya'akov Yosef challenges the traditional trajectory of biblical exegesis by suggesting that the Bible can only be saved if it points to the present, to the devotional needs of each reader in every generation (*be-khol et u-ve-khol zeman*). Although there were precedents to this reorientation (precedents he often cites), Ya'akov Yosef was doggedly devoted to making this the centerpiece of his approach, and, given that the *Toldot* was the first ḥasidic book in print, the approach of much of ḥasidic literature that followed. We need to read the Bible in this way, he implies, not only to bring the Bible to life but (also) to save us from the misdirected piety that had developed over the long period of exile. For Ya'akov Yosef, the Besht comes to offer us a new lens through which to read the Bible and to worship God, and both are mutually dependent on each other. That ḥasidic masters and their publishers seemed to follow this advice, coupled with the ultimate success of the movement against its traditional and progressive detractors, resulted in, among other things, a revivified Bible and a reenergized Judaism.

Chapter 2

The Case of Jewish Arianism: The Pre-existence of the Ẓaddik in Early Ḥasidism

He himself is before all things and in him all things hold together.
—Collossians 1:17

The creation of time and the question if anything precedes time (and thus creation) has been a matter of metaphysical speculation for millennia. Even before the introduction of Greek metaphysics to the Jewish theological orbit, the talmudic rabbis contemplated the ambiguous notion of pre-existence, that is, whether creation is a product of time, or whether all of creation is, in fact, equally created. The fifth chapter of *Pirkei Avot* (Avot 5:1–8) is perhaps the earliest rabbinic articulation of this question. Most of it reads as a laundry list of "tens," "sevens," and "fours"; ten utterances of creation, ten generations from Adam to Noaḥ, ten tests of Abraham, ten miracles in Egypt, etc. Culminating this imaginative flourish of "tens" we read that "ten things were created on the sixth day of creation between sunset and nightfall" (Avot 5:6). These things include the fissure in the earth that swallowed Koraḥ, the mouth of Balaam's donkey, Noah's rainbow, Moses' staff, and the worm that cut the stones in the Temple. In short, objects of miracle or divination. More striking we read a *beraita* cited in BT Pesahim 54b and Nedarim 39b that seven things came into being before creation, two being Torah (*Logos*) and the name of the messiah. This rabbinic sentiment could easily have been born from earlier notions of the pre-existence in Wisdom Literature where Wisdom (*Ḥokhmah*/Sofia) is said to exist before creation.[1] All this may not speak of pre-existence *per se* although that may depend on how we understand the process of creation as articulated in Genesis 1. At least one position holds that creation during the first six days was only *in potentia* and did not exist *in actu* until the creation of Adam on the sixth day.[2] Thus the things listed in the Mishnah as created *bein ha-shemashot* (at dusk) on the sixth day may have come into existence *before* the actualization of the rest of creation and thus technically be "pre-existent." The notion of the *Logos* being the "Firstborn Son of God," or "Man of God," or "Second God" already exists in Alexandrian Jewry as transmitted by Philo of Alexandria. This already suggests a pre-existence that does not imply or require coeternality. Here Ioan Couliano makes the relevant distinction. "The differences between God and Logos are those between the eternal, ungenerated, and incorruptible on the one hand, and simply 'deathless' (*athanatos*), generated, and incorruptible on the other."[3]

The topic of pre-existence also becomes a focus in the Israelite orbit in the early church's reflection of the Christ-event. Once High Christology became a central tenet of the church—perhaps most forcefully articulated in the Nicene Creed in 325 CE, "Christ was begotten as only begotten of the Father, God of God, Light of Light . . . [Christ was] begotten not made, consubstantial with the Father"—the pre-existence of Christ became a topic of theological reflection and vigorous debate. New Testament scholars argue about whether we can detect in Paul's epistles a gesture toward Christ's pre-existence, specifically in 1 Corinthians 15 and Philippians 2:6–11, known as Adam Christology (e.g., "The first man Adam became a living being; the last Adam became a life-giving spirit" [1 Corinthians 15:45]). References, oblique as they may be, in John and even more so in the gnostic-influenced Gospel of Thomas lend themselves more strongly to this position. Even though scholars such as James Dunn are highly skeptical as to whether in fact the New Testament supports a pre-existent Christ, it is certainly ambiguous enough to suggest that the pre-existent Christ that comes into focus with the Nicenes exists in a more diffuse form in the New Testament and then more strongly in Origen's *First Principles* before the

1 See, for example, on Helner Ringgren, *Word and Wisdom: Studies in the Hypostatization of Divine Qualities and Functions in the Ancient Near East* (Lund: Ohlsson, 1947), 99.

2 See, for example, BT Hulin 62b and Moses Nahmanides, *Persu'ah al ha-Torah* (Jerusalem: Mosad ha-Rav Kook, 1959), 32 to Genesis 2:5.

3 Ioan Couliano, *The Tree of Gnosis: Gnostic Mythology from Early Christianity to Modern Nihilism* (New York: Harper Collins, 1992), 122.

Nicean creed.[4] We should note that early Christians varied a great deal on the actual doctrine of Incarnation, especially as it relates to pre-existence. As Dale Martin writes, "Some Christians thought Jesus was divine, but of a more junior divine status than God the Father. Only eventually, through much theological debate and conflict, did the Christian Church come to believe that in order to be 'orthodox' one had to believe that Jesus was fully divine, of equal divine status with God the Father."[5] While Origen in his *First Principles* may have been the first early Christian to gesture toward a notion of non-identity of God (Father) and Jesus (Son), it was Arius (c. 256–336) and his followers who concretized this position in the early Church.[6] The Arian doctrine that argued that Christ was "made" before creation but not coeternal with God was the source of a great controversy in the early church. "That the son is unbegotten, not in any way part of Unbegotten, not derived from some (alien) substratum, but that exists by will and council before times and before ages, full of truth, and grace, of God."[7]

This doctrine also became known as subordinationism or the notion that Jesus and, in some cases, the Holy Spirit, are divine creatures not equal to God, existed among the many Christian Gnostics, such as the radical Cathars, Bogomilists, and other forms of Christianity that were influenced by Origen on this question.[8] In his *Thalia*, Arius writes, "The one without beginning established the Son as the beginning of all creatures. . . . The Son possesses nothing proper to God. . . for he is not equal to God, nor yet is he of the same substance." According to Arius, the Son is born from the Father before creation, but he is not coeternal with the Father the way the Niceans

4 See James D. G. Dunn, *Christology in the Making: A New Testament Inquiry into the Origins of the Doctrine of the Incarnation* (Philadelphia: Westminster Press, 1980), 113–28. On Origen see Origen, *On First Principles*, trans. G. W. Buttweworth (Gloucester, MA: Peter Smith, 1973), 108–15. On Nicene see Lewis Ayer, *Nicea and its Legacy: An Approach to Fourth-Century Trinitarian Theology* (New York: Oxford University Press, 2004), 52–61, 105–30.

5 Dale B. Martin, *New Testament History and Literature* (New Haven, CT: Yale University Press, 2012), 165. Martin is likely referring to the Arianism whose belief in the non-identity of Father and Son was deemed heretical at the council of Nicea.

6 Arius (c. 256–336) was a priest in Alexandria whose controversy with Bishop Alexander regarding the coeternality of the Son sparked a major rift in early Christianity. Aruis's thinking was influenced by Origen's *First Principles* that lends itself to a belief in the pre-existence but not coeternality of Jesus. Church leaders such as Eusebius of Nicodemia were supporters of the Arian position until it was marginalized through the Nicean Council. On this particular dimension of Arian doctrine see Lewis Ayers, *Nicea and its Legacy*, 15–20 and 105–30. Cf. R. P. C. Hanson, *The Search for the Christian Doctrine of God: The Arian Controversy* (London: T&T Clark, 2005), 3–18, 99–128, 318–81.

7 From Arius's *Thalia* cited in Hanson, *The Search for the Christian Doctrine of God*, 6.

8 See, for example, in Couliano, *The Tree of Gnosis*, 221–29.

preferred.[9] The Arian creed is finally effaced by the Niceans through the Nicean Creed in 325 CE. Through this, pre-existence became synonymous with coeternality with God as the orthodox doctrine of High Christology of the Catholic Church. Hence, when I use the term "pre-existent" in regard to the ḥasidic *ẓaddik* below, I do not refer to the post-Nicean linkage of pre-existence and coeternality. Rather, I leave open the possibility of what I will call an Arian reading of these ḥasidic texts that affirms pre-existence without coeternality, which, while not Nicean, is still incarnational.

The notion of pre-existence in early Judaism is examined by Daniel Boyarin in *Border Lines* and *The Jewish Gospels* in his reading of Daniel 7. Boyarin argues that the rabbis entertained the possibility of a kind of coeternal binitarianism.[10] He argues that the distinction between Judaism and Christianity in this early period was "not via the doctrine of God, and not even the question of worshipping a second God . . . but only in the specifics of the doctrine of this incarnation."[11] As Boyarin's focus is largely Christianity in the Gospels he does not address the Arian controversy that exhibits an inner-Christian debate about the nature of the incarnation. In any case, the early inner-Jewish controversy arguably does not survive the end of the rabbinic period in what became in the normative rabbinic imagination the heresy of "two powers in heaven."[12] The kabbalistic tradition, however, tells a different story. It is to Kabbalah that we must turn to view the persistence of pre-existence that informs ḥasidic literature. On medieval Kabbalah Elliot Wolfson states, "it may be said that the medieval Jewish mystics recovered the mythic dimension of a biblical motif regarding the appearance of God in the guise of the highest angels... which sometimes appears in the form of man."[13] The *Tikkunei Zohar* reads *Shekhinah* through the numerical value of the Tetragrammaton rendered as 45, equaling ADAM.[14]

---

9 See Ayers, *Nicea and its Legacy*, 54, 55.

10 See Daniel Boyarin, *Border Lines* (Philadelphia: University of Pennsylvania Press, 2006),
120–25; and Boyarin, *The Jewish Gospels: The Story of the Jewish Christ* (New York: The New Press, 2012), 50–59.

11 *Border Lines*, 125. See also, Boyarin, *The Jewish Gospels*, 43. Cf. Boyarin, *Border Lines*, 127.

12 See Alan Segal, *Two Powers in Heaven* (Leiden: Brill, 1977).

13 Wolfson, *Through a Speculum that Shines* (Princeton, NJ: Princeton University Press, 1996), 255.

14 See *Tikkunei Zohar*, introduction, 18a, and section #22, 65b, discussed in Wolfson, "Suffering Eros and Textual Incarnation: A Kristevan Reading of Kabbalistic Poetics," in *Towards a Theology of Eros*, ed. V. Burrus and C. Keller (New York: Fordham University Press, 2006), 360–61.

The early kabbalistic reflection on Metatron, the Zohar's reading of *eheyeh asher eheyeh* and *keter*, and the Lurianic rendering of Adam Kadmon, while not offering clear notions of Nicene pre-existence, certainly test the elasticity of creation *ex nihilo* (*yesh me-ayin*) that became standard Jewish nomenclature by the High Middle Ages. My focus here will be on the much later refraction of the kabbalistic imaginary in the form of ḥasidic zaddikism. It should be noted that while the medieval kabbalistic dalliance with pre-existence is largely contained in its cosmology and cosmogony, Ḥasidism draws this down into the corporeal in the person of the *ẓaddik* which in some ways brings kabbalistic metaphysics into closer proximity to Christianity's theories about the Christ-event. Below I examine a selection of a few early ḥasidic texts to illustrate my point, focusing specifically on the notion of pre-existence that reflects the Arian position of incarnation that separates pre-existence from coeternality.[15]

The complexity of ḥasidic zaddikism is well documented in scholarship.[16] While Jews rejected the doctrine of incarnation that fuses God and the savior ("Light from Light"), as close readers of medieval Kabbalah, particularly the Zohar, many ḥasidic masters do not accept the categorical distinction between God and the *ẓaddik* that is common in non-mystical Judaism.[17] Put otherwise, Ḥasidism, as I understand it, is not party to the Maimonidean paradigm as conventionally understood.[18] Elsewhere I argue that since Ḥasidism develops in modernity largely outside the "Christian gaze," that is, not invested in defending why Judaism is *not* Christianity (I suggest this is endemic to the modern Jewish project in

---

15 See in Hanson, *The Search for the Christian Doctrine of God*, 106–16.

16 For some examples see Arthur Green, "The Zaddik as Axis Mundi," *Journal of the American Academy of Religion* 45 (1997): 327–47. In terms of the doctrine of the *ẓaddik* as the only real innovation of Ḥasidism, see Mendel Pierkarz, *Be-Yemei Ẓemikhat ha-Ḥasidut* (Jerusalem: Mosad Bialik, 1978), and Piekarz, *Ḥasidut Polin* (Jerusalem: Mosad Bialik, 1990), 157–80. Cf. Moshe Idel, *Ḥasidism: Between Ecstasy and Magic* (Albany: SUNY Press, 1995), 189–208; and Immanuel Etkes, "The *Zaddik:* The Interrelationship between Religious Doctrine and Social Organization," in *Ḥasidism Reappraised*, ed. A. Rapoport-Albert (Portland, OR, and Oxford: The Littman Library of Jewish Civilization, 1997), 159–67. Following Max Weber, Stephen Sharot describes the *ẓaddik* as a "mystagogue." See Sharot, "Ḥasidism and the Routinization of Charisma," *Journal for the Sociological Study of Religion* 19, no. 4 (1980): 328.

17 See, for example, Yehuda Liebes, "The Messiah of the *Zohar*: On R. Shimon bar Yohai as a Messianic Figure," in *Studies in the Zohar* (Albany: SUNY Press, 1993), 1–84.

18 See Menachem Kellner, *Maimonides' Confrontation with Mysticism* (Oxford: The Littman Library of Jewish Civilization, 2006), 286–96.

Western Europe), it more freely engages in descriptions of God and the *ẓaddik* in ways that bring it in closer to proximity to Christianity, showing, perhaps, that the categorical theological division between the two religions is less sound than we think.[19]

I begin with a text from *No'am Elimelekh* from the third generation ḥasidic master Elimelekh of Lyzinsk (1717–1787). I begin with this text in order to illustrate what I could call a normative theory of cosmic zaddikism that approaches but does not traverse the border of the pre-existent *ẓaddik* that I will claim exists more baldly in the second series of texts by Dov Baer, the Maggid of Mezritch (d. 1772). In *No'am Elimelekeh* we read:

> . . . . We read, "We learn in b. T Haggigah" one does not infer from *arayot* with three, *ma'aseh bereishit* with two, and *ma'aseh merkavah* even with one. . . ." (Hagigah 11b). One can explain this in the following manner: God creates and makes the world to God's will. Opposite that, God creates the *ẓaddik* who can nullify divine decrees. Yet we can ask: how is this possible to nullify divine decrees that were already decreed in the supernal heavens? However, as I have written numerous times, we read in Psalms (Ps. 33:6) "with the word of God the heavens were made" [*be-davar ha-shem shamayim na'asu*]. This means that the *ẓaddik*, by means of engaging in Torah [the word of God] for its own sake [*li-shemah*] and drawing from this study new meaning [*meḥadesh ḥiddushim*], makes/creates [*na'asu*] new heavens and engages in the act of creation [*ma'aseh bereishit*]. Therefore, by force the decrees [of the old heavens] are nullified [*betaylin*] as they were now not part of the world that created [anew] by the *ẓaddik*.[20]

Here the *ẓaddik* is surely created and not coeternal with God but he is created in a manner that enables, perhaps empowers him, when encountering the word of God in purity (*osek be-torah li-shemah*), not merely to alter the existing creation but to create something new, thereby making the divine creation (creation as we know it from Genesis) mutable. The *ẓaddik* here becomes a creator by engaging the creation-blocks (the word of God-Torah) of God's creation. I would suggest considering the possible symmetry of the term *osek be-torah li-shemah* relating to the *ẓaddik* here with the term *sha'ashu'a* to describe God's playful engagement with Torah in

---

19 See my *Ḥasidism Incarnate: Ḥasidism, Christianity, and the Construction of Modern Judaism* (Stanford: Stanford University Press, 2014).

20 *No'am Elimelekh* (Jerusalem, 1976), 277.

Proverbs 8:30, 31, Psalm 199:24, and other places.[21] In both cases, Torah is used as a creative tool by the one who is intimate with it. The term *sha'ashu'a* in Kabbalah has overt erotic implications. I suggest the term *osek*, literally "involved or busy with," also implies a kind of proximity that gestures toward intimacy.

The notion of using language, here *lashon ha-kodesh*/the language of Torah, as the building blocks of creation is common in Ḥasidism and has its roots in rabbinic midrash.[22] It is used here by Elimelekh in very specific ways to describe symmetry and perhaps even unity between the *ẓaddik* and God. Note in this text the implied symmetry between the *ẓaddik* speaking Torah (*osek be-torah*) and God playfully engaging with Torah (*sha'ashu'a*). Another example can be found in the Maggid's meditation on the verse from Genesis, "And he [Jacob] took stones from that place and put them under his head" (Gen. 28:11).

> It is known that the "stones are [Hebrew] letters. When the *ẓaddik* prays with these letters and binds [*mekasher*] himself to the supernal wisdom [*ḥokhmah elyonah*], as is known, he has already entered the gate of eternity/nothingness [*sha'ar ha-ayin*]. He will elevate his heart until it is as if God's power is in it. At that moment he achieves complete nullity [*efes mukhlat*]. As such, everything is divine power [*koaḥ*] and his [the *ẓaddik*'s] speech is from the speech of God that created the world. The world of speech [*olam ha-dibbur*] is drawn from the supernal wisdom [*ḥokhmah*] which is the pleasure [*ta'anug*] and playfulness [*sha'ashu'im*] that God gets from the world. And now he [the *ẓaddik*] speaks only for the playfulness [*sha'ashu'a*] of God. And through this the letters return to their original source, which is the wisdom [*ḥokhmah*] from which they were drawn.[23]

God's playful engagement with Torah (Proverbs 8:30, et al.) is now expressed as the pleasure God receives from the *ẓaddik* while praying with words of creation as explained in *Sefer ha-Bahir*. And the prayer of the *ẓaddik* results in his folding into divinity (*efes mukhlat*) and returning the letters to their original place in the Godhead, assumedly, before creation. Here the prayer of the *ẓaddik* creates a similar result as to the *ẓaddik* who studies *torah li-shemah*.

21 See the discussion in Wolfson, *Aleph, Mem, Tau* (Berkeley and Los Angeles: University of California Press, 2006), 127–32.

22 See, for example, Genesis Rabbah, 18:4 and 31:8.

23 The Maggid of Mezritch, *Torat ha-Maggid*, 1:73a/b. Cf. 1, 76a.

On Christ's incarnation, Augustine suggests that the way beyond the word is through the word. Reading this into our *No'am Elimelekh* text, when the *ẓaddik* fuses with the word through pure engagement with it (*osek be-torah li-shemah*), he transcends the product of the word, or creation, becoming a creator of new worlds through the word. Reading Elimelekh of Lyzinsk this way we could ask whether through pure engagement (*torah li-shemah*) the *ẓaddik* actually becomes the word? I admit this may be too strong a reading but with it we could then understand why the *ẓaddik* now has the power to nullify what God created. We could ponder whether the term "creation" (*bara*) used to describe the *ẓaddik*'s coming-to-be in these texts is best read as "made" or "begotten" (to import for a moment Christian nomenclature). To cite one example, reading Nahmanides' rendering of Genesis 1:1, "*bereishit bara Elohim*," as a description of the higher *sefirah ḥokhmah* to the lower *sefirah binah*, Frank Talmage chooses to translate *bara* as emanate rather than create, a term that may gesture toward the Christian distinction between "made" and "begotten."[24] I would prefer a simpler Arian reading, that the *ẓaddik* is created but created in such a manner that by fusing with the word (*torah li-shemah*) he can cross over from a created being to a creating one. This crossover, from the immutable to the mutable, and back again, is precisely the foundation of incarnational thinking without Nicean coeternality. This locution does not bring us to the coeternal Christ of the Nicenes or even the binitarianism suggested by Boyarin, but it may come close to the Arian notion of Christ as a divine body lower than the Father but still pre-existent.

The following text in the name of the Maggid engages the identical notion of the *ẓaddik* as empowered to create. Here, however, I think we may cross the very border Elimelekh of Lyzinsk only approaches:

> I heard from the Maggid of Ravna, "*Adon olam ha-shem malakh be-terem kol* [Master of the world, the Name who rules before all was created . . .]." The word "*kol*" [all] is called *ẓaddik* [the righteous one] who achieves the generalities [*oseh kelali'ot*] of God with the people of Israel.[25] This is what it means when it says "before all [was created]": the *ẓaddik* nullifies divine

24 Frank Talmage, "Apples of Gold: The Inner Meaning of Sacred Texts in Medieval Judaism," in *Jewish Spirituality I: From the Bible Through the Middle Ages*, ed. Arthur Green (New York: Crossroads, 1986), 329.

25 The *No'am Elimelekh* text also includes a discussion of the term "*kol*" in a similar but not identical way. See *No'am Elimelekh*, 277a.

decrees. God, as it were, is not king, rather [God is king only] *with* the *ẓaddik*, which is why the *ẓaddik* has so much power [*koaḥ*]. This is what I heard . . .[26]

This reading of the popular liturgical poem Adon Olam moves us further than the previous text in *No'am Elimelekh* toward a notion of the *ẓaddik's* actual preexistence, by suggesting *be-terem*, that is, before all, the *ẓaddik* was created/*nivra*, suggesting a strange kind of incarnationalism I call Jewish Arianism. Its suggestion that God shares the throne with the *ẓaddik* (God, as it were, is not king, rather God is king only *with* the *ẓaddik*) should evoke Psalm 110:1, "The Lord said to my lord, sit at my right hand," that became a central text for High Christology in the early church and a source for the binitarianism Boyarin suggests in rabbinic literature.[27] Even if the *ẓaddik* is created (or "begotten") and not coeternal or consubstantial with God the Father, he is created before the rest of creation and thus has a divine status exhibited by his ability to alter divine creation. The *ẓaddik* here is no simple angelic emissary without a will but a divine entity, a willful authority that can alter a divine decree. "The will of God and the will of the *ẓaddik* become one [*na'aseh eḥad*]. That which the *ẓaddik* wants, God also wants, and thus he [the *ẓaddik*] can turn judgment into mercy. . . Only the words of the *ẓaddik* are bound to their source. Behind the words of the *ẓaddik* are literally [*mamash*!] the word of God out of which the heavens were created."[28]

Our text reads the word "*kol*" (all) as a proper noun (the *ẓaddik*) and in doing so, completely alters the grammar of the liturgical verse. Elsewhere we read, "God only dwells on one who humbles himself [*maktinin et aẓmo*], therefore the *ẓaddik* is called '*kol*' [כל] the language of a vessel [*keli*, כלי], as it is written, *Its capacity was 2,000 baths* [*alpayim bat yakhil*, יכיל]. This is the language of suffering [סבלות] that the *ẓaddik* suffers [סובל] God within himself [*betokho*]."[29] We no longer read *Adon olam ha-shem malakh be-terem kol*, "Master of the world, the Name who rules before all was created. . ." but "Master of the world, the Name who rules, before [everything] [*be-terem*], the *ẓaddik* [*kol*] was created. . . ."

26 Seer of Lublin, *Zikharon Zot* #7, cited in *Torat ha-Maggid* (Bnei Brak: Mishur Books, 2011), 2:442.

27 See Boyarin, *Borderlines*, 112–27.

28 The Maggid of Mezritch, *Torat ha-Maggid*, 1:99b, 100a.

29 *Torat ha-Maggid*, 1:118b. Apparently the meaning here is that the notion of "*kol*," or everything, is linked etymologically to vessel (*keli*), that which holds something within it. Thus the *ẓaddik*, who is "*kol*," becomes a holder (or sufferer) of God within himself. On the *ẓaddik* as "*kol*" in the Maggid see his *Maggid Devarav le-Ya'akov*, ed. R. Shatz-Uffenheimer (Jerusalem: Magnes Press, 1990), #601, 96.

The Maggid then follows with a paraphrase of the rabbinic dictum, "the *ẓaddik* nullifies divine decrees" (BT Mo'ed Katan 17b) as a prooftext and illustration of the *ẓaddik*'s pre-existence read into Adon Olam. That is, if the *ẓaddik* precedes creation, his divine status maintains the power to alter creation.[30]

This follows by introducing a caveat to divine kinship, the centerpiece of the verse (*ha-shem malakh*), which is founded on God's mastery of creation (*adon olam*). God is not king ("as it were") because God is not fully a master of creation: "I make decrees and [the *ẓaddik*] nullifies them" we read in BT Mo'ed Katan 17b. Our text lends itself to a kind of binitarian reading, making the *ẓaddik* a partner with God, "God is only king *with* the *ẓaddik*," since the *ẓaddik*, being "*kol*," was created "before" (*be-terem*) creation. This seems close to what we read in 1 Timothy 2:5: "For there is one God, there is also one mediator between God and humankind, Christ Jesus, himself human. . . ." While we can surely differ as to how literally to take our ḥasidic texts, the superhuman status of the *ẓaddik* is quite common in ḥasidic zaddikism and should not be summarily dismissed simply because it comes close to High Christology. The question as to how such heretical teaching, if it is indeed heretical, can emerge from a community deeply inside the normative tradition is a sociological question that is beyond the scope of this chapter. I would simply say that according to my larger thesis it is precisely because these individuals were thinking outside the Christian gaze and thus in a non-defensive or at least non-apologetic posture, their understanding of what was and was not acceptable may be quite different than ours.

For our limited purposes this text introduces a divine/*ẓaddik* symbiosis, perhaps symmetry, depending on how strongly we want to read it, that will serve our goal of viewing God not in a pure, perhaps Maimonidean, monotheistic sense but "*with* the *ẓaddik*" or through the *ẓaddik*. The *ẓaddik* is the part of this partnership who participates in the cross-over from immutability to mutability in the divine descent from heaven to earth, from the heavens to the people, and this is precisely a reflection of the *ẓaddik*'s "divine" pre-existent stature.

My argument is built on the assumption that the *ẓaddik* in the Maggid's teaching describes something other than a Creator/creature relationship.

30 The pre-existence of Jesus was most forcefully argued in the Gospel of John but absent in the other synoptic gospels and does exist in some form in the Gospel of Thomas. We should note that early Christians varied a great deal on the actual doctrine of incarnation. See Martin, *New Testament History and Literature*, 165. Martin is likely referring to the Arians, whose belief in the non-identity of Father and Son was deemed heretical at the council of Nicea.

That is, it is more than a text supporting theurgy (how humans can affect the divine).[31] By suggesting the *ẓaddik* as "*kol*" in Adon Olam, the *ẓaddik* may or may not be created but even if created certainly precedes creation. Thus we do not read, *be-terem kol yeẓir nivra* ("God ruled before everything was created") but perhaps *be-terem kol yeẓir nivra* ("before, there was the *ẓaddik*, who helped fashion creation"). When the *ẓaddik* then enters the world of creation he is already more than God's emissary in a representational or normative sense but as an extension of the divine. The king and his son (God and the *ẓaddik*) are, as it were, extensions of one another (perhaps a different version of "Light from Light"). The *ẓaddik* travelling to retrieve the divine embedded in creation, to "retrieve the sparks," is an extension, via a reversal, of God embedding Godself in creation.

While this reading can obviously be accused of being overly Christological, my intentions are precisely to illustrate the extent to which the ḥasidic texts examined here (which are not atypical, albeit perhaps somewhat evocative), born in their deep engagement with medieval kabbalistic literature, replete with texts that engage pre-existence on a cosmogonic and not human plane (*eheyeh asher eheyeh, keter*, or *Adam Kadmon*), and their focus on the re-personalization of God in the *ẓaddik*, can openly advocate a notion of the *ẓaddik*'s pre-existence without coeternality, thus suggesting an Arian reading of the *ẓaddik*. The creative twisting/misreading of the first line of Adon Olam leads me to believe the ḥasidic masters knew exactly what they were doing. The ḥasidic masters probably did not know of the doctrine of Christ's pre-existence, and almost certainly knew nothing of the Arian controversy, which may be precisely what enabled them down a similar path.

Another admittedly more oblique text from the Maggid's reading of Proverbs 8:30, a popular text in various forms of High Christology, lends itself to this perspective. Here the Maggid subtly inserts the *ẓaddik* into the pre-creation/existent space in the biblical and rabbinic imagination of God's taking delight (*sha'ashu'a*) in wisdom/Torah. We begin with the verse, "And I was with Him [*eẓlo*] as an *amon*, a source of delight [*sha'ashu'a*] every day [*yom yom*] rejoicing before Him at all times [*be-kol et*]" (Prov. 28:30).[32] I intentionally leave the word *amon* untranslated here as this will be the operative word in the Maggid's reading of the verse. The new *JPS Tanakh* translates *amon* here as "confidant," but as we will see, the Maggid uses it in a very different sense.

31 For example, see this approach in Moshe Idel's *Ḥasidism: Between Ecstasy and Magic* (Albany: SUNY Press, 1995), 103–46.

32 The term *sha'ashu'a* appears numerous times in the Writings, e.g., Proverbs 8:30, Psalms 119:24, 70, 77, 92, 143, 174. I will refer solely to its use in Proverbs 8:30 as that is the verse cited in the Maggid's text.

The term *sha'ashu'a* has been analyzed at length in various studies by Elliot Wolfson. Wolfson argues that *sha'ashu'a*, God's delight either with Godself (autoeroticism) or with wisdom/Torah, denotes the very act that constitutes beginning.[33] Wolfson suggests the term *sha'ashu'a* is an indication of eternality ("enduring in its recurrence, eternal in its transience"). It is not something that happens "before" but that, being pre-existent (*yom yom*), exists always (*be-kol et*), beyond the time/space modality. But after creation its existence, whatever it is God was delighting with before, embodies a kind of temporality. In Judaism this is the Torah received at Sinai. In Christianity it would be the incarnated Christ. As we will see below, the Maggid complicates the dichotomy, i.e., Judaism/Torah, Christianity/Christ, a dichotomy that Boyarin suggests is the *logos* theology of the rabbis, by inserting, but not substituting, the *ẓaddik* into this pre-existent space of divine delight (*sha'ashu'a*).

The act of *sha'ashu'a* is an act of beginning but also denotes that which was before beginning, in the *Bahir*'s language "two thousand years" in the lap of the divine before creation. Below, the Maggid deploys this term in a longer discussion about the various dimensions of God's love for his son/child. Curiously, wisdom/Torah, the object of God's delight before creation, now becomes "the torah of the *ẓaddik*," thus inserting the *ẓaddik* into this pre-existent space.

> Before Israel existed each *ẓaddik*, his torah and his works, was revealed to God. And from the beginning, immediately when Israel went up in God's mind, God there was already taking delight [*sha'ashu'a*] and pleasure [*ta'anug*], as it were, from every *ẓaddik* and his actions.[34] The proof of this is that we find God taking delight [*mista'ashe'a*] in the torah of the *ẓaddik*. . .[35] Rashi explains Proverbs 28:30 that the Torah grew in the lap of God for two thousand years. . .[36] The plain-sense meaning is that the Torah was made an *amon* [confidant] to God. But this is difficult to understand. God exists before everything [*kadmon m'kol ha-kadmonim*]. But according to our

33 See especially Wolfson, "Before Alef/Where Beginnings End," in *Beginning/Again: Toward a Hermeneutics of Jewish Texts*, ed. A. Cohen and S. Magid (New York: Seven Bridges Press, 2002), 142–50. Cf. Wolfson, *Language, Eros, Being* (New York: Fordham University Press, 2005), 278–85.

34 See *Torat ha-Maggid*, 1:117a: "God created the world so that he should have pleasure [*ta'anug*] from the *ẓaddikim*."

35 The notion of "delight" as related to the act of study appears in Psalms 119:92, "Were not your teaching my delight, I would have perished in my affliction."

36 Rashi actually does not say this. Rashi merely says that *yom yom* means "two thousand years." The explanation the Maggid attributes to Rashi here appears in *Sefer ha-Bahir* cited above.

> way we can explain it that wisdom/Torah was praising itself that it was a confidant of God, as it were, to mean that God was taking such pleasure and delight from the Torah, that is, the torah of every *ẓaddik* and his good works, which are the *miẓvot* written in the Torah, that they were to God as an artisan [*uman*] and sustenance [*parnasah*].[37]

I acknowledge at the outset that this text can easily fit into a more normative idea that it is the Torah that is created before creation, an idea that occurs numerous times in talmudic and midrashic literature. However, it is curious that the *ẓaddik*, appearing here as "the torah of every *ẓaddik* and his good works," *is* the confidant that is nurturing in God's lap "two thousand years [before creation]." Moreover, there is a subtle twist of the term *amon*, or confidant, in the Maggid's final comment. By shifting the letter *vav* from the third position to the second position of the word, the Maggid changes "confidant" (*amon*, אמון) to "artisan" (*uman*, אומן). This points to his earlier comment of the *ẓaddik* being a partner in creation itself based on the rabbinic dictum that the *ẓaddik* has the power to alter creation. It remains unknown why the Maggid appeared unsatisfied leaving wisdom/Torah as the pre-existent subject of divine delight and chose to insert the *ẓaddik* into that equation. However, elevating the *ẓaddik* to that supernal perch is yet another indication, in my view, of the Maggid's consideration of the *ẓaddik* as something that precedes creation, and that each *ẓaddik* in creation is an articulation of that pre-existent entity. Making "Torah" the "the torah of the *ẓaddik*" appears to move us beyond Boyarin's *logos* theology into the realm of what I am calling Jewish Arianism, an incarnational position that does not reach the bar of the Nicean demand of coeternality but is incarnational nonetheless.

The categorical distinction between Judaism and Christianity that is sometimes proffered by scholars often revolves around the doctrine of the incarnation. Included in this is the notion of Christ's pre-existence, coeternal with God the Father. The complex details regarding the nature of this unity that has occupied Christian theologians for centuries was largely uninteresting for Jews because the unity of Father and Son implied in the doctrine solidifies categorical incompatibility. This, of course, assumes the formulation of the incarnation in the Nicene Creed. What remains puzzling to some scholars of Ḥasidism is that ḥasidic articulations of zaddikism resonate quite strongly with incarnational thinking but reject any notion of coeternality. Yet they do, as I suggested above, gesture toward the *ẓaddik*'s pre-existence. What I am suggesting is that

37 *Torat ha-Maggid, Parshat Toldot*, 65.

if we look at ḥasidic zaddikism, particularly in the early ḥasidic teachings of the Maggid of Mezritch, as something more akin to Arianism, which understood the pre-existence of the Son (or, in Ḥasidism, the *ẓaddik*) as distinct from coeternality, zaddikism can be viewed as a form of incarnational thinking. As I said at the outset, it is highly unlikely that ḥasidic masters gleaned this from Christianity about which they knew little. Rather it was likely an articulation of similar inclinations in medieval Kabbalah that now coalesced around the doctrine of the *ẓaddik* at a time and place where Jews were able to theologize about the *ẓaddik outside* the "Christian gaze."

Chapter 3

The Intolerance of Tolerance: *Maḥaloket* (Controversy) and Redemption in Early Ḥasidism

"In [the] theoretical problem of the history of the spirit, we cannot give any consideration to *tolerance*, the duty of which is to understand and approve every point of view."
—Hermann Cohen, *Religion of Reason*

"Religion is, in the religious view, the exile of man."
—Martin Buber, *The Eclipse of God*

This chapter is devoted to exploring the status and place of controversy (*maḥaloket*) as a redemptive trope in early ḥasidic thought. I am not making any claim as to the nature of *maḥaloket* in Ḥasidism in general. Rather, I will be looking at *maḥaloket* through a narrow lens, based on a close reading of one early ḥasidic text. This text will be the occasion to highlight some substantive differences between ḥasidic theories of *maḥaloket,* as presented in that text, and the rabbinic notion of *maḥaloket* as tolerance, embodied in the words "these and these are the words of the living God."[1]

I am not interested in *maḥaloket* as a sociological phenomenon, although ḥasidic literature has much to say about that, but only as a

1 BT Eruvin 13b; BT Gittin 6b; BT Yevamot 14a; PT Berakhot 1:4; PT Kiddushin 1:1. Cf. Ephraim Urbach, "*Halakhah u-Nevu'ah*" [Hebrew], *Tarbiz* 18, no. 1 (1947): II, 12 and 23–27; and more generally Avi Sagi, *Eilu ve-Eilu: A Study on the Meaning of Halakhic Discourse* [Hebrew] (Israel, 1996).

devotional practice. Therefore, I will not focus on the polemical literature between ḥasidim and mitnaggedim in the late eighteenth century nor the later inner-polemical literature between various ḥasidic dynasties in the nineteenth century.[2] Rather, I will focus on how early Ḥasidism, through the lens of the "literary" Ba'al Shem Tov (known as the Besht), understood the notion of *maḥaloket* as a cosmic category and progenitor to redemption.[3] This will be based on a reading of the longest entry in *Keter Shem Tov*, an early compilation of Beshtian material, that views controversy as part of the divine cosmic realm and the object of *deveikut*.[4] This text sug-

2 For some notes on the inner-polemic of Ḥasidism, see Arthur Green, *Tormented Master: A Life of Rabbi Nahman of Bratslav* (Woodstock, VT: Jewish Lights, 1992), 94–123. On the ḥasidic–mitnaggedic polemics, see Mordecai Wilensky, *Ḥasidim u-Mitnaggedim*, 2 vols. (Jerusalem, 1970); and more recently, Allan Nadler, *The Faith of the Mithnagdim* (Baltimore, MD: The Johns Hopkins University Press, 1997), esp. 11–28, 151–70.

3 By "literary" Ba'al Shem Tov I simply mean the Besht as he was constructed by his disciples and used as an authority for later ḥasidic teaching. Neither the historical Ba'al Shem Tov nor the historicity of the teachings of the Besht is at issue here. I would suggest that the introduction "in the name of the Besht," so common in early ḥasidic collections of Beshtian material is a literary trope rooting a particular teaching in the source of ḥasidic teaching. This is not to say that authentic Beshtian material does not exist. Rather, in collections like *Keter Shem Tov* the assumption is that all its teachings are from the Besht. As has been shown by scholars, there is no real evidence to justify such a claim. For a comprehensive discussion on these matters, see Moshe Rosman, *Founder of Ḥasidism: A Quest for the Historical Ba'al Shem Tov* (Berkeley, Los Angeles and London: University of California Press, 1996).

4 *Keter Shem Tov* #320. *Keter Shem Tov* was collected, edited, and redacted by R. Aaron ben Zvi Hirsch of Optaw (Zolkiew), a disciple of R. Ya'akov Yosef of Polonnoye. It was first published in two volumes; volume one in Zolkiew, 1784, and volume two in Zolkiew, 1795. It was first published in one volume in Karetz in 1797. The Karetz edition became the source for subsequent editions. It contains material largely drawn from Ya'akov Yosef's *Ben Porat Yosef* and *Ẓofnat Pane'ah* and, to a lesser extent from the Maggid of Mezritch, *Likkutim Yekarim* (Lemberg, 1792). See A. Haberman, "*Sefer Zivat ha-Ribash ve-She'ar Likkutim ha-Kadmonim mi-Divrei ha-Besht*," in *Sefer ha-Besht* (Jerusalem, 1960), 38–49. Because it was largely viewed as merely a collection of previous material, while *Keter Shem Tov* was one of the more popular collections of Beshtian Ḥasidism, scholars of Ḥasidism did not take it seriously. This long excerpt is taken from the second volume and likely compiled from various sources and redacted by R. Aaron. In this sense it likely cannot be considered, in its entirety, as directly from the Besht but more accurately a product of his disciples filtered through R. Aaron. While *Keter Shem Tov* is a fairly early version of the teachings of the Besht, the second volume in particular contains teachings that do not exist in any previous source. Some were collected from oral sources and others, according to Gedalya Nigal, may very well be the product of R. Aaron himself. See Gedalya Nigal, "The First Source of the Literature on the Ḥasidic Story: On *Keter Shem Tov* and its Sources" [Hebrew], *Sinai* 79 (1976): 132–46. Interestingly, Nigal lists the sources of volume two of *Keter Shem Tov* from the first edition (Zolkiew, 1795) and has no listing for the lesson that serves

gests, against certain strains of rabbinic notions of controversy, particularly as constructed in post-rabbinic literature, that we should never strive to resolve *maḥaloket.* Rather, human devotion should perpetuate *maḥaloket* as an emulation of the divine realm.

The consequence of this reading extends beyond merely suggesting an alternative understanding of *maḥaloket* in ḥasidic literature. I will argue that this difference illuminates a much larger division between ḥasidic thought and classical Rabbinic Judaism, especially as envisioned by post-rabbinic thinkers. Moreover, it also exhibits a difference between ḥasidic anti-rabbinism and other forms of mystical anti-rabbinism in classical Kabbalah (e. g., *Tikkunei Zohar* and certain strains of Lurianic Kabbalah). I will argue that the Besht's re-reading of the rabbis and reconstruction of *maḥaloket* as ontological rather than historical is an attempt to reconstruct the rabbinic tradition in the image of nascent ḥasidic spirituality, creating a spiritualized rabbinism that offers a new *telos* to the entire project of Rabbinic Judaism.

The underlying assumption of this chapter is that Ḥasidism deviates sharply from the conventional rabbinic attitude on the issue of *maḥaloket*, particularly the way Rabbinic Judaism was reconstructed through the lenses of two foundational post-rabbinic texts, Sherira Ga'on's *Iggeret*, or "Letter on Rabbinic Literature and Transmission," and Maimonides' "Introduction" to his *Commentary on the Mishnah*. My claim is that early Ḥasidism, again only seen through the narrow window of this one example, understood the conventional notion of Rabbinic Judaism to argue that *maḥaloket* was a result of historical exile and the inattentiveness of the disciples of the rabbinic sages Hillel and Shammai. The source of this notion appears in numerous rabbinic passages but is expanded and codified in the writings of Sherira Ga'on and Maimonides. In *Keter Shem Tov*, the Besht emphatically rejects this idea and views it as antithetical to ḥasidic spirituality and as a misreading of rabbinic literature. Therefore, when I refer to "rabbinic notions of *maḥaloket*" in this chapter I am only referring to those ideas that were canonized and transmitted

---

as the basis of this chapter. The 1858 Lemberg edition contains this lesson, as do all subsequent editions. In the 1858 Lemberg edition, perhaps the earliest source of this lesson, it appears on 32a. All references to *Keter Shem Tov* in this chapter are to the 1987 Brooklyn edition published by Kehot. For a recent appraisal of some of these early collections, see Jacob Immanuel Schochet, *Tzava'at Harivash: The Testament of Rabbi Israel Baal Shem Tov* (Brooklyn, NY: Kehot, 1998), xi-xvii. On the importance of editors and redactors in Ḥasidism in general, see Zeev Gries, "The Ḥasidic Managing Editor as an Agent of Culture," in *Ḥasidism Reappraised*, ed. Ada RapoportAlbert (London and Portland OR, 1996), 141–55.

by these two post-rabbinic authorities. The wider rabbinic stance is far more complex.[5]

In the case of *Keter Shem Tov*, for example, numerous rabbinic dicta reflecting what may be construed as an "ontology of *maḥaloket*" closer to the Besht's reflections are conspicuously absent. What appears instead is a one-dimensional rabbinic notion that controversy is the result of human failure.[6]

I argue that the omission of these alternative rabbinic views in *Keter Shem Tov* is intentional and serves a polemical end, primarily toward mitnaggedic postures of *talmud torah* (Torah as the study of *maḥaloket*). That is, study is the quintessential religious act in a world without prophecy and serves as a substitute for the inability of individuals to achieve direct access to God. David Weiss Halivni succinctly summarizes this approach.

> Midrash represents distance from God, a clinging to the worlds of the past at a time when the living present word is not forthcoming any longer. It constitutes a substitute for divine intervention, through either revelation or prophecy . . . Canonization [sic] dried up the flow of direct information from God to man [sic] forcing man to rely on Midrash, an intellectual endeavor that anchors the present in the past. It divines God's will from words uttered by Him in the past, since man can no longer talk to, or be addressed by Him now.[7]

---

5 See, for example, Exodus Rabbah 28:6, 47:1; BT Megillah 12b; PT Peah 2:4; Tanhuma, "Yitro" 11; Tanhuma Va-Yera, 5. The nature of rabbinic *maḥaloket* and whether it represents a notion of pluralism has been the subject of many scholarly studies. See Urbach, "*Halakhah u-Nevu'ah*," esp. 6 and 7, and 50n; Sagi, *Eilu ve-Eilu*, esp. 73–117. An English summary of Sagi's work can be found in "Both are the Words of the Living God: A Typological Analysis of Halakhic Pluralism," *HUCA* LXV (1994): 105–36. Cf. Aviezer Ravitzky, *Ḥerut al ha-Luḥot* (Tel Aviv: Am Oved, 1999), 114–38; Reuven Kimelman, "Judaism and Pluralism," *Modern Judaism* 7, no. 2 (1987): 131–50; Michael Rosenzweig, "*Eilu ve-Eilu Divrei Elohim Hayyim*: Halakhic Pluralism and Theories of Controversy," in *Rabbinic Authority and Personal Autonomy*, ed. Moshe Sokol (Northvale, NJ, and London: J. Aronson, 1992), 93–122; Moshe Sokol, "What Does a Jewish Text Mean?: Theories of Elu ve Elu Divrei Elohim Hayim in Rabbinic Literature," *Da'at* 32–33 (1994): xxii-xxxi; and Aviezer Ravitzky, "The Question of Tolerance in the Jewish Religious Tradition," in *Hazon Nahum*, ed. J. S. Gurock, Y. Elman (New York: Yeshiva University Press, 1997), 359–90.

6 BT Sota 47b and BT Sanhedrin 88b.

7 David Weiss Halivni, *Midrash, Mishnah, and Gemara: The Jewish Predilection for Justified Law* (Cambridge, MA: Harvard University Press, 1986), 16. Halivni goes further to argue that many of the sectarian debates in the rabbinic period were likely focused on this question. Halivni argues that the closer a community felt to God, the more its canon was understood and the less it needed interpretation. On this, see Moshe Halbertal, *People of the Book: Canon, Meaning, and Authority* (Cambridge, MA: Harvard University Press, 1997), 32–44.

The Besht would not agree with the foundation of Halivni's assessment of the nature and purpose of the rabbinic enterprise. Rather than viewing study as a substitution for prophecy, the Besht envisions study (*maḥaloket*) as a vehicle for *deveikut*—a recovering of the prophetic experience—since God's Torah in heaven, as much as human Torah on earth (i.e., *talmud torah*), is built on the foundations of *maḥaloket*. In this sense, the Besht erases the opaque distinction between *talmud torah* and prophecy. As we will see, through a reading of Mishnah Avot 1:1 and 6:1, the Besht makes the case that prophecy, and not its absence, is the origin of *maḥaloket*.

Sherira Ga'on and Maimonides on the Loss of Univocality, Exile, and the Birth of *Maḥaloket*

In his famous *Iggeret*, Sherira Ga'on (906–1006 CE) presents perhaps the first post-rabbinic discussion about rabbinic transmission and authority.[8] This document was written as a response to questions from R. Jacob bar Nissim on behalf of the elders of Kairouan on many questions of rabbinic literature, including the history of rabbinic transmission and the literary format of the Jerusalem and Babylonian Talmud.[9] Sherira Ga'on makes his first claim about rabbinic *maḥaloket* when discussing the rise of R. Judah ha-Nasi (the Prince) and his circle of scholars:

> During all these years [the sages] clarified all the laws, which had been left unresolved in the academies due to the great loss that took place because of the Temple's destruction and the unresolved halakhic questions that had arisen during these troubled and confused times.[10]

---

8 For a general survey, see B. M. Lewin, ed., *Iggeret Rav Sherira Ga'on* (Haifa, Israel, 1921), esp. 1-lxxi. I consulted the edition including Hebrew and English by R. Nosson Dovid Rabinowich, *The Iggeres of Rav Sherira Ga'on* (Jerusalem, 1988). All page references will be from the Rabinowich 1988 edition. For his Hebrew translation see *The Iggeres of Rav Sherira Ga'on* (Jerusalem, 1991). See also Margarete Schlüter, *Aufwelche Weise wurde die Mishna geschrieben?* (Tiibingen, 1993); and Yaakov Elman's review of Schlüter's book in *AJS Review* 20, no. 1 (1995): 180–86.

9 *Iggeret*, "Introduction" (no pagination) and 27n, 36n. The polemical nature of Sherira Ga'on's *Iggeret* is significant to understanding its underlying message. On this see Michael Seth Berger, "The Authority of the Babylonian Talmud: Analysis of its Justification and a Proposal for a Contemporary Model" (PhD diss., Columbia University, 1992), 30, cited in Menahem Kellner, *Maimonides on the "Decline of the Generations" and the Nature of Rabbinic Authority* (Albany: SUNY Press, 1996), 20n37.

10 *Iggeret*, 14. Cf. 16 and the discussion in Kellner, *Maimonides on the Decline*, 19, 20.

Echoing a well known rabbinic dictum, Sherira Ga'on refers to the Talmud's description of the loss of univocality among the sages as resulting from the inattentiveness of the disciples of Hillel and Shammai.[11] The circle of Judah ha-Nasi began the process of reconstructing these discrepancies, sifting through the myriad of *maḥalokot* in order to "establish the correct version." The decision to document these "opinions," according to Sherira Ga'on, was Judah ha-Nasi's fear of further diffusion, citing the talmudic statement that "the hearts of Israel had become small and the wellsprings of wisdom had closed."[12] Sherira Ga'on's entire justification of Judah ha-Nasi's decision to document rabbinic debate and therefore create the Mishnah is founded on the most explicit rabbinic text on this approach, BT Sanhedrin 88b:

> Rabbi Yosi said, "Originally there was no *maḥaloket* in Israel . . . But when the disciples of Shammai and Hillel increased in number, disputes multiplied in Israel because their disciples did not study diligently [the words of their masters]. As a result, the Torah became as two *torot*."

The rise of controversy, according to this talmudic text, is due to the loss of tradition, implying that the tradition, if maintained, would have resulted in a univocal rabbinism, even as that rabbinism would have always contained deliberations that entertained various opinions. According to Sherira Ga'on, the rabbinic attempt to resolve differing opinions before the inattentiveness of Hillel and Shammai's disciples began with a search among various courts for the authentic tradition until it reached the High Court in the Temple. If no tradition was found, the court would render a decision taking into account all the information gathered from the various other courts. This means that dissenting opinions would be taken into account but the final court decision of the Sanhedrin would *de facto* become the correct and only opinion. The underlying point of this talmudic passage as read by Sherira Ga'on is the sharp distinction between the apparent univocal past of Temple legislation and the contentious and diffuse reality of Late Antique rabbinic society, placing the blame on the inattentiveness of the sages coupled with the confusion born from societal instability.[13]

By using this talmudic passage as a historical depiction of the break down of transmission and the birth of *maḥaloket*, Sherira Ga'on codifies

---

11 BT Sotah 47b and Bt Sanhedrin 88b. Cf. Rashi to Bava Mezia 33b s. v. "*bi-yemei*."

12 BT Sotah 49a and *Iggeret*, 14 and 73.

13 He uses a similar argument to justify the compilation and subsequent closing of the Talmud. See *Iggeret*, 58 and 60, and Kellner, *Maimonides on the Decline*, 19. Cf. Gerald Blidstein, "The Concept of Oral Law in R. Sherira's Epistle" [Hebrew], *Da'at* 4 (1980): 5–16.

this position as the source and justification of Judah ha-Nasi's project. That is, Judah ha-Nasi was able to sufficiently gather together all legitimate opinions on matters of law and sift out those that were not legitimate or reliable. Judah ha-Nasi's decision to document these opinions, ultimately resulting in the Mishnah, was due to his fear of a repetition of communal amnesia at which point even his collection of controversies would be lost. As the Talmud itself relates, Judah ha-Nasi is likened to Moses, and his academy is likened to a romantic vision of the Jewish past when reliable transmission was real.[14] Now, however, the univocality of the High Court is replaced by the multivocality of mishnaic discourse. The last line of Sherira Ga'on's chapter makes this point clear. "The sages after this, during the days of Rabban Gamliel[15] and his son Shimon, continued to debate the law. Disputes among the *tannaim* prevailed and it was impossible to teach the laws in a univocal manner."

The next section of the *Iggeret* begins as follows: "The days of Rabbi [Judah ha-Nasi], the son of Rabban Shimon ben Gamliel, were an opportune time. Rabbi arranged and wrote the Mishnah. The words of the Mishnah were like the words Moses heard from God (*mi-pi ha-gevurah*), they were like miracles and wonders."[16] I would suggest this last sentence is meant more as hyperbole than fact. That is, I seriously doubt whether Sherira Ga'on held Judah ha-Nasi to be a prophet, and surely not a prophet like Moses. The nomenclature of prophecy ("miracles and wonders") most likely refers to Judah ha-Nasi's ability to act as a cipher for previous traditions the way Moses acted as a cipher for God's command. Embodying the notion of a "pure vessel" removes the contamination of any biases of the redactor in the body of the text, enabling the text to speak in a voice of tradition rather than human creativity. The correlation between Moses and Judah ha-Nasi serves to equate the divine source of Moses' Torah (Sinai) and the traditional veracity of Judah ha-Nasi's compilation (Mishnah). The Torah speaks in a divine voice heard through the pure prophetic filter of Moses, and the Mishnah attests to historical reality not tainted by R. Judah ha Nasi's particular predilections.

According to Sherira Ga'on, however, Judah ha-Nasi did more than just emulate Moses. With the Mishnah, he saved Moses' Torah because Moses as a cipher, and the tradition he produced, could not survive the instability of Late Antique Jewish society. By compiling, ordering, and recording the

14 BT Gittin 59a.

15 The printed text has "in the days of Hillel and his son Shimon." Rabinowich changes it to R. Gamliel, which makes more chronological sense. See *Iggeret*, 19n25.

16 *Iggeret*, 20.

fragments of Moses' Torah, Judah ha-Nasi prepared Torah for its long dwelling in exile. As stated above, Sherira Ga'on adopts the rabbinic opinions cited above that *maḥaloket* was born out of inattentiveness and historical catastrophe.[17] The response to that historical catastrophe (i.e., the Mishnah) saved Torah by changing its course. Embedded in this new discourse of *maḥaloket* was the desire and hope to recover the univocal Torah of Moses. However, the tradition now recorded by Judah ha-Nasi, a tradition based on *maḥaloket*, could not, without prophetic intervention, recover the univocal tradition of Moses. For Sherira Ga'on, the foundation and context of the mishnaic project and Rabbinic Judaism, in both substance and method, was exile.

Maimonides' position is similar to Sherira Ga'on's in one sense and very different in another.[18] More important for our concerns, his position had a much wider impact on post-rabbinic attitudes toward *maḥaloket*, as his authority both as an exegete and jurist was far greater than that of Sherira Ga'on.

In his Introduction to the *Mishneh Torah*, Maimonides basically reiterates Sherira's position that the decision to redact the Mishnah as we have it today was the result of societal instability and the fear that traditions would be lost.

> He [Judah ha-Nasi] gathered together all the traditions, enactments, interpretations and expositions of every portion of the Torah, that had either come down to Moses, our Master, to have been deduced by the courts in successive generations. All this material he redacted in the Mishnah, which was diligently taught in public, and thus became universally known among the Jewish people . . . Why did Our Teacher, the Saint [Judah ha-Nasi], act so

17 Rabinowich makes a similar point. See *Iggeret*, 20, s. v. "a sign and a wonder." Although Rabinowich is not willing to conjecture as to what the figurative nature of the Moses/ Judah ha-Nasi correlation might be.

18 Kellner argues that Maimonides and Sherira Ga'on are quite different on the question of "the decline of the generations," an issue that has indirect relevance to our issue. Kellner locates the origin of the term in Sherira Ga'on and argues that Maimonides, unlike many of his medieval contemporaries, rejects the notion outright. Relevant to us, Kellner suggests that while Maimonides shares Sherira Ga'on's assessment about societal instability as the cause of the breakdown of rabbinic univocality, he disagrees with Sherira Ga'on that there is some inherent difference between the intellectual capacity of one generation and another that underlies the construction of rabbinic authority. Although this does not directly relate to the issue of the multivocality of Rabbinic Judaism, it is important in that it may impact Maimonides' notion of the messianic era and the intellectual capacity of Israel in that time. See Kellner, *Maimonides on the Decline*, 83–90.

> and not leave things as they were? Because he observed that the number of disciples was diminishing, fresh calamities were continually happening, and wicked government was extending its domain and increasing in power, and Israelites were wandering and immigrating to distant countries.[19]

Maimonides differs from Sherira Ga'on on two important counts. First, that the authority of the sages, and by extension the Mishnah and Talmud, is based on the sages' superior intellect. Second, on the origin and nature of *maḥaloket*. On the first count, Maimonides implies, contra Sherira Ga'on, that the authority of the Mishnah and Talmud is simply based on the historical fact that it was universally accepted by the Jewish people and not that the sages in the Mishnah and Talmud were by definition intellectually or spiritually superior to later rabbis and jurists.[20]

On the question of the origin of *maḥaloket*, Maimonides differs from Sherira Ga'on in that he significantly minimizes the spectrum of *maḥaloket* in the Mishnah and, in doing so, narrows the scope and distinctiveness of the mishnaic project from what preceded it. In opposition to Sherira Ga'on, he maintains that *maḥaloket* is not about the loss of transmission (*kabbalah*). "Those that think that judgments upon which there is *maḥaloket* also applies to matters of Mosaic tradition resulting from mistaken transmission or forgetfulness . . . this is very bizarre, incorrect, and does not square with our general principles."[21] Whereas he too bases his understanding of *maḥaloket* on the talmudic passage about the disciples of Hillel and Shammai, he understands the subject of the passage quite differently.

According to Maimonides, this talmudic passage does not relate to any traditions received from Moses, all of which Maimonides maintains remained intact. The talmudic passage in question only relates to those cases where there is no tradition and the sages had to rely solely on the use of hermeneutic principles to clarify matters of law. In cases with no tradition, the inattentiveness of the disciples of Shammai and Hillel resulted in an inability to properly implement the Mosaic principles of interpretation. This ultimately caused a proliferation of controversy in matters of Jewish law. According to Maimonides, what the disciples lost through dereliction

19 "Introduction to Mishneh Torah," in Moses Hyamson's bilingual edition edited according to the Bodleian Codex, *Mishneh Torah: The Book of Knowledge* (Jerusalem, 1965), 2b. Cf. Kellner, *Maimonides on the Decline*, 87, 88.

20 This is the basis of Kellner's thesis that Maimonides rejected the notion of the "decline of the generations," built on Sherira Ga'on's foundation of the ontological superiority of the sages versus later jurists. See Kellner, *Maimonides on the Decline*, 88.

21 R. Moses Maimonides, *Peirush al ha-Mishnah* (Jerusalem, 1969), 1:11 and 12 (my translation).

was not tradition but an intimate knowledge of the principles of interpretation necessary to adjudicate unprecedented cases and situations.

> "But when the disciples of Shammai and Hillel increased in number, disputes multiplied in Israel because their disciples did not study diligently [the words of their masters]." This is actually very clear. A discourse of two individuals equal in intellectual stature and knowledge of the general principles of interpretation will not result in *maḥaloket*, as long as they use one of the accepted principles [of interpretation]. And if such *maḥaloket* would result it would only be in very few cases, as we can see that Shammai and Hillel only disagreed in a few instances. This is because their method of study and their use of hermeneutic principles were very similar. It is also because each had identical [general] principles with which to enact interpretation. When the attentiveness of their disciples decreased and their legislative understanding of their teachers, Shammai and Hillel, weakened, the result was [an increase in] *maḥaloket* in many cases of legal deliberation. This was because each [disciple] ruled according to his intellectual capacity [*koaḥ sikhlo*] using the interpretive principles that were known to him. This was not their fault. We can't expect two individuals to argue according to the [elevated] stature of Joshua and Phineas. We should also not wonder about the *maḥalokot* of the sages, lamenting that they are not Shammai or Hillel, or even above them. God only required us to heed the sages in our generation, as it says, *and appear before . . . the judges that are in your time, and present your problem* (Deut. 17:9). This is the nature and origin of *maḥaloket*. It is not that there was a mistake in transmission in that one received the proper tradition and the other did not. As one contemplates these matters they will become clear. This is a great fundamental principle of Torah.[22]

Maimonides argues that there are five general ways by which law is determined in the Mishnah, only one of which yields *maḥaloket*.[23] He is in basic agreement with Sherira Ga'on's claim about redaction, that the decision to construct the literary documents, which became the Mishnah and Talmud, was the result of social conditions. However, regarding *maḥaloket* Maimonides disagrees with Sherira Ga'on in that he does not overtly view

22 Maimonides, *Peirush al ha-Mishnah*, 11f.

23 The five ways are: (1) traditions from Moses that can also be drawn out via biblical interpretation; (2) traditions from Moses that have no scriptural referent (*halakhah le-Moshe mi-Sinai*); (3) things on which there is no tradition and can only be drawn out through interpretation; (4) rabbinic decrees; and (5) rabbinic injunctions. Maimonides, *Peirush al ha-Mishnah*, 12. According to Maimonides only #3 results in *maḥaloket*.

maḥaloket solely as a result of persecution and societal instability but also (or primarily) a result of a deficiency in the educational program of the sages.[24] The distinction is that Sherira Ga'on wants to connect social decline with the intellectual nature of the sages while Maimonides does not. According to Maimonides, while correctly receiving the traditions originating in Moses' Torah, the disciples of Shammai and Hillel were deficient in fully absorbing the principles of interpretation that would enable them to accurately interpret unprecedented cases of law—they did not lose any traditions. Instead of lamenting this fact, as Sherira Ga'on does, Maimonides reads it as a natural and inevitable outgrowth of human legislation that is sanctioned by the Torah.[25]

According to Maimonides, the multivocality of the Mishnah only exists in cases where no tradition exists (as opposed to where no tradition can be found, as in the case of Sherira Ga'on), forcing jurists to rely solely on hermeneutic principles to determine the correct practice. The tolerance of *maḥaloket* according to this Maimonidean model is that God does not require us to recover the "true" law (that is, the law as given to Moses) in cases without tradition, but only to pay heed to those sages (more specifically the sages of the two Talmuds) who engage in the process of legal reasoning.[26] This is because without a tradition or a prophet we have no direct access to "original" divine will in these cases. That is, we have no way to recover any mistake a previous tradition might have made in legislating without the precedent of tradition. On this, Maimonides states, "Therefore I say that the law, although it is not natural, enters into what is natural. It is part of the wisdom of the deity with regard to the permanence of this species of which He has willed the existence, that He put into its nature that the individuals belonging to it should have the faculty of ruling."[27] Tolerance here is the result of both positions in a *maḥaloket* being the result of the human intellect. Therefore both are correct in the sense that both struggle to make sense, by means of divinely sanctioned principles of interpretation, something for which we have no definitive answer, that is, no tradition. An

---

24 Maimonides does, however, suggest that the loss of political independence did damage its spiritual life. See Aviezer Ravitzky, "To the Utmost Capacity," in *Perspectives on Maimonides*, ed. Joel Kraemer (Oxford: Oxford University Press, 1991), 223; Maimonides, *The Guide of the Perplexed*, 2:36; and Maimonides, *Mishneh Torah*, "*Hilkhot Yesodei ha-Torah*," 7:4.

25 For a similar view, see Rashi on BT Ketubot 57a, s. v. *ka mashma lan*. Cf. the important understanding of rabbinic *maḥaloket* in Rabbeinu Nissim of Gerona's *Derashot ha-Ran* (Jerusalem, 1977), 110–24.

26 On this, see Kellner, *Maimonides on the Descent*, 55–67.

27 *Guide* 2:40.

illegitimate ruling would be one where a received tradition is challenged by hermeneutic principles.[28] Since the principles in exile are defective while traditions are transmitted accurately, the sages cannot use defective interpretive skills to counter a received tradition. Maimonides maintains that this rarely occurs. The interpretive principles are generally implemented either to support a tradition, functioning descriptively, or to adjudicate cases where no tradition exists, functioning proscriptively.

The question as to how the messianic era will change this type of halakhic legislation is never made explicit by either thinker. It is unclear whether Sherira Ga'on and Maimonides would support a claim that the reemergence of prophecy would result in the resolution of all *maḥalokot*. From Sherira Ga'on's perspective one could argue that the restitution of Jewish sovereignty and prophecy could result in the recovering of lost traditions that would clarify disputed points in Jewish law. For Sherira Ga'on the defective nature of the Mishnah, i.e., the *maḥalokot* therein, is largely the result of lost traditions that Judah ha-Nasi could not recover as a result of societal unrest. The inability of later jurists to challenge earlier authorities, based on the notion of "the decline of the generations," is temporal—it will end with the coming of the Messiah. The recovery of lost traditions coupled with the elevated status of jurists in the messianic era could easily result in the resolution of unresolved *maḥalokot* in rabbinic literature.

The case of Maimonides is more complex for at least two reasons. First, because, unlike Sherira Ga'on, Maimonides has so much to say about the messianic era and the state of Torah at that time. Second, his comments, scattered throughout all his major writings and letters, are inconsistent. While Maimonides does argue that the messianic future will yield world peace, tranquility, and the freedom to pursue divine knowledge, resulting in a world that is "only interested in the knowledge of God," he adds the sober caveat that people will still only know God "according to their capacity as human beings."[29] More relevant to our concerns, Maimonides never spells out how that prophetic dimension of the messianic era will alter the way halakhic adjudication is now determined. When he unequivocally states in his *Commentary to the Mishnah* that the law will remain, does he mean "the law" in general, or the particular laws as they have been adjudicated and enacted until that point? If we accept Maimonides' principle that prophecy is an extension of, and not a break with, human reason, as prophet, the King Messiah may at best be able to clarify ambiguities about divine will that were previously unknown. This may include the proper

28 On this in rabbinic literature, see Urbach, "*Halakhah u-Nevu'ah*," 10, 11, and 20.
29 Maimonides, *Mishneh Torah*, "Laws of Kings," 12:1, 4, 5.

implementation of interpretive principles that can then be used to resolve standing rabbinic controversies or even to correct past mistakes.

On the question of metaphysics in the messianic era, given Maimonides' overt rejection of the miraculous nature of the messianic age in general, I suggest that it is highly unlikely that Maimonides imagined God's essence would be more disclosed to us in the messianic age than it is in the present.[30] What we know of God now, or at least what philosophers know now, is not very different from what will be known of Him in the future. At best, the defects in our present knowledge of God may be clarified and the correct opinions confirmed. Alternatively, the difference may be that the non-philosopher will know in the future what the philosopher knows now.[31]

However, the ambiguities in the law, the result of which is rabbinic *maḥaloket*, could easily be erased if jurists had a more accurate knowledge of how to apply the rules of interpretation. This is especially true if we accept Menahem Kellner's basic premise that Maimonides did not accept the Gaonic notion (which became canonized in post-rabbinic literature) of the "decline of the generations." Without a belief in the ontological inferiority of later sages, the only thing the messianic era needs to produce to bring about univocality in matters of law and to correct past errors is a social context that would enable sages to peacefully and meticulously go about the business of careful interpretation.

According to Maimonides, the messianic era will result in "a widespread increase in wisdom . . . because the righteous will gather together in friendship, and because goodness and wisdom will prevail."[32] In "Laws of Kings" Maimonides comes closest to claiming that in the days of the Messiah we will know that which is now unknown. However, the parameters of that new knowledge are never made explicit. "The one preoccupation of the whole world will be to know God. Hence they will be very wise, *they will know things that are now concealed* and will attain an understanding of the

30 See *Guide* 3:32. Maimonides writes, "Though all miracles change the nature of some individual being, God does not change at all the nature of human individuals by means of miracles." While the messianic era may result in a clearer and more precise understanding of the world and God's will, it will not result in an apprehension "beyond human capacity" now. That is, according to Maimonides, the messianic era is a corrective and not a transformative phenomenon.

31 Much of this rests on how one reads *Guide* 3:51–54. For one reading that suggests that the philosopher may know now what others will only know in the future, see Joseph Stern, *Problems and Parables of Law* (Albany: SUNY Press, 1998), esp. 15–49.

32 Maimonides, "Introduction to *Perek Helek*," *Peirush al ha-Mishnah*. Cf. Ravitzky, "To the Utmost Human Capacity," 227f.

Creator to the utmost human capacity . . ."[33] If we maintain a rational view that "things that are now concealed" are not, as some mystics would have it, esoteric doctrine but either: one, *ta'amei ha-miẓvot*, or two, the resolution of *maḥaloket*, we could argue that Maimonides would hold that the messianic future will create the context for a full and correct application of hermeneutic principles that would resolve rabbinic controversy.[34] This works according to Maimonides' realistic messianic posture, which is based on the principle that the messianic future will not alter human nature, but only create a context for more accurate and careful study of God's word.

In sum, this does not necessarily imply the complete resolution of *maḥaloket* in the future. However, given societal stability, relative peace, and the universal desire for knowledge of God, the messianic era could easily produce sages who would have the luxury of careful analysis that would yield a better knowledge of applying those legal principles to unprecedented situations. One could argue, therefore, that Maimonides might indeed agree that *maḥaloket*, at least the way we know it now, could end in the messianic era.[35]

The Besht and the Intolerance of Tolerance, or, The Ontology of *Maḥaloket*

The Besht rejects the idea that *maḥaloket* is a product of historical or even cosmic exile and therefore, I propose, rejects the idea that *maḥaloket* will be (or should be) resolved in the messianic era. I will extend this claim to

33 *Mishneh Torah*, "Laws of Kings," 12:5. While this can be, and has been, interpreted to mean esoteric knowledge, Maimonides' addition of "to the utmost human capacity" seems to problematize the mystical reading, unless, of course, one assumes that, as human beings, we have not achieved, through reason, such a level. Given Maimonides' rationalism, such a reading is hard to justify in his corpus.

34 Kellner suggests that this phrase means "a perfection in metaphysics." See Kellner, *Maimonides on the Decline*, 75, ". . . the Jews, with the advantage of always having had the Torah, will be very wise, will know things that are now concealed (i.e., it is a safe assumption that Maimonides means *ma'aseh bereshit* and *ma'aseh merkavah*), and will achieve an understanding of God (i.e., perfection in metaphysics) to the very greatest extent that humans can achieve." While this is indeed plausible, I am suggesting that perhaps Maimonides also means a renewed ability to utilize the thirteen principles of interpretation in order to resolve *maḥaloket* in rabbinic literature. Given that Maimonides was not bound by rabbinic authority in any definitive sense (at least according to Kellner), a renewed ability to implement principles of interpretation (which are, for Maimonides, Mosaic in origin) could easily lead to a resolution of *maḥaloket*.

35 I want to thank Menahem Kellner for helping me clarify some of these passages.

argue that he would also reject the idea that the culture of *maḥaloket* is a culture that promotes pluralism, if we define pluralism as the product of the indeterminacy of divine will.[36] That is, he would reject *maḥaloket* if we present it as the product of human society functioning with divine sanction but without the capacity to unequivocally maintain and transmit the Sinaitic Torah of Moses (Mishnah Avot 1:1). This severing of human society from the divine world is a position Ḥasidism contests on many fronts. While the Besht surely agrees with the talmudic idea of "these and these are the words of the living God," for him this rabbinic dictum does not point to the tolerance of *maḥaloket* by seeing the unified source of differing positions in God. Rather, he sees "these and these" as a call *for* the perpetuation and proliferation of *maḥaloket* as a way *to* God. Therefore, what I mean by the Besht's intolerance of tolerance is as follows. The conventional notion of *maḥaloket* as the foundation of religious pluralism is that the culture of *maḥaloket*, built on a belief in its unified source, enables human (Jewish) society to absorb differences without contentiousness, thereby producing tolerance. The belief is that maintaining the idea of the univocality of divine will, coupled with the divine sanction of the multivocality of the human struggle to live by that will, softens the sharp edges of controversy because the latter always sees the former simultaneously as its origin and as its goal. That is, the source of all *maḥaloket* "for the sake of heaven" is God (Torah) and the end of all such *maḥaloket* is redemption, the return of univocality to Israelite society. This creates a society that promotes the legitimacy of any struggle that inhabits the universe of divine will as refracted through the prism of rabbinic authority. If, however, *maḥaloket* is not viewed solely as the product of human struggle but constitutes the very fabric of the cosmos—that is, if *maḥaloket* is divine—the perpetuation of *maḥaloket*, providing it is "for the sake of heaven," is an act of *imitatio dei* and not simply a divinely sanctioned response to the eclipse of God (*hester panim*).

The Besht's unwillingness to use controversy as a model for tolerance is not simply the result of his fundamentalist worldview. Rather, it is because Ḥasidism is founded on three principles that the rabbinic model of "*maḥaloket* as tolerance," at least the way it is presented in post-rabbinic Judaism, is untenable. These three principles are: first, its de-historicized messianism; second, it adaptation of kabbalistic theosophy; and third, its focus on *deveikut* as self-redemption.

36 For example, see Sokol, "What Does a Text Mean?," xxxi-xxxiii.

Ḥasidic messianism contains subterranean antinomian strains that challenge or at least push the limits of the nomic roots of the rabbinic project, even as it supports and ardently defends the pietistic approach to Jewish practice.[37] It is true that rabbinic literature, especially when fantasizing about redemption, contains its own antinomian moments, presented more as hopeful musings rather than definitive statements of law or doctrine.[38] However, the dominance and influence of Maimonides' highly nomic messianism eclipsed (or repressed) many of those disparate rabbinic voices, re-presenting rabbinic messianism in the image of Maimonides' more normative posture.[39]

Ḥasidic Messianism, Self-Redemption, and the Democratization of *Deveikut*

Ḥasidic messianism is different than Maimonidean messianism and Maimonides' depictions of rabbinic messianisms in two distinct ways. First,

37 See the discussion by Gershom Scholem, "Redemption Through Sin," in his *The Messianic Idea in Judaism* (New York: Schocken, 1971), 91.

38 See BT Sanhedrin 92a ff. The unsystematic and non-authoritative statements of the sages regarding the messianic era are discussed in Ephraim Urbach, *The Sages: Their Concepts and Beliefs*, trans. Israel Abrahams (Jerusalem: Magnes Press, 1979), 649f; and Urbach, "Redemption and Repentance in Talmudic Judaism," in *Types of Redemption*, ed. R. J. W. Werblowsky and C. J. Bleeker (Leiden: Brill, 1970), 190–206. Maimonides had little tolerance for these rabbinic musings. In his "Letter on Resurrection," he states, "None of these things [i.e., what will happen in the messianic era], are foundations of the Torah, so one needn't be particular as to what people believe about them." See David Hartman, *Epistles of Maimonides: Crisis and Leadership* (Philadelphia: Jewish Publication Society, 1985), 211–23. Ravitzky notes that this citation does not relate to the notion of Messiah but to the particular musings about what will happen in the messianic era. Cf. Yeshayahu Leibowitz, "Messianic Redemption in the Teachings of the Rambam" [Hebrew], in his *Emunah, Historiah ve-Arakhim* (Jerusalem, 1982), 299f; Ravitzky, "To the Utmost Human Capacity," 237n37; and Amos Funkenstein, "Law, Philosophy, and Historical Awareness," in his *Perceptions of Jewish History* (Berkeley, Los Angeles and Oxford, 1993), 135.

39 It is duly noted that the dominance of Maimonides' rational influence over against less rational rabbinic messianic models has changed with contemporary Lubavitch rereadings of Maimonides. Although a thorough analysis and appraisal of Lubavitch's use of Maimonides to support their more mystically oriented messianic idea has not yet been written, Maimonidean scholars have often noted the way Lubavitch readings of Maimonides, besides being overtly apologetic, view Maimonides completely outside his philosophical context. On contemporary Lubavitch and messianism, see Naftali Loewenthal, "Contemporary Habad and the Paradox of Redemption," in *Perspectives on Jewish Thought and Mysticism*, ed. A. Ivry, E. R. Wolfson (Amsterdam, 1998), 381–402.

unlike Maimonides and Maimonides' presentation of the rabbis, ḥasidic notions of the messianic are less committed to the unchanging nomic structure so prominent in Maimonides' "realistic messianism."[40] More than just musing about the erasure of certain *miẓvot* in the redemptive future, characteristic of certain rabbinic positions, Ḥasidism creates a correlation between God and the *ḥasid* who achieves *deveikut*, that problematizes the whole notion of *miẓvot* as the exclusive frame of human devotion to God. In this sense, I think Martin Buber's intuition about Ḥasidism, setting aside his use of that intuition to push his own philosophical agenda, has more merit than is often thought in light of Gershom Scholem's critique.[41]

Ḥasidism's de-historicized messianism, especially in the early period, altered the centrality of redemptive hope so prominent in the rabbinic and Maimonidean models of devotion because Ḥasidism believed in the realization of "self-redemption" through the act of *deveikut* in the yet unredeemed world.[42] That is, the one who experiences *deveikut* is already living in a messianic world, albeit one that is temporary as a result of historical exile.[43] The object of hope in Ḥasidism is not solely or even primarily focused on a historical event. Rather, it is the hope in something that has already been experienced in the state of *deveikut*. The hope of Ḥasidism is not the unknown but the already known—it is the hope for the permanence of the experience already felt temporarily in the unredeemed world (i.e., *deveikut*). The early nineteenth-century Hungarian ḥasidic master, R. Issac Judah Jehiel Safrin of Komomo, aptly captures this notion of self-redemption as a prelude to historical redemption:

---

40 See Ravitzky, "To the Utmost Human Capacity," 221–56.

41 For Scholem's critique see Scholem, "Martin Buber's Interpretation of Ḥasidism," in his *The Messianic Idea in Judaism*, 228–50; and Rivka Shatz-Uffenheimer, "Man's Relation to God and World in Buber's Rendering of the Ḥasidic Teaching," in *The Philosophy of Martin Buber*, ed. Paul Arthur Schlipp and Maurice Friedman (LaSalle, IL: Open Court, 1967), 403–34, and Buber's reply, 731–41. For an analysis of Buber's reading of Ḥasidism, see Jerome Gellman, "Buber's Blunder: Buber Replies to Scholem and Shatz-Uffenheimer," *Modern Judaism* 20, no. 1 (2000): 20–40; and the discussion in Morris Faierstein, "Scholem and Ḥasidism," *Journal of Jewish Studies* 38, no. 2 (1987): 221–33.

42 For an example of this see *Keter Shem Tov*, #427, 53b/54a, where de-historicizing the historical depiction of the messianic era is viewed as the end of being captive among the nations.

43 Scholem characterizes *deveikut* in kabbalistic literature as "a state of personal bliss which can be attained without having recourse to the vast field of eschatology, utopianism, and Messianism." See his "*Devekut*, or Communion with God," in *The Messianic Idea in Judaism*, 204. When Scholem uses the term "messianism" in that essay he is referring specifically to historical messianism. Ḥasidic messianism cannot be understood solely through a historical lens but requires an existential perspective.

> In the case of collective (historical) redemption in the messianic era, we can say, *Let there be light, and there was light* (Genesis 2 1:3): that is, darkness and anguish are overcome beforehand. This is also the case with an individual. Before the final unveiling of redemption [one can experience the verse], *Come near to me and redeem me* (Psalms 69: 19). [This happens by means of faith in the fact that human suffering (the absence of God) is only a temporary phenomenon.] At that moment [i.e., when he experiences God in His absence] . . . he is redeemed.[44]

The redemptive hope as an outgrowth of self-redemption in early ḥasidic messianism is thus two-fold: one, the democratization of *deveikut*; and two, the permanence of *deveikut.*[45]

Although rarely overt and historical, messianism informs every stage of ḥasidic discourse, beginning with the Besht's self-redemptive messianic dream, which is arguably the very origin of Ḥasidism, what Simon Dubnow called "the manifesto of Ḥasidism."[46] Its de-historicized nature, perhaps best captured as messianic consciousness or, as Rivka Shatz-Uffenheimer coined it, "self-redemption," veils the fact that ḥasidic messianism, especially in early Ḥasidism, exhibits a consistent and emphatic belief in a transformative vision that will challenge and, in some cases, deconstruct the nomic system of halakhic Judaism as we know it.[47]

The anarchic and antinomian strains in messianism are not limited to mystical constructions of this idea. Therefore, in my view it would be inaccurate, or at least presumptuous, to understand the ḥasidic ambivalence

---

44 R. Isaac Judah Jehiel Safrin of Komomo, *Nativ Miẓvotekha* (Jerusalem, 1992), 4.

45 Safrin, *Nativ Miẓvotekha*, 204, 205.

46 The Besht's ascent as depicted in his "Holy Epistle" is the source of the long scholarly debate on ḥasidic messianism. See Isaiah Tishby, "The Messianic Idea and Messianic Trends in the Growth of Ḥasidism" [Hebrew], *Zion* 32 (1967): 1–45; and Scholem's response, "The Neutralization of the Messianic Idea in Early Ḥasidism," in *The Messianic Idea in Judaism*, 176–202. Cf. Ben Zion Dinur, *Be-Mifne ha-Dorot* (Jerusalem, 1955), 181–227. For more recent readings of the "Holy Epistle" and its relationship to messianism, see Rosman, *Founder of Ḥasidism*, 97–113, Moshe Idel, *Messianic Mystics* (New Haven, CT: Yale University Press, 2000), 213–20, and notes; and Mor Altshuler, "Messianic Strains in Rabbi Israel Ba'al Shem Tov's 'Holy Epistle,'" in *Jewish Studies Quarterly* 6 (1999): 55–70. For some recent studies more generally, see Immanuel Etkes, *The Beginning of the Ḥasidic Movement* [Hebrew] (Israel, 1998), 120–28; and Arie Morgenstern, *Mysticism and Messianism* [Hebrew] (Jerusalem, 1999), 180–208.

47 Rivka Shatz-Uffenheimer, "Redemption as Self-Redemption," in *Types of Redemption*, 207–12; Idel, *Messianic Mystics*, 235–47; and Scholem, "On the Neutralization," 186, "The experience of *deveikut* destroyed the exile from within, at least for the individual who achieved it—and it is an experience of the individual and not of the whole community that is spoken of in ḥasidic sources."

toward the rabbinic project simply as a result of its mystical inclination. The permanence and exclusivity of the law is also problematic for many who do not inhabit the spiritualistic universe of the mystics. For example, the legal theorist Robert Cover, while discussing the general phenomenon of messianism and its relationship to law, aptly stated, "Messianism requires a commitment that entails loss of present social life, authority, and reality in exchange for that which can only be imagined."[48] Most post-rabbinic forms of Rabbinic Judaism, however, largely structured on Maimonidean principles, reject, or at least de-emphasize, any apocalyptic notion that seriously destabilizes the nomic foundation of *halakhah*. Maimonides' strict nomianism is unmoving, even as it extends to the messianic future.

Rabbi Joseph Soloveitchik, in his *Lonely Man of Faith*, succinctly formulates this sentiment. "In short, God's word is *ipso facto* God's law and norm. Let me add that for Judaism the reverse would be not only unthinkable, but immoral, as well. If we eliminate the norm [i.e., the law] from the prophetic God-man encounter, confining the latter to its apocalyptic aspects, then the whole drama would be acted out by a limited number of privileged individuals to the exclusion of the rest of the people."[49] What Soloveitchik chooses to ignore is the fact that the ḥasidic notion of the "apocalyptic," i.e., *deveikut* or self-redemption, *does* include everyone, at least *in potencia*. In fact, the Besht, and more pointedly his disciple R. Ya'akov Yosef of Polonnoye, argued that it was the nomic elitism of Lithuanian Talmudism that excluded the masses and created an anti-democratic Judaism that

48 Robert Cover, "Bringing the Messiah Through the Law: A Case Study," in *Religion, Morality, and the Law*, ed. J. R. Pennock, J. W. Chapman (New York and London: NYU Press, 1988), 204.

49 Soloveitchik, "Lonely Man of Faith," *Tradition* 7, no. 2 (1985): 40. Soloveitchik's comments are a reflection of a similar sentiment expressed by Hermann Cohen, with whom Soloveitchik was quite familiar. In his *Religion of Reason out of the Sources of Judaism* (Atlanta, GA: Scholars Press, 1995), 339, Cohen writes, "Thus, sacrifice is, on the part of man, what creation and revelation are on the part of God. As revelation is the necessary means for this correlation, so also is the law. *Revelation and law are therefore identical* [my emphasis]. If the law were not the necessary form of achievement of the correlation between God and man, revelation would not be so either. Thus, God's law is a necessary concept of monotheism." Unlike Soloveitchik, Cohen does not mean *halakhah* when he says "law" in the sense that specific prescribed behaviors that comprise halakhic norms are not binding for Cohen. Rather, what is binding is the manifestation and embodiment of the two absolutes in Cohen's system: God as the idea of morality and the actualization of that idea in human action. While Cohen would also reject *deveikut* as a religious ideal, in fact his notion of correlation is antithetical to *deveikut*, he would do so for other reasons and not, as Soloveitchik implies, because it is undemocratic.

suppressed the messianic impulse.[50] While the fulfillment of the law may be democratic, knowledge of the law and thus the power to legislate is not, especially in a Jewish society that is founded on certain formalistic privileged classes.[51] While it is surely true that law is democratic in that everyone is equally obligated (except, of course, women, children, and slaves, in certain cases), *deveikut* is just as democratic in principle, perhaps even more so, since no segment of society is by definition excluded.[52] While it may be true that *deveikut* requires a devotional commitment that may be beyond many members of the society, it is potentially open to all who seek it.[53]

Whereas ḥasidic visions of the future often suggest a democratization of *deveikut*, I am not as familiar with similar approaches in terms of halakhic legislation (i.e., rabbinic authority). At least according to Maimonides, it

50 See Samuel Dresner, *The Zaddik* (New York: J. Aronson, 1960), 75–110. It should be emphasized that the populist tenor of Ḥasidism, while bearing a certain element of truth, is often overstated. See, for example, in Ada Rapoport-Albert, "God and the Zaddik as the Two Focal Points of Ḥasidic Worship," *History of Religion* 18 (1979): 296–325. Even though Rapoport-Albert exhibits the elitist nature of Ḥasidism, especially in its early period, in my opinion the polemical nature of ḥasidic discourse against the hierarchical structure of rabbinic society remains intact. While early Ḥasidism largely perpetuated the elitist structure of the *Kloyz* (closed fraternity) it also undercut elitist rabbinism by offering an alternative to *talmud torah* as the sole, or at least primary, avenue of Jewish devotion. Cf. the discussion on philosophy as a false foundation of devotion in R. Nahman of Bratslav, *Likkutei MoHaRan* 2:19.

51 For an example of this in the rabbinic institution of divorce law, see Aryeh Cohen, "Giddul's Wife and the Power of the Court: On Talmudic Law, Gender, Divorce, and Exile," *Southern California Review of Law and Women's Studies* 9, no. 2 (2000): 197–223.

52 See Martin Buber, *The Origin and Meaning of Ḥasidism* (Atlantic Highlands, NJ: Horizon Press, 1960), 60, 61. "One cannot understand the enormous influence that Ḥasidism exercised on the masses of the people if one does not recognize the 'democratic' strain in it, the tendency native to it to set in place the existing 'aristocracy' of spiritual possession the equal right of all to draw near to the absolute Being."

53 For Soloveitchik's response to the question of democracy and *halakhah*, see his *The Halakhic Mind* (New York: Free Press, 1986), 79 and 80. Cf. Soloveitchik, *Halakhic Man*, trans. L. Kaplan (Philadelphia: Jewish Publication Society, 1983), 42. "And more. Halakhic man's religious viewpoint is highly exoteric. His face is turned toward the people. The Torah, whether in terms of study or practice, is the possession of the entire Jewish community . . . The thrust of Halakhah is democratic from beginning to end. The Halakhah declares that any religion that confines itself to some remote corner of society, to an elite sect or faction, will give rise to destructive consequences that far outweigh putative gains." His critique of zaddikism comes in the next sentence. "No person, according to the Halakhah, needs the aid of others in order to approach God." But see p. 79: "The countenance of the rabbinic scholar testifies to a strength of mind and a spiritual stature that sheds its brilliant light near and far. His whole being is imbued with the dignity of uniqueness and individuality, and displays a *distinct streak of aristocracy* [my emphasis]."

will still be the sages (i.e., those who "know" Torah) who will maintain the power of halakhic legislation in the messianic future. Therefore, I think that Ḥasidism's messianic antinomianism is not solely the product of mystical reflection but also contains a social critique, challenging the anti-democratic and thus deficient nature of the conflation of rabbinic authority and divine will. Thus, even though Raphael Mahler's Marxist presentation of Ḥasidism in his *Ḥasidism and the Jewish Enlightenment* has largely been discredited, I think that ḥasidic messianism, while surely informed and even founded on mystical/pietistic principles, also contains a political dimension, one that protests against the exclusivity of the law as expressing divine will, especially as regulated and legislated solely by the elite class of rabbinic scholars.[54] A Marxist reading of ḥasidic polemics is not as foreign to the literature as many think. Part of Ḥasidism's messianic vision, and its success as a modern form of Jewish pietism, is its ability to eradicate such inequity by enabling access to God through *deveikut* to circumvent the legal system of *halakhah* without destroying the viability of the *halakhah* as such. While this pietism is surely not in the spirit of Marx's solution to class struggle, Ḥasidism's use of *deveikut* as "self-redemption" to equalize the inequity of rabbinic society is noteworthy.

The Doctrine of the *Sefirot*, the *Shekhinah*, and *Maḥaloket*

Living in the intellectual universe of theosophic Kabbalah, Ḥasidism fully adopted the cosmology of the diverse Godhead of *torat ha-sefirot* but was less intent on drawing the sharp distinction between the *sefirot* and *ein sof* common in the classical tradition. This is not to say that early Ḥasidism denied the doctrine of divine Oneness—it is to say, rather, that in Ḥasidism's particular interpretation of theosophic Kabbalah, divine Oneness is always in a dialectical relationship to and never distinct from divine plurality. The plurality of the Godhead is not a radically other dimension of divinity, it is a reflection of the very nature of the essence of God.[55]

54 Raphael Mahler, *Ḥasidism and the Jewish Enlightenment* (Philadelphia: Jewish Publication Society, 1985). While Mahler is mentioned in more recent scholarship on Ḥasidism, his work is not given its due. See, for example, Miles Krassen, *Uniter of Heaven and Earth: Rabbi Meshullam Feibush Heller of Zbarazh and the Rice of Ḥasidism in Eastern Galicia* (Albany: SUNY Press, 1999), 217n1.

55 There is an important connection between ḥasidic messianism and its adaptation of Kabbalah. Gershon Cohen has noted the different attitudes of Sephardic and Ashkenazic cultures on the question of messianism. Ḥasidism served as a crucial nexus between these two cultures in the modern period. Its acceptance of Lurianic Kabbalah

In this sense Ḥasidism's reading of Kabbalah delicately diffuses some of the dualistic Neo-Platonic strains present in classical Kabbalah. While the theosophic tradition may undermine earlier rabbinic notions of radical otherness between God and the world through the mediation of the *sefirot*, it maintains a basic dualistic worldview filtered through the double lens of Rabbinic Judaism and Neo-Platonism.[56] While the *Shekhinah* as divine indwelling plays a prominent role in the tradition of the Zohar, the classical kabbalist still has his eyes focused upward to the supernal realm, contemplating and witnessing the unfolding drama of divine emanation.[57] The role of the *Shekhinah* "in" the world yielding access to God "in" the world, while surely present in classical Kabbalah, becomes the focus of the mystic's relationship to God in Ḥasidism's emphasis on immanentism and *deveikut.*

While the notion of the plurality of the Godhead is what Rabbinites in the Middle Ages found so distasteful, and even heretical, about theosophic Kabbalah,[58] the basic dualistic nature of Kabbalah in terms of the relationship between *ein sof* and the *sefirot* remained surprisingly close to the less formalistic and less metaphysical dualism present in the rabbinic distinction between God and the world. The antagonism against Kabbalah was largely relegated to the breakdown of radical transcendence implied in *torat ha-sefirot* (the Godhead) and the way that cosmic plurality, as opposed to divine unity, became the focus of prayer and other forms of worship. While that shifting focus may indicate a change worth protesting, the classical

---

and subsequent adaptation of Sephardic kabbalistic tradition and customs (both theosophic and ecstatic) enabled Sephardism to become deeply embedded in eastern European Jewry. It would be worthwhile to examine how this plays out in ḥasidic messianisms versus other Ashkenazic messianisms not as influenced by Sephardic tradition. See Gershon Cohen, "Messianic Posture of Ashkenazim and Sephardim," reprinted in *Essential Papers on Messianic Movements and Personalities in Jewish History*, ed. Marc Saperstein (New York: NYU Press, 1992), 202–32.

56 See, for example, R. Azriel of Gerona's *Perush al Eser Sefirot* (*Sha'ar haSho'el*), printed as the introduction to R. Meir Ibn Gabbai's *Derekh Emunah* (Berlin, 1850). Cf. Scholem, "The Development of the Doctrine of the Worlds in the Early Kabbalists" [Hebrew], *Tarbiz* 2 (1931): 415–42 and 3, 33–66; and Moshe Idel, "Jewish Kabbalah and Platonism in the Middle Ages and Renaissance," in *Neoplatonism and Jewish Thought*, ed. Lenn E. Goodman (Albany: SUNY Press, 1992), 319–51.

57 *Shekhinah* as "divine indwelling" is of rabbinic origin, based on Scripture, although its meaning changes significantly in the kabbalistic reading. See, for example, Urbach, *The Sages*, 37–65. In later Kabbalah, see Elliot R. Wolfson, "*Tiqqun haShekhinah*: Redemption and the Overcoming of Gender Dimorphism in the Messianic Kabbala of Moses Hayyim Luzzato," *History of Religion* 36, no. 4 (1997): 289–332. Cf. Steven Schwarzschild, "*Shekhina* and Eschatology," in *In Pursuit of the Ideal*, ed. Menahem Kellner (Albany: SUNY Press, 1990), 235–50.

58 See, for example, *Teshuvot ha-Ribash* #157, especially s. v. *ve-haran*.

theosophic tradition mostly maintained a sharp division between *ein sof* and the *sefirot*, in some cases even utilizing the negative theology of medieval Islamic and Jewish philosophy to strengthen that distinction.[59] Access to God through the *sefirot* was tempered by the ineffability and unknowability of God as *ein sof*. It could be argued that the constant reiteration of *ein sof* as the source of all emanation saved the doctrine of the *sefirot* and later the *Shekhinah*, from the damning accusations of idolatry or pantheism. In this sense, it may be that the concept of *ein sof* contributed to saving Kabbalah from disappearing from the Jewish intellectual landscape.[60]

In its attempt to present a kabbalistic (or post-kabbalistic) worldview outside of Kabbalah's closed language and formalistic cosmology, early ḥasidic literature often blurred, unconsciously or not, the lines of demarcation between God and the *sefirot* in its attempt to create a context for the possibility of *deveikut* that required experiential access to some dimension of divinity.[61] Thus, while the unity of God (*ein sof*) is certainly maintained in ḥasidic literature, the lines separating *ein sof*, the plurality of the cosmos (*sefirot*), and the divine indwelling in nature (*Shekhinah*), are not as sharply or carefully defined as they are in the theosophic tradition.

I would argue that the reification of *maḥaloket* as part of the cosmic drama and not merely a consequence of human exile is another way Ḥasidism attempts to diffuse distinctions between our world and the divine world. Usually this is done by viewing the unity of this world through the dual lens of the *Shekhinah* and the divinity of the human soul. However, in *Keter Shem Tov* #320, viewing human *maḥaloket* as a re-enactment of a cosmic drama also creates symmetry between human beings and the cosmos through study that is useful in creating the necessary groundwork for *deveikut*. The plurality of human discourse becomes an extension of divine plurality—not in the ontological sense of emanation but in the contentious dialogical sense of *maḥaloket*. The human condition, so often viewed as the product of exile, now becomes a manifestation of the healthy state of the cosmos.

---

59 See Elliot R. Wolfson, "Negative Theology and Positive Assertion in the Early Kabbalah," *Da'at* 32–33 (1994): v-xxii. Ḥasidism does not spend a great deal of time on the identification of *keter* with *ein sof*, which was a controversy in medieval Kabbalah.

60 See Scholem, *On the Mystical Shape of the Godhead*, trans. Joachim Neugroschel (New York: Schocken, 1991), 38–41 and 46.

61 This is not to say that a purer form of kabbalism did not survive in ḥasidic circles. On the kabbalism of early Ḥasidism, see Menahem Kallus, "The Relation of the Baal Shem Tov to the Practice of Lurianic Kavvanot in his Comments to the *Siddur Rashkov*," *Kabbalah* 2 (1997): 151–65; and Louis Jacobs, *Turn Aside from Evil and Do Good* (Oxford, UK: Littman Library of Jewish Civilization, 1995), xv-xxxviii.

Deveikut and the Effacement of Radical Transcendence

Ḥasidism's implicit diminution of the focus on God's radical transcendence, a notion that underlies the rabbinic project, making *halakhah* the sole arbiter of the covenant ("God dwells *solely* in the four ells of halakhah," BT Berakhot 8a), results in a more pronounced affinity between God and humanity where the human being reflects rather than opposes the divine realm.[62] *Deveikut*, in all its complex manifestations, implies a human ability to commune with God from one's own humanness (admittedly understood as the divinity within) and not solely through the law.[63] This means that the unity of God and the disunity of human beings cannot be viewed in such

---

62 On radical transcendence as a model of Rabbinic Judaism through the lens of Mitnaggedism, see Mordecai Pachter, "Between Acosmism and Theism: R. Hayyim of Volozhin's Vision of God" [Hebrew], in *Studies in Jewish Thought*, ed. Sara O. Heller-Wilensky, Moshe Idel (Jerusalem: Magnes Press, 1989), 139, 157; Tamar Ross, "Two Interpretations of Zimzum: R. Hayyim of Volozhin and R. Shneur Zalman of Lyady" [Hebrew], in *Mekharei Yerushalayim* (1982): 153–69; and my "Deconstructing the Mystical: The Anti-Mystical Kabbalism in Rabbi Hayyim of Volozhin's *Nefesh ha-Hayyim*," *Journal of Jewish Thought and Philosophy* 9 (1999): 21–67.

63 For a provocative understanding of how *deveikut* can enable one to maintain a connection to God outside *mizvot*, see the lesson cited in the name of R. Dov Baer, the Maggid of Mezritch, in R. Hayyim Tshemowitz, *Be'er Mayyim Ḥayyim* (repr. Jerusalem, 1999), 1:194b. Cf. R. Shalom Noah Barzofsky of Slonim, *Netivot Shalom* (Jerusalem, 1982), 1:297. See also, Scholem, "*Devekut*, or Communion with God," 208–10, and 216; and Miles Krassen, *Uniter of Heaven and Earth*, 50–79. In this sense, Ḥasidism deviates from classical theosophic Kabbalah, which more strictly limits access to God through the *mizvot*. This is one reason why theosophic Kabbalah is so invested in *ta'amei hamizvot*. The notion of *deveikut* as a model of human worship outside *halakhah* is a leitmotif of Sabbateanism that mirrors Ḥasidism even as it is more explicit. As Scholem notes, "Unlike Sabbatianism, whose followers were determined to carry their doctrine to its ultimate conclusion, it was the genius of Ḥasidism that it knew where to set the limits." See "Redemption Through Sin," in *The Messianic Idea in Judaism*, 91. Idel makes this point even stronger. Regarding Sabbateanism he writes, "The classical nomian acts prescribed by halakha are now not the exclusive vehicles of theurgic activities, as in the theosophical-theurgical Kabbalah; rather, every activity as such is formed by a peculiar redemptive power" (*Messianic Mystics*, 204). I think this sentence could also describe early Ḥasidism. On challenging the internal connections between Sabbateanism and Ḥasidism, specifically regarding *deveikut*, see Mendel Piekarz, "Ḥasidism as a Socio-religious Movement on the Evidence of *Devekut*," in *Ḥasidism Reappraised*, 225–248. Martin Buber captures part of the essential nature of *deveikut* as a this-worldly spirituality open to all, in his distinction between religion and philosophy. See his, "Religion and Philosophy," in *The Eclipse of God* (Atlantic Highlands, NJ: Humanities Press, 1979), 35. "The religious essence in every religion can be found in the highest certainty. That is, the certainty that the meaning of existence is open and accessible in the actual lived concrete, not above the struggle with reality, but in it."

stark opposition—just as the world is, in essence, unified, God must be, in some way, diversified. Harking back to the second condition above, the implicit correlation between the Godhead and God in ḥasidic discourse also spills over into the correlation between God and the human being. If we are created in God's image, then God's image above must be likened to the human image below. If we reflect God (or, more precisely, the Godhead) then God reflects us. Even though the distinction between the categories of *sefirot* and *ein sof* are maintained in ḥasidic literature, the early masters are less formalistic than their kabbalistic predecessors in demarcating the distinction between divine unity and divine plurality.

The strong affinity ḥasidic masters make between God and the world or, in this case, God and Israel (since it is Israel and not humankind who are primarily the objects of the ḥasidic imagination), is not limited to a prophetic world but also applies in a post-prophetic world. Therefore, *maḥaloket* in Israel cannot simply be the product of the weakened human condition of exile or the inevitable outcome of the indeterminacy of divine will. It must also be an exercise that contains the potential, if enacted properly, to draw one into a relationship with the cosmos. For Ḥasidism and, I would argue, for Kabbalah in general, exile may have diminished the overt and public access Israel has to God's will (i.e., prophecy) but it did not erase the ability of the individual to commune with God.[64] In our ḥasidic text, the diversified nature of the human condition is also a reflection of God, and the inevitable multivocal outcome of human discourse is linked to the divine essence as emanated into this world. *Deveikut* is grounded in the symmetry between human discourse and the cosmos. To be engaged in *maḥaloket*, that is, to reflect and embody difference rather than non-difference, is an act of *imitatio dei* and not the result of the exilic condition of *deus absconditus*.

The Disappearing Bridge: Messianism, *Maḥaloket*, and the Collapsing Law

Using *Keter Shem Tov* #320, I am arguing that unity and harmony are not the goals of Ḥasidism for human society because they do not truly reflect

64 In fact, Scholem argues that this indeed may be Kabbalah's protest theology against the normative exilic nature of Rabbinic Judaism. For a depiction and critique of Scholem's historiosophy of Kabbalah, see Moshe Idel's analysis and critique in "On Rabbinism vs. Kabbalism: On Gershom Scholem's Phenomenology of Judaism," *Modern Judaism* (1991): 281–96.

the cosmos. Perfection is not exemplified here in univocality but plurality—not tolerant plurality but contentious plurality—the plurality of controversy. Nor is the goal, as some formulations of Rabbinic Judaism might have it, that controversy promotes tolerance in that it represents a liminal state of uncertainty, awaiting the reinstitution of prophecy when controversy will be resolved.[65] Ḥasidic messianism, as I understand it, refuses to view the messianic as tied solely and inextricably to history. Rather, ḥasidic messianism is lived in the act of *deveikut*, in our case, a state of redemptive controversy with oneself and with one's neighbor, whereby one emulates the *maḥaloket* of the Godhead (the cosmos being reified as a supernal *beit ha-midrash*).

The goal in the text that serves as the backbone of this chapter is to procure and perpetuate this redemptive controversy, what the rabbis call *maḥaloket le-shem shamayim*,[66] which I would translate from our ḥasidic perspective as "controversy as *imitatio dei* (*maḥaloket* as emulating in heaven)." For the rabbis, *maḥaloket le-shem shamayim* brings redemption because it assumes a unity of intention and focus on Torah as being given by "one shepherd."[67] In *Keter Shem Tov* #320 *maḥaloket le-shem shamayim* is redemptive because it unites human plurality with its divine origins. To be in conflict is to be in sync with the cosmic dis/order. This gives an ontological spin to R. Nahman of Bratslav's very personal lament, "*kol ha-olam maḥaloket*" (the entire world is made up of controversy).

I am also arguing that this ḥasidic stance wages a subtle attack on the rabbinic project as refracted through the collective lens of Sherira Ga'on, Maimonides and later mitnaggedic Judaism, the latter of which Ḥasidism deems as non-messianic or at least not-messianic-enough. What I mean here is that early Ḥasidism views the mitnaggedic focus on the primacy of Torah study (which is essentially the study of the Talmud or rabbinic *maḥaloket*) as an overly conservative messianic exercise. Mitnaggedic messianism is envisioned by early Ḥasidism as a "holding back," a conservative response to the dangers of apocalyptism in the aftermath of the Sabbatean

65 The possibility of the continuation of controversy after Messiah is plausible in Maimonides as well as other medieval jurists. See, for example, R. Eliezer of Beaugency as cited in H. H. Ben-Sasson, "The Unity of Israel According to 12th century Jewish Thinkers" [Hebrew], *Perakim Heker Toledot Yisrael* (Cincinnati, OH, 1971), 3:212–14. One could easily read Maimonides to agree with such a position. See his "Introduction to *Helek*," trans. J. Abelson in his "Maimonides on the Jewish Creed," *Jewish Quarterly Review* 19 (1907): 44. Cf. David Hartman in *Epistles of Maimonides*, 171–93.

66 See *Avot de-Rabbi Natan*, first version, chapter 40 (Vienna, 1887), 65a.

67 See BT Eruvin 21b; PT Sanhedrin 29c; *Sifrei Devarim*, #41 s. v. "*asher anokhi*."

heresy.[68] This is not to say that Mitnaggedism was not messianic at all—it was just not messianic enough.[69]

Robert Cover's comments on law illustrate this point. Cover claims that "[o]ne of the law's functions is to hold off the Messiah."[70] A religious worldview focused on the exclusivity of the law holds back the perennial danger of messianic activism that threatens the law by arguing that access to God is solely through the nomic system of laws and religious praxis. This "holding off," which I am suggesting is the nature of rabbinic/mitnaggedic messianism, is precisely what Ḥasidism found difficult to accept. For Cover the law is a bridge between what is and what can be, between the exilic character of indeterminacy, where law is needed, and the ultimate renewal of prophecy (whose context and content are unknown). According to Cover, the relationship between law and prophecy, that is, whether law will be necessary in a prophetic world, remains undetermined. More than a liminal stage of waiting, Cover argues that law is the bridge connecting the two historical moments, the known and the yet to be known.[71] But, Cover implies, the bridge may (or perhaps must) disappear once it is traversed. More strongly, law only functions properly when it contains the seeds of its own demise, since Cover maintains that law is always directed toward something outside itself—the law never has the law as its goal.[72] And, Cover further argues, the disappearing bridge is always possible at any moment in the process. The jurist must be aware of the anarchic roots of his nomic exercise, which, if successful, may collapse the legal process and give birth to a new society. I would suggest that this anarchic posture, the foundation of Cover's

68 Amos Funkenstein makes a similar argument regarding Maimonides' messianism. See Funkenstein, "Maimonides: Political Theory and Realistic Messianism," in *Perceptions of Jewish History*, 131–67.

69 In fact, it has been argued that the Vilna Ga'on was an ardent messianist and sent his disciples to Ereẓ Israel to prepare for the immanent redemption. Even if this is the case, mitnaggedic Judaism in subsequent generations did not follow this passion or, at least, did not construct its own hierarchy of Jewish values with immanent messianism as its focus. On the Vilna Ga'on and messianism see Arie Morgenstern, *Mysticism and Messianism: From Luzzatto to the Vilna Gaon* [Hebrew] (Jerusalem, 1999), 275–327; and an abbreviated English version in *Essential Papers on Messianism and Messianic Movements*, 433–55.

70 Robert Cover, "The Folktales of Justice: Tales of Jurisdiction," in *Narrative, Violence and the Law: The Essays of Robert Cover*, ed. M. Minow, M. Ryan, A. Sarat (Ann Arbor: The University of Michigan Press, 1995), 187–95. Cf. Cover, "Bringing Messiah Trough Law," in *Religion, Morality and the Law*, 209. Cf. Gordon Tucker, "The Sayings of the Wise are Like Goads," *Conservative Judaism* (Summer, 1993): 21–30.

71 See Cover, "The Folktales of Justice," 175, 176.

72 See Cover, "Nomos and Narrative," in *Narrative, Violence and the Law*, 101.

jurisprudential theory, has a correlate in Ḥasidism's overtly pietistic and largely veiled antinomianism.[73]

The rabbinic model of *maḥaloket* as tolerance, especially as post-rabbinic jurists and scholars envision it, maintains a belief in the eventual advent of the Messiah while advocating a mentality of "not-yet." In this sense, rabbinic *maḥaloket* is an act of protecting the law by diverting attention away from the future. For example, discussing the messianism of the sages in Palestine in the aftermath of the Bar Kokhba revolts in the first century CE, Gershon Cohen calls the rabbinic messianic posture "a quiescence [of] passive resistance."[74] Rabbinic discourse quiets the messianic impulse for activism, relegating redemption to the hope of a distant future that has no substantive content in the exilic world of law. *Maḥaloket,* the cornerstone of the Mishnah and Talmud, represents such an exilic quiescence on the question of redemption.[75]

While law may be a bridge in Cover's metaphor, the rabbis dictate that traversing that bridge must be done without looking to or thinking much about the other side. This is embodied in the rabbinic dictum, "three things come [most often] when they are not expected: Messiah, a lost article, and a scorpion."[76] According to one reading of this passage, it is not that Messiah can come *when* unexpected but *only when* he is not the focus of our attention. Nomic life remains the sole focus of religious devotion even as it leads its practitioner to an unknown, perhaps a-nomic or antinomian future.

I think this is one way of reading the rabbinic myth of God's sanctioning, and even enjoying, rabbinic controversy in the oft-cited talmudic

---

73 Cover, "Nomos and Narrative," 114 and 115. The notion that the nomos of inheritance is broken again and again in Genesis points to what he sees as the tenuous nature of law in general. "To be an inhabitant of the biblical normative world is to understand, first, that the rule of succession can be overturned; second, that it takes a conviction of divine destiny to overturn it; and third, that divine destiny is likely to manifest itself precisely in over turning this specific rule" (117). Even though the Bible serves as the basis and foundation of Jewish law, Cover notes: "the biblical narratives always retained their subversive force—the memory that divine destiny is not lawful" (119).

74 Cohen, "Messianic Postures of Ashkenazim and Sephardim," 220–22.

75 See, for example, Baruch Bokser, "Messianism, the Exodus Pattern, and Early Rabbinic Judaism," in *The Messiah*, ed. James H. Charlesworth (Minneapolis, MN: Fortress Press, 1992), 239–58.

76 BT Sanhedrin, 97a. The rabbinic play is that "*hesek ha-da'at*" can mean either "unawares" or "forgetting." One way to read this passage is that the phrase "*hesek ha-da'at*" relating to the scorpion is a warning to be constantly aware, lest you will be in danger of its life-threatening venom, whereas when referring to messiah means "forgetting," i.e., Messiah will come only when we cease focusing on him.

discussion of the Oven of Aknai.[77] By constructing a myth where God smiles on human controversy and refuses to intervene to resolve *maḥaloket* (i.e., "the Torah is not in Heaven"), the rabbis comfort us by claiming that, while our indeterminacy is "other than God" (in this case, even against divine directive) and thus exilic, it is still the will of God.[78]

This is even more explicit in BT Temurah 16a, a fascinating rabbinic depiction of the death of Moses and the subsequent loss of 300 laws resulting from communal mourning and Joshua's unwillingness to take the opportunity to clarify questions of law immediately before Moses' departure. Joshua goes up to heaven in an attempt to recover those lost laws.

"The Holy One, blessed be he, said to him [Joshua] 'It is not possible to tell you these laws. Go and occupy yourself in war.'" In another part of this text, Israel asks Joshua to go up to heaven and recover these lost laws (apparently it was Joshua's fault since he didn't take the opportunity to ask Moses to disclose all he knew before he died). Joshua replies (to Israel): "*It is not in heaven* (Deut. 36:13). [Later] they ask Samuel. He replies, *These are the commandments* (Numbers 36:13)."[79]

The Talmud is adamant about the fact that it is functioning in a lacuna, a realm where prophetic clarity is impossible. The indeterminacy of divine will seems woven into the very fabric of the rabbinic project. On this reading, the tolerance of the rabbis is built on the assumption of a normative and not a messianic society, a society that simultaneously stakes its claim on the eventuality of the Messiah and the directive not to think about him. The absence of any absolute (exile) and the belief in the eventual emergence of an absolute (Messiah) yields a "tolerance of waiting" enacted in the discourse of rabbinic debate. This is coupled with an unsystematic theology that is committed to a sharp distinction between God and the world that, unlike many kabbalists, does not dwell upon any (experiential) symmetry between God and humanity.

This last point is crucial. As discussed earlier, the sages in the rabbinic period largely maintained a sharp distinction between God and the world.

---

77 BT Bava Mezia 59b. Cf. Rabbeinu Nissim to BT Berakhot 19b, cited in Urbach, "*Halakhah u-Nevu'ah*," 11. Most recently, see Jeffrey Rubenstein, *Talmudic Stories: Narrative Art, Composition, and Culture* (Baltimore, MD: Johns Hopkins University Press, 1999), 34–63 and notes.

78 BT Bava Mezia 59b. "R. Nathan met Elijah and asked him: 'What did the Holy One, blessed be He, do at that moment [i.e., when R. Jeremiah argued that since the Torah was not in heaven the sages did not need to pay heed to a heavenly voice dictating law]?' He replied, 'He [God] laughed saying: 'My sons have defeated me, my sons have defeated me.'"

79 See also Sifra, ch. 13; and PT Megillah 1:8; PT Megillah 1:5. Cf. Urbach, "*Halakhah u-Nevu'ah*," 3–6, 8.

God is one and the world is many. God is perfect; humanity is imperfect.[80] The bridge is the law that is humanly constructed, or legislated, with divine sanction, in order to bridge that which can never be fully bridged without prophecy. God's will is unified while his law, in this world, is diversified. This is precisely because law without prophecy can only be as perfect as the human beings who transmit and/or legislate it, even as God sanctions that legislation. Rabbinic authority is built on the foundation of God's sanction of human legislation according to divinely given hermeneutic principles. The outcome of the proper implementation of those principles *de facto* becomes divine will. But, the rabbis claim (at least through the lens of many medieval jurists following Maimonides), this imperfection is, in actuality, the law's perfection—controversy is the human mirror of divine truth in a world where divine truth is effaced. And losing oneself in this exilic truth protects society against the messianic activism that threatens to destroy exile and its Torah.

God praises human controversy as an act of living covenantally without Him and, through that, living with Him.[81] The rabbis thus claim that *maḥaloket* (the natural outcome of indeterminate jurisprudence) is a human enterprise that God sanctions, embodied in the famous verse and dictum about *maḥaloket*: "The Torah is not in heaven" (Deuteronomy 30:12; and T. B. Bava Mezia 59b). Because, I assume, if the Torah *were* in heaven (or, according to mystical formulations, the concealed Torah [*Torah kedumah*] that *is* in heaven) it would be univocal.[82]

On this reading, commitment to the indeterminacy of divine will in a post-prophetic world is a metaphysical foundation of rabbinic authority. However, it is not only about the loss of prophecy. It is also that the loss of prophecy results in a metaphysical transformation whereby human beings,

---

80 The rabbinic unwillingness to entertain correlations between God and the world (or humanity) is later used by anti-Christian polemicists who argue that the Christian notion of incarnation is theologically outside any Jewish notion of metaphysics. The kabbalists, and later Ḥasidism, problematize that polemical stance in the notion of *torat ha-sefirot* and the *Shekhinah* as divine indwelling. Buber, in particular, noticed the way ḥasidic immanentism had the potential to change the Jewish-Christian debate. See his "Spinoza, Shabbtai Zvi, and the Besht," in *The Origin and Meaning of Ḥasidism*, 89–112.

81 See David Hartman, *A Living Covenant* (New York: Free Press, 1985), 32–41.

82 The notion of the Primordial Torah (*Torah kedumah*) in heaven that is concealed in the realm of *Ḥokhmah* is an idea that was made popular by the anonymous kabbalistic text *Sefer Temunah* (Karetz, 1784). See Scholem, *Ha-Kabbalah shel Sefer haTemunah ve-shel Avraham Abulafia*, ed. J. Ben-Shlomo (Jerusalem, 1969), 1–84. Cf. Idel, "Types of Redemptive Activity in the Middle Ages" [Hebrew], in *Messianism and Eschatology*, ed. Zvi Baram (Jerusalem, 1984), 253–79.

having no symmetry with the heavens, are severed from their divine origins.[83] The only connection is law, embodied in study and practice. The elitist foundation of this authority is that the rabbis alone are the arbiters of divinely sanctioned *maḥaloket* (i.e., *le-shem shamayim*), for only they are able to enact the necessary thirteen hermeneutic principles of interpretation. This exclusive right of interpretation and subsequent legislation prevents three things from happening, exhibiting rabbinic orthodoxy, messianism, and theology: (1) It prevents the valorization of controversy outside the discourse of Torah, a discourse the sages construct and exclusively inhabit. This is a foundation of rabbinic orthodoxy. (2) It prevents the false resolution of *maḥaloket* in a premature messianic figure who would claim to have the capacity and authority to resolve *maḥaloket* via prophecy. As long as God smiles on *maḥaloket*, *maḥaloket* and not prophecy is God's will. This is rabbinic quietistic nomian messianism. (3) It prevents the collapse of the strict distinction between God and world, serving as a foundation of the rabbinic distinction between Judaic monotheism and Gentile idolatry and solidifying the necessity of the law as the exclusive vehicle of covenantal expression. This is a cornerstone of rabbinic theology.

Together these three measures enable and empower the perpetuation of exile—an exile that is normative. While never losing sight of its messianic potential, the law functions as blinders, protecting its adherents from looking beyond it. For the rabbis, exile and controversy are inextricably bound together. "*Eilu ve-eilu . . .*" ("These and these are the words of the living God") indeed contains a rabbinic redemptive hope, but one that is staunchly rooted in the exilic mentality of human frailty and the silencing of the divine voice.[84]

Perhaps partially compensating for their limitations, the sages construct an ideology founded on the rabbinic advantage over prophecy, removing the prophet from the process of halakhic legislation, either by making him a sage or by marginalizing the prophetic voice as having legislative authority.[85] This is summarized by Ephraim Urbach when he says, "In sum (according to this investigation), the prophets did not legislate halakhah (*lo hidshu*

83 It is interesting to note that the rabbis do not seem overly concerned whether the prophetic world that is foreign to them will constitute a different metaphysical reality. That is, is exile only a change in God's relationship to Israel or is it also a change in the very nature of existence?

84 This is similar to the way David Hartman envisions Rabbinic Judaism. See his "Torah and Secularism," reprinted in *A Heart of Many Rooms* (Woodstock, VT: Jewish Lights, 1999), 71–89. Cf. Hartman, *A Living Covenant*, 204–28, 256–77.

85 See BT Yevamot 102a, Pesahim 13a, 34a, Hulin 124a, Bava Mezia 59b, *Sefer haḤinukh* #492; and more generally in Urbach, "*Halakhah u-Nevu'ah*," 20.

halakhot) or make decrees according to prophecy but only as those halakhot or decrees could be reached (by them) from logical deduction (*sevara*), casuistry (*pilpul*), or via tradition (*kabbalah*). This results in the following conclusion: if we relate to the words of the prophets with the same value as the sages, we cannot use the prophets as a source for *derash* like the worlds of the Torah."[86] By lowering the status of prophetic literature from Torah to rabbinic discourse, and by lowering the status of the prophet by making his law subject to rabbinic method, the sages create the foundation for the adage: "the sage is preferred to the prophet."[87] This position is made even more explicit in Maimonides' "Introduction" to his *Commentary on the Mishnah*.[88] In response to the question of the status of *bat kol* (a heavenly voice) in relation to prophecy and in matters of determining *halakhah*, some sages diminish the halakhic authority of prophecy (which no longer existed) and, in doing so, diminish the status of the rabbinic *bat kol* (i.e., the Torah is not in heaven).[89] This was surely not a unanimous position in rabbinic literature, as Urbach carefully shows. However, this strain of rabbinic thinking did become informally canonized in Maimonides, and impacted post-rabbinic constructions of Rabbinic Judaism.

In sum, the rabbinic infatuation with exile, its theology of radical difference, and its case for the authority of Torah over prophecy ("the sage is preferred to the prophet"), all contribute to a theory of *maḥaloket* that is a result of human error, albeit error that God tolerates and even celebrates. I will argue that the Besht challenges all of these claims—not by diffusing *maḥaloket* and vying for the presence of divine unity in our contentious world, but by reifying human *maḥaloket* as part of the nature of God.

The Text: *Keter Shem Tov* #320

In *Keter Shem Tov* #320, the Besht constructs his theory of *maḥaloket* by reading one mishnah in *Pirkei Avot* with another mishnah in that same tractate (Avot 1:1) as its subtext. Avot 6:1, the beginning of a supplementary chapter to Mishnah Avot, also called *Kinyan Torah* ("On the Acquisition of Torah"), begins as follows:

86 Urbach, "*Halakhah u-Nevu'ah*," 13 (my translation).

87 BT Bava Batra 12a. Cf. *The Responsa of Rabbeinu Asher*, principle 68, #23, and Urbach, "*Halakhah u-Nevu'ah*," 9.

88 See the discussion in Urbach, "*Halakhah u-Nevu'ah*," 20.

89 Urbach, "*Halakhah u-Nevu'ah*," 19–21 and 23–27.

> The sages taught in the language of the Mishnah. Blessed be He who chose them and their Mishnah [*be-mishnatam*]. Rabbi Meir says, "all those who busy themselves with Torah for its own sake [*torah li-shemah*] will merit many things. Not only this, but he is worthy of the whole world. He is called friend, beloved of God, and a lover of God."

The Besht begins by claiming that this mishnah is dealing with the cornerstone of the mishnaic project—those who study the same material and reach different conclusions (*de'ot shonot*).[90] That is, this auxiliary chapter in Mishnah Avot is the source of the rabbinic culture of debate (*talmud torah*), declaring that God blesses rabbinic controversy (*maḥaloket*). However, the Besht implies, this mishnah and the entire chapter that follows problematize the first mishnah in Tractate Avot (1:1) that speaks of the apparent uninterrupted transmission of Torah from Moses and subsequently to the forerunners of the rabbis. If the transmission from God to Moses was immaculate, he asks, how can there be so many differences on matters of law and practice in the Mishnah? Put another way, how can Avot 1:1 square with his reading of Avot 6:1? He continues, "if God is One, Alone, and Unique [is it not so that] His Torah must be of one mind?" The question, of course, is one that the rabbis ask themselves. Cognizant of that fact but wholly unsatisfied with their answer, the Besht reproduces that rabbinic answer refracted, and thus caricatured, through the lens of Sherira Ga'on and Maimonides.

> It should not come into one's heart, Heaven forbid, that Torah was forgotten in Israel [this is Sherira Ga'on's view], resulting in each sage [*tanna*] speaking from his own perspective according to the thirteen hermeneutic principles [this is Maimonides' view]. We should also not think, Heaven forbid, that the Torah we have now is not the pristine Torah.[91] Rather, the mishnah that we study is the same mishnah that was taught by God in heaven, in the same language, and with the same names of the sages.

The Torah of controversy that is blessed in Avot 6:1 must be the very same immaculate Torah that Moses received at Sinai described in Avot 1:1[92] It is

90 See also R. Moses Alsheikh, *Yarim Moshe, Be'ur le-Masekhet Avot* on Avot 6:1, reprinted in *Masekhet Avot—Bavli Yerushalmi* (Warsaw, 1851).

91 This is a somewhat strange locution. Perhaps the Besht is referring to the kabbalistic idea of *Torah kedumah* from *Sefer Temunah*, which states that the Torah we have is only one dimension of the pristine Torah of *Ḥokhmah* that will only be revealed in full in the messianic era.

92 It seems highly unlikely that this comes from R. Ya'akov Yosef of Polonnoye. See, for example, a completely different view in Ya'akov Yosef's *Ẓofnat Pane'ah* (Brooklyn, NY, 1991), 206c.

noteworthy that the Besht's depiction of the rabbinic position is a conflation of the rabbinic dictum in BT Sanhedrin 89b with Sherira Ga'on's *Iggeret* and Maimonides' comment in his introduction to his *Commentary to the Mishnah* (pp. 11, 12). The Besht intentionally presents the rabbis through the lens of Sherira Ga'on and Maimonides in order to make their position on *maḥaloket* a rabbinic principle that he will contest and ultimately reject. His admittedly fantastic counter-claim should not be so easily dismissed as a ḥasidic fancy. In fact, the notion that *maḥaloket* is born in heaven is supported by other rabbinic voices that the Besht intentionally suppresses in his own presentation for reasons that will become clear later on. It is also quite curious that he has no interest in bolstering his own position with *Tikkunei Zohar*'s blatantly anti-rabbinic posture.[93] Both of these omissions exhibit, in my view, his intent to reconstruct Rabbinic Judaism in the ḥasidic image rather than use the rabbis as the antithesis of his own project.[94]

The Besht's attack on the rabbinic posture of *maḥaloket*, using the strong language "Heaven forbid!," is founded on his position that the rabbinic view of the inattentiveness of the disciples of Hillel and Shammai as the origin of rabbinic *maḥaloket* would nullify the veracity and utility of Avot 1:1. What use is a description of an uninterrupted transmission from God to Moses when that transmission is erased by human error and unrecoverable without the Messiah? The teachings of the sages can only survive, according to the Besht, if the mishnah about *maḥaloket* (Avot 6:1) can exist without effacing the mishnah about uninterrupted transmission (Avot 1:1). His reading intends to create that link. In doing so, however, he counters the rabbinic notion of *hester panim* (the eclipse of God) as a foundation of, and the condition for, the centrality of rabbinic authority and the cause of *maḥaloket*.

The Besht's interpretation of Avot 1:1 is recast according to his belief in the ontology of *maḥaloket* expressed in his reading of Avot 6:1. In the following excerpt, he is more explicit in rejecting the rabbinic solution to controversy, suggesting that Moses, as a true and faithful vehicle of transmission, embodies the very controversy that the mishnah exhibits. "*Moses received Torah from Sinai* (Avot 1:1). Moses is the acronym for *Maḥaloket Shammai* and Hillel.[95] Do not say that *maḥaloket* is caused by the inattentiveness of the disciples of Shammai and Hillel [this is the

93 See Pinhas Giller, *The Enlightened Will Shine* (Albany: SUNY Press, 1993), 59–79.

94 See more on this at the conclusion of this chapter .

95 Note that "*Maḥaloket Hillel ve-Shammai*" is the description of "*Maḥaloket leshem shamayim*," described in Avot de-Rabbi Natan discussed earlier.

rabbinic position]. Rather, controversy is precisely what Moses received at Sinai."[96]

Simply making Moses the recipient of *maḥaloket* does not satisfy the Besht's critical project. He also wants to view the act and culture of *maḥaloket* as a cosmic and creative foundation of the world. He accomplishes this by recasting Israel's relationship to God as being more than the result of being recipients of his Torah. He argues that the righteous among them (which he reads as the sages of the Mishnah) are also partners in the very creation of the world.

> The sages said, "God took counsel with the souls of the righteous when He created the world, for they were *the potters who dwelled in Neta'im . . . with the King in his work* (Chronicles I:4, 23)."[97] *And God formed the man* (Genesis 2:7). This means God chose to create man according to the characteristics of the creators, i.e., the souls of the righteous [thus he formed the man from the created righteous men].[98] Therefore [before reciting the Shema] we say, "He who loves Israel" in the Evening Prayer and "He who has chosen Israel with love," in the Morning Prayer. What is this "love?" Scripture says, *Hear O Israel the Lord your God.* This means the Lord who is Your God is the Lord who is One [i.e., who was one with you before creation]. When He was alone [with you] in His world [i.e., before creation] he was uniquely your God [since you were in/with Him before creation].[99]

---

96 This appears in numerous other places. See R. Natan Shapira's *Megalleh Amukot* (Lemberg, 1858), #74. Cf. R. Efrayim of Sudylków, *Degel Maḥaneh Efrayim*, 199a; and R. Nahman of Bratslav, *Likkutei MoHaRan* 1:56, 8. Cf. Arthur Green, *Tormented Master*, 116 and 130n62.

97 *Mesudat David*'s commentary ad loc. lends support to the Besht's ḥasidic reading. He states, "the dwellers (i.e., creators) were those who made clay vessels in the place where planting took place. They were masters of boundaries, that is, they built fences and walls." Given the Mishnah's description of the sages as "builder of walls" (*asu sayag le-Torah*), these "fences and walls" could easily be read to mean "masters of the halakhah."

98 There are two main sources of this midrash, neither of which corresponds exactly to the Besht's rendition. See Bereishit Rabbah (T. Albeck ed.) 8:7 and Midrash Tanhuma (S. Buber ed.), "*Toledot*," 11, 66b. The Tanhuma version, although quite different linguistically then the citation in *Keter Shem Tov* most resembles it in substance. One important distinction between Tanhuma and *Keter Shem Tov* is that only the latter (in line with Bereishit Rabbah) uses the Genesis 2:7 verse. In this sense alone, the language and context of *Keter Shem Tov* is more compatible with Bereishit Rabbah than Tanhuma.

99 *Keter Shem Tov*, 43d, 44a.

This last comment about covenantal love connects God's covenant with Israel with the Mishnah's statement in Avot 6:1, i.e., that those who busy themselves with Torah are "beloved and lovers of God." According to the Besht's use of the midrash in Genesis Rabbah as an intertext to Mishnah Avot 6:1, the sages in question are no longer (only) the earthly sages of the Mishnah but (also) the souls of the righteous (or the supernal roots of those early sages) who were created before Genesis and are partners in the creation of the world. Note that the "righteous souls" described in the midrash are not identified there as the "sages of the Mishnah." By coupling those anonymous righteous souls in the midrash, who aid in creation, with the mishnaic sages in the Mishnah, who engage in *maḥaloket*, the Besht accomplishes two things. First, he locates *maḥaloket* in the cosmos before creation. Second, he reads God's love of the sages as a pre-Genesis covenant, a *berit* of *maḥaloket*. God does not only sanction *maḥaloket*—he creates with it. It is this pattern of creation (the sages of the Mishnah) and its results (*maḥaloket*) that is transmitted to Moses.

It is noteworthy that the Besht's ontology of controversy is based on the extension of a classic kabbalistic trinity linking God, his emanation (*torat ha-sefirot*), and his covenant with Israel (*berit*). In this covenantal construction, however, Israel is not the nation of Israel but the souls of the righteous in heaven now understood by the Besht as the sages of the Mishnah. The rest of Israel's entry into a covenant with God is through the intermediary of those sages. This is the foundation of the Besht's notion of *talmud torah* (Torah study) as an act of *deveikut*. Study is not merely the fulfillment of God's will—it is an emulation *of*, and a unity *with*, the partners of God's creation.

Divine Oneness is expanded from a purely ontological category to a relational one, now a description of the exclusivity of covenant and not only of divine essence. The souls of the righteous, who are the sages of the Mishnah, create the world and have a loving relationship with God before creation by means of engaging in *maḥaloket* (because, in essence, that is what the sages do, both in heaven and on earth). God's pre-genesis covenant with the souls of the righteous is a covenant of *maḥaloket*. The outgrowth of this covenant is creation. The nature of the world is thus founded on controversy as a reflection of God's unique relationship (*berit*) with those souls created before the world and those same souls who, through *maḥaloket*, create the world.

This type of divine plurality is different than the zoharic and later Lurianic notion of the plurality of the Godhead where the *sefirot* are initially emanated in one unified line (*shurah*) and become fragmented as a result of the breaking of the vessels (*shevirat ha-kelim*) and human sin. In the Besht's model, at least as described in *Keter Shem Tov*, there is no pre-controversy period where the sages are all in agreement or cosmic time when the *sefirot* are all aligned. The birth of the sages, i.e., the creation of the souls of the righteous, is the birth of controversy. This happens before creation—it is not as a result of comic rupture or historical exile.

This ontology of *maḥaloket* directly challenges the rabbinic claim (again refracted through the prism of Sherira Ga'on and Maimonides) that controversy is a human phenomenon resulting from *hester panim* and human delinquency. According to this rabbinic model, *maḥaloket* could easily be resolved when prophecy is restored. For the Besht, however, it cannot, as prophecy is that which gives birth to *maḥaloket*! Moses, the archetypal prophet (and rabbi), is the very embodiment of *maḥaloket*. When the Mishnah says, "the sages taught [*shanu ḥakhamim*]," *Keter Shem Tov* reads this to mean that "God taught Moses the sages" (*shano ḥakhamim*).[100] That is, God taught Moses the very same controversy that we have before us in the Mishnah, even using the names of the sages in question. Controversy is not the product of human frailty but the very fabric of divine creativity. As a faithful servant, Moses so embodies God's teaching that he is named "*Maḥaloket Shammai ve-Hillel*."

Deveikut: Unity With Supernal *Maḥaloket*

The idea that the *maḥaloket* of the sages is part of God's Torah transmitted to Moses (Avot 1:1) also serves as a foundation for the Besht's notion of study as a vehicle for *deveikut*. *Deveikut* here is not to God or even to the *Shekhinah*—it is *deveikut* to the particular sage whose opinion is being studied. This is because the earthly sage is not merely expressing his opinion but voicing the cosmic roots of that opinion, the source of which is God.

> This is what is meant, "The sages taught in the language of the Mishnah [*shanu/o ḥakhamim be-lashon ha-Mishnah*]." It means the names of the sages were taught in the language of the Mishnah. The language of the Mishnah states, "this is permitted, this is forbidden, this is pure, this is impure." Do not bother asking, "Since God is One shouldn't His will in the Mishnah be

100 The unvocalized nature of the Hebrew language, resulting in words only made up of consonants, allows one to read/vocalize the same word in numerous ways. Thus "the sages taught" can be rendered "God taught (Moses) the sages" with no change in the word root. This common word play is a fundamental tool of midrash and is adopted and expanded in post-rabbinic homiletic literature.

> one?" The sages [respond to this query and] say, "Blessed be He who chose the sages and their Mishnah." This means God Himself taught the Mishnah the way it is taught now with the names of the various sages; this is a portion of their Torah and this is a portion of their souls and roots in the supernal chariot above . . . When one studies with fear and love he attaches himself to that sage and studies with him. This means he attaches himself to that sages' source and light in the supernal chariot, as the Zohar (2.110b) says, the word *tanna'im* (sages) is also *etanim* (strong ones), as it says, *For the strong ones are the foundation of the earth* (Micha 6:2).[101]

There are two main points in this text, one overt and the other hidden, the latter of which strikingly exhibits the way in which ḥasidic masters create classical texts by grafting parts of one text onto another and then use the "created" text as a prooftext to support a particular viewpoint. This creative hermeneutical act of constructing primary texts when a text cannot be found to support a particular position is not uncommon in post-rabbinic homiletics.

Both points in our text deepen the Besht's claim about *maḥaloket* and redemption. The first point here is that the object of *deveikut* is not God but a member of the supernal academy where the discourse of *maḥaloket* is ongoing. Identifying with and learning from an ancient sage who is engaged in the act of *maḥaloket* achieves *deveikut* with that sage and through him, with God. This motif reflects, but also significantly departs from classic theosophic ideas about attaching oneself to a particular *sefirah* or *parẓuf* (*sefirotic* cluster) during prayer.[102] Even though the *sefirot* in Kabbalah are distinct fragments of a unified God and often seem in opposition to one another, they are not usually presented as engaged in anything resembling *maḥaloket*. At most, their oppositional nature is the product of cosmic discord and dysfunction resulting from the fractured nature of the supernal

---

101 The Besht's rereading of this verse is significant here. The *JPS Tanakh*, following standard commentaries, reads "*etanim*" modifying "mountains" in the first part of the verse. Hence, "Hear, you mountains, the case of the Lord, you firm foundations of the earth." The Besht wants to read "*etanim*" as "*tanna'im*" (using the intertext of the Zohar), referring specifically to the sages in heaven who are partners in creation. Therefore, he reads *atanim* as a proper noun, *foundations of the earth* as its modifier. The making of nouns out of modifying adjectives is a common practice of the theosophic Kabbalah, particularly the Zohar, and one of its fundamental hermeneutic principles.

102 In other places, the Besht does seem to adopt the more conventional kabbalistic position by stressing that the one who studies is connecting with the letters being studied. But even in such a locution he remarks that "the letter is the soul" but does not specify the nature of that soul. In our text, the soul is clearly the souls of the sages of the Mishnah. See, for example, *Keter Shem Tov* #127, 16d.

realm. Israel unifies these disparate cosmic forces through the performance of *mizvot* accompanied by contemplative practices.[103] In the Besht's teaching here, study does not facilitate a unification of the cosmic forces but an identification of the contentious supernal rabbi with the diligent student. By superimposing a particular reading of kabbalistic theosophy on the Mishnah, the Besht constructs the cosmos as a forum for the rabbinic enterprise of *talmud torah* and, in doing so, reifies *maḥaloket* as a divine act to be emulated. The discord of the cosmos now refracted through mishnaic *maḥaloket* is no longer the exilic state of creation in need of repair (*tikkun*), but a vehicle for redemption that serves as the object of the *ḥasid*'s *deveikut* to God through study. In this instance, engaging in *maḥaloket* is an expression of the self-redemption so prominent in early Ḥasidism.

The second point in this text is concealed under the guise of a Zohar text that, as we will see, does not exist as the Besht cites it. This section of the text has two parts. The first part comes from the section of the Micha verse that is not cited by the Besht. The second part is the Besht's reconstruction of the Zohar passage used to interpret that verse.

The frame of the Micha verse is the prophet's description of a relationship between God and Israel that is founded on *maḥaloket*. The Hebrew terms for controversy (*riv, viku'aḥ*) permeate the entire sixth chapter of Micha. In a strong sense, this chapter is about a *maḥaloket* between God and Israel, each side justifying the legitimacy of its own position. More than providing a context for the Zohar's word play, the verse in Micha also draws the reader into the *maḥaloket* between God and Israel that does not end in reconciliation. The sixth chapter of Micha does not conclude with any reconciliation between God and Israel so common in prophetic literature. That reconciliation only comes at the conclusion of the Book of Micha. In isolation, chapter six can easily have been seen as a chapter dealing solely with unresolved *maḥaloket*. This, I think, was how the Besht wanted his reader to understand his use of the verse.

He would have us believe that the Zohar uses a word play between *etanim* (strong ones) and *tanna'im* (early rabbinic sages) as an interpretation of Micha 6:2. In truth, however, this is not the case. Although it is true that the

103 On this, see Lawrence Fine, "The Contemplative Practice of Yihudim in Lurianic Kabbala," in *Jewish Spirituality II*, ed. Arthur Green (New York: Crossroad, 1987), 64–98, and Fine, "The Study of Torah as a Rite of Theurgic Contemplation in Lurianic Kabbala," in *Approaches to Judaism in Medieval Times*, ed. David Blumenthal (Atlanta, GA: Scholars Press, 1988), 3:29–40. Cf. Daniel Matt, "The Mystic and the Mitzvot," in *Jewish Spirituality 1*, ed. Arthur Green (New York: Crossroad, 1986), 364–404; and Morris Faierstein, "God's Need for the Commandments," *Conservative Judaism* 35 (1982): 45–59.

word play of *etanim/tanna'im* appears on the same page as the Micha verse in the Zohar (2.110b) it is completely disconnected from that verse. In fact, the word play in the Zohar about *etanim/tanna'im* refers to another verse entirely, a verse in Numbers communicating Balaam's final conversation with Balak (Numbers 24:21): "He [Balaam] saw the Kenites and, taking up his theme, he said, 'Though your abode is strong [*etan moshavekha*] . . . yet the Kenites shall be consumed, when Asshur takes you captive.'" The Zohar (2.110b) comments:

> We learn oral law from this opening [of *yesod*, the corona of the phallus or *ateret yesod*]. We must know this. This is what is called *tanya* [we learn or it is taught], as it says, *atan moshavekha* ["your abode is strong"]. The term *beraita* [a standard opening of a rabbinic statement] means something outside [*bar mi-gufa*, lit. outside the body, the phallus].[104] *Etanim* are *tanna'im* who stand and support [the cosmic structure of *ze'ir anpin*, the cosmic body and the written law] from the outside [i.e., from the oral law or *beraita*]. Now one must know; when they [the sages][105] are engaged with the written law they are called *etanim*, when they are engaged with the oral law they are called *tanna'im* [they speak from the outside]. This has now been clarified.[106]

Toward the bottom of that same page the Zohar takes up interpreting the verse in Micha cited in *Keter Shem Tov*: "Here you mountains, the case

104 That is, *ateret ha-yesod,* or the opening at the end of the phallus that is considered distinct from the rest of the divine body (*tiferet* or *ze'ir anpin*). On this, see Elliot R. Wolfson, *Through a Speculum that Shines* (Princeton, NJ: Princeton University Press, 1994), esp. 336–345.

105 The Zohar, of course, is not referring to the sages at all but rather to the relationship between *ze'ir anpin* and *malkhut.* I am interpolating the Besht's use of this passage and interpreting *etanim/tanna'im* to refer to the sages.

106 The Zohar teaches that the pillar of the written law enables the oral law to be taught. Most likely this refers to verses in Scripture that are used as the foundation for rabbinic teaching. The sages employ hermeneutic techniques to these verses and create oral law. The rabbis of the oral law, specifically of the mishnaic period, are called *tanna'im.* They are able to function because of those (*etanim*) who support them through the study of the written law. This is, of course, not referring to two groups of people. The sages are both *etanim* and *tanna'im.* This is interesting to consider in the context of the medieval debate about Biblicism between Ashkenazim and Sephardim. The Sephardim were vocally critical of certain trends in Ashkenazi Judaism in the High Middle Ages against the study of the Bible in favor of exclusive study of the Talmud. On this see Frank Talmage, "Keep your Sons from Scripture: The Bible in Medieval Jewish Scholarship and Spirituality," in *Understanding Scripture: Explorations of Jewish and Christian Traditions of Interpretation*, ed. C. Thoma and M. Wyschogrod (New York and Mahwah, NJ: Paulist Press, 1987), 81–101.

of the Lord, strong [*etanim*] foundations of the earth [*moshvei areẓ*]." As is often the case in kabbalistic exegesis, the Zohar changes the word *etanim* in the verse from an adjective modifying the noun "foundations of the earth" to a noun separate from foundations of the earth. The verse now reads, "the strong [*etanim*] are the foundations of the earth." The *etanim*, whoever they are, are literally *the foundations of the earth*, giving sustenance to the world and serving as the catalyst between God and His creation. The Zohar, however, does not tell us who these *etanim* are. Remember, in the previous passage in the Zohar, the *etanim* are depicted as the sages who study the written law. This is learned out of the verse in Numbers and not the verse in Micha.

Given that the Zohar creates a noun from an adjective but does not give the noun a definitive identity, the meaning of the noun is wide open. The Besht proceeds to define this noun in his re-reading of the Zohar, using it as the lynchpin connecting the sages to the cosmic roots of creation. As a close reader and witness of the Zohar's reading of Scripture, the Besht takes license to connect the Zohar's reading of *etanim* in Micha, whose identity is undetermined, to its earlier connection of *etanim* and *tanna'im* referring to Numbers 24:21 above. While this may seem entirely plausible from a midrashic/homiletic point of view, the Besht does not present it as such. Rather, he cites the *etanim/tanna'im* correlation and then simply cites the Micha verse as its prooftext, as if the Zohar bases such a correlation on the Micha verse.

This cannot simply be explained as a lapse in the Besht's memory, confusing the upper part of the Zohar page from its bottom portion. While this is surely plausible, given that many of these teachings were delivered orally without the aid of written texts, I would say that in this case there is a curious underlying reason for such a veiled hermeneutic move. The Besht needs to unify these two Zohar passages in order to support his position that the souls of the righteous in Genesis Rabbah, who have become the sages in the Mishnah through the intertext of Mishnah Avot 6:1, support the world through *maḥaloket*. Each Zohar text separately could not support such a reading.

In the first part of the Zohar, both *etanim* and *tanna'im* are the sages. Their different attributes depend on whether they are engaged with the written or oral law. There is no mention of any part they play vis-a-vis creation of the world. In this first section, there is no indication that these sages (be they *etanim* or *tanna'im*) are anything more than earthly sages. The Zohar's interpretation of Micha 6:2 speaking about "foundations of the earth," (the prooftext of the second Zohar passage) does not talk about the interchangeability of *etanim* and *tanna'im* mentioned in the first part of the passage. Yet this is precisely the connection the Besht needs. By citing the passage about *etanim* and *tanna'im* and then substituting Micha 6:2 for Numbers 24:21 as its prooftext, the Besht connects the sages of the Mishnah to the "foundations of the earth," thus supporting his idea of the ontology of *maḥaloket* in the Zohar.

As already mentioned, this phenomenon of creating texts with a particular end in mind and then using the "new" texts as a prooftext to support that end is widespread in Ḥasidism and other Jewish homiletic literature.[107] This example is particularly telling in that the Besht uses rabbinic and kabbalistic literature to carve out a position that is both non-kabbalistic and anti-rabbinic.

Its non-kabbalism is that his idea of ontological *maḥaloket* is not in concert with later kabbalistic cosmology (particularly in the sixteenth century) that claims that the fragmented Godhead is the result of rupture or sin and that, in the future, all existence will fold back into its roots in *ein sof*.[108] As stated above, in the Lurianic system that serves as the backbone of ḥasidic mysticism the initial emanation of the *sefirot* after *ẓimẓum* and before the rupture of the vessels (*shevirat ha-kelim*) was linear and harmonious. The fracturing of the cosmos occurred with the rupture and then again with the sin of Adam and Eve. For the Besht the cosmos is constructed out of contentious souls engaged in the *maḥaloket* of God's will. This supernal culture of *maḥaloket* is not only cosmological—it is cosmogonic. It existed before creation, according to the Besht's reading of Genesis Rabbah, and subsequently became the Platonic pattern of God's creation. There is no harmony outside God that is transformed or altered by means of a mythic or historical event.

As for its anti-rabbinism, the Besht explicitly and emphatically rejects the rabbis who claim that *maḥaloket* is a creation of human failing or the loss of prophecy. More to the point, the Besht rejects the postrabbinic depiction of the rabbis (in particular Sherira Ga'on and Maimonides) as correlating *maḥaloket* with exile. In fact, for the Besht *maḥaloket* is not something to be transcended but is precisely the object of *deveikut*, self-redemption, and the goal of the religious life.

In order to accomplish this unconventional reading, however, the Besht had to create his own Zohar text and then use it to support his highly anti-classical position. As mentioned above, while later strata of the Zohar

---

107 For a striking example of this, see R. Jonathan Eybeshuetz, *Tiferet Yonatan* (Brooklyn, 1974), 24c, on the binding of Isaac.

108 See Isaiah Tishby, *Torat ha-Ra ve-ha-Kelippah* (Jerusalem, 1984), 91–105; and 134–43.

(*Tikkunim* and *Ra'aya Meheimana*) contain fairly overt anti-Rabbinite positions, many of which would have supported the Besht's subliminal anti-Rabbinite position, he chooses to base his reading on a classic depiction of the oral law in the Zohar against what he understands to be the rabbinic position of the oral law. That is, that the oral law is God's Torah without any univocality. In my view, the reason for this tact was carefully calculated. The Besht did not want to polemicize against the rabbis as much as challenge a particular interpretation of the rabbis that had become canonical. He wanted his reading of the rabbis to be viewed as a corrective to the Sherira/Maimonidean model that he believed was flawed in that it severed human activity (*maḥaloket*) from the nature of the cosmos.

The notion of *maḥaloket* as a human act invalidated Torah study (*maḥaloket*) as a model for *deveikut* because it separated human devotion from the life of the cosmos. However, instead of presenting a critique of the rabbis the Besht, at least according to *Keter Shem Tov* #320, re-presented the rabbis in the image of nascent ḥasidic spirituality, making the canonized view of the rabbis (Maimonides and Sherira Ga'on) a mistaken formulation of what the rabbis sought to achieve. Therefore, he intentionally avoided alternative rabbinic positions in the two Talmuds and more explicit polemical kabbalistic positions in the *Tikkunei Zohar* that would have supported his claim, instead favoring a reading of the foundational texts of rabbinic transmission, i.e., the Mishnah. His reading of the Mishnah was done through lenses created by de-contextualizing and then re-contextualizing a composite of midrashic and kabbalistic sources coupled with the creation of a "new" Zohar text that served as his final prooftext. What resulted was that Avot 1:1, the classic rabbinic declaration of transmission and rabbinic authority, is now squared with Avot 6:1, the mishnaic text describing *maḥaloket*. The latter text is re-read through a midrashic/kabbalistic lens, advocating an ontology of *maḥaloket* that makes controversy part of the very fabric of creation and the substance of the Sinaitic transmission.

This is not to suggest there is no anti-rabbinism here. I think that pietistic anti-rabbinism underlies the entire ḥasidic project, especially in its early phases. However, Ḥasidism's anti-rabbinism is quite different from the anti-rabbinism of earlier Kabbalah or Sabbateanism that is largely founded on contesting doctrinal and literary traditions or protesting rabbinic interpretations of history.[109] In *Keter Shem Tov* #320, the Besht clearly believed

109 Moshe Idel has a different understanding of the difference between ḥasidic and pre-ḥasidic mystical messianism. See his *Messianic Mystics*, 235–47. Given the complex and variegated nature of ḥasidic discourse, I feel both models (at least) can be legitimate readings of the ḥasidic tradition.

deeply in the rabbinic corpus and the efficacy of rabbinic literature as a vehicle for *deveikut.* Although he accepted the Kabbalah as authoritative and favored viewing rabbinic literature through mystical, quasi-kabbalistic lenses, he surely did not seek to substitute Kabbalah for the Talmud. However, he strongly contested particular constructions of the rabbinic corpus. In this text his contestations were two-fold.

First, he contested the notion that access to God is exclusively through the law, and second, he contested the post-rabbinic construction of rabbinic literature as an exilic form of Jewish creativity that obligates in a world of divine absence (*hester panim*). For the Besht the culture of *maḥaloket* that is rabbinic literature *is* divine presence and not just a divinely sanctioned practice in lieu of the absence of prophecy. The study of the Torah enables the reader to engage in the supernal activity of controversy and attach themselves to the cosmic roots of any particular *maḥaloket* and thus experience (self)redemption.

In this sense, the rabbinic corpus is not exilic but redemptive—it experientially connects one to the contentious nature of the transcendent realm. He would, I assume, oppose any synthetic method of Torah study, be it *pilpul* or otherwise, that attempts to resolve *maḥaloket* and show the seamless nature of the talmudic text. Rather, according to the reconstructed text attributed to the Besht in *Keter Shem Tov* #320, the proliferation of contentious study, both in what the text says and how it is read, is the root of the Besht's vision of the cosmos and the individual's access to God.

This reading rejects the notion that *talmud torah* is the quintessential religious act for the Jew only or even primarily *because* he/she can no longer experience God directly through prophecy. For the Besht, and Ḥasidism in general, this idea exhibits a deep misunderstanding of the Mishnah's intention. According to *Keter Shem Tov* #320, this mistaken notion is born from a misunderstanding of Avot 1:1 (resulting from the Sheririan/Maimonidean matrix) as depicting an immaculate transmission that was lost during the unstable period of exile. According to the Besht, the advocates of such a position are, in the final analysis, the ones who are anti-rabbinic.

Chapter 4

The Ritual Is Not the Hunt: The Seven Wedding Blessings, Redemption, and Jewish Ritual as Fantasy in R. Shneur Zalman of Liady

"Do passive indolent women make the best wives?"
—Mary Wollstonecraft

Ritual studies occupies a major place in the contemporary study of religion. The anthropological and theoretical work of scholars such as Margaret Mead, Emile Durkheim, Sigmund Freud, Claude Levi-Strauss, Victor Turner, and Clifford Geertz has placed the study of ritual at the center of understanding the emergence, development, and survival of culture.[1] More recently historians of religion such as Catherine Bell and

I want to thank Rabbi Dr. Aubrey Glazer with whom I studied and debated part of this homily during the spring and summer of 2004 in Toronto, Canada, immediately preceding his marriage to Elyssa Wortzman. His passion and insight are much appreciated. Any errors are solely my own.

1 See Emile Durkheim, *The Elementary Forms of Religious Life* (New York: Free Press, 1965), 337–65; Claude Levi-Strauss, *The Naked Man*, trans. J. and D. Weitman (New York: Harper & Row, 1981); Clifford Geertz, *The Interpretation of Cultures* (New York: Basic Books, 1973); Sigmund Freud, "Obsessive Acts and Religious Practices," in The *Standard Edition of the Complete Psychological Works of Sigmund Freud*, ed. I. Strachey (London: Hogarth, 1953), 9:117–27; Victor Turner, *The Forest of Symbols: Aspects of Ndembu Ritual* (Ithaca, NY: Cornell University Press, 1967).

Jonathan Z. Smith have taken this initial research and applied it more specifically to religious ritual, that is, to acts that are performed within a framework of devotional practice and/or are determined by their practitioners to have some dimension of transcendent or supernatural meaning and significance.[2] These acts are humanly constructed, and thus "historical," but the actors claim they point to an unhistoricized dimension of reality, a dimension unrealized and, in some cases, only accessed *through* ritual.

The application of ritual studies to Judaism from a theoretical perspective is in its early stages. A fairly recent book by Ithamar Gruenwald is one of the first devoted exclusively to ritual theory and Judaism.[3] This chapter has a much narrower focus. It is devoted to one section of one ritual and based on one lengthy homily and some subsequent comments by an early ḥasidic master's interpretation of that ritual. My intention here is not to give a broad interpretation of Jewish ritual but only to illustrate how this particular ritual, interpreted through this ḥasidic lens, supports the notion of ritual as unrealizable fantasy rather than a reflection of reality. Through such a lens we can see how this ḥasidic master understands the tension created through the ritual—perhaps created by the ritual—displacing the resolution to some unknown (and perhaps unattainable) future.

The ritual in question is the Jewish marriage ceremony, a layered ritual consisting of two basic legal components (the betrothal, or *erusin*, and the marriage, or *kiddushin*) and various non- or quasi-legal components that

---

2 See Catherine Bell, *Ritual Theory, Ritual Practice* (New York: Oxford University Press, 1992), esp. 19–46 and 182–95; Bell, *Ritual: Perspectives and Dimensions* (New York: Oxford University Press, 1997); Ronald C. Grimes, *Readings in Ritual Studies* (New York: Prentice Hall, 1995); and Jonathan Z. Smith, *To Take Place: Toward Theory in Ritual* (Chicago: University of Chicago Press, 1987).

3 Ithamar Gruenwald, *Ritual and Ritual Theory in Ancient Israel* (Leiden: Brill, 2003). Cf. the review of Gruenwald by Jonathan Klawans in *AJS Review* 29, no. 1 (April, 2005), 163–65; Moshe Hallamish, "The Place of Kabbala in Ritual" [Hebrew], in *The Rituals of Israel: Sources and Development*, ed. D. Sperber (Jerusalem: Mossad ha-Rav Kook, 1998), 3:289–311; Moshe Idel, "Some Remarks on Ritual and Mysticism in Geronese Kabbala," *Journal of Jewish Thought and Philosophy* 3 (1993), 111–30; Lenn Goodman, "Rational Law/Ritual Law," and Moshe Sokol, "Mitzvah as Metaphor," both in *A People Apart: Chosenness and Ritual in Jewish Philosophical Thought*, ed. Daniel H. Frank (Albany: SUNY Press, 1993), 109–228; Yakov Travis, "Kabbalistic Foundations of Jewish Spiritual Practice: Rabbi Ezra of Gerona on the Kabbalistic Meaning of the *Miẓvot*" (PhD diss., Brandeis University, 2002), 108–46; and Elliot Wolfson, *Language, Eros, Being* (New York: Fordham University Press, 2005), 246–55.

accompany the implementation of these two legal criteria.[4] More specifically, it focuses on the liturgical component of the marriage ritual, the seven blessings that accompany, and conclude, the ceremony.[5]

As is the case with many religious rituals, the Jewish wedding ceremony serves as a motif or metaphor for a more formative moment in the myth or history of that culture. In this case, the wedding is viewed as a metaphor for the theophany at Sinai (Exodus 19–21), imagining the covenant of Israel with God in heterosexually erotic terms.[6] The midrashic depiction of Sinai as the "wedding" of God and Israel results in the wedding ritual adopting the trappings of that event, e.g., the Torah as the vehicle of the covenant is embodied in the bridegroom and bride, and the ritual space of the *ḥuppah* becomes Sinai. That is, the midrashic correlation is reciprocal, Sinai is a wedding and any common wedding becomes Sinai.

The liturgical component of the wedding ceremony includes a statement of intent of the bridegroom to consecrate the bride solely to him (in the traditional ceremony the bride is silent and is "acquired" by the bridegroom, an idea that will become significant later on) and the recitation of seven

---

4 For an explication of the ritual and its legal components in the rabbinic period see Michael Satlow, *Jewish Marriage in Antiquity* (Princeton, NJ: Princeton University Press, 2001), 162–77; and Judith Hauptman, *Re-Reading the Rabbis* (Boulder, CO: Westview Press, 1998), esp. 60–73.

5 The seven blessings are commonly called *sheva berakhot* but also called *birkhat ha-ḥatanim* ("the blessings of the bridegroom") since halakhically (legally) the whole ritual and subsequent celebration serves to cheer the bridegroom and not the bride. See R. Azaria Berzon, "*Birkhat Ḥatanim*," *Tehumin* (Alon Shvut, Israel, 1985), 6:101–17. This legal foundation only strengthens Shneur Zalman's kabbalistic interpretation. On the seven blessings see Rabbi Shaul Yisraeli, "On the Blessings of the Groom and the Participation of Women in Them" [Hebrew], *Barka'i* 1 (Summer, 1983): 163–66. In English see Joel B. Wolowolsky, "Women's Participation in Sheva Berakhot," *Modern Judaism* 12 (1992), 157–65.

6 See BT Ta'anit, 26b; *Mekhilta de-Rebbe Yishmael, Yitro, be-Ḥodesh* (Horowitz, Rabin ed.), 214. Cf. Tosefta Bava Kama 7:4; Satlow, *Jewish Marriage*, 50–57; Arthur Green, "The Song of Songs in Early Jewish Mysticism," *Orim: A Jewish Journal at Yale* 2 (1987), 49–63; Green, *Keter: The Crown of God in Early Jewish Mysticism* (Princeton, NJ: Princeton University Press, 1997), 78–87; and Henry Glazer, "The Marriage as Metaphor in Jewish Theology: A Mirror of God's Nature and its Relation to Israel" (PhD diss., The Jewish Theological Seminary, 1997), 30–46. The classic prophetic text describing the relationship between Israel and God as a wedding can be found in Jeremiah 2:2: "I accounted to your favor, The devotion of your youth, Your love as a bride—How you followed Me in the wilderness, in a land not sown."

blessings recited by prominent guests or family members.[7] This chapter will focus on the seven blessings as interpreted by the early ḥasidic Grand Rabbi Shneur Zalman of Liady, patriarch of the ḥasidic dynasty known as Ḥabad or Lubavitch.[8] I will attempt to show that his ḥasidic/kabbalistic interpretation of the seven blessings illustrates that the religious ritual in question does not conform to reality but, in fact, acknowledges, by implication, that the act being ritualized (i.e., marriage) by definition fails to live up to the expectation the ritual constructs, just as exile (the reality of Israel) shows that Sinai is a moment of covenantal reciprocity that fails to reflect the reality of the covenant established there. Hence this ritual is not, in fact, a devotional moment inaugurating a human decision (in this case, marriage) but illustrates that the event in question fails before it begins.[9]

In his essay "The Bare Facts of Ritual" Jonathan Z. Smith argues that rituals often present unrealistic and unrealizable portrayals of certain behaviors.[10] One example Smith employs is an elaborate sentimental depiction of a hunting ritual among Finnish tribes. The "hunting ritual" describes and enacts detailed ways in which the animal is addressed during the hunt and specifies certain ways it must be killed (bloodlessly, painlessly, and never when the animal is asleep or hibernating). The ritual and accompanying

7 The blessings read as follows: (1) Blessed are you, O Lord our God, King of the universe, who has created the fruit of the vine. (2) Blessed are you, O Lord our God . . . who has created all things to His glory. (3) Blessed are you, O Lord our God . . . who has created man (Adam). (4) Blessed are you, O Lord our God . . . who has made man in His image, after His likeness, and out of His very self. You have prepared unto him a perpetual fabric. Blessed are you, O Lord, who has created man. (5) May she who is barren (Zion) be exceedingly glad and rejoice when her children are united in her midst in joy. Blessed are you, O Lord, who makes Zion glad through restoring her children. (6) May You gladden the beloved friends (the married couple) as You made glad Your creature (Adam) in the Garden the jubilant voice of bridegrooms from their nuptial canopies, and of the young from their feats of song. Blessed are you, O Lord, who gladdens the bridegroom and the bride of Eden in the ancient time. Blessed are You, O Lord our God, who gladdens the bridegroom and the bride. (7) Blessed are you, O Lord, King of the universe, who has created joy and gladness, bridegroom and bride, rejoicing, song, pleasure and delight, love and friendship, peace and fellowship. May there soon be heard in the streets of Jerusalem the voice of joy and gladness, the voice of the bridegroom and the bride.

8 The homily appears his *Siddur Tefilot me-Kol ha-Shanah* (hereinafter TMKHS; Brooklyn, NY: Ozar ha-Ḥasidism, 1981), 125–36. For a popular and schematic history of the Ḥabad dynasty see Chaim Dalfin, *The Seven Chabad-Lubavitch Rebbes*, ed. Dov Baron (Northvale, NJ: Jason Aronson, 1998).

9 On the rabbinic notion of the "ideal marriage" see Satlow, *Jewish Marriage*, 225–45. This includes rabbinic texts expressing the notion of the ideal spouse.

10 See Jonathan Z. Smith, "The Bare Facts of Ritual," in his *Imagining Religion: From Babylon to Jonestown* (Chicago: University of Chicago Press, 1982), 53–65.

"liturgy" describe the passive role the hunter plays in the process, seeing himself as a vehicle for returning the animal to its "Supernatural Owner." In short, the ritual depicts an environmentally friendly and humanitarian rendering of the hunt. In reality, however, these same tribes do not conform to the ritual they practice. In the real hunt, the tribesmen kill in much more conventional ways, trapping and sometimes bludgeoning the animal to death, killing bears while they hibernate, and so forth. That is, they blatantly act in ways that contradict the ritual. How does one make sense of the obvious discrepancy between the ritual and the reality? Smith argues that (1) the practitioners of the ritual are acutely aware of the discrepancy between ritual and reality and are not apologetic about it; and (2) the discrepancy is the very origin and basis for the ritual:

> I would suggest, among other things, ritual represents the creation of a controlled environment where the variables (i.e., the accidents) of ordinary life may be displaced precisely because they are felt to be so overwhelmingly present and powerful. Ritual is a means of performing the way things ought to be in conscious tension to the way things are in such a way that this ritualized perfection is recollected in the ordinary, uncontrolled course of things. . . . . [Ritual] relies . . . for its power on the perceived fact that, in actuality, such possibilities cannot be realized.[11]

On this reading, ritual does not reflect reality but contradicts it such that the shortcomings of reality (bludgeoning a bear to death while it is hibernating due to the real fear that otherwise the bear might kill you) are tempered by the projection of a more perfect humanitarian model enacted in the "ritual of the hunt." Rituals create controlled environments void of the dangers of reality, enabling a society to fantasize about how it would like to live (and how it believes it should live) while mired in the complexities of its own frail existence. Sacred space is part of that controlled environment. In housing the ritual it accentuates the distinction between the real and ideal. In describing the hunting ritual, Smith argues that the ritual that precedes the hunt is not an attempt to create a model that can be replicated in the hunt itself. In fact, the principle of the ritual is that "the ritual is unlike the hunt."[12] The world created by the ritual is not only distinct from the real, it creates a model that, given the nature of the presently "real," simply cannot exist. Smith suggests, "There is a 'gnostic' dimension to ritual. It provides the means for demonstrating what we

11 Smith, "The Bare Facts of Ritual," 63.

12 Ibid., 64.

know ought to have been done, what ought to have taken place . . . ritual thus provides an occasion for reflection on and rationalization of the fact that what ought to have been done was not, what ought to have taken place, did not."[13] I will argue that in Judaism, a religion that has a strong redemptive component, the non- or even anti-reality of the marriage ritual is constructed as a prefiguring of a messianic future, projecting an ideal redemptive moment into the mundane and fallen state of human affairs. Thus the seventh blessing of the wedding ceremony, concerning a redeemed Jerusalem, frames the previous six.

In his commentary to the *siddur* (the classic text of Jewish liturgy) R. Shneur Zalman offers a kabbalistic interpretation of the seven blessings that accompany the wedding ceremony. The blessings constitute the center of the liturgical part of the ritual, recited under the *ḥuppah* (the sacred space) while holding the cup of wine used to consecrate the marriage (the sacred object). The blessings celebrate three moments: the creation of the human being (Adam/man) in God's image, the joy of marital union, and the commandment to procreate. They conclude with a blessing of the future joy of wedding celebrations in a redeemed Jerusalem when the collective covenant between God and Israel will mirror the particular covenant of the bride and the bridegroom.

Shneur Zalman uses the language of these blessings as an occasion to reflect on what is occurring in and through the marriage, drawing heavily on two motifs: the rabbinic utilization of the wedding as a metaphor for Sinai, and procreation (more specifically, the sexual act), the formal *telos* of the marriage ritual. Thus Sinai (i.e., Torah) and the sex act (in all its biological details) become reflections of one another. The rabbinic metaphor of Sinai/*ḥuppah* is hyperliteralized and elevated to an ontological status. In his depiction of the ritual, Shneur Zalman constructs a reality far from the real and messy nature of human relationships. In fact, according to his reading, the ritual creates a reality that undermines the very possibility of any spousal relationship accomplishing the goals set out in the ritual. The ritual is framed as a future-oriented expectation; a fantasy of accomplishing something that cannot be accomplished in this world. As we will see, in his reading one of the functional purposes of marriage is the limitation and thus control of male sexual desire through the objectification of the pious wife ("the woman of valor" of Proverbs 31:10) who dutifully serves her husband, summarily submitting to her status as catalyst and object. This is not merely an ideal to aspire to; it is a

13 Smith, *To Take Place: Toward Theory in Ritual* (Chicago: University of Chicago Press, 1987), 109.

fantasy that cannot exist because the de-eroticized passive wife is not the compelling object of sexual desire (the seductive maiden in Song of Songs stands in contrast to the "woman of valor who is a crown to her husband" in Proverbs 12:4).

Human Bodies as Torah: Sex as Interpretation

The beginning of this homily introduces the well-known rabbinic depiction of the wedding as the metaphor for Sinai.[14] In midrashic literature, this correlation serves as a covenantal frame whereby Sinai is viewed as an event founded on love, Eros, and a binding commitment. It is not that Sinai is the origin of the rabbinic ritual of marriage but rather the rabbinic ritual of marriage binds God and Israel to their Sinai commitments. Shneur Zalman writes that at Sinai sometimes Torah is the bridegroom and Israel the bride and sometimes Israel in the bridegroom and Torah the bride. "When one studies Torah to fix his soul [*tikkun ha-nefesh*] the Torah is the bridegroom who emanates [downward] and the divine soul receives that light and is thus the bride. When he studies Torah for its own sake it is the opposite. Israel is the bridegroom who draws light from *ein sof* to Torah and Torah receives it and is called the betrothed."[15] The interpretive frame here seems to be one of mutual reciprocity, each party serving to fulfill the needs of the other. This ostensible egalitarian (or proto-egalitarian) approach is problematized in what follows.[16]

---

14 For a discussion of this metaphor within kabbalistic exegesis, see Wolfson, *Circle in the Square* (Albany: SUNY Press, 1995), 7–10.

15 TMKHS 125a. The notion of gender reversals between God and Israel is not uncommon in kabbalistic literature. See, for example, in Wolfson, *Circle in the Square*, 79–121; and Wolfson, *Language, Eros, Being*, 46–58 and 333–71. Specific to our concerns, we read, "To be sure, kabbalists portray ritual, with a special focus on liturgical practices, in terms of gender transformations that render fluid the distinction between male and female—Jewish men are feminized so that the divine female may be masculinized and the antediluvian androgyny restored…" (*Language*, 49).

16 For a more apologetic approach to this whole question, focusing on the Ḥabad tradition that emerges from Shneur Zalman, see Naftali Lowenthal, "'Daughter/Wife of Hasid'—Or: 'Ḥasidic Woman?'" *Jewish Studies* 40 (2000), 21–28; and Lowenthal, "Women and the Dialectic of Spirituality in Ḥasidism," in *Within Ḥasidic Circles: Studies in Ḥasidism in Memory of Mordecai Wilensky*, ed. I. Etkes, D. Assaf, I. Bartal, and E. Reiner (Jerusalem: Bialik Institute, 1999), 7- 65 [English section]. More generally see Ada Rapoport-Albert, "On Women in Ḥasidism," in *Jewish History: Essays in Honor of Chimen Abramsky* (London: Halban, 1988).

Shneur Zalman's ḥasidic/kabbalistic interpretation hyperliteralizes the rabbinic metaphor of *Sinai/ḥuppah*, viewing the bridegroom and bride as two dimensions of Torah—the written law (Tanakh) and the oral law (its rabbinic interpretation).[17] He frames this discussion by noticing a liturgical difference between the second and third blessing. The second blessing begins with the liturgical formula using the word "Blessed [are Thou] [*barukh*]," while the third blessing begins with *barukh* and also concludes with the standard liturgical formula of *barukh*. The second blessing is uncharacteristic of standard liturgy (not having a concluding sentence beginning with *barukh*). He argues this unconventional blessing corresponds to Adam (the male) while the third more conventional blessing corresponds to Eve (the female). He explains:

> The notion of bridegroom and bride hints at the written law and the oral law. The written law does not explain any *miẓvah* in its fullness but only hints at it in writing . . . the oral law is fully disclosed . . . this is a metaphor for the male and female. The egg is initially formed into an embryo through the male semen in the womb of the woman. The "whiteness" of the father [the seminal drop] is completely undifferentiated, white and without blemish. It has no distinguishable form. . . . When this drop is disclosed [through insemination] in the womb of the mother it takes on form and appendages like a head, feet, and arms [begin to grow]. So too the oral law is called *malkhut* which is the world of disclosure [*alma de-etgalyah*].[18] It interprets and explains how each *miẓvah* is done. This is not the case with the written law where the *miẓvot* are in a state of concealment, like the seminal drop.[19]

There is an ostensibly seamless transition from the Torah (written and oral)—alluding perhaps to the rabbinic midrash, arguing that both were given at Sinai—to sexual consummation or insemination and procreation as the *telos* of marriage refracted through the lens of the wedding liturgy. The ritual has two referents—first the act of procreation and second the metaphor of Sinai (Torah). Shneur Zalman merges these two and then reads one through the lens of the other. The ritual points to procreation through the vision of Sinai, the bodies are the texts that create "religion"

17 In the rabbinic mind both were given at Sinai. See Midrash Sifra to Leviticus, "*be-Har Sinai*." The rabbinic depiction of the status of the oral law as equal or superior to the written law is discussed in David Weiss Halivni's *Midrash, Mishnah, and Gemara: The Jewish Predilection for Justified Law* (Cambridge, MA: Harvard University Press, 1986).

18 See *Tikkunei Zohar*, 17a.

19 TMKHS, 132c.

(another Jew who is also an embodiment of Torah and the process by which Torah is extended) through their actions upon each other. Sinai/the *ḥuppah* is not only the place where the Torah is given—it is where it is (re)created. The *ḥuppah* is simultaneously Sinai and the nuptial bed. Revelation is sexualized and sex becomes the creative/revelatory act that produces Torah.

But of course this romantic image does not hold the reality of the gender life in traditional Judaism nor does it correspond to the biological make-up of the bodies engendered here. The prohibition of women to engage in Torah is specific to the oral law, while a woman studying the written law is, for many jurists, permissible.[20] For the male, it is the oral law (Talmud) that dominates his devotional life, and it is he, and not she, who "explains and interprets" the life of *mizvot*. Biologically it is the female's genitals that are "concealed" while the male organ is "disclosed," a biological fact that is not lost on the rabbinic or kabbalistic tradition.

The ritual is thus interpreted here as envisioning a world inverse from our own. Women embody that which is forbidden to them. Men are represented (the written law as the undifferentiated and concealed seminal drop) by that which is antithetical to their charge as arbiters of Jewish law and practice.[21] The creative and interpretive skill (here depicted biologically) is ostensibly taken away from men and given to women. The ritual that should inaugurate the devotional roles of each gender turns the social structure on its head. As Smith suggests, "the ritual is unlike the hunt."

The correlation between man/woman and written/oral law is expanded later in this homily. There, however, the engendering is bent somewhat. The feminine now becomes the *zaddik* (the righteous male) who carries the will of God through his oral teaching.[22] The bride now transmorphs into

---

20 See, for example, R. Yehiel Michel Epstein, *Arukh ha-Shulkhan* V: "*Yoreh De'ah*," 2.46, and R. Israel Meir ha-Kohen, *Likkutei Halakhot* (St. Petersburg, 1918) to BT Sotah 20a; and R. Moshe Feinstein, *Iggrot Moshe*, "*Yoreh De'ah*" (Brooklyn, 1973), 1:137, 2:102, and 3:73b. Cf. the sources in Shoshana Zloty, *And Your Children Shall be Learned* (New York: Jason Aronson, 1993), esp. 227ff, and Norma Baum Joseph, "Jewish Education for Women: Rabbi Moshe Feinstein's Map of America," *American Jewish History* 83, no. 2. (1995), 207–209.

21 In fact, there are prohibitions regarding the study of the written law without its interpretive (oral law) tradition. See Frank Talmage, "'Keep Your Sons From Scripture': The Bible in Medieval Jewish Scholarship and Spirituality," in *Understanding Scripture: Explorations of Jewish and Christians Traditions of Interpretation*, ed. Clemens Thoma and Michael Wyschogrod (Mahwah, NJ: Stimulus Books, 1987), 81–101.

22 The feminization of the male in his relationship to the (masculine) deity is common in classical kabbalistic literature and also has its correlate in Christian mystical literature. See Moshe Idel, "Sexual Metaphors and Praxis in Kabbala," in *Jewish Family: Metaphor and Memory*, ed. David Kraemer (New York: Oxford University Press, 1989), 197–221.

Israel at Sinai and this homily now returns to what we cited at the outset—the feminine and masculine are fluid categories. The wedding canopy now becomes the mountain and the blessings invoke God as the male whose will is being inherited by the female (the bridegroom turned *ẓaddik*). The question then is: when Israel (or the *ẓaddik*) becomes the female, what becomes of the "real" woman who stands under the *ḥuppah*? Before answering that question we need to see how this transgendering occurs in our text.

> There is an advantage of the oral law over the written law in that the oral law reveals the will of God [*raẓon elyon*]. From the written law [alone] we cannot know how to make phylacteries or *ẓiẓit* (ritual fringes). From the oral law the will of God becomes manifest without any addition or subtraction, as is known. It is also known that divine will is a contracted form of God Himself [*ba'al raẓon*], as it is written, *Open up your hand and sustain all of life, your will* (Psalm 145:17).[23] That is, *all of life* [*kol ḥai*] is the *ẓaddik*, the life of the world, the last dimension of all divine emanations [who carry your will]. From the *ẓaddik*, the divine will is drawn from its source [who is God, unified and one and above all will and wisdom]. As it is written, *May it be your will*, or *makers of His will*.[24] That is, the *ẓaddik* makes divine will by means of contraction [*ẓimẓumim*]. Therefore, one should understand that since the oral law draws divine will from its source, saying this is ritually clean [*kosher*] and this is pure [*tahor*], this must also contain a dimension of the source of that will [i.e., God]. This is not the case with the written law, which does not reveal the will [of God], but it is concealed in wisdom [*ḥokhmah*], hints, and crowns.[25]

The "female" who embodies the oral law in the previous citation is now envisioned as the feminized (yet still male) *ẓaddik* who carries the divine message in his teaching ("this is kosher, this is *tahor*"). The wedding ceremony moves back to Sinai where Israel is feminized in relation to a masculine deity.[26]

---

23 The hyperliteral and awkward translation is intentional in an attempt to exhibit how it is being read by Shneur Zalman. A more idiomatic translation would be, *Open up your hand and sustain the world with your will.*

24 This usually refers to angels. See BT Sota 39b. But see Abraham ibn Ezra to Psalm 33:4 where this locution is also connected to *ẓaddik.*

25 TMKHS, 134b.

26 The text continues to offer a reason why the female produces a male child and the male produces a female child. The point is to substantiate the seemingly counterintuitive notion of the female serving the male function of explicating Torah (the oral law).

> We find that the feminine is actually rooted in the masculine and the masculine is rooted in the feminine. It is only in their formation [as physical male or female] that they are transformed. By means of these parables you will know that the oral law is the foundation of the origin of [divine] will, which is in the realm of the masculine, and the written law is founded on the feminine. . . . This is why [the final blessing] concludes, "to bring joy to the bridegroom *with* [*im*] the bride." That is, the essential joy is the joy of the bride who, in their roots, is the opposite. The female bride is thus above the place of the masculine emanation. This is the meaning of, *A wife of valor is a crown to her husband* . . . (Proverbs 12:4). The crown refers to the root of the husband. He is masculine now but feminine in his root.[27]

Shneur Zalman had given us two ways of understanding how the feminine (the oral law) is higher than the masculine, but in both cases the lofty feminine is, in essence, masculine. In this first case, the feminine is a manifestation of the male (*ẓaddik*). It is the *ẓaddik*, as arbiter of the oral law, who serves as the feminine carrier of the masculine God (the *ba'al raẓon*). Thus the perfection of the female is only when she/he becomes male. In the second case, the feminine (oral law) is higher than the masculine because in essence the feminine is masculine in its roots.[28] Thus it is the male who carries the divine will and it is the male who interprets Torah. The woman, as rooted in the masculine, is thus closed, concealed, and ineffectual. What Shneur Zalman has done is to take any positive assessment of the feminine exemplified in the wedding blessings and make them manifestations of the male. We must now ask, "What becomes of the flesh and blood female bride whose illustrious femininity has now been taken by her male partner?"

The Expression and Diffusion of the Masculine and the Bride as Object

In the previous section we viewed how the male bridegroom is transgendered to become either the "female" *ẓaddik* (in relation to God) or rooted in the "positive" femininity as interpreter of (the closed and concealed) written

---

While an interesting comment about the fluidity of gender, it is not essential to my argument. See TMKHS, 134b (middle section).

27 See TMKHS, 134b (middle section).

28 The masculine root of the feminine is common in Lurianic Kabbalah, the tradition that plays most prominently in Shneur Zalman's thinking. See, for example, Hayyim Vital, *Likkutei Torah* (Vilna, 1880), 21; and Wolfson, *Language*, 94. Cf. Charles Mopsik, *Les sexes des ames* (Paris: Editions de l'eclat, 2003).

law.[29] In some sense, both cases point back to the relationship between the male and God/Torah; that is, both are dominated by the Sinai experience. Does the bride under the *ḥuppah* also experience a transgendered state? My answer is no. I suggest she is un-gendered. By that I do not mean that she loses gender completely but that she loses any sovereignty that positive engendering entails. She becomes the object through which the male can embody his erotic desire that he then turns away from her and toward God. As noted above, this homily is based on the incongruity between the second and third blessing of the seven wedding blessings. The second blessing opens with "*barukh*" but does not conclude with "*barukh*"; and the third blessing opens with "*barukh*" and concludes with "*barukh*." That is, it has a seal (*ḥatimah*) creating an enclosed (and enclosing) whole. The third blessing thus embodies the earthly bride. She is the seal of her husband, the receptacle of his "blessing" and/or the object of his desire. Shneur Zalman uses this structure as a frame to discuss the nature of desire, pleasure, and joy (*simḥah*). The expression of desire is facilitated through *ẓimẓum* (contraction) initiating the downward flow of divine light (and human desire) toward its object—the world or the wife. In reference to God and Israel, this *ẓimẓum* is a consequence of *miẓvot*. The performance of *miẓvot* arouses divine (male) desire that emanates into the world (via *ẓimẓum*) as reward and thus pleasure for Israel. Sin prevents divine flow and is thus the source of pain.

> These are the divine decrees. Through *miẓvot* Israel is able to arouse God to act in ways that result in joy and kindness. Sins have the opposite effect. … By means of potencies [*gevurot*] and *ẓimẓum* [the contraction of] divine light descends to give pleasure and joy through the performance of *miẓvot*. … Metaphorically we can see that human pleasure is also dependent on will. If one does not have the desire to eat he will not experience pleasure, whereas if he desires it, he will experience pleasure. … It is known that joy [*simḥah*] comes from pleasure, that is, the disclosure of that which is concealed in the essence of the source of the emanation.[30]

---

29 I am in agreement with Wolfson that the "female" *ẓaddik* is not a "womanly man" but rather very much a man who has absorbed the roots of the feminine to serve in a particularly passive (yet still male) role. In fact, here it is only through his maleness as bridegroom that he can become the (feminized) *ẓaddik*. See *Language*, 94 and especially 465n327.

30 TMKHS, 135a.

The connection between pleasure and will serves as the model of healthy relation. Pleasure resides dormant and concealed in either God or the human and it is only through desire (that is, the manifestation of will to instantiate desire) that the act of *ẓimẓum* and thus disclosure is evoked. While Shneur Zalman chooses to express this in the context of divine will, *miẓvot*, and human appetite,[31] we should remember this is all an interpretation of the wedding ceremony, the teleology of which is the sexual encounter of the bridegroom and the bride. Thus Eros is the conspicuously absent frame of reference, and the pleasure for food described here is likely a stand-in for sexual pleasure, a common trope in rabbinic and later mystical traditions.[32] Shneur Zalman continues:

> *Ẓimẓum* can take on many forms and through this we can understand the seal. [For example] the signature/seal of writing is a limitation [denoting that] this is as far as *ẓimẓum* can go. As long as something is not signed/sealed it can always change direction. One can also understand metaphorically that one can draw playfulness/Enjoyment [*sha'ashu'im*][33] from its [concealed] essence without any limit or telos. This is like a person who enjoys a particular food. He can experience desire for the pleasure [in a particular food] to the point that he even eats that which is extraneous [*pesolet*] and bad [*ra*] in it. He can also experience pleasure from that [extraneous] matter because pleasure emanates from the roots of enjoyment that can be drawn down even in something that is not in and of itself pleasurable. A final seal is required so that the pleasure that is drawn from its roots in Enjoyment will have one particular destination. Any other destination should be despised and viewed as disgusting.[34]

And again:

> The notion of "opening" [*petiḥah*] with "*barukh*" enables the source of emanation to contract itself so much that the pleasure will be disclosed from its concealed state. . . . But the seal is *malkhut*, as we explained, because once

31 On the kabbalistic connection between human appetite, pleasure, and sexuality see Joel Hecker, *Each Man Ate an Angel's Meal: Eating and Embodiment in the Zohar* (Detroit, MI: Wayne State University Press, 2005).

32 For example, see Genesis Rabbah's reading of Genesis 39:6 that Potiphar gave Joseph everything "except his bread." The sages render "bread" (*leḥem*) a euphemism (literally, "refined language") for sexual partner, in this case, Potiphar's wife.

33 On the erotic dimension of *sha'ashu'im* see Wolfson, *Circle in the Square*, 12ff, and *Language*, 274–82.

34 TMKHS, 135a.

> something is fully disclosed there is [also] extraneous [desire for pleasure]. In order that this extraneous pleasure not be drawn to something foreign, the pleasure must be directed toward one particular thing . . . This is achieved by means of the seal in the blessing that is sealed with "*barukh*."[35]

In these two excerpts Shneur Zalman discloses his understanding of the difference between the second and third blessing and, by extension, the essential difference between bridegroom and bride and, more generally, he reveals the true vocation of the physical bride under the wedding canopy. The male here (represented by the kabbalistic understanding of the word "blessing" [*barukh*] as a sign of emanation) enters the wedding canopy with his desire still concealed but aroused and ready for disclosure. The ritual not only provides the context for him to begin the process of *ẓimẓum* (enabling his innate desire to become manifest). The ritual, in fact, is constructed precisely for that purpose. Yet at the same time the ritual is envisioned as Sinai, a moment where he (aspiring to emulate the ideal type—the *ẓaddik*) must be feminized to carry the message of divine will disclosed (i.e., the oral law). So the bridegroom must be male and female at the same moment. His maleness unfolds in his desire to emanate (here seminal emission is more than a metaphor; it is the biology of the metaphysics). Yet this desire, that is, maleness unhindered, can or perhaps invariably will lead to licentiousness and the uncontrolled desire to experience pleasure even in those things that are forbidden (i.e., other women). So the physical bride, now stripped of her constructive femininity (this was transferred to the male as the *ẓaddik* in the midrashic rendering of the *ḥuppah* as Sinai or in the notion of his roots being feminine)[36] plays the role of the seal [*ḥatimah*].[37] That is, she is the stop-gap that prevents the overflow of his male desire. She says (by *not* saying, her silence will be discussed below), "here and nowhere else." In saying that she strips him of pure masculinity, she limits his maleness by making herself the sole object of his desire. The price is that she sacrifices her Eros in order to limit his and her sacrifice may, in turn, diffuse the arousal of

35 TMKHS, 135a.

36 On this point Wolfson notes, ". . . but suffice it here to underscore that in kabbalistic lore the uroboric quality is also associated in a distinctive way with the feminine and particularly with the imaginal symbol of the *Shekhina*, but in this context the matter must be seen from an androcentric perspective; the positive aspects of femininity are valenced as masculine and the negative as feminine" (*Language*, 68).

37 On the functional dimension of the bride as a vehicle for her husband's devotion to God in the kabbalistic tradition, see Moshe Idel, "Female Beauty: A Chapter in the History of Jewish Mysticism," in *Within Ḥasidic Circles*, 317–34. Cf. Wolfson, *Language*, 49–50.

his desire that it would be redirected to God. Put differently, he needs her as object to become the *ẓaddik* but when she is merely object he cannot become the *ẓaddik*.

This may also have at least two negative consequences in the real world of human relationships. First, she becomes the sole object of his Eros by legal decree, thus she can also be a source of resentment and sexual frustration; and second, as a seal she loses her sense of independence and sovereignty that may very well be the source of her attraction (it is the unmarried maiden who is the object of desire in Song of Songs. The wife in Proverbs 31:10 is defined as the "wife of valor," faithful and serving).[38] The way I am reading Shneur Zalman's rendition of the seven wedding blessings, the bride may become an object of desire that is not that desirable—or, the very status of "wife" (wife of valor) may require her to sacrifice her desirability. Her objectification as a "wife of valor" may be the source of her de-eroticized status. And it is this de-eroticized subservience that makes her role as the sole object of his desire problematic.[39] Why? Not only because it may blemish their intimate marital relationship (this may also be true) but because his own "desire" for God is to some extent a product of his ability to draw down pleasure from the roots of Enjoyment and feminize that in order to be a servant of God. If she does not continue to arouse that male desire in him, he will not have the requisite desire for God.[40]

One could argue that if (male) pleasure was not necessary for the process of feminization into a *ẓaddik*, marriage would not be a goal in the Jewish devotional life. But in this case, if he does not desire his wife, he cannot be a *ẓaddik* because he will not draw from the repository of desire and pleasure, that is, there will be no will that can initiate the process

38 On Song of Songs in Kabbalah more generally see Arthur Green, "The Song of Songs in Early Jewish Mysticism," *Grim* 2 (1987), 49–63; and Elliot Wolfson, *Language*, 334–71.

39 For another perspective on the fragmented nature of the feminine as it emerges from the masculine gaze see Moshe Idel, "The Beloved and the Concubine: The Woman in Jewish Mysticism" [Hebrew], in *Blessed That I Was Made a Woman?: The Woman in Judaism from the Bible to the Present*, ed. D. Ariel, M. Lebovitz, and Y. Mazor (Tel Aviv: Sifrei Hamad, 1999), 23–84.

40 Thus we read in Zohar 1.228b that the *Shekhinah* only dwells with a man who has an earthly woman. This is also likely drawing on the oft-cited story told by Rabbi Isaac of Acre (thirteenth century) about the man who waits his entire life for the princess to submit herself to him in the graveyard and through this desire he is transformed into a righteous man. One version of the story states, "and R. Isaac of Acre wrote there his account of the deeds of the ascetics, that he who does not desire a woman is like a donkey, or even less than one, the point being that from the objects of sensation one may apprehend the worship of God." See as cited in Elijah da Vidas, *Reishit Ḥokhmah*, "Gate of Love" (Jerusalem, 1984), 426.

of drawing down desire that can then be transferred back to God. If he desires women other than his wife he will never be able to feminize that desire and direct it toward God—he will remain hopelessly in the realm of unhindered masculinity.[41] How then can the bride be both a passive seal and an erotic mate? This may be one of Shneur Zalman's dilemmas, and his metaphysical understanding of the wedding ritual may reflect that uncertainty. To return once again to Smith, "the ritual is not the hunt." Put differently, what may emerge from this is that the medieval Jewish rejection of Christian celibacy that colors earlier kabbalistic literature simply does not work here.[42] For the aspiring devotee, marriage may not be an adequate "Jewish" answer to Christian asceticism but there may also be no other alternative.

The Jewish wedding ceremony has all the necessary criteria of a religious ritual: sacred space (*ḥuppah*),[43] liturgy (the seven blessings), a text (the *ketubah* or marriage agreement),[44] religious objects (wine), and historical memory (breaking the glass commemorating the destruction of Jerusalem). It is also reified to represent the quintessential moment in Jewish religious/mythic history—the covenant between God and Israel forged at Sinai. But more than that, it conforms to Jonathan Z. Smith's theory of ritual as fantasy—it has an inverse relationship to reality. On Shneur Zalman's reading it reflects the male tension of reality, the erotic desire for the female and the desire for God as incompatible impulses that

---

41 It does not go unnoticed that this is a wholly heterosexual model. And yet, the homoeroticism of Kabbalah is also quite prevalent. On Kabbalah and the heterosexual matrix see Yehuda Liebes, "Zohar and Eros" [Hebrew], *Alpayyim* 9 (1994): 67–115; and Moshe Idel, "Sexual Metaphors and Praxis in Kabbala," 197–224. On homoeroticism and Kabbalah see most recently Wolfson, *Language*, 324–32; and Mopsik, *Les sexes des ames*.

42 On the kabbalistic rejection of Christian celibacy, see Scholem, *Major Trends in Jewish Mysticism* (New York: Schocken, 1941), 235. Elliot Wolfson has challenged this generalization and argued that the focus on marriage as an act of spiritual significance does not reject the notion of celibacy *in toto* but attenuates the ascetic lifestyle by using, and transforming, the sexual act. See Wolfson, *Language*, 255 and 363–71. Cf. David Biale, *Eros and the Jews: From Biblical Israel to Contemporary America* (New York: Basic Books, 1990), 101–20.

43 The custom of the *ḥuppah* the way it is presently practiced is quite new to Jewish ritual, likely originating in the sixteenth century. See R. Moshe Isserles (Rama) to *Shulkhan Arukh*, "*ha-ezer*," 55:1. Cf. Samuel B. Freehof, "The Chuppah," in *In the Time of Harvest: Essays in Honor of Abba Hillel Silver*, ed. D. J. Silber (New York: Macmillan, 1963), 186–93.

44 On the history of the *ketubah*, see Moshe Gaster, *The Ketubah* (New York: Herman Press, 1923); and Mordecai Akiva Friedman, *Jewish Marriage in Palestine* (Tel Aviv and New York: JTS Press, 1980), 1:1–47.

are, nonetheless, dependent upon one another. Judaism's decision not to institute celibacy as convention left the aspiring devotee of God with little other choice but to marry.[45] This may be a case where communal/tribal survival trumps devotional practice. Yet marriage, both in terms of its familial responsibilities and its evocation and simultaneous limiting of masculine desire, presents itself as a challenge as much as a blessing for the aspiring devotee of God.

Ritual Reversal: The Sinai "Wedding" as Betrothal, the Imperfection of Reality, and the Ritual as Fantastic Ideal

Just as Smith suggests with the Finnish hunters, I argue Shneur Zalman (and others like him) were quite aware of the tension between the edifying fantasy of Jewish ritual and the messy reality of lived existence. In our case, marriage depicted through the wedding ceremony (according to Shneur Zalman) and the reality of marriage as a lived phenomenon exist in perennial tension. This is not simply because human beings fail to live up to the standard of the ritual—it is because the ritual is constructed with deep contradictions that we, as humans, are constitutionally unable to resolve. Moreover, the ritual, as a product of human creativity (and as interpreted through the human imagination), is constructed in full awareness of its incongruity with reality. As Smith suggests, this may precisely be the point. That is, that ritual creates the "work" for the community to overcome this chasm but "it relies, as well, for its power on the perceived fact that, in

45 The question of asceticism and celibacy in classical Judaism is a topic of considerable debate. For some informative studies see David Berger, *The Jewish-Christian Debate in the High Middle Ages: A Critical Edition of the Nizzahon Vetus* (Philadelphia: Jewish Publication Society, 1979), esp. 27ff; David Weiss Halivni, "On the Supposed Anti-Asceticism of Simon the Just," *Jewish Quarterly Review* 58 (1968), 243–52; Steven Fraade, "Ascetical Aspects of Ancient Judaism," in *Jewish Spirituality I: From The Bible to the Middle Ages* (New York: Crossroad, 1986), 253–88; Eliezer Diamond, *Holy Men and Hunger Artists: Fasting and Asceticism in Rabbinic Culture* (New York: Oxford University Press, 2003); and Elliot Wolfson, "Martyrdom, Esotericism, and Asceticism in Twelfth-Century Ashkenazi Pietism," in *Jews and Christians in Twelfth-Century Europe*, ed. J. Van Engenand, M. Signer (Notre Dame: University of Notre Dame Press, 2001), 171–220; Wolfson, "Re/Membering the Covenant: Memory, Forgetfulness and the Construction of History in the Zohar," in *Jewish History and Jewish Memory: Festschrift for Yosef Hayim Yerushalmi*, ed. E. Carlebach, J. Efron, and D. Myers (Hanover and London: University of New England Press, 1998), 214–46; and Wolfson, *Language*, 296–332.

actuality, such possibilities cannot be realized."[46] I have argued that Shneur Zalman's interpretation of this ritual puts this tension into stark relief and that this tension, to some degree, exposes a crack between the legal obligation to marry and the spiritual trauma it creates. First, he integrates the Sinai metaphor as ontology by envisioning the two marriage partners as embodiments of Torah. In one sense, this only raises the stakes. Marriage in principle becomes more than human relation, it becomes the center of one's spiritual existence and the criteria for one's devotional success. Yet the reality of marriage as envisioned by Shneur Zalman is far more complicated. Second, he takes the maiden and makes her a seal (*ḥatimah*), stripping her of her feminine allure (she no longer embodies the oral law—that is now "masculinized" and given to the *ẓaddik*), rendering her a functional object limiting male desire. Elliot Wolfson's assessment of the zoharic worldview seems appropriate here. ". . . It becomes abundantly obvious that the zoharic author is promoting a purely instrumentalist view of the woman as one who provides the space—and hence the symbolic significance of referring to a wife as the 'essence of the house'—in which the male can cohabit, discharge his seminal overflow, and thereby unite with the *Shekhina*."[47]

In this homily, the earthly bride occupies a category shared by food and *miẓvot*—all three are objects *of* relation but not partners in relation. They are vehicles to evoke male desire that is then to be redirected to divine worship. In reality, of course, this is not the case. Jewish marriages are no better or worse than marriages in other cultures. Women play important roles in the Jewish family and society. Even though the legal structure of the Jewish marriage requires the male to "acquire" the woman (from her father's house)[48] in reality women generally do have a voice, a constructive role, and sometimes considerable influence even against the will of their husbands or the society in which they live. Even the rabbis in the talmudic period, not always known for their positive assessment of women, state regarding the Sinai event, "Go and inquire of the daughters of Israel whether they want to receive the Torah for the way of men is to follow the opinion of women, as it says, *Thus it has been spoken to the House of Jacob* (Exodus 19:3), this refers to women, *and declare unto the sons of Israel*, this refers to men."[49]

46 Smith, "The Bare Facts of Ritual," 63.

47 Wolfson, *Language*, 83.

48 See Mishnah Kiddushin 1:1. See Michael Satlow, *Jewish Marriage*, 68–92; and Judith Hauptman, *Re-Reading the Rabbis*, 60–73.

49 See *Pirkei d'Rebbe Eliezer*, chapter 41. As to not overstate the point, see Judith Wegner, *Women as Chattel? The Status of Women in the Mishna* (New York: Oxford University

The zoharic metaphysics that is transplanted in Shneur Zalman's description of the Jewish wedding is simply not a reflection of what it ostensibly represents, not in our time and not in his time. So what is going on here?

Smith argues that rituals are artificially controlled environments constructed precisely because they cannot be fulfilled. They exhibit, among other things, the frustration a society feels toward the chasm between what they want to happen and what they know must happen. In the case of the Finnish hunters the ritual conveys the desire for a more edifying, humanitarian, and righteous hunt. The real hunt is otherwise. In Shneur Zalman's description of the Jewish wedding, the seven blessings offer us a window into the anxiety of evoking and then limiting sexual desire, having only an object to fulfill that desire. The erotic desire evoked through this "object," facilitated through the institution of marriage, must then be transformed through transgendering the bridegroom into a female (the *ẓaddik*) and then into divine worship. The fantasy of the ritual is that somehow those three components (bride as seductress, bride as submissive stop-gap, bridegroom as male and then female) can work without interference. The reality, as one can expect, is quite different.

Smith concludes his essay by suggesting that these tribesmen simply enact something they know can never exist, and that ritual at most illustrates the tension of the real and the ideal. Judaism's emphasis on redemption enables it to simply project all unrealizable phenomena to a transformed future. In a shorter commentary on the seven blessings that follows this homily Shneur Zalman presents us with a juxtaposition of exile and redemption through the lens of betrothal and marriage and Sinai that clarifies some of the more opaque elements of the larger homily and further affirms its place in Smith's model of ritual. As we will see, here the ritual is not describing the actual marriage at all but pointing to (1) the fact that the wedding taking place is imperfect and (2) the wedding alluded to in the ritual is a future wedding in the time of redemption when the tension between the ideal and the real will be resolved and when the wife of valor can also be the virginal maiden.

The liturgical context of this discussion is based on noting the difference between the description of joy described in the sixth and seventh blessings. The sixth blessing concludes, "Blessed are you God, who brings

Press, 1988). But even here one could argue that the rabbis' legal writings were also constructing a "fantasy" that never really existed and may have in fact been a reaction against the reality they lived. Cf. Daniel Boyarin, "Women's Bodies and the Rise of the Rabbis," in *Jews and Gender: Studies in Contemporary Jewry* 16, ed. Jonathan Frankel (Oxford: Oxford University Press, 2000), 88–100.

joy to the bridegroom *and* the bride." The seventh blessing concludes, "Blessed are you God, who brings joy to the bridegroom *with* the bride." Shneur Zalman notes, "When it says, 'who brings joy to the bridegroom *and* the bride' it is referring to this time of exile. When it says, 'who brings joy to the bridegroom *with* the bride,' this refers to the future, that is after 'the voice of the bridegroom and the bride will be heard' (part of the seventh blessing). However, before the voice of the bridegroom and the bride will be heard [that is, before the bride speaks] we say, who brings joy to the bridegroom *and* the bride."[50] The ritual thus concludes by noting its incongruence with reality. The seal of the final blessing points to the tension between the ritual and the real. As the explanation continues it appears as if Shneur Zalman is offering a proto-feminist resolution to this tension.

> The difference between these two locutions [the conclusion of the sixth and seventh blessings] is that when one says "who brings joy to the bridegroom *and* the bride," the joy comes from the bride who is the repository of joy [*u-mimenah ikar ha-simḥah*] and she brings joy to her bridegroom. But when we say, "who brings joy to the bridegroom *and* the bride," it is the bridegroom who brings joy to the bride.[51]

In the future, then, the bride reveals her concealed source of joy. Only then does she have a voice ("the voice of the bridegroom and the bride will be heard") and can be the source of joy, and perhaps Eros, for her bridegroom. That is, only in the future will the bride be both beautiful maiden and subservient wife. The distinction between exile (now) and redemption (the future), between the tension and anxiety of the real and its resolution takes a strange turn. The real wedding, it turns out, is not a wedding at all but only a betrothal. This is because of the twofold purpose of the ideal wedding: (1) the simultaneous objectification of the bride as erotic object and the nullification of the bride as erotic partner; and (2) the arousal of male Eros and the feminization of the bridegroom as a "female" (*ẓaddik*) for God—is simply impossible to achieve and Shneur Zalman knows it. So now the wedding ritual no longer embodies the event taking place but points to an unknown future when the "wedding" will finally take place.[52]

---

50 TMKHS, 138a.

51 Ibid.

52 See my "When Will the Wedding Take Place?," in *One God, Many Worlds: A Festschrift in Honor of R. Zalman Schachter-Shalomi*, ed. N. Miles-Yepez (Boulder, CO: Albion Books, 2015), 95–106.

Interestingly but predictably, this *all* comes from the imperfect state of the Sinai event.

> There is betrothal [*erusin*] and there is marriage [*kiddushin*]. "It is written, *Moses commanded us in the Torah, an inheritance* [*morashah*] *to the community of Jacob* (Deut. 33:4). Do not read, *inheritance* [*morashah*] but rather betrothal [*me'ursah*]."[53] And so it is written, *Go out and see King Solomon, daughters of Zion, whose mother crowned him on the day of his wedding* [*ḥatunato*], *on the day of his joy* (Song of Songs 3:11). This is all the theophany at Sinai which only has the status of a betrothal, which is called *ḥatunato*.[54] It is not a wedding [*kiddushin*] because *kiddushin* will only take place in the redemptive future, as it is written: *For He who made you shall penetrate you, His name is the Lord of Hosts, the Holy One of Israel will redeem you.* (Isaiah 54:5) . . . .[55] The difference between betrothal and marriage is like the difference between internality and externality. Even though there was a revelation of the light of *ein sof* at Sinai in the ten commandments the light was still [only] in an external state. . . . The internal nature of Torah, its concealed secret called "explanations of the *miẓvot*" was not revealed at all at Sinai and will only be revealed in the future . . . .[56]

The Sinai event, now presented as the preliminary stage in the process of full "penetration" (the engaged couple allow themselves to express attraction to one another but not to engage in sexual penetration) becomes the setting for the wedding ritual as a ritual that points to the marriage but recognizes the impossibility of achieving its goals (the engaged can never consummate the union). The verse from Song of Songs, using the image of the crown (*atarah*) is now drawn to another use of that term describing

53 Midrash Exodus Rabbah 33:7.

54 But see R. Shlomo Yizhaki (Rashi) on Song of Songs 1:2, who suggests that this song is the song sung by Israel when they are in the state of exile and mourning. R. Shalom Noah Barzofsky (a late twentieth-century ḥasidic master) reads Rashi to mean that the desire of the song is an expression of a desire that is evoked precisely when the individual feels distance from the lover (i.e., the distance between Israel and God in the state of exile). See Barzofsky, *Netivot Shalom* to Numbers (Jerusalem: Yeshivat Beit Avraham M'Slonim, n.d.), 192.

55 The colloquial translation renders the Hebrew term *bo alayakh* as "espouse." The term more literally means "to penetrate" in a sexual way and I think this is the intention of its use in this homily.

56 TMKHS, 138a.

the "the wife of valor" (*eishet ḥayil*). In Kabbalah the *atarah*, the corona of the penis (*ateret yesod*), is used to describe the *malkhut* or the feminine.[57]

> But in the future it is written, *The wife of valor* [*eishet ḥayil*], *the crown of her husband*—(Proverbs 12:4). This crown represents *malkhut* who is a *wife of valor*. She will be the crown of her husband, who is *ze'ir anpin*[58] and she will embody the verse, *whose mother crowned him on the day of his wedding* [*ḥatunato*], *on the day of his joy* (Song of Songs 3:11) during Sinai. In the future he will get this crown from *malkhut* [in Song of Songs he gets it from his mother!] who is called "the one who receives" because the light of *malkhut* will rise above the realm of *ze'ir anpin* . . .[59]

In the future, then, the bride will also be the maiden—she will come alive from her dormant state of silence (she will have a voice) and arouse his desire for God.[60] I suggest the giving of the voice to the bride is symbolic of her transformation (back) into the maiden; she now becomes "the good [submissive] wife" who is also the seductress. The silencing of the bride under the *ḥuppah* accompanies her wearing a veil, an idea that denotes a subservient social and sexual status in Islam. It should be no surprise that in many communities the ritual of the wedding ceremony begins by the bridegroom veiling the bride, silencing her, thus making her a "woman of valor."[61] This final excerpt brings this to a conclusion.

> This is what the liturgy means when it says, "May it be soon that we hear in the forests of Jerusalem . . . the voice of happiness, the voice of the bridegroom

---

57 See Wolfson, *Through a Speculum That Shines* (Princeton, NJ: Princeton University Press, 1996), 357–68; and Wolfson, *Language*, 71and 73. On the raising of *malkhut* to *keter* and its possible gender implications see Arthur Green, *Keter: The Crown of God in Early Jewish Mysticism* (Princeton, NJ: Princeton University Press, 1997), 156–61; and more recently "*Shekhina*, the Virgin Mary and the Song of Songs: Reflections on a Kabbalistic Symbol in Historical Context," *AJS Review* 16 (2001), 1–51.

58 *Ze'ir anpin* is a kabbalistic construct referring to cosmic man. Although it is more complicated than that, for the purposes of this text this general definition will suffice.

59 TMKHS, 138a.

60 The relationship between Song of Songs and Sinai is a significant part of this text, albeit it remains unexplained. On the rabbinic idea that Song of Songs was actually a description of Sinai, fortifying the marriage metaphor with divine covenant, see Saul Lieberman, "Mishnat Shir ha-Shirim," in *Jewish Gnosticism, Merkavah Mysticism, and the Talmudic Tradition*, ed. Gershom Scholem (New York: JTS, 1960), 118–26; Daniel Boyarin's critique of Lieberman in "Two Introductions to the Midrash of Shir ha-Shirim" [Hebrew], *Tarbiz* 56 (1987): 479–500; and Green, *Keter*, 78–87.

61 The veil plays a prominent role in kabbalistic teaching, symbolic (and not so symbolic) of this state of concealment. See, for example, in Wolfson, *Language*, 224–33.

> and the voice of the bride."[62] In our present state of exile *malkhut* is only that which receives from her husband, "she has no independent reality." Hence, her prayer is called "the prayer of silence" because the bride has no voice. . . . This is why the bridegroom says to the bride "behold you are sanctified to me"[63] and the bride is silent and this very silence is the sanctification. It would seem she should also speak? ... [She is silent] because in the present [state of exile] *malkhut*, who is called bride, is subjugated and nullified to her husband. Hence her voice is not heard, not in prayer and not in the wedding ritual. Her silence is her sanctification. However, in the future when *malkhut* rises to *keter* and she will be a crown for her husband [*ateret ba'alah*] then she will influence *ze'ir anpin* and she will have an independent voice that emanates outward. . . . [The reason this is not now] is because marriage is all a state of betrothal, the light [drawn down] is only external light . . .[64]

I mentioned above that one could read this whole homily from a proto-feminist perspective. I think this is a mistake for various reasons. First, the fact remains that Sinai, now rendered as betrothal and not marriage, remains binding. That is, the silencing of the woman in the ritual is a reflection of Sinai (*halakhah*) and thus embodies the promise that in some future era women will attain a voice. In my view this is no consolation even as the final blessing gives us a prelude to her voice. In fact, this blessing can be interpreted as a tool of oppression since her silence can be viewed as the prerequisite for redemption and thus women are relegated to a passive role in order to further a process that may, at some undetermined future, result in their taking on an active role. One could say that redemption rests on her silence. This again brings us back to the ritual as fantasy, as Shneur Zalman knows that although the bride symbolically remains *silent* during the ritual, that silence is broken the moment the couple begin their life as husband and wife.

Second, in the text cited above distinguishing between betrothal and marriage where we read that in the future the woman (*malkhut*) will rise to *keter*,[65] the example Shneur Zalman brings of the redeemed *malkhut* is not the woman (the bride) but the *ẓaddik* (perhaps the pious bridegroom). "This can be understood by the fact that in the messianic future the angels will say 'Holy!' to the *ẓaddikim*. This is because the roots of their souls

62 This is part of the seventh blessing.

63 This is the proclamation the bridegroom says to the bride to verbalize the acquisition, "Behold you are sanctified to me with this ring according to the laws of Moses and Israel."

64 TMKHS, 135b. Cf. Moses Nahmanides, *Commentary to the Torah* on Exodus 16:6.

65 On this see *Tikkunei Zohar*, 11b.

are in *malkhut* that will rise above [the angels] and dwell in *keter* that is called 'their origins.' Therefore the angels will say to them 'Holy!.'"[66] Is it not inconsequential that the example Shneur Zalman chooses to describe this reversal of gender positioning in the future is the (feminine) *ẓaddikim*. The redeemed woman, or bride, is presented as a man who has successfully integrated the feminine as a source for his devotion to God. When *malkhut* is absorbed into *keter*, she takes the form of the male *ẓaddik*.

Finally, there is an implied distinction made here between Proverbs 31:10, *A wife of valor who can find?* and Proverbs 12:4, *A wife of valor who is a crown to her husband*. The second verse appears to be the fantasy of the first. The first is included in the liturgy sung at the Friday night dinner table. The male thanks God for giving him a wife who has prepared such a beautiful meal. But perhaps the Eros of Shabbat (in some communities the entire Song of Songs is recited as part of the Friday evening liturgy, interestingly juxtaposing the *wife of valor* verses likely recited within the same hour!) is better captured in Proverbs 12:41, a desire not adequately fulfilled in Proverbs 31:10. If only, this reading suggests, the wife of valor in Proverbs 31:10 was the wife in Proverbs 12:4.

Closer to our concerns, I suggest the deflection to the future in the seventh blessing illustrates the tension between the real state of marital relationships and the ideal state of marriage as the ultimate metaphor for covenant. The wedding ceremony fails to embody this metaphor because it requires contradictory things of the bridegroom and the bride. Shneur Zalman downgrades the Sinai metaphor introduced by the rabbis to a betrothal, the arousal of desire that remains unfulfilled, awaiting a redemptive future. Sinai now becomes a metaphor for exile rather than covenantal fulfillment. In traditional Jewish societies, the period of engagement is significant yet quite frustrating and precarious. The bride has been chosen but not yet consecrated to her husband. She is silenced by him (she is no longer in search of a husband) but not yet a vessel for his desire (there is no physical intimacy). She arouses the desire of her bridegroom yet she is not yet able to help transform that desire into a desire for devotion (feminizing him) because she is not yet a physical vessel for him. Betrothal, like Sinai, is a covenant not yet fulfilled.

In portraying the conventional "wedding" at Sinai as only a betrothal, Shneur Zalman addresses the tension between the ritual and reality. How

66 TMKHS, 138b. The correlation between the rise of *malkhut* to *keter* and the *ẓaddik* is predictable given the zoharic tradition that Shneur Zalman was intimately familiar with. When *malkhut* becomes *keter* she is envisioned by *Tikkunei Zohar* as the crown on the head of the *ẓaddik*.

can the bridegroom be a man for the bride and a "woman" for God? How can the bride be a "good [submissive] *wife/ wife of valor*" and a seductive maiden? How can she seduce him, arousing his desire, if she is silenced? In truth, neither the bride nor the bridegroom can achieve the ends intended in the ritual, either for themselves or for each other. This is the point of the seventh blessing. Only in the seventh blessing does the ritual acknowledge the failure of the entire enterprise, as the seventh blessing reveals how the ritual and the reality are incompatible. Only in the seventh blessing does the liturgy acknowledge that the survival of the institution of marriage is dependent on the belief in a future when it could actually work (or even take place!). The promise of the future, however, does not resolve the dilemma; it only puts it into starker relief. If there is no belief in redemption, would the Sinai covenant be worth it? If there is no belief that the bride could be both a *wife of valor* and a seductive maiden, would marriage be worth it? If the bride cannot be both a woman with a voice and a vessel for her husband's erotic devotion to God, the wedding/Sinai metaphor collapses. The futuristic and "fantastic" core of the ritual as understood by Shneur Zalman may tacitly acknowledge that, in the present, *she* cannot be both (woman of valor and maiden) and thus *he* cannot be both (male for her, female for God).

Marriage works and it does not work. It works because the bride functions to limit the expression of male Eros ("here and NOWHERE else!") that is required for divine worship. It does not work because that very function requires her silence and the subsequent de-eroticization of her seductive status ("HERE and nowhere else!"). In short, real marriage is as broken as the Sinai tablets. Once again, Smith is correct: "the ritual is not the hunt," and, like the Finnish tribesmen (according to this reading of Shneur Zalman's homily), the Jewish wedding ritual is deeply conscious of that tension. Only the fantasy of the future can hold the present together—but the future does not make marriage in the real world any easier; albeit for other reasons it may still be necessary.[67]

67 For example, see Satlow, *Jewish Marriage*, 3–41.

Chapter 5

Nature, Exile, and Disability in R. Nahman of Bratslav's "The Tale of the Seven Beggars"

Ḥasidism can be described as a Jewish revivalist movement beginning in the latter third of the eighteenth century in the provinces of Podolia and Volhynia of Eastern Europe (what is now largely known as Ukraine). Its enigmatic and mysterious founder, Rabbi Israel ben Eliezer, known as the Ba'al Shem Tov ("Master of the Good Name," 1700–1760), used earlier Jewish traditions of Kabbalah and medieval pietism as a foundation for what can be called a Jewish renewal of devotion and praxis based on joy and ecstasy.[1] The Ba'al Shem Tov's charismatic personality and his reputation as a faith healer and miracle worker attracted other Jewish mystics and pietists and even some prominent rabbinic figures to his circle of disciples. Many of these disciples became the inner circle of the Ba'al Shem Tov's admirers.[2] After his passing in 1760, some of these figures began to develop circles of their own, migrating into Poland, Lithuania, White Russia, Hungary, and other parts of Eastern Europe, spreading the Ba'al Shem Tov's popular pietistic message of serving God with joy

1 For a discussion on Ḥasidism in light of earlier models of Jewish mysticism, see Gershom Scholem, *Major Trends in Jewish Mysticism* (New York: Schocken, 1941), 325–50; and Moshe Idel, *Ḥasidism: Between Ecstasy and Magic* (Albany: SUNY Press, 1995), 45–102.

2 See Moshe Rosman, *Founder of Ḥasidism: A Quest for the Historical Ba'al Shem Tov* (Berkeley, Los Angeles, and London: University of California Press, 1996), 1–94; Immanuel Etkes, *The Besht: Magic, Mysticism, Leadership* [Hebrew] (Jerusalem: Zalman Shazar Institute, 2000), 54–87 and 122–62; and Simon Dubnow, "The Beginnings: The Ba'al Shem Tov (Besht) and the Center in Podolia," reprinted in *Essential Papers on Ḥasidism*, ed. Gershon Hundert (New York: NYU Press, 1991), 25–57.

and challenging the asceticism of earlier pietistic movements and the hierarchical rabbinical societies that had come to dominate the Eastern European Jewish landscape.[3]

While Ḥasidism after the Ba'al Shem Tov largely grew out of two of his most prominent disciples, Rabbi Dov Baer of Mezritch (Miedzyrzecz) and R. Ya'akov Yoseph of Polonnoye, the Ba'al Shem Tov's family also produced some masters who gained prominence outside the circles of these leading figures. The two most prominent members of the Ba'al Shem Tov's family were his grandsons Rabbi Barukh of Medzhibozh (1750–1812) and Rabbi Moshe Hayyim Ephraim of Sudilkov (1737–1800), both of whom were sons of the Ba'al Shem Tov's daughter 'Odel. In the next generation, 'Odel's daughter Feige (the sister of Barukh and Moshe Ḥayyim) gave birth to a son, Nahman, who would become the celebrated ḥasidic master Nahman of Bratslav.[4]

At the century's close, ḥasidic dynasties were beginning to emerge in many parts of Eastern Europe, mostly in Poland, Hungary, and Galicia. The Ba'al Shem Tov's family, however, stayed close to their birthplace in Ukraine. While not attracting large numbers of Jews like the disciples of the Mezritch circle, these ḥasidic masters, most notably R. Nahman of Bratslav, had a tremendous impact on early Ḥasidism. Independent, rebellious, and sometimes audacious, Nahman rose to become one of the most celebrated ḥasidic masters of any period. This chapter is dedicated to an analysis of one aspect of his thinking—his relationship to the natural world, exile, and his use of the mythic fable as an alternative mode of communicating his complex ideas, complimenting his homilies and the more informal advice he offered his students, much of which was posthumously published.

As great-grandson of the Ba'al Shem Tov (known as the Besht), Nahman was reared in the shadow of the first generations of Eastern European ḥasidic masters. However, as opposed to most other ḥasidic masters who emerged as leaders through discipleship, Nahman claimed to be a self-made *ẓaddik*, never attributing his stature to any master other than his great-grandfather, who died in 1760, a decade before he was born. The audacity of Nahman's claim to be a self-made *ẓaddik* caused a mixture of admiration

---

3 See Ada Rapoport-Albert, "Ḥasidism After 1772: Structural Continuity and Change," in *Ḥasidism Reappraised,* ed. Ada Rapoport-Albert (London and Portland, OR: The Littman Library of Jewish Civilization, 1997), 76–140; and Simon Dubnow, "The Maggid of Miedzyrzecz, His Associates, and the Center in Volhynia," reprinted in Hundert, *Essential Papers on Ḥasidism*, 58–85.

4 For a history of the birth and childhood of the young Nahman, see Arthur Green, *Tormented Master: A Life of Rabbi Nahman of Bratslav* (1979; Woodstock, VT: Jewish Lights, 1992), 23–62.

and animosity among his peers, culminating in a controversy that nearly ripped apart the nascent ḥasidic movement in Poland and Ukraine.[5]

Nahman's collected teachings, *Likkutei MoHaRan* (1808) and *Likkutei MoHaRan Tinyana* (1811), serve as the backbone of his thought. Various hagiographic and aphoristic works published posthumously supplement these two volumes.[6] In addition, Nahman is renowned for a series of thirteen tales he told near the end of his short life (he died of tuberculosis at the age of thirty-nine), which are viewed as the culmination of his entire intellectual oeuvre. While much scholarship has been done on these tales, the relationship between the tales and his homiletic writings is still in question. In this chapter I will explore that relationship, arguing, against earlier readings, that the tales do not always reflect his earlier work but often change his earlier thinking, specifically on the binary way he presents many of his ideas in *Likkutei MoHaRan*. The tales offer a more dialectical rendering of those ideas, using the genre of fable as a tool to nuance the texture of his religious anthropology.

This chapter will focus on Nahman's view of nature and the natural world, both as it is presented in *Likkutei MoHaRan* and again in his final tale, "The Seven Beggars." In his homilies, nature (and natural law) is viewed as exilic because it represents false security, logic, and a vision of the world severed from the constant influx of divine effluence. It is presented as the binary opposite of miracle. In the tale, nature is viewed in a more dialectical fashion. Through a close reading of a portion of the tale, I will argue that nature is represented in the tale as human disability (all seven beggars are inflicted with a specific disability) and, while rectifying the false view of nature as independent of God, nature/disability is not viewed in stark opposition to miracle as perfection. Rather, the disability and thus imperfection of each beggar becomes the source of his very perfection. The nullification of one (nature) does not bring about an understanding of the other (miracle), as is implied in his homilies. Rather, a deep understanding of nature (presented as the reason for the beggars' disability) enables one to see how the natural world, as exilic, already contains within it the elements of redemption.

5 On this, see Joseph Weiss, "Nahman on the Controversy about Him" [Hebrew], in Joseph Weiss, *Studies in Bratslav Ḥasidism* (Jerusalem: Mosad Bialik, 1974), 42–57; and Green, *Tormented Master*, 94–134.

6 On the publication of these texts and other Bratslav texts, see Weiss, *Studies in Bratslav Ḥasidism*, 251–77; Gershom Scholem, "*Kuntrus 'Eleh Shemot:* The Books of MoHaRan of Bratslav and the Works of His Disciples" [Hebrew] (Jerusalem, 1928). Compare the recent bibliographical study of traditional and scholarly literature of Bratslav Ḥasidism: David Asaf, *Bratslav: An Annotated Bibliography* [Hebrew] (Jerusalem: Zalman Shazar Institute, 2000). Asaf's study is the most comprehensive bibliographical study to date on Bratslav literature and an indispensable tool for anyone working in Bratslav Ḥasidism.

Nature, reconstrued and reconstructed, becomes the vehicle *for* and not the impediment *to* redemption. However, unlike his great-grandfather's quasi-pantheistic appropriation of nature, Nahman maintains the Neoplatonic dualism common in medieval Kabbalah and pietism, suggesting that one can, through prayer and joy, understand how nature and miracle are dependent upon, and not in opposition to, one another. The dialectic of deformity and perfection in the tale is a revision of this dualism that does not simply collapse into a mystical monism.

The Tales as the Final Failed Attempt for the End

In the summer of 1806, immediately preceding and then following the tragic death of his infant son Shlomo Ephraim that spring,[7] Nahman of Bratslav announced to his disciples, "*ikh vel shoyn onheybn mayses dersteyen*" (the time has come for me to begin to tell stories).[8] In the years following that proclamation, Nahman told thirteen stories, which were transcribed and published as *Sippurei Ma'asiyot* in Ostrog in 1816[9] (five years after Nahman's death on October 15, 1810) by his scribe and most

7 On the death of his son from tuberculosis and its effect on his life, see R. Avraham Hazan, *Avnekha Barzel* (Jerusalem, 1961), 30n32, and *Ḥayyei MoHaRan* (Jerusalem, 1991), 199, 200n151. Cf. Mendel Piekarz, *Studies in Bratslav Ḥasidism* (Jerusalem: Mosad Bialik, 1972), 78–81.

8 This statement is considered a paradigm shift in Nahman's life and his teaching by both disciples and scholars alike. The most comprehensive studies of the stories can be found in Yaakov Elstein's "Structuralism in Literary Criticism: A Method and Application in Two Representative Ḥasidic Tales" (PhD diss., University of California, Los Angeles, 1974); Martin Irving Mantel, "Nahman of Bratslav's Tales: A Critical Translation from the Yiddish with Annotations and Commentary" (PhD diss., Princeton University, 1977); Joseph Dan, *Sippur ha-Ḥasidi* (Jerusalem: Keter, 1975), 132–87; Renie G. Haidenberg and Mikhal Oron, *From the Mystical World of Nahman of Bratslav* [Hebrew] (Tel Aviv: Papirus, 1986); Piekarz, *Studies in Bratslav Ḥasidism*, 132–50; Green, *Tormented Master*, 337–71; Abraham Berger, "Approaches to Nahman and His Tales," *Studies in Jewish Bibliography, History, and Literature in Honor of I. E. Kiev* (New York: Ktav Press, 1971), 11–19; and, most recently, David Roskies, *A Bridge of Longing: The Lost Art of Yiddish Storytelling* (Cambridge, MA: Harvard University Press, 1995), 20–58. The stories have been translated into many languages. The most well-known translations are by Martin Buber into German, in 1909, and by Adin Steinsaltz, Aryeh Kaplan, and Arnold Band into English. For more references, both scholarly and popular, see Green, *Tormented Master*, 367, 368n1. For a historical overview on these and other translations, see "The Text and the Translation," in Arnold Band, *Nahman of Bratslav: The Tales* (New York: Paulist Press, 1978), 43–48.

9 The text was originally published with *Shivḥei ve-Siḥot ha-Ran*; additional material by and about Nahman was later published separately. Also included in this first printing were numerous lessons from *Likkutei MoHaRan* that were not included in the first

cherished disciple R. Nathan Sternhartz of Bratslav.[10] Most scholars agree that these tales constitute the culmination of Nahman's creative thinking,[11] deepening many of the essential themes presented in his Torah discourses, published in two volumes as *Likkutei MoHaRan.*[12]

Here I will focus on various sections of the final tale in *Sippurei Ma'asiyot*, "The Tale of the Seven Beggars." Told over the period of a few weeks, and culminating a few months before Nahman's death, it is unanimously viewed by scholars and disciples as the most obscure and difficult of the thirteen tales.[13] In many ways, this final tale is Nahman's last will and testament, incorporating recurring themes in the other tales, all contributing to form Nahman's overarching "theology of exile" and his prescription for redemption. It is an unfinished tale, as were numerous other tales, its finale intentionally concealed for the messianic future.[14]

---

printing. See R. Avraham Hazan, *Avnekha Barzel*, 74n62; and Chaim Kramer, *Between Fire and Water* (Jerusalem and New York: Breslov Research Institute, 1992), 255.

10 R. Nathan Sternhertz is usually known in scholarly literature as R. Nathan of Nemerov because he was a leading rabbinic figure in that city before becoming a disciple of Nahman. However, after becoming a disciple of Nahman, he explicitly stated that he wanted to be known as R. Nathan of Bratslav (Breslov), and he is referred to as such by adherents to the Bratslav tradition. He is buried in Bratslav, a short distance from Nahman's grave in Uman, and his grave remains a shrine for Bratslaver *ḥasidim*.

11 It is not only scholars who took this view. Nathan was recorded as saying, "In the eulogies [for me] they will say, 'Here is the man who printed *Sippurei Ma'asiyot.*' This will be my great honor." See *Siaḥ Sarfei Kodesh* (Jerusalem, 1991), 3:155.

12 This is true in the Bratslav tradition as well. Most of the traditional commentaries on the tales explain them according to *Likkutei MoHaRan, Likkutei Eiẓot, Likkutei Halakhot,* and subsequent Bratslav literature. See, for example, Nahman of Cheryn's *Rimzei Ma'asiyot*, perhaps the most widely read commentary on the tales, and R. Avraham Hazan's *Ḥokhmot u-Tevunot.* The former is published at the end of standard bilingual editions of the tales. For discussions of these commentaries, see Piekarz, *Studies in Bratslav Ḥasidism*, 147–50.

13 See Dan, *Sippur ha-Ḥasidi*, 145ff; Green, *Tormented Master*, 360–67; Mantel, "Nahman of Bratslav's Tales," 223–39. On the importance of the story, see *Siḥot ha-Ran*, 149–51, and *Ḥayyei MoHaRan*, "Conversations Relating to His Stories," 189–90. "The Tale of the Seven Beggars" was told over a period of a few weeks. The first part was told on Friday evening, March 10, 1810, when Nahman's lung ailment was worsening. The story of the third day, the story of the heart and the spring discussed later in this chapter, was told a few days before the death of his young son Shlomo Ephraim. The story of the sixth day was told on April 10, 1810. The story of the seventh day was never told. Nahman died on the intermediate days of the festival of Sukkot that year, October, 15, 1810. See *Yemey MoHaRan* (The Life of R. Nathan of Bratslav), 1.42; and Kramer, *Between Fire and Water*, 172–74. For an elaborate description of his final days and hours, see *Yemey MoHaRan*, 1.62–66.

14 See Elisheva Schoenfeld, "The Story of the Seven Beggars of Nahman of Bratslav," in *Fourth International Congress for Folk-Narrative Research in Athens: Lectures and Reports*

"The Tale of the Seven Beggars" illustrates Nahman's tortured relationship to nature and the natural world. From his homilies one can easily see how he is simultaneously enraptured and repelled by nature, viewing it as a place of solitude and peace yet also seductive and theologically precarious. Reared in the early period of Ḥasidism and profoundly influenced by the Besht's exaltation of nature as a forum and vehicle for divine worship, Nahman struggled with the mystical monism of his great-grandfather and the pietistic dualism that attracted him in the traditional literature he read. As a result, Nahman's assessment of nature is far more complex than that of his great-grandfather. In his collected homilies, he returns to a model of assessing nature more in concert with classical Kabbalah and medieval pietism, viewing nature as exilic because it represents order and fate in opposition to miracle (the suspension of order) and free will (prayer or the human ability to override natural law).[15]

The tension of nature being both beautiful and demonic emerges again and again in this final tale, resonating with the themes in his homiletic discourses. However, in the tale the polarities of good and evil begin to collapse. The seven beggars, all of whom are deformed, appear twice in the tale, first to bless the children to "be like them" (with no explanation), and then again at the end of the tale to give marital gifts to the children (in the form of a story), explaining why their deformity is an illustration of their perfection. My reading of the tale will incorporate various comments from the homilies in an attempt to see the ways in which Nahman's mythic turn to fantasy transforms his dualistic view of nature and miracle to a dialectic of the human struggle for God, who is ontologically *beyond* nature but experientially *in* nature.[16] This realization does not result in the nullification of nature nor does it yield a view, closer to the Besht, that one can experience God *through* nature. Rather, it is the foundation of an exile of sadness, an ability to retain joy even in the depths of exile because one

(Athens, 1965), 459–65; Michal Oron, "Exile and Redemption: An Analysis of the Tale of the Seven Beggars of Nahman of Bratslav" [Hebrew], *Davar, Literary Supplement* 9 (September, 1979): 14–15; and Aviad Lipsker, "The Bride and the Seven Beggars: On the Question of the Sources of the Story 'The Seven Beggars'" [Hebrew] *Jerusalem Studies in Jewish Folklore* 13–14 (1992): 229–48.

15 Another important early ḥasidic example of the relationship between nature and miracle can be found in R. Levi Isaac of Berdichev's *Kedushat Levi*, "Second Sanctification on Purim" (Jerusalem, 1966), 6b–9d. The original publication of *Kedushat Levi* (Slovita, 1818) only included his comments on Purim and Hanukkah, both of which speak about the nature of miracle. The later editions, beginning with the 1836 Berdichev edition, include his more extensive commentary on the Torah. Subsequent editions include his comments on Purim and Hanukkah at the end of the book, with new page numbers.

16 See, for example, in *Likkutei MoHaRan* 1.7, 1; 1.8, 7; 1.250; 2.10, 7.

holds a primordial memory of a pre-exilic past. Joy never effaces or erases sadness—it lives deeply within it.

A Structural Introduction

The difficulty of this tale lies not only in its highly symbolic/mythic character (which is true of all of the tales) but more specifically in its complex structure, comprising a dizzying network of stories within stories, each internal story serving simultaneously as an independent unit and part of the larger mosaic of the tale as a whole. It has been a long-standing belief among close readers of the tales that their esoteric nature can be divided into four distinct categories, the first two biographical, the third literary, and the fourth theological.[17] While the fourth approach has usually been the theater of traditional commentaries, my reading is closest to this approach as it seeks to navigate a two-way path between the homilies and the tales. Traditional commentaries usually read the tales through the homilies. I will argue that we can also reverse this equation. That is, since the tales change what is written in the homilies, the homilies should also be (re) read through the tales.

The underlying assumption of most traditional commentaries is that the tales are mythological representations of kabbalistic symbols deeply couched in folklorist themes, told (and then written) specifically for the purposes of "waking up those who are asleep."[18] The tales thus serve as a literary embodiment of "descent for the sake of ascent," a concept with roots in Lurianic Kabbalah and Sabbateanism and popularized in early

---

17 This approach has been documented most thoroughly by Joseph Dan and Yaakov Elstein. Mantel notes that Dan is largely following Nahman of Cheryn's *Rimzei Ma'asiyot* by fleshing out the literary structure and substance according to kabbalistic literature. Mantel prefers a more comparative analysis, showing the ways in which the literary framework of the story resembles folk tales of Ukraine and Eastern Europe (*marchen*). Cf. Mantel, "Nahman of Bratslav's Tales," 223–39.

18 *Likkutei MoHaRan* 1.60, para. 6: "You wake a person up through tales, tales which take place in the midst of years, representing one of the seventy faces [of the Torah]. Some people have fallen so low that they can only be aroused and awakened by means of tales of 'ancient days,' the place where all seventy faces derive their sustenance." Cf. Green, *Tormented Master*, 345–46. This lesson was given on Rosh Hashanah 1807, after Nahman had already begun his storytelling. See Nahman of Cheryn, *Pe'arparot le-Ḥokhmah* (Brooklyn, NY, 1976), 3la-33a.

Ḥasidism's notion of zaddikism.[19] According to this, the tale was the way of the *ẓaddik* lowering himself to the language of the people in order to arouse and elevate the remaining sparks embedded in their souls as a precursor to the messianic era. This does not mean that the tales were bereft of all the complexity and nuance of classical kabbalistic theosophy. They always function on various levels simultaneously.

To decipher the tales one must be intimately acquainted with the Zohar and Lurianic Kabbalah, both of which serve as the urtext of Nahman's own imagination, mystical ideology, as well as his homiletic discourses.[20] Scholars and disciples agree that Nahman's imagination was fed by zoharic symbolism and Lurianic myth and that his tales represent his unique "remythologization" of kabbalistic literature that could not be accessed by the non-initiate.[21] In this sense, the *ẓaddik*, who is the teller of the tale, serves as a translator of mystical lore to the simple Jew in order to arouse him or her to divine worship. In doing so, the hidden sparks embedded in their souls are uplifted and reunited with their divine source. Coming at the end of his life (when he knew his death was near), and perhaps drawn from Shabbatai Zevi's failed messianic descent into the netherworld (i.e., his conversion to Islam), coupled with his infatuation with fantasy, these tales serve as Nahman's final contribution to the messianic project that was a central part of his identify as a self-made *ẓaddik*. More strikingly, it is, perhaps, the reluctant acknowledgment of his failure to achieve his messianic goal.

---

19 The descent of the *ẓaddik* is paradigmatic in early Ḥasidism. See Arthur Green, "Typologies and Leadership and the Ḥasidic Zaddik," in *Jewish Spirituality II: From the Sixteenth-Century Revival to the Present*, ed. Arthur Green (New York: Crossroads Press, 1989), 127–156; and Joseph Weiss, "The Beginning of the Way of Ḥasidism" [Hebrew], *Zion* 16 (1951): 89–103. Cf. Mark Verman, "Aliyah and Yeridah: The Journeys of the Besht and Nahman to Israel," in *Approaches to Judaism in Medieval Times*, ed. David Blumenthal (Atlanta, GA: Scholars Press, 1988), 3:159–71.

20 Scholars, of course, acknowledge this as well. See, for example, Joseph Dan, preface to *Nahman of Bratslav: The Tales*, trans. Arnold J. Band (New York: Paulist Press, 1978), xiii-xix; Green, *Tormented Master*, 340–44.

21 On this, see Roskies, *Bridge of Longing*, 29; Dan, preface to *Nahman of Bratslav: The Tales*, xvii: "Still, we do find major Kabbalistic elements, especially the Lurianic concepts of mythological history and mystical redemption, serving as major motifs within the tales. But there is a basic difference between 'using' Kabbalistic ideas and 'expressing' them in the tales: those elements which are present in the tales ceased to be building blocks of a mystical theology and became chapters in the mystical biography of Nahman's soul. . . . This process of identification in a deep spiritual way with cosmic developments is rare, but not impossible, in both mystical and literary creative work."

The Symbiosis of Nature and Disability

"The Tale of the Seven Beggars" revolves around various themes, each becoming manifest in different ways.[22] One of the central themes in the story is the apparent deformity of each beggar and the way each beggar explains to the two children in the story (representations of Israel) that his deformity is not a deformity at all but an illustration of his perfection. My claim is that the theme of physical deformity in the tale alludes to Nahman's attitude toward nature in *Likkutei MoHaRan.* In his homiletic discourses, the term *teva* (conventionally translated as nature) is almost exclusively pejorative, suggesting a view of the natural world independent of any higher source. Nature appears perfect, Nahman argues, in its stability and predictability. Yet, this appearance of perfection, which is illusory, is actually the source of its imperfection. Alternatively, *olam* (world) is a term that refers to the natural world in a constant state of renewal. It implies that nature is unstable, dynamic, and unpredictable—in short, miraculous. In *Likkutei MoHaRan*, nature (*teva*) is the imperfect and exilic perception of the world (*olam*). In "The Tale of the Seven Beggars" the (apparent) deformity of each beggar is viewed as the result of an inability to see the world as *olam.* That is, it is the result of the world seeing them only in relation to nature (*teva*). This can be illustrated through his notion of higher wisdom and lower wisdom in *Likkutei MoHaRan*:

> There are two kinds of wisdom, higher wisdom and lower wisdom. Lower wisdom draws from higher wisdom. The Torah is the embodiment of higher wisdom. Worldly wisdom, which is lower wisdom, draws from this higher wisdom. When worldly wisdom is severed from higher wisdom (Torah) the result is the diminishing of the moon, which is the exile of the *Shekhinah.*[23]

According to Nahman, exile is the state when wisdom becomes severed from that which sustains it. This also applies to nature (*teva*), which is the exilic state of the world (*olam*). It should be emphasized that nature is not

---

22 The tale embodies the same methodology as Nahman's homiletic writings. Terms are expressed and then tied into other terms via association (*beḥinot*), creating a complex terminological labyrinth used to create a frame for his lesson. On this, see Nahman of Cheryn, *Pe'arparot le-Ḥokhmah*, 2a-2d; and Green, *Tormented Master*, 285–87. Cf. my "Associative Midrash: Reflections on a Hermeneutic Theory in Nahman of Bratslav's *Likkutei MoHaRan*," in *God's Voice from the Void: Old and New Studies in Bratslav Ḥasidism*, ed. Shaul Magid (Albany: SUNY Press, 2001), 15–66.

23 *Likkutei MoHaRan* 2.101.

identical with the natural world—it is only a false perception of it. Finally, Nahman implies that exile is false security while redemption is perpetual insecurity.[24] The "security of exile" rests on the fact that we are seduced into believing the ultimate truth of our rational, scientific vision of the world. This security is not rejected because it is ontologically false as much as it sublimates the longing for redemption. The maintenance or revival of longing requires destabilizing the security that lies at the heart of reason. The unfolding of the tale is Nahman's way of destabilizing these conventional notions, problematizing our system of values in an attempt to take his reader from the exilic state of false security to the instability of renewal.[25] "To arouse those from sleep," the expressed intention given for telling stories, can now be understood as awakening the longing for redemption by destabilizing the human inclination to believe in security, which, by definition, is false. As I will suggest later, "sleep" is not only a state of the disciples of reason but can also describe those who succumb to the false security of faith.

This is the foundation of my reading of "The Tale of the Seven Beggars." Unlike most of the classical commentators, who stick more closely to the explicit themes in the tale, I think Nahman's relationship to nature and the natural world in his homiletic discourses underlies much of the tale, even as the tale never overtly mentions nature per se. However, the tale reveals a more dialectical understanding of nature than we find in *Likkutei MoHaRan*. In his homilies, nature (*teva*) must be overcome as a prelude to redemption, as nature represents coincidence and fate, the very opposite of prayer and miracle. In the tale, this dualism is changed, or at least diminished. At the end of the tale, the children once again experience joy when they understand that the apparent unnaturalness of the beggars, i.e., their deformity, is really their perfection: that is, that exile and suffering do not stand in contradiction to divine election but hold the key to redemption because exile creates the longing to pray and prayer holds the potential to change nature and thus to redeem the world.

24 Exile is a complex term in Nahman's thinking, especially in the tales. For a more textured definition, see my discussion earlier in this chapter. Here I only mean that exile, as alienation, requires longing as the vehicle for reconciliation. The security of exile threatens the continuation of this longing.

25 What I mean by this is that the turn toward redemption in Nahman's eyes is a revolutionary move, turning the world on its head to reveal the illusions of exile. The "security of exile" rests on the fact that we are convinced that what we think is true is in fact true. This security is the most dangerous dimension of exile because it diminishes the longing for redemption. This is, for Nahman, the fundamental malaise of modernity.

The Prelude of the Tale as the Universal Stage of Jewish Redemption

Before moving to the analysis of the tale, a few brief remarks are in order on the literary structure of the tale, playing close attention to the way the structure impacts my reading. "The Tale of the Seven Beggars" can be divided into three major sections, the final section including six subsections, each subsection itself comprised of numerous sub-subsections. The first section of the tale is an unfinished prelude about a king and his son. There are three characters in the prelude: the king, the son, and the wise men in the king's country. The setting of the prelude is a grand ball celebrating an anonymous king handing over his kingdom to his son. The king interrupts the joyous occasion to tell his son two things. First, that his son's tenure as king is solely dependent upon his remaining in a state of constant joy (*simḥah*). Second, as a stargazer, the king predicts that in the future his son will lose his kingdom because he is not worthy, that is, he could not maintain the perpetual state of joy required for his kingship. However, the king warns his son that he should still be joyous, even in losing his kingdom, implying that true joy should never be contingent upon anything other than divine will. If God wills that he should lose his kingdom, that too should be cause for joy.[26]

The second part of the unfinished prelude draws an important connection between joy and wisdom, or, alternatively, between sadness and false wisdom—a recurring theme in Nahman's writings—by telling us some details about the son's tenure as king.

> The prince [the son] was a wise man, he loved wisdom dearly, and gathered around him many wise men. Whosoever came to him with some sort of wisdom was highly esteemed by him. . . . Since wisdom was so esteemed, everyone adopted wisdom and the whole kingdom engaged in the practice of wisdom. . . . Because of this wisdom, the wise men of the land fell into heresy and drew the prince into their heresy. . . . Only the wise men and the prince became heretics. And since the prince had goodness in him because

26 See *Rimzei Ma'asiyot*, 17a: "One who is unable to maintain the state of joy at the time of great despair [losing the kingdom], it is fitting that he should be dethroned because fitness for kingship necessitates maintaining joy even in the time of despair" (my translation). Nahman of Cheryn's comment implies that authentic joy cannot be contingent upon an external event or circumstance but needs to be an orientation toward all possible circumstances. For Nahman of Cheryn, it is joy and not wisdom that is an absolute value.

> he had been born with goodness . . . he always remembered, "Where am I in the world and what am I doing?" And he would groan deeply and remember, "What is this? . . . What's happening to me? Where am I in the world?" Yet, no sooner had he begun to use his reason than the heretical ideas were strengthened within him. . . .

As a lover of wisdom (*ḥokhmah*), the son mistakenly allowed wisdom to become exclusively equated with the good.[27] The consequence of this absolute love of wisdom was that the educated classes in the kingdom fell into heresy (*apikorsis*).[28] Nahman uses the term *ḥokhmah* as a distortion of true wisdom infused with faith, similar to his use of the term *teva* (nature) in *Likkutei MoHaRan*. The severing of wisdom (higher wisdom, Torah) from what sustains it (lower wisdom, science) is the beginning or at least the condition of heresy. The son, however, never became a heretic like the other wise men. Because he was "of good character," a concept Nahman never explains but which seems to reflect the notion of the innate goodness of the simple Jew so common in Ḥasidism, he never stopped asking the essential questions of human existence, even in light of the answers wisdom provided. Yet, even as he was never completely seduced by wisdom into believing that it provided adequate answers to these questions, as soon as he began to reflect rationally on these questions, he again fell into heresy.[29]

27 See *Likkutei Eiẓat*, "*Ḥakirot*," 4: "Sometimes individuals involve themselves in 'wisdom' for frivolous purposes. For example, for honor, money, etc. . . ." Cf. *Rimzei Ma'asiyot*, 18. Nahman's description of wisdom here, as in many other places, is sarcastic. This sarcastic thread filters through all of the tales and plays the most prominent role in the tale "The Wise Man and the Simpleton" (*Likkutei MoHaRan* 1.64). This also seems to be a comment about the Jewish infatuation with the Enlightenment. That is, the Jew is easily drawn to the security of reason but, as a result of his/her innate goodness, is never fully convinced by it. Thus, while the Jew may think he/she is being accepted by the Gentile world, like the son, he/she is forever estranged from their surroundings (the wise men).

28 For the connection between heresy and nature, see *Likkutei MoHaRan* 1.52: "There are heretics who say that the world is necessary [*meḥuyav*]. According to their mistaken opinion they imagine that they have wondrous proofs . . . . In truth it is just empty breath because only God is a necessary Existent. All the worlds are only contingent existents. . . ." Cf. *Likkutei MoHaRan* 2.7, para. 9; and Maimonides, *Mishneh Torah*, Laws on the Foundation of the Torah 1.1, para. 2.

29 The son represents the redeemable heretic spoken about in *Likkutei MoHaRan* 1.64. For a translation and discussion of the two types of heretic in Nahman, see Green, *Tormented Master*, 312–22. Mantel understands the son's response, "where am I in the world," as "the first niggling of penitential regret," thereby introducing repentance into the narrative. See Mantel, "Nahman of Braslav's Tales," 226. While this may be true, prayer, as depicted in the screams of the children in the forest, does not appear in the prelude.

This is Nahman's narrative description of a particular kind of exile of the Jewish people. Israel is caught in a circle that it cannot transcend. The only thing that will save them is the advice of the king, i.e., to remain in a perpetual state of joy. However, for some unknown reason, the son could not absorb his father's advice. As long as he lived in the world of false wisdom, joy always eluded him.

For Nahman, misunderstanding and misappropriating the limits of reason is the struggle that produces exile and alienation. Everyone in the tale is in exile—the king's son, the wise men, the beggars, and the children (who serve as the main characters in the body of the tale). All exiles, however, are not the same. There are three distinct types of exile in the tale, each one carrying its own unique qualities and challenges.[30]

The first type of exile is the exile of the wise men in the prelude. It is an unredeemable exile, one that does not contain longing and therefore can never bring about redemption. For Nahman it is the exile of the Nations, particularly in the modern world. Because it holds the promise of logic and reason as the answers to all questions, it is an exile that does not contain suffering or sadness, both of which result from a feeling of incompleteness. For Nahman, sadness is the underside of longing. This is the most dangerous kind of exile, likened to the "black hole" of existence (*hallel ha-paneui*) in *Likkutei MoHaRan* 1.64, the place where God is absent.[31] This exile is terrifying to Nahman, yet plays no part in redemptive history. Therefore, it disappears from the narrative after the prelude. There is no correlate to the wise men in the body of the tale.

The second type of exile is the exile of the son in the prelude, replicated in the children in the tale. It is an exile of longing for that which is unknown; it is an exile of sadness.[32] This exile can be overcome through prayer, which Nahman maintains changes nature (*teva*) into world (*olam*) by recognizing

30 The notion of three distinct types of exile is not new in Nahman. This idea exists, in a very different form in early Ḥasidism. See, for example, R. Ya'akov Yoseph of Polonnoye, *Toledot Ya'akov Yoseph*, "*parashat ve-ethanan*," 178d, and *Sefer Ba'al Shem Tov*, "*parshat balak*," 2:474–75.

31 See *Likkutei MoHaRan* 1.64. Cf. my "Through the Void: The Absence of God in Nahman of Bratslav's *Likkutei MoHaRan*," *Harvard Theological Review* 88, no. 4 (1995): 495–519; Green, *Tormented Master*, 285–336; Weiss, *Studies in Bratslav Ḥasidism*, 109–149; and, most recently, Mordecai Pachter, "Studies in Faith and Heresy in the Teachings of Nahman of Bratslav" [Hebrew], *Da'at* 45 (2000): 105–34.

32 The correlation between sadness and exile goes back to rabbinic literature and takes center stage in early Ḥasidism. See, for example, the Besht's rebuke to his disciple R. Ya'akov Yoseph about his excessive fasting. "This [fasting] is the way of depression and sadness. The *Shekhinah* does not inspire one through sadness but only via the joy [*simḥah*] of performing *miẓvot*" (*Shivḥei ha-Besht*, 49). Even though *Shivḥei ha-Besht* was first

the instability of reason, enabling the reconciliation between higher and lower wisdom to emerge. This is the exile of Israel, embodied in the king's son, who is "of good character" and the children, who wander aimlessly in search of happiness, always in danger yet always protected. The place of wandering is the forest, a part of the natural world that simultaneously holds the potential for all kinds of sustenance and untold dangers. In this sense, the prelude is the universal model of exile that becomes particularized in Israel in the children in the forest. Note that the son in the prelude is never redeemed, as are the children in the tale. He appears forever caught in the cycle of reason and longing, unable to pray and thus unable to achieve the necessary tools to transcend his situation.

The third type of exile is the exile of the beggars. This is also the exile of the *ẓaddik*. This is an exile that is more deeply felt than the other two because the *ẓaddik* has a memory of the world before exile. The exilic experience of the *ẓaddik* is that he has to live in the world *before* redemption with the memory *of* redemption. The role of the *ẓaddik* (the beggars) is that he can teach those stuck in the second exile how to overcome it. The king in the prelude introduces the exile of the *ẓaddik*. He warns his son that joy, and joy alone, can achieve a return to the kingdom. The beggars are more developed embodiments of the *ẓaddik* in the prelude, revealing the true nature of this third exile, the exile of redemption. Perhaps the king in the prelude represents all the *ẓaddikim* before Nahman. While he holds the answer to his son's dilemma, he can do no more than programmatically tell him how to survive. Finally, his advice is not enough to save his son. The beggars, however, do much more. They sustain the children in the forest and then teach them the key to the third exile under the wedding canopy by telling them stories. As tellers of stories, the beggars represent Nahman as the *ẓaddik* who is a storyteller.

The second important trope of the tale, after exile, is the notion of heresy, which is understood in unique ways in Nahman's overall discourse.[33] The difference between the wise men in the prelude (who are unredeemable heretics) and the king's son (who is a redeemable heretic) can be understood in light of the discussion of the "two types of heretics" in *Likkutei*

published in 1815, more than five years after Nahman's passing, many of its traditions were widely known before that time. See Rosman, *Founder of Ḥasidism*, esp. 187–211.

33 On this, see Green, *Tormented Master*, 285–336; Piekarz, *Studies in Bratslav Ḥasidism*, 21–55; Weiss, *Studies in Bratslav Ḥasidism*, 109–50; Joseph Weiss, "Sense and Non-Sense in Defining Judaism: The Strange Case of Nahman of Bratslav," in *Studies in East European Jewish Mysticism*, ed. David Goldstein (Oxford, UK: Oxford University Press, 1985), 249–69; and my "Through the Void."

MoHaRan 1.64. In this lesson the first type of heretic (the king's son in the tale) is one who falls into a redeemable heresy. "Even though he should have fled it [heresy], he may find a way to be saved from there. God can be found there, if one looks for him and seeks him out." The second type of heretic (the wise men in the tale) is far more dangerous. "It seems that his opinion is a most profound one, even though it is all based on a wrong interpretation. . . . There is no answer to this heresy: it comes from the void, from which God, as it were, has withdrawn himself." The first type of exile discussed above embodies the second type of unredeemable heresy. The second type of exile, the exile of sadness, embodies the first type of heretic, the son in the prelude and the two children who are lost and alienated, yet always respond to the question, "where are you from?" with "we don't know." They never stop longing, even in the midst of the joy of their wedding at the conclusion of the tale.[34] The second type of heretic (who is in the first type of exile) is unredeemable because, convinced of his own logic, he stops asking questions. This heretic is presented in the prelude (the wise men) and then disappears from the narrative, as it plays no role in the redemptive message of the tale.

There may be another reason why the second type of heretic disappears in the body of the tale. The frame of the tale, presented in this prelude, is that of temporal exile.[35] The body of the tale intends to overcome the dilemma of the king's son (temporal exile) via the bride and groom's confrontation with the deformed (and unnatural) beggars, all of whom show the children how to achieve the absolute value of joy (*simḥah*) even, or precisely, in exile.

For Nahman, the act that brings one from exile to redemption, from sadness to joy, is prayer. Exile is temporal by definition, as its existence is contingent on the possibility of redemption. Prayer actualizes the "possibility of redemption" by facilitating a dramatic change in the worshiper's perspective of nature, resulting in the transformation of sadness to joy. The second unredeemable heretic in *Likkutei MoHaRan* 1.64 has no part in this process. His exile is permanent, holding no possibility of redemption because

34 See *Rimzei Ma'asiyot,* 18: "Meriting the gifts from each beggar is the result of the greatness of the children. However, all that the children merit is the result of their longing and yearning" (my translation). In this comment, Nahman of Cheryn makes the important connection between the son in the prelude and the children in the body of the tale.

35 Nahman's notion of the redeemable and unredeemable heretic plays an important role in his assessment of secularism and modernity. See Mendel Piekarz, "The Episode of Uman in the Life of Nahman of *Bratslav*," in Piekarz, *Studies in Bratslav Ḥasidism,* 21–55.

he does not feel the longing for things to be other than they are. Therefore, he does not experience exile, as he views his state as permanent and complete. Seduced by the certainty of his own rational view of the world, he is lost, according to Nahman. The depth of his so-called exile is exhibited by the fact that he does not feel sadness, as sadness is a response to the experience of imperfection. The second type of heretic in *Likkutei MoHaRan* 1.64 and the wise men in the prelude have no need for prayer, the condition of prayer being brokenheartedness (*shevirat ha- lev*) and longing.[36]

For our purposes, the most significant point in the prelude is the connection Nahman draws between reason and sadness, which is never developed in the body of the tale but serves as its subtext. Through the king's warning to his son that joy be the sole criteria for kingship, i.e., redemption, Nahman suggests that redemption is only possible when the sadness indicative of the second type of exile is confronted and overcome. Sadness is rectified, although not nullified, through prayer and overcome through joy.[37] Joy for its own sake, resulting from humanity's recognition of the divine source of human and natural life, overshadows the second type of exile, diminishing the first type of heresy. When the beggars bless the children to "be like them" in the forest and then explain the blessing under the wedding canopy as a marital gift, they are blessing them to embody the third kind of exile, the exile of the *ẓaddik.*

This kind of exile is unique in that it does not contain sadness, as we know it, but does contain longing, because it contains the memory of the world before exile and the recognition that this is the place to which the world will ultimately return. The eclipse of sadness in the *ẓaddik* is not because he doesn't feel longing. It is because he mimetically knows that his experience of longing will bear fruit. The disability of the beggars is not about their personal deficiency; it is that, as *ẓaddikim*, they are estranged from the exilic world, even as they are an integral part of it. The *ẓaddik* laments the fallen state of the world by carrying it on his shoulders as he walks through the world deformed. He participates in the redemptive process by helping others overcome the seduction of reason by giving them the gift of joy—the joy the king told his son about in the prelude. The gift they give is the memory of a world before exile—even before creation—a world that will be the culmination of their suffering. But, the beggars add, one can

36 On brokenheartedness as the foundation for prayer, see *Siḥot ha-Ran*, 31, and *Likkutei MoHaRan* 2.25 and 47. On the connection between prayer and redemption, see *Likkutei MoHaRan* 2.71.

37 See the discussion in Azriel Shochet, "On *Simḥah* in Ḥasidism" [Hebrew], *Zion* 16 (1951): 30–43.

experience that world here, in exile, through joy. The first type of heresy becomes the third type of exile when reason becomes subsidiary to prayer and false security (fate) yields to redemptive instability (miracle).[38]

"Be Like Me": The Blessing of Primordiality

The body of the tale opens with a description of two children lost in a forest. Hungry for food, the children scream for help. They are approached by seven beggars, one at a time, all of whom have a physical disability: one is blind, one deaf, one stutters, one has a twisted neck, one is hunchbacked, one has no hands, and one has no feet. Each beggar gives the children bread to eat, temporarily alleviating their suffering, and then departs saying, "be like me," without ever explaining what that means. The children continue to wander, ultimately becoming beggars themselves. Finally, they end up at a fair celebrating the birthday of an anonymous king (a reference taking us back to the prelude). All the beggars of the land (not only the seven beggars) are gathered at this fair. Seeing the children, who are now also beggars, they decide that it would be fit for them to marry since they are orphaned and have no other family. The beggars at the fair raise a wedding canopy and designate the children as bride and groom. Under the wedding canopy the children joyously recall all the favors that God bestowed upon them during their wanderings in the forest. Their joy is immediately interrupted, however, by the memory of the beggars who gave them food and helped them survive. They cry out longingly (a reference to prayer), "How do we find the first beggar, the blind beggar, who brought us bread in the forest?" At that moment, the blind beggar emerges from the crowd and blesses the children by telling them a story, illustrating that his blindness is not a deformity but a state of perfection. Then he blesses the children to "be like him" and disappears.

---

38 See Adin Steinsaltz, *The Tales of Rabbi Nahman of Bratslav* (Northvale, NJ: Jason Aronson, 1993), 254. Steinsaltz reads the prelude in a similar manner but misses, in my opinion, the complexity of the interplay between sadness and exile. His depiction is that the prelude replays another tale, "The Wise Man and the Simpleton," where Nahman develops the notion that the pursuit of wisdom as an end in itself (i.e., as an absolute value) leads to heresy. The focus here, however, is less about the distortion of wisdom and more about the failure of such wisdom to produce joy (*simḥah*). For Nahman, redemption is an emotional state and not a correct opinion. Sadness is exilic because it reverses the redemptive process of human perfection.

The wedding continues in this manner for seven days. Each day the children begin joyous and then become sad, longing for another beggar, who arrives to bless them, telling them an elaborate story to illustrate why his deformity is really not a deformity at all. The children are joyous at the arrival of each beggar yet their joy disappears the next morning as they long for the next beggar. The tales that each beggar tells are intricate and elaborate, all of which explain their deformity as the result of some vision, hearing, or memory of the primordial past or a time before exile. Before departing they give this memory as a gift of joy to the couple. While this gift works in that it brings the children joy, the gift never lasts because the children mix that memory with the memory of another beggar, who is deformed, thus bringing their joy to an abrupt and crashing halt.

The body of the tale contains two main parts: 1) the second type of exile exhibited in the king's son in the prelude is revisited in the lost children who are alienated in the forest, crying (i.e., praying) for sustenance; and 2) the appearance of the beggars in the forest and then again under the wedding canopy. The beggars (the *ẓaddik*) teach the children the way to the third type of exile (the exile of the *ẓaddik* that the king alludes to in the prelude but can never quite communicate to his son) through the renewal of joy contained in their blessings. The body of the tale draws the reader more deeply into Nahman's exilic anthropology by reading his prescription for redemption. This redemptive process emerges in three significant points in the body of the tale: 1) the lost children in the forest, exiled but longing; 2) the disabled seven beggars who reveal the nature of their disability; and 3) the joy of the wedding that is still unfulfilled because the seventh beggar, the beggar without feet, never arrives. In this unfinished tale the expression of joy remains temporal in that the final beggar (the Messiah) tarries.[39]

However, the notion that longing is the vehicle for joy becomes the prescription for surviving the exile. Each day the wedding ends in joy, but each morning that joy disappears as the bride and groom lament the absence of the next beggar. The king's warning to his son in the prelude that perpetual joy is the sole criteria for kingship, i.e., redemption, looms over the entire narrative as it loomed over Nahman's tortured life. The dependence on the *ẓaddik* is paramount. Without the *ẓaddik* (the beggars) reminding the children of the world before exile, the children

39 The significance of the beggar without feet as the Messiah relates to Nahman's emphasis on dance as a redemptive act, one that can elicit joy like no other act. On this, see Michael Fishbane, "To Jump for Joy: The Rites of Dance According to Nahman of Bratslav," *The Journal of Jewish Thought and Philosophy* 6 (1997): 371–87.

could never get beyond the son in the prelude. Only the *ẓaddik* keeps messianism alive. Only the *ẓaddik* prevents redeemable heresy from the fate of unredeemable heresy. Only the *ẓaddik* prevents the son's exile from becoming the wise men's exile. Only the *ẓaddik* can teach the children the redemptive way of suffering.

The overarching theme of the tale, which appears in many different guises, is that wisdom (*ḥokhmah*) and nature (*teva*) are the sources of human imperfection and the perpetuation of exile.[40] This imperfection initially emerges in the description of the deformity of each beggar in his or her first encounter with the children in the forest, and is resolved in their subsequent meetings with the children under the wedding canopy. At that auspicious moment each beggar reveals that his deformity is really his perfection, implying that perfection appears imperfect in a world that it is imperfect.[41] The correlation between wisdom and nature serves as the two poles of exile; but this correlation lies beneath the surface of the tale, never fully disclosed.

Before attempting to disclose the implicit connection between wisdom and nature in the tale, I will briefly review Nahman's views about "nature (*teva*) as exile" explained in *Likkutei MoHaRan*. Perhaps the most succinct statement on this issue appears in *Likkutei MoHaRan* 1.150:

> The pain of Israel in exile is the result of the absence of the consciousness of God [*da'at*] and the belief that everything is dependent upon nature [*teva*], coincidence [*mikrim*] and fate [*mazal*]. This is the cause of Israel's pain. If they knew that everything was the result of providence [*hashgaḥah*] [and not nature] they would not suffer any pain at all. In truth, Israel is rooted above nature. It is only when they sin, God forbid, that they become subject to the laws of nature.

Nature (*teva*) for Nahman is a view of the world that is unchanging and necessary (*meḥuyav*). *Likkutei MoHaRan* 1.7 speaks about exile as a deficiency of faith, true faith being the belief in the temporality of nature, which is constantly destabilized via miracle, providence, and prayer. The possibility for miracle requires the acknowledgment that the world, even as it appears ordered, is unstable. This is nothing new. What Nahman contributes is that prayer is the devotional act that creates this possibility in the human psyche for such a posture. To pray properly, Nahman suggests, requires two things:

40 Nahman uses "wisdom" in a pejorative sense. It is like the Yiddish *ḥokhmas*, which implies deception, the appellation *ḥokham* almost meaning "wise guy." See Weiss, *Studies in Bratslav Ḥasidism*, 25; and Green, *Tormented Master*, 331n12.

41 On this, see Elisheva Schoenfeld, "The Seven Beggars of Nahman of Bratslav" [Hebrew], *Yeda Am* 11, no. 30 (1965): 65–78.

1) a suspension of reason; and 2) an act of protest against reason. "Miracles are above nature, prayer is above nature. This is because nature is necessity and prayer changes nature." The children scream in the forest in protest against their "natural" fate of starvation.

> Prayer encapsulates miracle, which is not the way of nature [*derekh hateva*]. Sometimes nature necessitates that something will occur and prayer reverses that occurrence . . . those people who deny miracles, and say that everything flows according to the laws of nature, in effect they destroy prayer, for prayer is miraculous in that it changes nature. They also impair faith, because they deny divine providence [which is also miraculous]. They also impair the Land of Israel as this land is the land of miracles. . . . [42]

World (*olam*) as opposed to nature (*teva*) represents a perspective of the natural world infused with divine will in a constant state of renewal and transformation. Both nature (*mada*, science) and logic (*higayon*, philosophy), two dimensions of false wisdom, or *ḥokhmot ḥiẓoniyot* (extraneous wisdom), are embedded in the realm of necessity (*meḥuyavut*), which Nahman believed denies the transcendent character of the creation. There is a correlation here between the false wisdom or logic (depicted as reason) of the wise men in the prelude of the tale and nature in the body of the tale in the appearance of the seven beggars. As deformed, each beggar seems imperfect, yet the beggars' stories all teach how their deformity reflects the very attainment of perfection.

For Nahman, both wisdom (*ḥokhmah*) and nature (*teva*) hold the illusion of truth precisely because they *claim* to resolve the essential questions of human existence, either by observation (empiricism) or human intellection (logic). The danger of both is the susceptibility of imperfect beings to see them as paths toward perfection by incorporating them as absolute values. Both are exilic in his eyes not because they are false in any objective sense but because they diminish joy, resulting in either sadness (*aẓvut*) or hopelessness (*ye'ush*).[43] The connection between reason (*ḥokhmah*) and sadness (*aẓvut*) is often alluded to but never made explicitly in the tale, but it does play a prominent role in Nahman's homilies and the hagiographic stories about him. It appears that the correlation is built on his assumption that wisdom can never achieve that which it claims, always failing to realize expectations, leaving one disillusioned and subsequently hopeless.

42 *Likkutei MoHaRan* 1.9, 5.

43 *Azvut*, perhaps best translated as depression or the demonic (*sitra aḥra*). For its connection to hopelessness see *Siḥot ha-Ran*, 41, and *Likkutei MoHaRan* 2.25.

Wisdom itself is not exilic. It is only exilic when it holds the expectation of resolving the essential questions of human existence.[44] The mistake of the son in the prelude was not to love wisdom *per se* but to elevate it to an absolute value. This is because the son did not pray—as prayer (as a protest against reason) will always prevent the overextension of reason that is so seductive in the natural world. However, being "of good character," the son was able to avoid the fate of the wise men, perhaps a surreptitious reference to the Jewish Enlightenment Nahman became so familiar with at the end of his life.[45]

Another example of wisdom and nature as the cause of sadness can be seen in Nahman's understanding of divine election. He argues that from a logical and empirical standpoint the election of Israel can be easily and convincingly construed as a fallacy, because for him, the Gentiles are successful and Israel is in a constant state of subjugation and humiliation. Therefore, it is both to the advantage of the Gentile and logically defensible to claim that Israel is no longer God's chosen people. In a sense, Nahman is advocating, from the perspective of reason, a kind of Hegelian supersessionism whereby Judaism and the Jewish people are negated through history. From a logical and empirical (i.e., historical) perspective, the Gentile's (i.e., Christian) argument against God's covenant with Israel in exile is valid. If Israel would submit to this logical evaluation of its fate, however, its covenant would indeed be nullified and its exilic consciousness would move from the first heretic to the second, ending the quest *for* redemption and thereby erasing the possibility *of* redemption. The son would become one of the wise men. Whereas wisdom in the prelude to our tale yields personal sadness and exile, the empirical observation of the natural world potentially yields submission to the collective subjugation of exile, destroying the possibility of turning sadness into joy and exile into redemption.[46] At that point, the children in the forest (Israel) would no longer hear the exile of the *ẓaddik* (the beggars' blessing "be like me") because they would no longer have the requisite longing necessary to hear him. If the children did

---

44 In this sense, Nahman is echoing Pascal (contra Descartes), who he most probably did not know, that skepticism can teach us about the things reason cannot achieve, such as answering the basic questions of human existence, i.e., "Who am I?" See Blaise Pascal, *Pensees* (New York: E. P. Dutton and Company, 1996).

45 See Piekarz, *Studies in Bratslav Ḥasidism*, 21–55.

46 See *Likkutei MoHaRan* 1.17, 1, where Nahman gives us a description of *am segulah*, the biblical depiction of Israel as chosen. "This is like the '*segulah*' of healing. Even though naturally a particular medicine will not necessarily work [lit., nature cannot determine the efficacy of healing] healing [*segulah*] is higher than nature, which the human intellect cannot comprehend."

not scream in the forest, they would have never met the beggars and would have collapsed into nature (fate) and disappeared forever.

The Gift of Primordial Memory

The lost children in the forest embody the second type of exile, expressed in human anguish and prayer. Each time they get hungry, they "scream and cry" (*geshreien un gevent*). Even though it is not given significant attention in the tale, the screams of the children play an important role in the narrative. The screams represent authentic (primal) prayer, introducing the most important theme in the body of the tale that is absent in the prelude.[47] The forest introduces us to the natural world, simultaneously a place of beauty and seduction. The potential tragedy of the natural world is that observing it through the lens of natural law can seduce one away from recognizing God as its source, resulting in a belief in the independence and absolute status of nature (*teva*). Lost in the forest, the children exist outside of civilization. Being children, they cannot survive independently, as they are not trained in foraging food for themselves. The natural consequence (i.e., nature without miracle) should be that these two children starve and die in the forest. In protest of nature and fate, however, they scream for sustenance. This scream is their prayer that "change[s] nature [*meshaneh ha-teva*]," breaking through the illusory boundaries of necessity and fate, resulting in the appearance of the beggars who save them.[48] In *Likkutei MoHaRan* 1.55, para. 4, Nahman states, "prayer is founded upon the faith that everything is in God's hand, even altering nature." Drawing on kabbalistic teaching, he further argues that prayer (*mayyim nukvin*, feminine arousal) activates the creative power of God (*mayyim dekhurin*, masculine arousal), renewing divine creativity and nullifying the perceived necessity of natural law (*olam keminhago noheg*). Nahman's message is strikingly straightforward. Prayer changes fate by activating a renewal of creation (*ḥiddush haolam*), nullifying the perception of natural order upon which fate is founded. It is not that nature is nullified in this equation. Moreover, we are not dealing with

47 On the importance of the scream and song in Bratslav Ḥasidism, see Pachter, "Studies in Faith and Heresy in the Teaching of Nahman of Bratslav."

48 See especially *Likkutei MoHaRan* 1.8, para. 7, where Nahman presents three distinct but interrelated categories: 1) nature-order; 2) world-renewal; and 3) prayer-creativity. Prayer contains the potential to activate the renewing power of "world," which then overcomes the order of "nature."

a concept of transcending nature or even nullifying the physical (*hitpashtut ha-gashmiut*), so common in early Ḥasidism.[49] Nahman's interests are existential and not ontological. The beggars are trying to teach the children about living and surviving *in* the world, perceiving and evaluating their external environment by understanding that exile and redemption are existential states as much or more than states of reality.[50] This point stands at the center of the story and serves to nuance Nahman's more blatantly negative appraisal of nature in *Likkutei MoHaRan*. In his homiletic lessons we are taught that nature stands diametrically opposed to miracle, that science stands in opposition to prayer, that exile is the result of being seduced by reason. Although all of these assumptions are, in principle, maintained in the tale, the tale explains the ways in which this exilic stance can be rectified by changing one's orientation toward the natural world while living in it. The tale creates a solution to exile and heresy while remaining a part of the exilic world. Prayer (the screams of the children in the forest and their longing at the wedding) opens up the possibility of witnessing miracle. Miracle is not something different from nature—it is a new way of understanding it. The juxtaposition of the themes (reason, exile, sadness, nature, deformity) with the tale's characters (the king's son, the children, the beggars) yields a more dialectical rendering of Nahman's dualistic thinking.

The wedding of the children in the final scene of the tale begins by bringing the reader back to the first scene of the children lost in the forest. Just as their longing for food and prayer in the forest resulted in the appearance of the blind beggar, the blind beggar immediately appears when they long for him under the wedding canopy. The blind beggar enters, stating that "[previously, i.e., in the forest] I offered you my blessing but today I bestow this upon you outright as a gift. You should be as old as I am." Instead of simply vanishing, as he does in the forest, he remains and reveals the true nature of his deformity. "You think I am blind? Not at all. It is just that the entire world does not amount to the wink of an eye [*heref eyin*] to me." Then he embellishes his paradoxical claim with a story, which is replicated in different ways by all of the six subsequent beggars who appear at the wedding. The blind beggar says that "he is very old yet hasn't begun to live," which is

49 See, Miles Krassen, *Uniter of Heaven and Earth* (Albany: SUNY Press, 1998), esp. 106–21.

50 For a detailed analysis of this in early Ḥasidism, see Rivka Schatz-Uffenheimer, "Self-Redemption in Ḥasidic Thought," in *Types of Redemption*, ed. R. J. Z. Werblowsky and C. J. Bleeker (Leiden: Brill, 1970), 207–12.

the "outright gift" he gives to the children.[51] The proof of his claim unfolds in a story he tells which describes the beggar's memory as remembering "nothingness" (*ayin*), i.e., a memory of the world before creation.

> Once people set sail upon the seas in many ships. A tempest arose and destroyed the ships but the people were saved. The people came to a tower. . . . They called upon each other to recite an old tale, one that he has remembered from his earliest recollection, that is, what he remembered from the inception of his memory. . . . And I [the blind beggar] . . . declared, "I remember all those tales and I remember nothingness." They all declared, "That is a very old tale, older than all the others." . . . [Then a great eagle came and addressed all those shipwrecked.] And to me [the blind beggar] the great eagle said, "You come with me because you are just like me in that you are extremely old and yet very young. And you have not yet begun to live, though you are very old. . . ."

The blind beggar is the oldest of the group. However, because of the exile he also "hasn't yet begun to live" because the element of *ayin* (nothingness), the root of creation, remains concealed for the future redemption. He is blind because his vision, or more precisely his memory of perfection (*ayin*) makes it impossible for him to envision imperfection (the natural world). By seeing the end in the primordial beginning, he cannot bear to witness the imperfect process toward that completion. His blindness is thus his unwillingness, and not his inability, to see.

The blind beggar's story rests on the relationship between perception and memory. How does one live with memory and not be thrown into despair? As discussed, for Nahman the deepest exile is the exile of the *ẓaddik* (the third type of exile). This exile is a feeling of alienation from the exilic world resulting from an experience, memory, or vision of the world before exile (i.e., perfection). Only the truly righteous experience this exile that serves as the necessary bridge to redemption. The one who feels in exile in the exilic world (and appears to others as abnormal, i.e., deformed or disabled) is more capable than others to direct the world toward completion be cause only he has a memory of the end in the beginning. His deformity is an externalization of his memory of perfection (the world before creation/exile).

The important lesson of this third exile is that it is an exile of joy—not in place *of* sadness, but a joy *in* sadness. It brings us back to the king's warning

51 Each beggar begins to tell his tale by making a logically incongruous statement, thus challenging logic as a way of seeing the world and enabling the children to comprehend the ways in which imperfection in this world is often a sign of perfection.

to his son in the prelude that he should maintain joy even though he loses the kingdom, because joy is the only way to retrieve the kingdom. The children are like the son in that they long to be redeemed, and thereby experience sadness, but cannot maintain joy long enough to live joyously in the sadness. In some sense, they are stuck in the dualistic cycle that joy and sadness are binary opposites. The beggars, as the *ẓaddik*, come to teach them otherwise. The opaque message of the king to his son in the prelude is now disclosed. One must be joyous in exile by remembering his tenure as king. This memory of his stature before exile will enable him to retain joy in sadness, eliminating his continual fall into heresy, thus securing the renewal of the kingdom. It is only the tale (both Nahman's tale and the specific tales of the beggars) that makes this possible.

For Nahman, the *ẓaddik* (always a reference to himself) is the most tragic figure of all because he must live joyously in an exilic world while maintaining a memory of redemption (the primordial world before exile).[52] It is this anxiety that makes the *ẓaddik* always occupy the margin of insanity, a psychological abnormality that Nahman transfers into the physical disability of each beggar. When the blind beggar says, "be like me," he is attempting to move the children from the second type of exile (longing for redemption) to the third and final type of exile, the exile of joy in sadness, the bridge to redemption achieved by realizing the memory of nothingness, the world before exile.

For the sake of brevity, I will skip the next beggar, the beggar who cannot hear, and move directly to the beggar who stutters. The beggar who stutters appears at the wedding to bless the couple. He tells them that he stutters because he cannot speak words that are not praises of God, or more precisely, "[he cannot speak] words that contain no perfection." He is the master of "words of perfection," he claims, which he illustrates in his ability to clearly recite complex riddles and divine praises with no impediment. His mastery of riddles and divine praises is proven with a story about a heart and a spring.[53]

> A heart existed at one end of the world. At the other end of the world was a mountain. On top of that mountain there was a spring. The heart longed for the spring, yet could never ascend the mountain, for when it did it lost

52 On the concept of suffering in Nahman, particularly the fate of suffering of the *ẓaddik*, see Martin Mantel, "The Meaning of Suffering According to R. Nathan of Nemerov" [Hebrew] *Da'at* 7 (1981): 109–18.

53 For a fascinating literary reading of "the heart and the spring," see Dov Sadan, "The Heart of the World," in *Bein She'elat le-Kinyan* (Tel Aviv: University of Tel Aviv Press, 1968), 137–57.

> sight of the spring. Hence, it had to be content gazing upon the spring from afar while longing to unite with it. The spring also longed for the heart. This mutual yearning of the heart for the spring and the spring for the heart sustained the world. The problem was that the spring didn't really exist in time [i.e., it was either above or before time—an allusion to its primordial status]. Therefore, each day the heart gave the gift of one day's time to the spring so that it could exist in time and be the object of its longing, which in tum sustained the world.

This ambiguous gift of time is now explained as consisting of a collection of songs and poems of kindness that an unidentified Man of Kindness delivered to the spring each day. These songs, an allusion to the prayer of the *ẓaddik*, are rooted in the place before created time (the nothingness [*ayin*] of the blind beggar) and thus constitute the gift of time, a time that must be renewed daily. The spring on the mountain, or the effluence of divinity into the world, is the source of life that is in a constant state of renewal. It is renewed by prayer, more precisely by the prayer of the *ẓaddik*, or the stuttering beggar, which is facilitated by the longing of the heart. The stuttering beggar says that he travels the world and collects all kinds of songs of praise and gives them to the Man of Kindness, who creates praises from them and gives them to the spring each day so that it can remain in time and continue to be the object of the heart's longing which, in turn, sustains the world. Therefore, he is the source of the gift of time, the state of constant renewal that sustains the world.

The story of the stuttering beggar, retold here in abbreviated form, takes place amidst a larger debate among "men of science" each of whom take credit for their inventive discoveries, utilizing natural resources for human consumption (iron, silver, and other metals). The stuttering beggar intervenes in the debate of the scientists and claims superiority over all the scientists because he is the master of time, as opposed to each scientist who is only the master of "an hour of time," or one small component of nature. The stuttering beggar then turns to the couple and blesses them to be like him, that is, to utilize prayer to access the power which sustains the longing between the heart (the yearning for divine presence) and the spring (the source of divine wisdom).

As discussed above, for Nahman prayer is that which activates the creative power of world (*olam*) over nature (*teva*). To pray is to hold the gift of time (the master of the day—the one who prays), as opposed to utilizing a component of time (the master of the hour—the scientist). Like the blind beggar, the stuttering beggar has access to that which is above nature, the unity of which is the source of joy and redemption. By collecting these "songs of praise," the stuttering beggar can appreciate the natural world by seeing the extent to which nature is sustained by longing: the heart for the spring, the human being for God. Prayer, the human response to longing, should not yield sadness, as it does in its exilic form (the second exile), but joy in sadness (the third exile/the beggars/the *ẓaddik*), as it maintains existence. The stuttering beggar blesses the children that they should recognize their longing as redemptive, taking them from the second to the third exile.

The stuttering beggar, like his predecessors, is perfect (and thus appears deformed) because he has access to that which is beyond the created world ("the songs of praise" before time). Therefore, he is, unlike the wise men, never satisfied but, unlike the son, never hopeless. All the beggars have access to the source of creation, the memory of nothingness, or its sustaining power, the gift of renewal that is rooted in the primordial nothingness (*ayin*) before creation. The deformity of each beggar is the result of being confined to the natural world which each has already transcended by means of perfecting a particular virtue. Thus, from the perspective of the imperfect world, perfection appears deformed. The *ẓaddik* is always a deformed creature as he refuses to submit to nature. More precisely, he is deformed because he carries the burden of transforming the children to see the world "otherwise."

It is clear that the inner frame of the body of the tale, as opposed to the outer frame of the prelude, is based on prayer. The fact that the prelude contains no reference to prayer is significant. The prelude is the presentation of the second exile, the exile of sadness, the inability of the son to overcome the sadness that resulted from his loss of the kingdom. The son and the wise men represent two foci of humanity. Israel, while potentially embodied in the son, is only fully disclosed in the children in the body of the tale, where the story moves from the universal to the particular. The Gentile world, represented in the wise men or the son in the prelude, lives either in the false security of reason or is caught in the endless cycle of longing and heresy.

As discussed above, the construct of prayer for Nahman is that prayer opposes both reason (logic) and nature (fate). In the following text from *Likkutei MoHaRan* 1.217, the juxtaposition of prayer and nature is made explicit in a way that deepens our understanding of the stuttering beggar, connecting his story back to the unfinished prelude:

> The philosophers call nature [*teva*] the "mother of all existence" [*em kol ḥay*]. However, through prayer we nullify nature. Nature is necessity, prayer changes nature. Thus the eighteen benedictions [of prayer] exclude the blessing to wipe out the heretics [the nineteenth benediction inserted at a later time]. By

> means of the eighteen [benedictions, the letter representation of eighteen as *ḥet, yod,* i.e., life] we nullify nature as necessity and simultaneously debunk the heretic [the subject of the nineteenth blessing].

In the prelude and the tale itself, we have three villains: the philosopher or lover of wisdom, the heretic, and the scientist. Each, to varying degrees, bases their knowledge on reason (logic) or nature (science). Each beggar represents another way of debunking one or all of those villains, either by the memory of origins (the blind beggar), the songs of praise (the stuttering beggar), or, as we will presently see, the one who lives on the edge of space (the hunchback). The songs of praise, which the stuttering beggar hears and collects, are simultaneously the prayers that sustain the world (*meḥadesh ha-olam*) and the prayers that "change" the world (*meshaneh teva*).

The identification of maintenance and change is significant here. If the world would be void of prayer, that is, if Israel, or perhaps more accurately the *ẓaddik*, would disappear, nature (as necessity) would collapse. The illusion of nature as necessity only exists because there are those who pray and, in doing so, create the condition for the illusion. The illusion, as exile, exists because of the longing for redemption. While prayer makes the illusion possible, the beggars are telling the children that the more one sees that the illusion is dependent on prayer, the more one is able to live joyously in nature, manifesting the third exile, the exile of the joy in sadness. As this posture becomes more prominent, the notion of nature (as necessity) collapses in the mind of the worshiper. The power of renewal (*ḥiddush*) inherent in prayer results in breaking the illusion of necessity (*meḥuyavut*). To pray requires a bracketing of the necessity of nature. The heart and the spring in the stuttering beggar's tale is a metaphor for the dialectic of human prayer, simultaneously creating the condition for nature and dissolving it.

The final beggar I will discuss is the hunchback who appears on the fifth day of the wedding. The hunchback claims that he appears deformed because he carries so much weight on his shoulders. In a brilliant interpretation of the midrashic image of "the little-that-holds-much" (*ha-mu'at heḥezik et ha-merubeh*),[54] Nahman presents this beggar as the one who carries the entirety of space, only appearing to be a hunchback. In truth, the hunchback claims, he carries the world on his back. The hunchback illustrates this with a story. The story is about a group of people who want to travel to a special tree whose branches hold all the birds of the world and whose shade provides a

---

54 See Genesis Rabbah 5.7, in *Midrash Bereishit Rabbah*, ed. J. Theodor and C. H. Albeck (Jerusalem, 1965), 36–37.

resting place for all the world's animals.[55] The tree is rooted in three virtues: faith, reverence, and humility. The root of the tree is truth (*emet*, EMT).[56] Only those who achieve these three virtues can reach the tree. The hunchback is included in the group of journeymen who finally merit seeing this tree in the distance. The journeymen soon realize, however, that even as they see the tree they cannot reach it because the tree doesn't really exist in space; it exists on the edge of space, between space and nothingness.

> And I [the hunchback] was also there with them. So I declared to them: "I can lead you to the tree. For this particular tree has no space; it is entirely above [superior to] the earth's space. And yet, the trait of "the little that holds much" still involves some space. . . . And my "little that holds much" is at the very edge of space, and beyond it there is no space at all. . . . That is why I can lead all of you to this tree which is totally above the space it stands on.

The tree is the place of true virtue that encompasses and nurtures the disparate elements of creation. It embodies a transformed view of nature, reminiscent of Isaiah's redemptive vision of Israel because all the birds of the world can rest there peacefully and the entire animal kingdom can enjoy its shade without conflict. True virtue does not exist in the center of space

---

55 See *Likkutei MoHaRan* 1.15, para. 5, where Nahman interprets the talmudic Rabba bar bar Hanna story about the tree that contains all virtues and that dwells at the edge of space. Cf. Mantel, "Nahman of Bratslav's Tales," 236–37. The connection between Nahman's interpretations of the Rabba bar bar Hanna fantasy stories in Talmud Bava Batra and *Sippurei Ma'asiyot* is a desideratum. Green alludes to this in *Tormented Master*, 342–44.

56 The importance of the tree being EMT is that *emet* is composed of three letters of the Hebrew alphabet, the first, middle, and last letter. Based on the kabbalistic notion, rooted in Midrash, that God created the world with the Hebrew letters, *emet* is a linguistic sign of the entirety of existence. See, for example, in Elliot R. Wolfson, "The Tree that Is All: Jewish-Christian Roots of a Kabbalistic Symbol in *Sefer HaBahir*," *Journal of Jewish Thought and Philosophy* 3 (1993): 31–76. The tree is a central motif in both the Talmud and the Zohar; see, for example, Babylonian Talmud Ta'anit 7a, and the tree as the *Shekhinah* in *Saba de-Mishpatim*, Zohar 2.105a-108b. Cf. the exegesis of R. Pinhas ben Yair in Zohar 3.200b–202b; Yehuda Liebes, "Sections of the Zohar Lexicon" (PhD diss., Hebrew University, Jerusalem, 1976), 107–31; Liebes, "Zohar and Eros" [Hebrew], *Alpayyim* 9 (1994): 27n46; and Pinchas Giller, *Reading the Zohar: The Sacred Text of the Kabbalah* (Oxford and New York: Oxford University Press, 2001), 58–60. These and other examples are brought and discussed in Giller, "The World Trees in the Zohar," in *Trees, Earth, and Torah: A Tu B'shvat Anthology*, ed. Ari Elon, Naomi Mara Hyman, and Arthur Waskow (Philadelphia: Jewish Publication Society, 1999), 128–34; and Michael Fishbane, "The Book of Zohar and Exegetical Spirituality," in *Mysticism and Sacred Scripture*, ed. Steven T. Katz (Oxford and New York: Oxford University Press, 2000), 103–105.

(in nature) but only on the very margins where space comes into being, the meeting place of the infinite and the finite.[57] While a certain element of virtue can be achieved in nature, thus resulting in the journeymen seeing the tree from a distance, the longing for righteousness, which is beyond virtue, can only be achieved in the place where the world meets its infinite source. According to Nahman, a moral order, reflecting natural law, may perhaps create a moral society, but it can never fulfill the longing for true virtue and thus cannot be the harbinger of redemption. This is because the view of nature as *teva* (natural law) is the epitome of imperfection. It is the center and not the margin of space.

Moving back to the central motif in the tale, that sadness is the perpetuation of the second type of exile: as long as the aspiration for virtue is sought solely in the center of space (i.e., in nature), it will always yield sadness. Perhaps this is another allusion to Nahman's distinction between world (*olam*) and nature (*teva*) discussed earlier. World (*olam*) is the intermediary between the infinite (God) and the finite (nature). The recognition of the constancy of divine effluence into nature, embodied in the concept of *olam*, enables one to maintain the connection between nature and God. To carry space, as the hunchback does, is to retain the consciousness of the world's constant state of renewal. To see the world as *olam* is to inhabit that edge of space where the tree of virtue, and true joy, reside.

The virtues of faith, reverence, and humility stand at the center of classical Jewish conceptions of righteousness. Nahman was living at a time (late eighteenth, early nineteenth century) when philosophical debates were underway concerning the relationship between natural law and morality/ethics.[58] Although it is unlikely that he has firsthand knowledge of these debates, it

---

57 This is in contrast to earlier kabbalistic views that understand holiness as the center rather than on the margin. See, for example, Rabbeinu Baḥya ben Asher, *Kad va-Kemaḥ*, "Shabbat," in *Kitvei Rabbeinu Baḥya*, ed. Hayim Dov Chavel (Jerusalem, 1970), 12a. Cf. a relevant summary of Baḥya's position in Reuven Kimmelman, "Introduction to Lekha Dodi and to Kabbalat Shabbat" [Hebrew], *Jerusalem Studies in Jewish Thought* 14 (1998): 433: "Jerusalem is the center of the world, Shabbat is the center of the week. Everything that is in the center is holy. Everything on the margin is profane. The desecration of the Sabbath is a desecration of the center by making it marginal." For Nahman, the center is the materiality of nature, the place of God's deepest concealment. The margin is the place where the finite and the infinite meet.

58 This was true in Jewish Enlightenment circles as well. After his move to Uman, Nahman had sustained dialogue with some of the leading Enlightenment figures in Uman. It is therefore likely that he had some exposure to some of these ideas. See Piekarz, "The Episode of Uman in the Life of Nahman of Bratslav," esp. 49–55.

is likely that he at least knew of their existence.[59] His notion here that virtue dwells on the edge of space and not in its center may reflect a surreptitious response to some of the Enlightenment ideas he may have heard during his residence in Uman, which was a maskilic center in the early nineteenth century. In conventional kabbalistic thinking, the more material the world becomes, the more God becomes concealed. Materiality is often defined as a condition for *deus absconditus*. The upper levels of space—in kabbalistic nomenclature, the world of the *sefirot*—are the realms where God's presence is most profoundly felt. The message of the hunchback is that true virtue (faith, reverence, humility) is founded upon the consciousness of divine effluence, which is only evident as one approaches the boundaries of space itself. It is at the edge of space when nature becomes most unstable, where natural law succumbs to miracle. The attainment of true virtue is not achieved solely through the practice of the law, which exists in the center of space, but only by approaching the margins of space where nature dissolves into miracle. At best, the law serves as a vehicle for that virtue.

In conclusion, I have offered a reading of part of this complex tale as a window into Nahman's exilic anthropology, arguing that the tale reworks his dualistic notion of nature and miracle in his homilies. I used various examples from his homiletic writings, not as prooftexts for the tale, but rather to illustrate the extent to which the tale problematizes some of his apparently more straightforward opinions in these writings. I argued that it is not nature that is exilic but the human being who, for numerous reasons, cannot see how order is conditioned on miracle—that is, how nature is redemptive.

Nahman relates that he began to tell stories to "wake people up from their slumber." I assume this statement was also directed to his disciples, men of deep faith who were intimately familiar with his ideas. Perhaps those sleeping were not only those lost in the cyclical nightmare of reason but also believers who had become overly secure in their belief? That is, perhaps Nahman was trying to communicate that the dichotomy between security and perpetual instability is not identical with those who live by reason or faith. Even, or perhaps precisely, the faithful are vulnerable to the compelling tendency for false security. Even believers can be the son and not the children in the tale.

---

59 See Piekarz, *Studies in Bratslav Ḥasidism*, esp. 27–32. Piekarz traces Nahman's relationship to the Uman "heretics" (*maskilim*) during this final period of his life. While traditional literature cites the existence of a cemetery of Jewish martyrs as the reason for Nahman's choice to move to Uman, the city was also a center of Enlightenment activity. For an alternative view, see Yakov Travis, "Adoring the Souls of the Dead: Rabbi Nahman of Bratslav," in *God's Voice from the Void*, 155–92.

As he faced his own death and confronted the limited influence of his message, by both skeptics and disciples alike, perhaps he became concerned, even agitated, that his listeners did not fully grasp the complexity of his discourses. Perhaps he felt this was because the genre of homily was not the best vehicle for communicating his ideas. The tale, his final attempt at being understood, became his last word, representing all he had previously taught in the form of fantasy, whose allusive images would forever spark the imagination and make readers believe they have not fully understood what lies beneath. Perhaps the tale serves to awaken its readers by evoking the longing to fully comprehend the narrative that always eludes full disclosure.

Nature, characterized in almost demonic language in *Likkutei MoHaRan*, is presented in our tale in a much more textured light. The beggars are redeeming the world by changing the way the children see the natural world. Revealing to them the source of their disability does this. The beggars never negate the world, or the reality of their deformity, only an exilic perception of it. This is illustrated in my suggestion that the tale presents three realms of exile: the exile of the unredeemable heretic, the exile of the redeemable heretic, and the exile of the *ẓaddik*. The second exile of sadness (the king's son in the prelude, the children in the tale, and the redeemable heretic in *Likkutei MoHaRan*) and the exile of joy (the beggars/the *ẓaddik*) serve as the two relevant poles of Nahman's vision of the world and the vocation of Israel. The blessings each beggar bestows on the children are directed toward overcoming the false view of nature and the absolute status of reason, both of which are indicative of the second realm of exile.[60]

Each beggar holds only one piece of the redemptive puzzle. False wisdom, which resulted in the exile of the king's son in the prelude, is coupled with a false view of nature as necessity (*meḥuyavut*) in the body of the tale. The beggars seek to heal the imperfections of civilization by drawing it back to the source of life, the root of true wisdom, and the true appreciation of nature in a perpetual state of renewal. The vehicle toward this end is prayer, the devotional act that is conditioned on the bracketing of nature as necessity.[61]

60 This also is the foundation of the first exile, the exile of the unredeemable heretic.

61 Nahman often speaks of prayer as a weapon, using the terms "bows" and "arrows." See, for example, *Likkutei MoHaRan* 1.2, 1, and 2.83. Interestingly, the bow in both lessons represents the phallus (Joseph as the *sefirah* of *yesod*, in 1.2, and *tikkun ha-berit*, or sexual purity, in 2.83), while the arrows represent prayer. The power of prayer as the battle against sadness and exile also plays a role in various interpretations of the prelude of our story. In an attempt to connect the prelude to the body of the tale, Nahman of Cheryn states: "Since the people of the country [in the prelude] were solely involved in wisdom (*ḥokhmot*), they completely forgot the art of war. That is, how to wage the great war in this world which is the battle against the evil inclination" (*Rimzei Ma'asiyot*, 18).

The blessings of the beggars are blessings of perfected virtue that manifest as deformity in exile. As opposed to what the children may have thought, each beggar's statement, "be like me," meant in their first encounter in the forest, under the wedding canopy the blessings become clear when they become gifts. The gift is that each beggar reveals the source of his particular virtue, which appears as his deformity. As a result, each beggar revalues the couple's conception of normalcy and wellbeing, resulting in joy. Each day of the wedding the couple's sense of reality is turned upside down as the apparent disability of each beggar becomes the reflection of his perfection. The joy that ensues indicates the slow retrieval of the joy lost by the king's son in the prelude to the tale.

This process of retrieval is never complete and the tale remains unfinished. This is because the seventh beggar, the beggar without feet, never arrives.[62] The couple remains in exile, living a life in tension between joy and longing. The king's son remains in exile, struggling between his legitimate questions and his heretical answers. Israel remains in exile, never fully overcoming the deception of nature as fate and necessity, still lost in the seductive world of rationality. Finally, Nahman remains in exile, a messianic figure who lived out his last debilitating days without ever achieving overwhelming acceptance outside his closed circle of followers.[63] A few months after finishing this unfinished tale, Nahman left the world of nature he struggled so passionately to transform. As to the legitimacy of his messianic claim, we will have to wait for the seventh beggar to arrive.

Cf. Steinsaltz, *Tales of Rabbi Nahman of Bratslav*, 255, where he comments that there is no textual basis for this reading. However, given that the prelude contains no mention of prayer (the tools of the great war in Nahman), and the body of the tale is founded upon prayer as the antidote for sadness, heresy, and exile, Nahman of Cheryn's insertion is well founded.

62 On this see Fishbane, "To Jump for Joy," cited in n. 39 above.

63 Although Nahman and Bratslav Ḥasidism had a profound impact on Ḥasidism in general, Nahman achieved only moderate success during his short life. Most of his teachings were published posthumously and his audacious and extreme personality led to controversy inside and outside the circles of early Ḥasidism. His creative mind and unique perspective attracted many from the neo-ḥasidic movement in the late nineteenth and early twentieth centuries, including Martin Buber, Samuel Abba Horodetzky, Hillel Zeitlin, Yehudah Leib Peretz, Adin Steinsaltz, and Areyh Kaplan, among others. The Breslov Research Institute in Jerusalem has done a remarkable job translating, reprinting, and interpreting his teachings to the larger popular audience. My deep thanks to Moshe Mykoff of the Breslov Research Institute, my friend and perennial *ḥavruta*, for his ear, his heart, and his love of "Rabbeinu's" teaching.

Later Ḥasidism

Chapter 6

Modernity as Heresy: The Introvertive Piety of Faith in R. Areleh Roth's Shomer Emunim

"There are two, and in the end only two, types of faith. To be sure there are very many contents of faith, but we only know faith in two forms."

—Martin Buber

Jewish discussions about the nature and fabric of faith are often elusive because faith (*emunah*), even as it served as a foundation for Judaism throughout the ages, often became eclipsed by the centrality of study and praxis.[1] In the Middle Ages and early Modern period, Jewish intellectual energy was focused largely on the elaboration and study of the Law. Even though an extensive body of metahalakhic literature[2] did pursue the nature of faith (rather than solely the content of faith), Jewish literature is still somewhat bereft of a systematic analysis of faith as a matrix of the devotional life.[3] While we do see such discourse in the medieval pietist tradition,

1 For a general discussion of Jewish faith, see Louis Jacobs, *Principles of the Jewish Faith* (New York: Basic Books, 1964) and Jacobs, *Faith* (New York: Basic Books, 1968).

2 I am borrowing this term from Professor Isadore Twersky, who suggested this category as a way of approaching non-halakhic literature in Medieval and early Modern Judaism. His most comprehensive definition of this term and its implications for Jewish intellectual historians can be found in "Talmudists, Philosophers, Kabbalists: The Quest for Spirituality in the 16th Century," in *Jewish Thought in the Sixteenth Century*, ed. B. Cooperman (Cambridge, MA: Harvard University Press, 1983), 431–59.

3 This becomes evident when perusing the extensive literature on Principles of Faith (dogma) in medieval Jewish thought. Much of this discussion centers around the content

where faith (*emunah*) and trust (*bitaḥon*) are treated as focal points of Jewish worship, the fulfillment of the Law almost always overshadows faith as an independent concept. In the ḥasidic tradition, beginning in the mid-eighteenth century, the issue of faith as a mode of worship and as a topic set apart from its content (i.e., what one must believe) emerged as an important issue.[4] Whereas the medieval philosophical discussions largely treat the content of faith or Principles of Faith,[5] ḥasidic discourse subtly reformulates the faith discussion toward a sophisticated psychological and phenomenological analysis of what it means to believe and what effect such belief has on the spiritual life of the individual.[6]

This chapter will be devoted to the work of one particular ḥasidic master, Rabbi Aaron (Areleh) Roth (1894–1947), whose book *Shomer Emunim*, first published in 1942, has become a classic part of the devotional corpus in the contemporary ḥasidic world.[7] Roth is perhaps best known as the leader

---

of faith, or what must be believed, rather than the nature of faith and how it serves as a vehicle for *avodat ha-shem*. See, for example, S. Schechter, "The Dogmas of Judaism," *Studies in Judaism* (Philadelphia: Jewish Publication Society of America 1905), 147–81. For an overview of the Principles of Faith debate in the Middle Ages, see M. Kellner, *Dogma in Medieval Jewish Philosophy* (Oxford, UK: Oxford University Press, 1986).

4 See, for example, Martin Buber's "The Faith of Judaism" in *Mamre* (London: Oxford University Press, 1946), 1-17. Buber invokes a Lutheran faith typology of "belief in" as opposed to "belief that" to describe the differences between Jewish faith and Christian faith in his *Two Types of Faith* (New York: Macmillan, 1951). For a study of this dichotomy see H. H. Price, "Belief 'In' and Belief 'That,'" *Religious Studies* I (1965): 5–27. For another similar treatment see Leo Baeck, *This People Israel: The Meaning of Jewish Existence* (Philadelphia: Holt, Rinehart and Winston, 1965), 25, "Faith is therefore not a commanded faith . . . but a commanding faith. It is not a demand to accept truth without question; it is not surrendering oneself to overpowering emotion; it is neither orthodoxy nor ecstasy. It is the choice of one's stand and the way (*wege*) . . . ." For a critique of this highly subjective formulation see E. Berkowitz, "Faith and Law," in his *Major Themes in Modern Philosophies of Judaism* (New York, 1974), 141–48.

5 For a recent discussion which cites many medieval and early modern Jewish positions on the Principles of Faith debate, see Marc B. Shapiro, "Maimonides' Thirteen Principles: The Last Word in Jewish Theology?" *Torah u-Madda Journal* (1993): 187–242. But see A. Altmann, "Are There Dogmas in Judaism?" in *The Meaning of Jewish Existence: Theological Essays 1930–1939* (Hanover and London: Brandeis University Press, 1990), esp. 108–12. Altmann's more theoretical analysis casts a much wider net in his reading of medieval attitudes toward dogma and the Jewish relationship between dogma and *emunah*.

6 This phenomenon is not limited to Ḥasidism. The Mussar Movement in the eighteenth and nineteenth centuries focused on the experience of faith and its relation to devotion. On the relationship between these two models, see M. Piekarz, *When Ḥasidism was Flourishing* [Hebrew] (Jerusalem, 1978), 96f.

7 Its popularity as a devotional tract is underscored by its numerous reprintings and the early appearance of an abbreviated version, entitled *Mevakesh Emunah* (Jerusalem, 1943).

of what began as a small ḥasidic court in the Jerusalem neighborhood of Me'ah She'arim and has grown to become one of the most influential forces in Israeli ultra-Orthodoxy.[8] He was also one of the ideologues behind the anti-Zionist movement among ultra-Orthodox Jews, both in Israel and America.[9] His popularity as a spiritual leader and ideologue overshadows, in my view, his most innovative contribution to the history of ḥasidic literature: his provocative and unique interpretation of faith (*emunah*) in his *Shomer Emunim*. This work did not go completely unnoticed in the academic study of Ḥasidism. Gershom Scholem deemed Areleh one of the three figures in his generation who came closest to an authentic mystical personality.[10] It is therefore peculiar that ḥasidic scholarship, as popular as it has become in the last thirty years, has completely overlooked this work as a subject of in-depth study.

---

8 For an ethnographic study of the contemporary Toldot Aaron community in Jerusalem, see D. Meijers, *Ascetic Ḥasidism in Jerusalem: The Guardian-of-the-Faithful Community of Mea Shearim* (Leiden: Brill, 1992). Meijer's study does not deal with the ideological underpinnings of the community but looks at their familial and communal patterns of behavior.

9 His work strongly influenced R. Yoel Teitelbaum, the previous Satmar Rebbe and architect of post-war anti-Zionism in the ultra-Orthodox community. See his *Va-Yoel Moshe* (Jerusalem, 1978) and the study of his ideology by A. Ravitsky, "'Forcing the End': Zionism and the State of Israel as Antimessianic Undertakings," in *Jews and Messianism in the Modern Era*, ed. Jonathan Frankel (Oxford, UK: Oxford University Press, 1991), 34–67, and Ravitsky, "*Ha-Ẓafui ve-ha-Reishut Netunah*," in *Yisrael Likrat ha-Me'ah ha-21*, ed. A. Hareven (Jerusalem, 1984), 135–97. Areleh moved to Satmar (Sate Mare) after his marriage (about 1920) and began attracting the interest of younger *ḥasidim*. When he later moved to Hungary to avoid controversy, he was supported by R. Hayyim Elazar Shapira, the Rebbe from Munkacz, the leader of the struggle against Zionism in Eastern Europe. On the anti secularist and anti-Zionist ideology of R. Hayyim Elazar Shapira see Allan L. Nadler, "The War on Modernity of R. Hayyim Elazar Shapira of Munkacz," *Modern Judaism* 14, no. 3 (1994): 233–64. The connection between Satmar and Areleh's sect (Toldot Aaron) remained intact. After his brief stay in Jerusalem in 1947 and subsequent immigration to America, R. Yoel Teitelbaum remained the honorary Chief Justice (*av beit din*) of the Edah Ḥaredit, the ultra-Orthodox judicial system in Jerusalem strongly influenced by the Toldot Aaron community.

10 See G. Scholem, "Thoughts on the Possibility of Jewish Mysticism Today" [Hebrew], *Devarim be-Go 1* (Tel Aviv: Am Oved, 1976), 76, "There is only one case in the generation before the Holocaust of a zaddik who rose solely on his own merit and not as the result of family inheritance. I am speaking about Areleh Roth and his court . . . Just as R. Kook's *'Orot Ha-Kodesh* represents a contemplative world view which is unique, *Shomer Emunim* of Areleh Roth is one of the most startling Jewish documents of our time . . . These two individuals (Areleh and R. Kook), men of stature and spirit, were still able to [creatively] illuminate and develop their ideas which identify with the world of Kabbala which preceded them."

Before beginning in earnest, a last introductory point is in order. The uniqueness of Areleh's contribution is highlighted by placing it within its historical context. This "contextualization" of *Shomer Emunim* should not be viewed as a scholarly exercise, which would be frowned upon by the traditional community for whom it was composed. Areleh himself, as well as his son-in-law and successor R. Abraham Isaac Kahan, stressed the importance of the extenuating circumstances of their respective generations as both the reason for writing this work as well as a necessary pre-requisite for understanding it.[11] In a somewhat startling assertion in "The Small Introduction" to *Shomer Emunim*, Areleh writes:

> Sages will say, what good is this new book to me? Is it not better for me at this time to study a book of the previous righteous ones [*ẓaddikim*]? However, I have already written in the introduction to my *Shulḥan ha-Tahor*[12] that physical healing coincides with spiritual healing. For example, regarding medication for physical ailments we know that we can often no longer use the medications of previous generations as a result of the different nature [of individuals], the different climate [*avirim*] and our different physical constitutions. This is true in spiritual matters as well. It is often impossible to adhere to the spiritual advice that we received from previous generations as they were holier, purer and full of holy wisdom [*da'at de-kedoshah*]. Their leaders were holy and not as dependent upon the physical world . . . This is not the case with us, who are deprived of knowledge, empty of mind, heart and strength. This is coupled with the anguish [*ẓarot*] of our generation which flows like water and rivers. The holy wisdom has already been emptied and the seduction of the world gains strength every day without limit until we have forgotten the devotion of the previous righteous ones. We are like a dreamer who wakens from his dream and asks himself whether it [the dream] was real or not. This is the state that we are in as the result of the great wave [of oppression], the concealment of holiness and the greatness of our sins.[13]

This challenge to the relevance of traditional *mussar* literature, even as it is justified by traditional means, is quite suggestive. Whether Areleh is

---

11 See R. Abraham Isaac Kahan, "Preface from the Publisher," 3ff. Areleh's entire introduction (*hakdamah*) is devoted to this very issue.

12 *Shulḥan ha-Tahor* is Areleh's ḥasidic commentary on the dietary laws. It was first published in Sate Mare (Satmar) in 1933 and has been reprinted many times.

13 *Shomer Emunim* 79b. Cf. R. Abraham Isaac Kahan's introduction to *Tikvat ha-Geulah* (Jerusalem, 1993), 2b.

making his claim vis-a-vis all pietistic literature or only about his particular contribution, it is evident that he viewed his work as addressing his particular community in a way that previous literature of this sort could not. He further writes, "I have seen and contemplated the situation in our time . . . [and decided] that I should write words which would help, with the Will of God, each and every one to strengthen themselves in all manners [of devotion] and not to despair. The underlying principle is faith, the root of all roots . . . ."[14] Although he rarely speaks about particular events in his contemporary world, it is clear that the overarching issues of secularization in general and, more specifically, secularization of the Jewish community in the form of Zionism, present a unique problem, one which points toward the final test before the messianic era.[15] Again, this in itself is not new. In fact, it was the basis of much of traditionalist anti-Zionist literature at that time. As we will see, the uniqueness of Areleh's position vis-a-vis his traditionalist contemporaries is the highly messianic tenor of his discourse.[16] The decade of the 1920s in Palestine witnessed the immigration of the Second and Third Aliyah, in the opinion of scholars of this period, the first true immigrations of the enlightened Zionist community.[17] The Old Settlement in Jerusalem, led by R. Hayyim Zonnenfeld and R. Israel Diskin, were staunchly attempting to protect the insular framework of their respective communities.[18] An ideological opponent of these great figures, the first chief rabbi of Palestine, R. Abraham Isaac ha-Kohen Kook, fought to embrace the secular influx while protecting the authentic nature of traditional Judaism. Kook's provocative ideology is founded

14 *Shomer Emunim* 8a.

15 See R. Abraham Isaac Kahan's introduction to *Tikvat ha-Geulah* 2b, "Specifically in this time, because of our many sins Satan has succeeded in establishing the State of Israel on the foundation of heresy and non-belief. He succeeded in destroying and confusing thousands upon thousands of Jews. All of this has confused their minds and weakened their faith, specifically in the coming of the Messiah. We need mercy from heaven in order to strengthen ourselves against this." *Tikvat ha-Geulah* is a reprint of Areleh's "Essay of Faith" in *Shomer Emunim* with a new introduction by R. Abraham Isaac Kahan.

16 The messianism of Areleh is present but not pervasive in *Shomer Emunim*. It becomes a central topic of discussion in his *Mevakesh Emunah* (Jerusalem, 1943), where faith is viewed as a prerequisite for redemption. This work is worthy of a separate study.

17 See I. Bartal, "Eastern European Jews and *Erez Yisrael:* Immigration and the Structure of the Old Settlement" [Hebrew], *Cathedra* 16 (July, 1980): 3–27. Cf. Menahem Friedman, *Ḥevrah ve-Dat* (Jerusalem, 1977), 33–73, 129–46.

18 For a comprehensive analysis of this historical period see M. Friedman, "The Old Ashkenazi Settlement in Palestine During the British Mandate" [Hebrew] (Phd diss., Hebrew University, 1972) and his more concise *Ḥevrah ve-Dat*.

upon a vision of inclusion and expansion, believing that he was standing on the cusp of the messianic era.[19] Zonnenfeld and Diskin, suspicious of this messianic optimism, viewed the influx of secular Jews to Palestine as a threat to the cohesiveness of their communities, built largely on an ideology of protection against the demonic forces of modern secularism.[20] Areleh, who was himself a new immigrant from his native Hungary, not being a descendant of a rabbinic dynasty, was not a major player in this vehement debate. However, as we will see, he was an interesting amalgam of both positions. On the one hand, he shared the introvertive pietism of Zonnenfeld and Diskin as well as their utter intolerance of Zionism and secularism (which they all viewed as synonymous). Yet, reared in a ḥasidic court in Hungary,[21] he shared Kook's love of mystical doctrine.[22] More important, like Kook he viewed his generation as the last before the messianic era and presented his solution to the problem of the secularization of the Holy Land as a way to hasten the coming of the Messiah.[23] Although this presentation will not be a comparative study of Kook and Areleh (although such a study would be opportune), it is worthwhile to note that, despite the similarities in their diagnosis of Palestine in the early 1920s, their respective prognoses are mutually exclusive. The messianic

19 There are many studies, mostly in Hebrew, which deal with the messianic optimism of R. Kook. For two English contributions, see B. Ish-Shalom, *Rav Avraham Yizhak Ha-Cohen Kook: Between Mysticism and Rationalism* (Albany: SUNY Press, 1993), esp. 132–37; and J. Gellman, "Zion and Jerusalem: The Jewish State in the Thought of R. Abraham Isaac Kook," 276–89, and Ella Belfer, "The Land of Israel and Historical Dialectics in the Thought of R. Kook: Zionism and Messianism," 257–75, both in *Rabbi Abraham Isaac Kook and Jewish Spirituality*, ed. L. J. Kaplan and D. Schatz (New York: NYU Press, 1995).

20 See Friedman, *Ḥevrah ve-Dat*, 87–110.

21 Areleh studied with various ḥasidic masters in Hungary, including R. Israel of Viznitz, R. Yesakhar Dov Rokeah of Belz, and, most importantly, R. Zvi Elimelekh Shapira of Bluzhov. The Bluzhov dynasty, now led by R. Israel Spira of Bluzhov, was recently popularized in Yaffa Eliach's *Ḥasidic Tales of the Holocaust* (New York: Vintage, 1982). For a hagiographic study of Areleh, see Elijah Hayyim Steinberg, *Uvdah de-Aaron* (Jerusalem, 1948).

22 Although Areleh's stance vis-a-vis secularism is the polar opposite of R. Kook's stance, in the following passage he exhibits a quasi-mystical justification for heretical doctrine. See *Shomer Emunim* 88a, "God created the world so that everything would be concealed, in order to [give mankind] free choice [*beḥirah*]. This is the purpose of creating man in this lowly world. Do not pay attention to the success of the evil ones, the evil of Israel, in their temporary fortune. As a result of their choice, all of the [holy] sparks that fell into the depths will be cleansed. All of the worlds will be repaired by means of the holy seed, whose roots are in the highest realms of existence . . ."

23 *Shomer Emunim* 4b, 5a (top).

optimism which apparently motivated Kook's willingness to embrace the secular and, by doing so, reveal its spiritual core, is absent in Areleh's writings.[24] However, Areleh is also beyond the traditional approach of Zonnenfeld and Diskin, both of whom functioned within the confines of what may be called an "exilic mentality," focused on maintenance rather than innovation.[25] As fundamentalist and stringent as Areleh's approach may be, his ideology is, in my view, anything but an ideology of exilic maintenance. Or, to put it another way, for Areleh maintenance itself had a subliminal messianic motivation.

Parting from the more traditionalist approach that the present is only a reconstituted version of the past,[26] Areleh asserts that the contemporary world suffers in ways unprecedented in Jewish history. This stance is common in messianic movements in Judaism, each of which views its generation as the culmination of pre-messianic oppression. Areleh's attitude is not limited to the intensification of external oppression and persecution, but more poignantly directed at the internal defilement and degenerative state

24 Rav Kook's optimism influenced his stance on modernity in general and modern Jewish scholarship in particular. See, for example, his qualified tolerance of Bible criticism in *Iggerot ha-Rav Kook*, 3 vols. (Jerusalem, 1961), letter #134, 1:163.

25 See Scholem, "On the Possibility," 76. This is also the basic posture of the Satmar Rebbe, R. Yoel Teitelbaum, whose anti-Zionism does not contain the same messianic undertones of his mentor, Areleh. It should be noted that Areleh's approach shuns any hint of innovation, a posture popularized by another Hungarian leader, the Hatam Sofer, in his oft-cited statement, "innovation is forbidden by the Torah." Yet, if we posit that Areleh viewed his generation as unique, wouldn't that by definition necessitate an innovative solution? Moreover his statement, cited above, that the advice of the past generations often cannot treat the ailments of the present implies to me that "innovation" in some form is necessary. This does not imply reformation or liberalization. Quite the contrary, the inwardness and stringency of a community can also fall under the rubric of innovation (*ḥiddush*). On this, see T. Fishman, "On Gender-Specific Commandments: On the Interplay of Symbols in Society," *AJS Review* 17, no. 2 (1992): 199–245.

26 Nahmanides' adaptation of the statement, "the actions of the fathers are signs for the children" (*ma'aseh avot siman le-banim*), became a signpost for traditionalist views of history in Medieval and post-Medieval Judaism. For its rabbinic source, see Midrash Tanhuma, *lekh lekha*, 9. Cf. *Nahmanides' Commentary on the Torah*, ed. C. Chavel (Brooklyn: Judaica Press, 2005), l:180, on Genesis 32:4, "All that occurred to our father with his brother Esau will always occur to us with the sons of Esau." Cf. his comment to Genesis 12:6 and his Introduction to Exodus in vol. 1, 279, and the discussion in A. Funkenstein, *Perceptions of Jewish History* (Berkeley: University of California Press, 1993), 110–17. See also Rabbeinu Bahya ben Asher, *Kad ha-Kemaḥ*, "the Light of Hanukkah," Sukkah, in *Kitvei Rabbeinu Baḥya* (Jerusalem, 1969), 269, 276.

of the Jewish people.[27] His argument makes three basic claims. His first claim is founded on a highly romanticized vision of the Jewish communities of the past as "standing against all of the tests of faith. In every generation Israel was holy, pure in the mind and the body . . . they were believers, sons of believers. In every exile, persecution and decree they accepted the yoke of heaven with love."[28] Although such a statement is not uncommon in traditionalist circles, here it is presented as a frame in which to view the present internal state of the Jews as worse than the biblical Sodom, "worse than any time in history since the Jews have become a nation."[29] As we will see, this degenerative state, which he labels "the fiftieth level of defilement,"[30] is a necessary prerequisite for the emergence of the messianic age. Working off the rabbinic dictum that the Messiah will come either when "all are righteous or all are sinners,"[31] Areleh presents his world as the latter part of the rabbinic equation and thus the final stage of exile. The unprecedented nature of modern society is, for him, the extent to which heresy has permeated the Jewish psyche and the fact that it has become normative and accepted rather than deviant behavior.[32] This assertion is driven home for him by the influx of secular Zionists who were building a secular Jewish

27 He is, of course, not original in his claim that Jewish secularization is the reason for Jewish tragedy. This is the basic framework of Jewish responses to suffering and only recently (with the emergence of post-Holocaust literature) is that assertion being challenged. Cf. D. Hartman, "Rabbinic Responses to Suffering," in *A Living Covenant* (New York: Free Press, 1985), 183–204.

28 *Shomer Emunim* 2a. Cf. *Tanna de-vei Eliyahu*, ch. 20. See also R. Joseph Ya'abatz, *Or ha-Ḥayyim* with *Ma'ein Ganim* of R. Zvi Elimelekh Shapira of Dinov (Zolkiew, 1848), chapter 2. Part of this is quoted in the gloss to *Shomer Emunim* 95a.

29 *Shomer Emunim* 12a, "Oy! Look what has happened to us. The Great Hunter [has come upon us], the evil inclination, helped by his soldiers who have alienated themselves from our people and increased heresy and abandonment. This [tragedy] has not happened since Israel became a nation." Even though the biblical story of Sodom occurs before the Jews became a nation, the rabbinic vision of Sodom as the worst possible place on earth emphasizes the desperate situation of the present. Cf. *Shomer Emunim* 11b and 52a, "We are now in a state [of defilement] which hasn't existed since Israel became a nation, anguish from every side, the increase of evil ones, outsiders [*ḥiẓonim*] and heretics (*apikorsim*), [all of whom] seduce us from all sides."

30 *Shomer Emunim* 100a-101b.

31 BT Sanhedrin 98a, "R. Yohanan said, 'The son of David will come only in a generation that is either altogether righteous or altogether wicked'..."

32 *Shomer Emunim* 11b, "It has gotten to the point now, in our generation, that the purpose of the poison of the multitude of the nations [*erev rav*], the souls of Sodom and Gomorra and the generation of the Tower of Babel has been fulfilled. They all seek to destroy and swallow the entire world with their falseness and seduction." His use of the term *erev rav* (mixed multitude) here is significant in that later on he deems any Jewish non-believer a descendant of the *erev rav* and thus not a Jew. The danger of the *erev rav*

State in the Holy Land.[33] The third claim follows on the heels of the image of Sodom in his second claim. Later in *Shomer Emunim*, Areleh returns to the notion of the degenerative state of the present as unique in that it is the first extended period in which the Jewish people did not have righteous ones (*ẓaddikim*) to rescue them from the seduction of evil.[34] This component strengthens the biblical image of Sodom above. In the biblical story of Sodom, Abraham convinces God to save the city of Sodom if he can find ten righteous individuals (Genesis 18:22–33). Even though he ultimately fails, this episode is often cited in rabbinic parlance to exhibit the power of the *ẓaddik* to intervene in divine decrees and rescue the worthy or innocent from the punishment of evil.[35] Quite uncharacteristic of the Hungarian Ḥasidism in which Areleh was reared, he laments that his generation is void of these types of "true" *ẓaddikim*, all of whom "have gone to their resting place and left us wanting and empty."[36] In a move reminiscent of *mussar*

---

in Jewish traditional literature has always been that they constitute an internal part of the Jewish People and are thus able to wield a profound influence on the community.

33 See *Shomer Emunim* 3b, where he claims that the influx of evil into the body of Israel continued "numerous generations until the trembling of the Land in the year 1914. At that time, *the foundations of the mountains shook, rocked by His indignation* (Psalms 18:8). The foundations of our fathers were weakened . . ." This apparently is a reference to what led up to the Balfour Declaration (1918) and its aftermath, which was a victory for the Zionists and therefore, according to Areleh, a victory for the serpent of modernity.

34 See *Shomer Emunim* 90a-91a.

35 On the motif of, "The *ẓaddik* decrees and God complies, God decrees and the *ẓaddik* nullifies [the decree]," see *Midrash Yalkut Shemoni* on 2 Samuel 370a, *Sifrei on Numbers*, #135, Numbers Rabbah 14:4. Cf. the interesting dialogue between Abraham and the biblical King Malkizedek (based on Genesis 15:18) where Malkizedek questions Abraham's decision to attempt to save Sodom in R. Mordechai Joseph Leiner of Izbica's *Mei ha-Shilo'ah* (Brooklyn, 1984), 1:7b/c.

36 *Shomer Emunim* 91a. This is remarkable in that the leader of the Hungarian, Galician tradition, R. Elimelekh of Lyzinsk, was perhaps the most provocative proponent of zaddikism in all of ḥasidic literature. Areleh cites a list of "true" *ẓaddikim*, including the Ba'al Shem Tov, the Maggid of Mezritch, R. Elimelekh of Lyzinsk, and "his student" R. Menahem Mendel of Riminov, whose line ended with the generation of Areleh's father, R. Samuel Jacob Roth. This statement is curious on numerous counts. First, although R. Menahem Mendel of Riminov was viewed as a leading figure in Galician and Hungarian Ḥasidism in the early nineteenth century, he is hardly the last (or most important) in the line of R. Elimelekh of Lyzinsk. Second, one of the constant challenges to Areleh's acceptance as a ḥasidic leader was the fact that he was not a descendant of a ḥasidic line. One of the reasons he left Satmar in Hungary and settled in Bergsas, Czechoslovakia, was the vehemence of this polemic against him. See Elijah Cohen Steinberg, *Uvdah d'Aaron* and *Encyclopedia of Ḥasidism* [Hebrew], "Names," Isaac Alfasi (Jerusalem, 1986), 175–77. Areleh also composed works which featured R. Menahem Mendel of Riminov. The first, *Menaḥem Zion* (Satmar, 1935), contains stories about R. Menahem Mendel of Riminov and his student R. Zvi Hirsch. The

literature, Areleh states that the burden of responsibility rests solely on the individual. The glorious days of the intervention of the *ẓaddik* no longer apply.[37]

In sum, the unprecedented nature of his generation is the combination of 1) the vehemence of external persecution, 2) the infiltration of heresy into the very body and psyche of the Jewish people, and 3) the absence of any "true" *ẓaddik* who could save the Jews from the fate of evil and defilement. Interestingly, Areleh rarely deals with the threat of external persecution as a test of faith for the Jews.[38] This is, for him, a normative phenomenon which always existed and will remain intact until the messianic era.[39] More important, it is far less threatening to the core of the covenant than the two other factors, i.e., the latent acceptance of heresy and the lack of Jewish spiritual leadership as celestial advocacy.[40] The introvertive nature of Areleh's piety is a direct response to the threat of internal Jewish annihilation, not the threat of physical or spiritual annihilation from without. Secularism as heresy had defiled the very fabric of Jewish life and Jewish devotion. By embracing or even tolerating modernity, the Jew destroys the "precious jewel" (*even yakar*) which is the Jewish covenant and primary faith (*emunah peshutah*).[41] Thus the way of saving Jewish faith, the "root of roots" of

---

second, *Derekh Ẓaddikim* (Jerusalem, 1967), contains short inspirational essays (*divrei mussar*) and stories about ḥasidic *ẓaddikim* from the Ba'al Shem Tov to R. Zvi Hirsch of Riminov.

37 Although Ḥasidism often laments the bygone days of the great masters, it still views its present masters as inheriting some remnant of the past. The nullification of the *ẓaddik* in the ḥasidic tradition exists primarily in the early and mid-nineteenth-century Polish ḥasidic tradition of Pryszucha and Kotzk.

38 Note that this treatise was written in the early 1940s before the effects of the Holocaust were widely known. Compare this with his contemporary, R. Kalonymus Kalman Shapira's *Eish Kodesh*. See Nehemia Polen, *The Holy Fire: The Teachings of Rabbi Kalonymus Kalman Shapira* (Northvale, NJ: Jason Aronson, 1994). Though Kalonymus Kalman does do battle with the forces of the Enlightenment in his *Mevo She'arim*, and *Eish Kodesh*, the latter consisting of collected sermons given in the Warsaw ghetto, focusing on the Nazi genocide as a test of Jewish faith.

39 See *Sifrei on Numbers*, ed. Horowitz, #59, 65, in the name of R. Shimon bar Yohai: "It is an axiom, Esau hates Jacob." For a late theological formulation of this midrashic idea, see R. Nathan Zvi Berliner, "*Sa'ar Yisrael*," printed at the end of his *Commentary to Song of Songs* (Jerusalem, 1967), 58a-67b.

40 *Shomer Emunim* 13b, where Areleh speaks of the "beginning and end" of faith as being challenged by the biblical Amalek, the demonic force which seeks to destroy the faith of the Jews. See also his "Sermon on Redemption," ch. 5, in *Shomer Emunim*, 2:333a-356b.

41 I have translated *emunah peshutah* (lit. simple faith) as primary faith throughout this chapter. My contention is that Areleh understands *emunah peshutah* as a primary stage of faith experienced at Sinai which then became concealed in order to protect it from contamination by the demonic forces of the intellect. He juxtaposes this type of faith to

the covenant, is by protecting this core from the claws of modernity. It is only this core which still remains untarnished. The structure and nature of his solution now needs to be addressed.

II

In light of the above observations, it is not surprising that the fundamental issue preoccupying Areleh in *Shomer Emunim* is the attempt to isolate the core of Jewish belief in order that it may be protected from contamination from the extraneous forces of evil. Areleh begins his discussion by creating a provocative architectonic of faith. The core of this faith itself is viewed as part of the Jewish psyche, distinct from and independent of Torah and *miẓvot*. This distinction is drawn out in a reading of the statement in B. Talmud Shabbat 138b, "In the future Torah will be forgotten in Israel!"[42]

This means [it will be forgotten] by particular individuals, not by the nation as a whole. Also, the term Torah in the above passage refers only to the 613 *miẓvot*, as it states in Talmud Makkot 23b.[43] These [613] do *not* include, God forbid, the *miẓvah* of *emunah*, which is the *miẓvah* of *I am the Lord your God* and *You shall have no other Gods before me*, which are only alluded to in the counting of the 613. This [faith] will never be forgotten because we received *emunah* directly from the mouth of God,[44] in His glory and from His essence.[45]

---

a secondary stage of intellectual faith, which, although an essential part of the authentic Jewish experience, is susceptible to the defiling nature of human weakness.

42 "When our rabbis entered *Kerem b'Yavneh*, they said, 'In the future, Torah will be forgotten in Israel, as it says, (Amos 8:11, 12) *A time is coming, says the Lord GOD, when I will send a famine upon the land; not a hunger for bread or a thirst for water, but for hearing the words of the LORD. Men shall wander from sea to sea and from north to east to seek the word of the LORD, but they shall not find it* . . .' R. Shimon says, 'God forbid, that the Torah should be forgotten.'"

43 Actually, the relevant passage appears in 24a, ". . . *Moses commanded us Torah, an inheritance for the congregation of Jacob* (Deut. 33:4). '*Torah*' being the letter value equal to 611; *I am the Lord your God* and *You shall have no other gods* are not counted because we heard them directly from the mouth of the Almighty [*mi-pi ha-gevurah*]." Cf. Zohar 3.264b, "*Hear O Israel, the Lord Our God, the Lord is One*, this is the fundamental principle of the Torah. *You shall have no other gods* . . . is only to protect Israel from turning from *I am the Lord Your God* . . ."

44 Makkot 23a.

45 *Shomer Emunim* 9a. For another ḥasidic reading see R. Mordecai Joseph of Izbica, *Mei ha-Shiloah* (Brooklyn, NY, 1984), 22b, and my discussion in *Ḥasidism in Transition:*

The unique quality of faith represented here serves as the backbone of Areleh's entire treatise. There are a number of implications suggested here worth noting. First, the distinction of Torah from *emunah* and the talmudic disclosure of the vulnerability of Torah directly addresses the diagnosis of his environment. The potential for evil to infiltrate into the Jewish community and cause the separation between Torah and Israel is a real possibility recognized by the architects of the tradition. However, the covenant itself is not threatened by such an occurrence because *emunah*, being independent from Torah, is not subject to the talmudic warning mentioned above.[46] His justification for this is interesting. The vulnerability of the relationship between Torah and Israel results from the fact that Israel only received the Torah through a medium, i.e., Moses.[47] Thus, as much as they may have accepted the Torah intellectually and even emotionally, they could not fully integrate the experience of Torah psychically. However the first two commandments which, according to rabbinic tradition, were received directly from God, entered into the innermost parts of those who stood at Sinai.[48] This experience, which he views as the core of *emunah*, could not be forgotten as it was not merely the experience of an event but a moment of direct encounter between God and the people which was transformative

---

The Ḥasidic Ideology of R. Gershon Henokh of Radzin in Light of Medieval Jewish Philosophy and Kabbala (Phd diss., Brandeis University, 1994), 456–63.

46 See also *Shomer Emunim* 49b.

47 This idea appears in a slightly different form in R. Yonatan Eybshutz's *Ya'arot Devash*, vol. 1 (Jerusalem, 1984), sermon for the 7th of Adar, 1777, 158–61. Eybshutz uses the figure of Moses to distinguish between the coercive reception of Torah at Sinai (where Moses was present) as opposed to the volitional reception of Torah in the episode of Purim (when Moses was absent) suggested in the Talmud.

48 Areleh accepts the rabbinic assertion that the Jews who stood on Sinai represent the entire collective soul of Israel. Therefore, all who are Jews, throughout postSinaitic Jewish history, "stood at Sinai." Therefore, a non-believing Jew is an oxymoron. This seemingly bizarre notion may be implied by Maimonides in his *Iggeret Teiman* (Epistle to the Jews of Yemen) when he says, "These trials [attempts by Islam and Christianity to convert us] are designed to test and purify us, so that only the saints and the pious men of the *pure and undefiled lineage* [my emphasis] will adhere to our religion and remain within the fold, as has been stated: *Anyone who invokes the name of the Lord shall be among the survivors* [Joel 3:5]. This statement makes it clear that they are not numerous, and that they are the descendants of those who were present at Sinai, witnessed the divine revelation, entered into the covenant of God, and took it upon themselves to do and obey, declaring, *we will do and we will obey* [Exodus 24:7] . . . God has given assurance He is an adequate guarantor and informed them that not only did all the persons who were present at Sinaitic revelation believe in the prophecy of Moses and in his Law, but that their descendants would do likewise until the end of time." For the text in English, see A. Halkin, D. Hartman, *Crisis in Leadership* (Philadelphia: Jewish Publication Society of America, 1985), 102–103.

in nature. To borrow a Hegelian formulation, for Areleh, Torah is comparable to Jewish consciousness, *emunah* to Jewish self-consciousness.[49] The experience of the direct encounter with the divine forever changed the way in which Jews viewed themselves. To forget *emunah*, according to Areleh, would be tantamount to questioning one's own existence.

One familiar with medieval Jewish literature on the issue of faith will immediately be reminded of the oft cited controversy between Maimonides and Nahmanides on the question as to whether faith is a commandment or not.[50] Areleh, certainly aware of this medieval debate, makes no reference whatsoever to this discussion. His reason may reflect the distinction I suggested at the outset between "belief in" and "belief that."[51] The medieval philosophical debate is focused on the model of "belief in," i.e., belief as a posture in relation to something or some set of principles. This is surely true in the case of Maimonides, whose provocative Thirteen Principles of Faith dominated the philosophical debate on this issue. Yet even Nahmanides, whose position on the legitimacy of principles of faith is far less certain, views faith as a posture toward an idea. His critical comment against Rashi on Genesis 1:1 is founded on the assumption that faith "in" Creation is fundamental enough to Judaism to justify beginning the Torah with the account of Creation.[52] His polemical sermon "*Torat Ha-Shem Temimah*" is largely devoted to defending the need for a belief "in" Creation *ex nihilo* against the Aristotelian challenge of eternity.[53] Areleh means something very different when he speaks about *emunah*.[54] *Emunah* in *Shomer Emunim* is not a posturing in relation to anything outside itself. Rather, it is viewed as the core of the Jewish soul, built upon

49 See G. W. F. Hegel, *The Phenomenology of Spirit*, trans. A. V. Miller (Oxford, UK: Clarendon, 1977), 58–138, and J. Hyppolite, *Genesis and Structure of Hegel's Phenomenology of Spirit*, trans. S. Cherniak and J. Heckman (Evanston, IL: Northwestern University Press, 1974), 143–56.

50 See Moses Maimonides' *Sefer ha-Mizvot*, positive commandment #1, and the gloss of Nahmanides, *Mishneh Torah*, "Laws on the Foundation of the Law," 1:1. Cf. A. Nuriel, "*Musag ha-Emunah ezel ha-Rambam*," *Da'at* (1979): 43–47.

51 See above, n. 4.

52 See Nahmanides' critique of Rashi on Genesis 1:1. For an interesting ḥasidic alternative to both Rashi and Nahmanides, which ultimately offers a different solution to Rashi's query, see R. Moshe Teitelbaum of Ohel, *Yismaḥ Moshe*, 2 vols. (rp., New Jersey, 1989), on Genesis, 3b–4b.

53 See, "*Torat ha-Shem Temimah*," in *Kitvei Ramban*, ed. Chavel (Jerusalem, 1963), 1:141–65. A full English translation appears in *Ramban: Writings and Discourses*, ed. and trans. C. Chavel (New York: Shilo, 1978). Much of this is a frontal attack on Maimonides statement in the *Guide* (2:25) that Judaism does not stand or fall on the belief on creation *ex nihilo*.

54 On the question of R. Nahman of Bratslav's dialectical faith, which may have influenced Areleh, see A. Green, *Tormented Master* (Woodstock, VT: Jewish Lights, 1992),

the direct experience of God at Sinai. It is also not a decision or a memory. Accordingly, Jewish non-belief is not a viable category for Areleh. If belief is not a choice but an innate part of the Jewish psyche how can non-belief exist among Jews?[55] Given the overpowering influence of heresy and non-belief among Jews living in his world, this is of central importance and, as we will see, becomes a pivotal dimension of his thinking.

The above overview of Areleh's distinction between faith and Torah is merely the preamble to his vision of *emunah*. The second part of his analysis places his initial presentation under closer scrutiny to delineate three basic categories: faith achieved through vision, hearing, and intellection.

Beside the vision and hearing [of God] achieved at the giving of the Torah, there was also a realm of *emunah* [achieved] through the lofty apprehension of a higher wisdom [*da'at elyon*]. This is the highest level of *emunah*. With it God opened up all the gates of heaven and all of the worlds and showed them, as it were, that none [alt. nothing] existed beside Him [*ein od melivado*] . . . All present [at Sinai] saw according to their ability and the extent to which they suffered the exile of Egyptian oppression without abandoning God. "The extent to which one toils on the eve of the Sabbath is commensurate with the amount one eats on the Sabbath." The apprehension at Sinai was commensurate with the faithful struggle each endured [in Egypt]. He saw and heard commensurate with his preparation . . . Just as we received *emunah* at Sinai in these three ways—seeing, hearing and intellectual-imaginative apprehension [*hasagat ha-da'at*]—*emunah* can be revealed in our hearts today in these same three ways . . .[56]

285–337; and my, "Through the Void: The Absence of God in R. Nahman of Bratzlav's *Likkutei MoHaRan*," *Harvard Theological Review* 88, no. 4 (1995): 495–519.

55 Martin Buber, *Two Types of Faith* (Syracuse, NY: Syracuse University Press, 2003), 40, "The separation, which is announced in Israel's Scriptures, cannot be between those who have faith and those who have not, because there is here no decision of faith or unbelief. The separation here is meant to take place between those who realize their faith, who make it effective, and those who do not." I would venture to say that Areleh would essentially agree with Buber's assertion, although he would suggest that the Buberian separation may also be between those who truly stood at the foot of Sinai and those who constitute the mixed multitude (*erev rav*) and thus do not share the existential experience of primary faith.

56 *Shomer Emunim* 50a. The three models are defined as follows: "Seeing: if a person sees with his inner eye [*ein ha-sekhel*] or through empirical vision that God performs a particular miracle for him. Or, he sees that God changes nature to comply with the will of a *ẓaddik*. Or, he sees the passionate devotion of a *ẓaddik* which strengthens his own faith . . . Hearing: if he hears the torah of a *ẓaddik* or tales of a *ẓaddik*'s devotion. Or, he hears the stories of miracles performed by God. After hearing this, *emunah* becomes engraved in his heart with emotion. This is the aspect of hearing." The third category, intellectual-imaginative apprehension, occurs by being unconsciously aroused to serve

The empirical (ocular, audible) and intellectual-imaginative types of faith continue to function in the present as the Sinai experience reverberates throughout the generations. Yet, these three modes of faith are all relational or veridical, i.e., their veracity is always dependent upon some external object. By definition they are also vulnerable to influences by the external forces of evil.[57] Hence Areleh continues:

"However, sometimes, God forbid, this intellectual-imaginative faith [the highest of the three] can be obstructed as the result of our many sins, especially the sins of our youth.[58] As a result, knowledge [*da'at*] becomes hidden until, God forbid, one's sensitivity is concealed."[59] This [sensitivity]

God without knowing where the arousal came from or by the memory of a vision or the oral transmission of some miraculous event.

57 In his *Kuntres Zava'ah* Areleh, addressing his *ḥasidim*, writes, "It is common knowledge that [in the days of] the Temple it was not necessary to believe that there was a Creator. With the help of God, they saw it empirically . . . each one, in his proper time, saw and felt divinity, with the help of God." See *Shomer Emunim* 78a-79a.

58 These are generally understood to be sins of a sexual nature, sins of desire, and "extraneous thoughts" regarding women. The purity of sexual behavior is of utmost importance for Areleh. *Tikkun ha-yesod* or *tikkun ha-berit*, both referring to sexual conduct, are viewed as central pillars of Areleh's community. Areleh composed a two-volume study on this topic, entitled *Taharat ha-Kodesh*. The first volume, published in 1964 in Jerusalem, deals with his attitudes toward proper sexual conduct. The second volume, published in 1968 in Jerusalem, focuses on ideas of sexual purity throughout the ages, beginning with rabbinic material but focusing primarily on ḥasidic literature from the generation of the Ba'al Shem Tov. The conventional Jewish connection between sexuality and youth is based on the verse, *since the devising of a person's mind is evil from his youth* (Genesis 8:21). Both halakhic and metahalakhic literature view one's youth as a time of unbridled passion. This interpretation squares with Areleh's subsequent statement in the above quote that *da'at* becomes hidden. In the kabbalistic tradition, the *sefirah da'at* is connected to *yesod*, the phallus, and is often referred to as "the higher phallus." Cf. Zohar 1.15a, 2.2a. This is likely to have been based on medieval scientific notions of the mind being the source of the semen, which travels through the spine during sexual relations. The idea of spermatogenesis probably existed in ancient Persia and is mentioned by the Greeks Alcmaeon of Crotona and Diogenesis Laertius and is found in Hippocratic writings as well. Cf. D. Jacqart, C. Thomasset, *Sexuality and Medicine in the Middle Ages*, trans. M. Adamson (Princeton, NJ: Princeton University Press, 1988), 53f. This perhaps influenced the later sixteenth-century Safed tradition which suggests that sexual relations bring about forgetfulness, a concealment of *da'at* or *hesekh ha-da'at*, caused by the production of semen. Cf. Gershom Scholem's *Annotated Zohar* (Jerusalem: Magnes Press, 1992), 1512, cited and developed in E. R. Wolfson, *Through a Speculum That Shines* (Princeton, NJ: Princeton University Press, 1994), 389n236. This is used in a novel interpretation by R. Mordehai Yoseph of Izbica as to the reason why Er and Onan, the sonsin-law of the biblical Judah, refused to sleep with Tamar, their dead brother's wife. See *Mei ha-Shilo'ah*, 1:15d, 16a.

59 See, e.g., in *Shomer Emunim* 93b, "Also the concealment of concealment [*hester betokh hester*] . . . specifically in the blemish of sexual behavior [*middat ha-yesod*] the result being forgetfulness."

is the catalyst for faith in divine Providence and the many miracles that occur at every moment . . . This is particularly true in a time when God's presence is concealed [*hester panim*] which is the concealment of concealment [*hester betokh hester*] because of our sins.[60] This leads to the disappearance of individuals who have the capacity for knowledge and spiritual sensitivity. Also, we lose those who would give their lives in their worship [*mesirat nefesh*], all as the result of our sins.

> However, we know that there is yet another level of apprehending faith, which is primary faith [*emunah peshutah*], a faith not based on reason.[61] This is a faith we received from our forefathers. . . . This eternally stands with us like a strong pillar. It is impossible to fall from this faith as God has already promised us that it will stand forever, as will be explained in the midrash later on.[62]

The new category of primal faith is introduced to verify the eternal nature of the covenant, which is not susceptible to external defilement.[63] However, it also raises numerous issues which need to be addressed. First, how is this primal faith integrated into Areleh's earlier comment about faith being rooted in the first two commandments (the direct experience of God) as

60 For a full treatment of *hester panim* in *Shomer Emunim*, see 91b–94a.

61 I have translated *emunah peshutah* as "primary faith," rather than the more literal "simple faith," as it better represents the nature of Areleh's argument. Areleh's *emunah peshutah* is not likened to the simple faith of R. Nahman of Bratslav, for example, which is closer to an innocent or childish faith. This type of simple faith is also portrayed in R. Nahman's tale "The Wise Man and the Simpleton." Cf. *Sippurei Ma'asiyot: Rabbi Nahman's Tales*, trans. Aryeh Kaplan (Jerusalem, 1993), 160–96. Areleh has something else in mind which will serve as the foundation for his distinction between Abraham and Moses, to be discussed later in this chapter.

62 *Shomer Emunim* 51a. The midrash he is referring to is Exodus Rabbah 23:5, which states that the Israelites only merited praising God at the sea (*shirat ha-yam*) because of the faith exhibited by Abraham, their forefather. Thus the act which carries the Israelites from Egypt (exile) to Sinai (revelation/redemption) is a faith which precedes the experience at Sinai.

63 This bifurcation of faith in Areleh is often strikingly similar to Buber's "two-faith theory" in his *Two Types of Faith*. See, for example, Buber on 35, "We believe and know, that it is not two expressions of faith, but of two kinds of faith. For the first, faith is a position in which one stands, for the second it is an event which has occurred to me, or an act which one has effected or effects, or rather both at once." For Buber, the first kind of faith, or the faith of the Bible and early Judaism and Christianity, was faith as an existential stance (a faith that) and not faith in relation to something, i.e., doctrine or event. The latter faith was the faith in the Church and also the faith of Jewish principles (*ikkarei emunah*), which, according to Buber, are both influenced by the Hellenistic and not the biblical notion of faith.

opposed to the remaining commandments (via Moses)? Second, this new category of primal faith needs to be integrated into the dichotomy suggested between faith and Torah as two independent sources of Truth suggested above. Third, a subtle bifurcation is implied between Moses (Torah) and Abraham (faith) (as the representative of pre-Sinaitic religion), one which is not uncommon in ḥasidic literature, but has a unique and highly nuanced formulation in *Shomer Emunim*.[64] A final question raised by the category of primal faith is the status of Jewish non-belief. That is, if belief is something inherited rather than chosen or achieved,[65] wouldn't non-belief and non-Jewishness become synonymous? This question becomes even more pressing when viewed in light of Areleh's historical circumstances and the vehement anti-Zionism which grew out of his teachings.[66]

III

One of the clearest examples of Areleh's distinction between these two models of faith (apprehended and inherited) emerges from his reading of a midrashic statement about Moses' reaction to the Golden Calf:

---

64 For the most recent discussion of the place of Abraham (as representing preSinaitic Judaism) in ḥasidic thought, see A. Green, *Devotion and Commandment: The Faith of Abraham in the Ḥasidic Imagination* (Cincinnati, OH: University of Pittsburgh Press, 1989).

65 There is an important distinction to be made between faith being "chosen" or "achieved," a distinction which served as the basis for considerable medieval debate. On the question as to whether belief can be commanded, Hasdai Crescas, opposing the Maimonidean position of belief as commandment, argues that belief cannot be commanded because it is not the result of free will. See Hasdai Crescas, *Or Adonai*, Preface, 3a, ". . . the term *miẓvah* and its structure can only apply to something which is subject to will and choice. If it will be concluded that belief and opinions [*emunot vede'ot*] were not subject to will and choice, it follows that the term *miẓvah* cannot apply to them." For Maimonides' position, see the discussion in I. Twersky, *Rabad of Posquières: A Twelfth-Century Talmudist* (Cambridge, MA: Harvard University Press, 1962), 282–86. The status of Areleh's argument in this debate is uncertain. Can one argue that Areleh's primary faith is also not the product of choice and therefore not a commandment? Is so, the result would differ from Crescas's conclusion. Whereas for Crescas, faith may not be able to determine heresy since it is not given a choice, for Areleh, primary faith also may not be able to determine heresy, but it may be able to determine one's Jewishness!

66 For example, when visiting one of the leading families of the faction of *Naturei Karta*, led by the widow of R. Amram Blau, I noticed a small sign on the front door which said in English, Hebrew, and Arabic, "A Jew, not a Zionist."

> Another explanation: *Hear, O Israel*. What reason did Moses have for saying this point [at this particular time; my addition], *Hear O Israel*? The Rabbis say, "It is like a king who betrothed himself to a noble woman with two precious stones; when one of them was lost the king said to her, 'You have lost one, take care of the other.'" So God betrothed Israel to himself with the words, *We will do* [*na'aseh*] *and obey* [*nishma*] (Ex. 24:7). When they lost *We will do* in making the Golden Calf, Moses said to them: You have lost the *We will do*, observe then *We will obey*. Hence the assertion, *Hear O Israel*.[67]

Areleh responds with the following interpretation:

> It is brought in the Midrash Song of Songs (1:15), *Oh, give me the kisses of your mouth* (1:2). If Israel did not ask Moses, *you speak to us . . . and we will hear* [*ve-nishma*]; *but let not God speak to us, lest we die*[68] (Exodus, 20:16) they would have heard the entire Torah directly from God. They would never have forgotten it and the powers of evil would have never had dominion over them. But, since they already said, *you speak to us . . . and we will hear* [*ve-nishma*], evil returned to them, they suffered the episode of the Golden Calf,[69] and they became vulnerable to forgetting.[70] They returned to Moses and said, "he should kiss us with His mouth as before so that we will once again desire to hear his voice."[71] Moses responded, "this is not possible until

67 Deuteronomy Rabbah 3:10. Note a similar interpretation of Sinai and the Golden Calf used as a critique of Israel in pseudo-Paul's Epistle to the Hebrews 4:2, 3:16ff., and 5:19, "For good news came to us just as to them [the Israelites]; but the message which they heard did not benefit them, because it did not meet with faith in the hearers" (4:2).

68 There is an interesting correlation here between Israel's statement to Moses, fear of death, and God's command to Adam not to eat of the Tree of Knowledge, *for as soon as you shall eat of it, you shall die* (Genesis 2:17). The fear of death that the Israelites express is the result of their mortality, which was the punishment for the sin in the Garden as well as the reason for their exile. Cf. Genesis 3:22, 23, *And the Lord God said, "Now that the man has become like one of us, knowing good and bad, what if he should stretch out his hand and take also from the tree of life and eat, and live forever!" So the Lord God banished him from the Garden of Eden, to till the soil from which he was taken.* I would suggest that the sin in the Garden is the intertext to the episode of the Golden Calf in this midrashic rendition. Israel's fear, lest we die, may be the inverse of God's warning, *you shall die*.

69 I intentionally offered the literal translation, "they suffered the episode . . ." because it transmits what I think is Areleh's intention, i.e., that the power of evil is so pervasive that it infiltrates every element of Jewish existence except primal faith.

70 Although the midrashic use of "forgetting" may be literal, Areleh brings to it the kabbalistic notion of the concealment of *da'at* discussed above.

71 The midrashic rewriting of Song of Songs 1:2 is significant here. The verse itself has the individual asking her lover directly for the kiss. Israel, no longer able to address God

> the future [redemption] when we will [witness] the verse, *I will pour my Torah into their innermost being and inscribe it on their hearts . . .* (Jer. 31:33)" . . . If they wouldn't have sinned they would have fulfilled the entire Torah in a spiritual manner[72] the way it will be fulfilled in the future, it should come quickly in our time. This is what the Midrash means when it says, "you lost the *We will obey*." As a result the Torah was wrapped in a sack.[73] However, we still have the *We will hear*, which are the words, *I am the Lord your God and You shall have no other God . . .* We heard these voices and flashes from the mouth of God and the souls of Israel rose up with every word. The engraving of these words will remain forever with us . . .[74]

The Midrash uses the biblical poles of *we will do* and *we will obey* (lit. hear) to suggest that the loss of one, because of the Golden Calf, does not imply the loss of the other. Alternatively, sin does not invalidate the possibility of obedience in the future. The covenant contains a "safety net" which incorporates deviant behavior without having it destroy the divine/human relationship. Areleh offers a far more radical interpretation. The act of the Golden Calf destroyed the possibility of a direct encounter with God and subsequently forced the covenant to be reformulated, "in a sack," concealed and vulnerable to both forgetting and the demonic forces of creation. More significantly the poles of *we will do* and *we will obey* become the archetypes of Torah and primary faith. The element of the covenant which was damaged in the episode of the Golden Calf was *we will do*. Hence the Torah no longer carries the infallible nature of perfection. However, the alternative,

---

directly as the result of the Golden Calf, asks for the reinstitution of direct contact with God through Moses.

72 The spiritual manner to which Areleh refers is likely to be the way ḥasidic literature interprets the Torah of the Patriarchs and Matriarchs. This purely spiritualized Torah is initially motivated by the rabbinic assertion that Abraham performed all of the 613 commandments. This spiritualized model is also used to describe the Torah of Redemption in the medieval Kabbalah and Sabbatean doctrine, both of which may have influenced ḥasidic authors. For an example of this, see A. Cardozo, *Iggeret Magen Avraham* (Jerusalem, 1937), 134, as quoted in G. Scholem, *The Messianic Idea in Judaism* (New York: Schocken, 1971), 65.

73 This locution probably comes from BT Sanhedrin, "He who recites a verse from Song of Songs and treats it as a [secular] air . . . brings evil into the world, *for the Torah put on sackcloth*, appears before God and complains, 'Your children have made of me a fiddle played by scoffers . . .'" The talmudic discussion fits nicely into Areleh's critique of modern Torah scholarship, some of which indeed treats Song of Songs (as well as other sacred Scripture) in a secular manner. Compare with *Shomer Emunim* 54b, "When the *we will obey* was lost, the Torah was dressed in sackcloth, but the *we will hear* remained. These are the words, *I am the Lord Your God* and *There shall be no other . . .*"

74 *Shomer Emunim* 54a.

we will obey, was not damaged by the act of deviance but remained in its pristine state as a pure experience of God. The vocation of the "faithful" is to integrate and utilize the pure form of untainted faith into the vulnerable nature of Torah.[75] Moreover, the vulnerability of Torah rests in the intellect, which was convinced that Moses' disappearance was permanent, thus justifying to the Israelites that the Golden Calf was a viable alternative.

Even as Areleh distinguishes between the vulnerability of Torah and the immutability of primary faith, the latter only serves to purify and protect the former. The vulnerability of Torah rests on the fact that, as a written document, it can be studied without primary faith and thus defiled and distorted. To exemplify this point, he uses the oft-cited zoharic passage about the biblical narrative being the garment of Torah, leading level by level to the soul of Torah.[76] Although the Zohar and later the *Tikkunei Zohar* use this formulation to argue that the esoteric tradition is the soul of Torah or the only vehicle to reach the soul of Torah,[77] Areleh, not being interested in the exoteric/esoteric debate, suggests another interpretation. He invokes a Beshtian tradition to give an alternative reading to the zoharic formulation.

> See, my precious brothers, from the words of the Zohar, [about] the one who studies the holy Torah with this [primary] *emunah*, which contains the inside and the inside of the inside until eternity [*ein sof*]. He will merit in the future the soul of the soul of Torah.[78] The Ba'al Shem Tov explained the verse, *The*

---

75 The notion of faith being the archetypal *mizvah* did not originate with Areleh, but is adopted from earlier ḥasidic traditions. See R. Menahem Nahum of Chernobyl, *Me'or Einayim* (Jerusalem, 1984), "*likkutim*," 235a/b.

76 Zohar 3.152a. See a complete translation in *Zohar: The Book of Splendor*, ed. G. Scholem (New York: Schocken, 1963), 12lf. Cf. M. Fishbane, "The Garments of Torah-Or, To What May Scripture Be Compared," in *The Garments of Torah: Essays in Biblical Hermeneutics* (Bloomington: Indiana University Press, 1989), 33–46.

77 Late medieval and early modern Jewish mystical literature is replete with polemical tracts arguing for the superiority of Kabbalah. See, for example, Moses Cordovero, *Or Ne'erav*; R. Hayyim Vital's, "Introduction to *Sha'ar Hakdamot*" (printed as the introduction to *Eiẓ Ḥayyim*); R. Moshe Alsheikh, *Ayelet Ahavim*; and R. Moses Hayyim Luzzato's *Ḥoker u-Mekubal* and *Miḥemet Moshe*. For an analysis of the polemical nature of the later strata of the Zohar in particular, see Giller, *The Enlightened Will Shine: Symbolization and Theurgy in the Later Strata of the Zohar* (Albany: SUNY Press, 1993), esp. 59–81. Cf. R. Naftali ben Ya'akov Elhanan Hertz, *Emek ha-Melekh* (Amsterdam, n.d.), second introduction.

78 This refers to the redemptive Torah that cannot be apprehended until the messianic era. "But the truly wise, those who serve the highest King and stood on Mount Sinai, pierce all the way through to the soul, to the true Torah which is the principle of all. These same individuals will in the future be vouchsafed to penetrate to the very soul of the soul of the Torah." Cf. Zohar 3.152.

> *Torah of God is perfect* [*temimah*] . . . That is, it is still perfect [*tamim*] in that no one in creation has yet apprehended anything close to its great depths.[79]

The integration of the Beshtian notion of the Torah which is perfect [*tamim*] and the zoharic soul of Torah is very suggestive. The complete reference to the Besht's statement yields an even sharper correlation.[80] The Besht is reported to have said,

The hidden light is still *tamim* [perfect]. No one except perhaps a very few have ever apprehended it. *The Torah of God is perfect* . . . this means that this [perfect] realm of Torah is called the Torah of God and not the Torah of Moses. *Temimah*: this means that it is not the way of the many to reach this level. However, in our generation each complete individual [*adam ha-shalem*] must strive to reach this level.[81]

The perfection of the Torah of God as opposed to the Torah of Moses in the Besht's statement suggests that the former is untouched by mankind, concealed only to be revealed in the future.[82] The zoharic "soul of the soul of Torah" is similar, although the Zohar implies that only through the soul of the Torah, i.e., the Zohar itself, can the redemptive Torah be realized.[83] Areleh adds yet another component, one which is absent in both the Zohar

---

79 *Shomer Emunim* 81b, 82a.

80 See R. Menahem Nahum of Chernobyl, *Me'or Einayim* 161a.

81 An earlier precedent to the Besht's statement can be found in R. Abraham Azulai's *Ḥesed le-Avraham* (Jerusalem, n. d.), 2:11, 49–51, cited in Fishbane, *Garments of Torah*, 35, "But when mankind will rise up from its physical condition to a subtler [spiritual] state, so will the material manifestation of the Torah be altered and its spiritual essence be apprehended in even higher levels of reality . . . [Then] the concealed faces of the Torah will shine and the righteous will meditate on them. But in all this the Torah remains one [and the same] . . . [for] its essence never changes." Cf. another version of this statement in R. Ya'akov Yosef of Polonnoye, *Toldot Ya'akov Yosef* (Jerusalem, 1973), 1:123d, and R. Meshullan Feibush Heller of Zbaraz, *Yosher Divrei Emet* (Jerusalem, 1974), 4b, in the name of Menahem Mendel of Premishlan.

82 This is what is implied in its initial formulation in *Tikkunei Zohar*. See *Tikkunei Zohar im Peirush ha-Gra* (Jerusalem, 1979), 5b, "There is a Torah of Creation [*beriah*] and a Torah of Emanation [*aẓilut*]. The Torah of Creation is (Proverbs 8:22): *The Lord created me at the beginning of His course* . . . The Torah of Emanation is (Psalms 19:8): *The Torah of the Lord is perfect* [*temimah*], *renewing life* . . . and, *You must be complete* [*tamin*] *with the Lord your God* (Deut. 18:13)." On the term *tamim*, the Gra comments, "In its soul there exists no blemish."

83 The Jewish mystical formulations of Torah in general and the study of Torah as a redemptive act is a complex issue. See L. Fine, "Recitation of Mishnah as a Vehicle for Mystical Inspiration: A Contemplative Technique Taught by Hayyim Vital," *Revue des etudes juives* (1982): 1–2, 183–99, and M. Idel, "The Concept of Torah in Heikhalot Literature and its Metamorphosis in Kabbalah" [Hebrew], *Jerusalem Studies in Jewish Thought* 1 (1981): 23–84.

and the Besht. He suggests a triadic formula between 1) the innermost parts of the zoharic Torah, the yet unrevealed "soul of the soul of Torah"; 2) the Beshtian formulation of the perfect yet unknown Torah; and 3) his notion of primary faith as the inherited remnant of the direct experience with God at Sinai. Whereas the Zohar suggests that the study of the esoteric tradition will yield the unfolding of "the soul of the soul" of Torah, Areleh, in true ḥasidic fashion, argues that only through the study of the exoteric garment relying on the pristine primary faith (*emunah peshutah*) can the innermost dimensions of Torah be revealed. The study of Torah without this element of primary faith will lead to heresy (or, perhaps *is* heresy) in that the unity of Torah with the direct experience at Sinai is severed.

Areleh's definition of heresy is an important component in his presentation. As stated above, heresy is the act of study which is not integrated with primary faith. This faith is based on 1) the divine nature of Torah and 2) the belief that the sages correctly interpret that Torah (*emunat ḥakhamim*).[84] "One of the 48 ways in which the Torah is acquired is through faith in the sages [*emunat ḥakhamim*] (Mishnah Avot 6:5). By means of faith in the sages and binding oneself to [their words], one binds oneself to the realm of Moses, who embodies knowledge [*da'at*]. Through that, one is bound to the *da'at* of God."[85] The difference between legitimate Torah study and heresy is the difference between analytic and synthetic methodology. The analytic method attempts to break Torah into distinct components, historically determined and affected by external influences. This is how Areleh interprets the talmudic prediction that "Torah will be forgotten in Israel." *Wissenschaft* scholarship, so prominent in his day, was seen as the epitome

---

84 Both of these principles are included in Maimonides' Thirteen Principles of Faith. It is interesting that Areleh never evokes Maimonides in this regard. Perhaps it is because Maimonides' focus on the intellect as the matrix of divine worship counters Areleh's vision of the intellect as the very realm where defilement takes place. See, for example, Areleh's statement in *Shomer Emunim* 55a, "[It states in BT Baba Mezia 84a] that 'the beauty [*shufrah*] of Abraham was similar to the beauty [*shufrah*] of Adam.' This comes to teach us that one who acts from the trait of truth and simplicity [*emet* and *temimus*, the traits of Jacob] will receive the light of the image of God [*ẓelem elokim*]." For the rabbinic source of Jacob as *emet* and *tamim*, see BT Yevamot 61a. Compare with kabbalistic sources in E. R. Wolfson, "The Image of Jacob Engraved Upon the Throne: Further Reflection on the Esoteric Doctrine of the German Pietists," in Wolfson, *Along the Path* (Albany: SUNY Press, 1995), 1–62. Compare this to Maimonides' view of *ẓelem elokim* in *Guide for the Perplexed* 1:1. On the larger issue of faith in the sages in Jewish thought, see S. Rosenberg, "*Emunat Ḥakhamin*," in *Jewish Thought in the Seventeenth Century*, ed. I. Twersky, B. Septimus (Cambridge, MA: Harvard University Press, 1978), 285–343.

85 *Shomer Emunim* 49a.

of defiling the holy because it severed the connection between the direct experience of *I am the Lord your God* and *You shall have no other gods*, i.e., the Beshtian Torah of God from the Torah of Moses, which is the result of the Golden Calf. The counter methodology of synthesis is that which purifies the defiled Torah and unifies primary faith with the vulnerable Torah of Moses. Areleh defines the entire process of Torah study as the attempt to reveal the underlying unity in traditional Jewish literature.[86] Modernity is defined as the attempt to sever the connection between primary faith and Torah and, through analysis, to sever Torah from its divine source.[87] This heretical position of Torah study is countered by his interpretation of study as integrating primary faith, defined either as the first two commandments, the zoharic soul of the soul of Torah, the Beshtian Torah of God (as opposed to the Torah of Moses) or the synthetic method of traditional Torah study (*emunat ḥakhamim*) as opposed to the "modernization" of Torah by way of analysis. His counter-modern proposal contains two elements. First, it stands in unequivocal opposition to the modernization of Torah and, second, its primary focus is to protect the untouched "precious jewel" of primary faith by means of an introvertive piety even as the vulnerable "faith of knowledge" becomes defiled and blemished.

The predominance of Areleh's primary faith theory is founded on his important insight that the protection the *ẓaddik* once offered the Jewish people is no longer available. Statements like, "because of our sins, we are an orphaned generation, all manners of holiness no longer abide [with us],"[88] resonate in his treatise. In fact, it is plausible that his entire ideology of primary faith is built on the assumption that the righteous no longer protect the sanctity of Israel. "Know my brother, it is not only the *ẓaddikim* [who can bring one to the source], but every individual who asks from God with truth [*emet*] and simplicity [*temimut*] can be bound by God to the highest

86 *Shomer Emunim* 88a–89b.

87 This assertion is strikingly similar to the critique of modern Torah scholarship offered by R. Isaac Breuer in *Der neue Kuzari* (Frankfurt, 1934), 337 and 244, 249. For an English study of Breuer, see Alan Mittleman, *Between Kant and Kabbala* (Albany: SUNY Press, 1990), esp. 113–23. Another twentieth-century ḥasidic critique of modern scholarship can be found in the writings of R. Kalonymus Kalman Shapira of Piaseczno, one of the ḥasidic masters of the Warsaw ghetto, who was deported to Treblinka, where he subsequently perished just a short time after the liquidation of the ghetto. See Kalonymus Kalman Shapira of Piaseczno, *Mevo ha-She'arim*, printed in *Hakhsarat Avrakhim* (Jerusalem, 1972), esp. 18a–26b. Kalonymus Kalman presents a much more systematic critique of modern scholarship than we find in *Shomer Emunim*. For a study in English of Kalonymus Kalman, see Polen, *The Holy Fire*.

88 *Shomer Emunim* 89a.

source."[89] This plea of Areleh to an orphaned generation is the basis for his notion of inherited faith, a throwback to the individualistic faith of Abraham in place of the Mosaic model, which had the *ẓaddik* (Moses) interceding on Israel's behalf. "Now, in this generation, the fundamental repair [*tikkun*] depends on the strength of *emunah*. It should be a primary faith [*emunah peshutah*] . . . this is what we received from our ancestors. This is what we received from Abraham, who is called the leader of all believers. This is the faith that is inherited in every generation, a stake that can never be uprooted."[90] The subject of the verse in Habbakuk (2:4), *A righteous man will live in his faith*,[91] is alternatively depicted as Moses or Abraham, depending upon whether Areleh is speaking about the ideal world of Mosaic Judaism or the real world of orphaned (Abrahamic) Judaism. In the true Mosaic model, the primary faith of direct communication, *I am the Lord your God* and *You shall have no other gods*, is embodied in the *ẓaddik*. The underlying principle here is that Moses was the only individual able to withstand a direct encounter with God.[92] The primary faith of Abraham is inherited through Moses and thus transmitted to the people. However, when speaking about the orphaned generation of his contemporary world where the *ẓaddik* is absent, Areleh reverts back to the pre-Sinaitic primary faith of Abraham that each individual inherited through that one transcendent moment at Sinai.[93] This primary faith did not filter down into the Torah of Moses, i.e., the other 611 commandments, and only functioned as long as the *ẓaddik* as catalyst was present. Perhaps as a consequence of the Golden Calf and the need for the second set of tablets, a bifurcation took place between the Abrahamic faith and the Torah, "clothed in sackcloth." In such a world, the only path toward holiness, the only way to purify the defiled Torah is by means of this primary faith, the non-rational, supra-intellectual faith of Abraham.

---

89 *Shomer Emunim* 90b.

90 Ibid. Areleh's use of the word *avoteinu* (lit. fathers) implies the Patriarchs of Genesis as opposed to the leadership of Moses. Moses' generation was not an orphaned one but a generation guided by the leadership of a "faithful shepherd" who directed them in the ways of God. Abraham represents an individual who lived in a world without leadership, a world where the recognition of God was concealed and the world defiled with idolatry. He is viewed by tradition as the one who begins to reveal God's providence through his simple faith. Cf. Moses Maimonides, *Mishneh Torah*, "Laws of Idolatry" 1:1–6.

91 I have altered the translation suggested in the *New JPS Tanakh*, which reads, *But the righteous man is rewarded with life*, to highlight Areleh's subtle use of the passage.

92 See Maimonides, *Mishneh Torah*, "Laws on the Foundations of the Torah," ch. 8.

93 This notion of an "orphaned generation" may revert back to the Ba'al Shem Tov himself in the quote cited earlier where the Ba'al Shem says that "in our generation" we must strive to achieve the knowledge that was concealed from the previous generations.

At this juncture, we have a convergence of the first two commandments at Sinai and the pre-Sinaitic faith of the Patriarchs (represented by Abraham). Primary faith, the "root of roots" which begins with Abraham, is transmitted through the first two commandments, yet retreats when the collective intellect of Israel sins in the desert.[94] The experiential component returns with the reappearance of Moses (bearing the second tablets), but only remains as long as the *ẓaddik* (i.e., Moses) leads the people.[95] Once this is no longer the case, the orphaned generation, already living a life of Torah defiled by heresy and distortion (i.e., the Golden Calf), must utilize the primary faith concealed in their own consciousness in order to remain pure and to repair the world. When Areleh comes to speak about his present generation, he consistently refers to the idea of pristine Abrahamic faith:

> At present we are in a state [of defilement] and darkness which hasn't existed since Israel became a nation; anguish from all sides, the concealment of divine presence [*hester panim*], the influence of evil ones, outsiders [*ḥiẓonim*] and heretics [*apikorsim*] who seduce us from all sides; he who strengthens himself in his faith in God is praised and glorified and will receive unlimited merit, as it is written, *Behold, his spirit within him is not upright, but a righteous one will live in his faith* (Habakkuk 2:4).[96] This is established by means of the *emunah* which we inherited from Abraham, primary faith without reason. This is only accomplished by means of the simple will of the love of God which is implanted within us as an inheritance from our fathers and [contains] the strength of our belief in God, as it states in the midrash, "this is the faith that they [Israel] inherited."[97]

94 The kabbalistic term "retreat of consciousness" (*histalkut ha-moḥin*) usually refers to the three highest *sefirot*: *keter*, *ḥokhmah*, and *binah*. This higher consciousness is alluded to in *Shomer Emunim* to define the primary faith rooted in the experience of the first two commandments at Sinai. Although Areleh rarely uses kabbalistic terminology, this particular notion of retreat is based on the zoharic and later Lurianic concept of the retreat of the first three elements in any sefirotic cluster when threatened by extraneous forces (*kelippot*).

95 This notion of Moses is taken largely from the zoharic corpus. See, for example, *Tikkunei Zohar* 122a.

96 In this context, this verse is taken to mean that even when the spirit is not upright, faith will enable the righteous to endure.

97 *Shomer Emunim* 52a. The midrash referred to at the end of the above citation appears in Midrash Song of Songs Rabbah 4:8, "How did the Israelites merit [being made a gift to the Messiah brought by the nations]? It is by reason of the merit that they gained when they sang the Song of the Sea. R. Nahman said, 'It was by reason gained by the faith with which Abraham believed. *And he [Abraham] believed in the Lord* (Genesis 15:6)." Note that while the midrash presents these two possibilities (and various

According to Areleh, the only way to overcome the threat of defilement and darkness which pervades every dimension of modern society is to revert to the pristine faith of Abraham. Apparently this faith was both genetically inherited and experienced at Sinai, but had retreated or was concealed as a result of the episode of the Golden Calf. The *ẓaddik*, viewed as a spiritual descendant of Moses, was able to maintain this primary faith and transmit it to the community. Areleh's concern rests on his belief that the *ẓaddik* is no longer able to transmit pre-Sinaitic faith to his community.[98] Hence it becomes incumbent upon each individual to look inward and find the hidden core of primary faith dormant within each Jewish psyche. It is only this untouched and untainted "root of roots" that can insure the survival of the Jewish soul, the pure Torah, and the messianic era.

IV

The above discussion on the nature and fabric of primary faith according to Areleh enables us to attempt to understand his solution to the problems of his generation. His overarching claim that modernity is heresy and his ideological and behavioral prescription of introvertive piety now need to be addressed.

His uncompromising statements concerning the necessary aversion to heretical teaching or even viable teaching that comes from a heretic are founded on a philosophical and mystical principle which *ḥasidim* adopted from the Middle Ages.[99] Generally, this position argues that

---

other alternatives, as well) as opposing one another, Areleh cleverly invokes another midrashic tradition in Exodus Rabbah 23:5, where the Israelites only merit singing the Song of the Sea because of Abraham's faith. Hence, in Areleh's reading, the two possibilities in the Song of Songs Rabbah text are complementary not contradictory.

98 The *ẓaddik* becomes a model for the individual who also must go through a similar process. Cf. *Shomer Emunim* 52a, 53b, "*The righteous one lives in his faith* (Hab. 2:4). The *ẓaddik* sustains himself through *emunah*. Sometimes in primary faith, sometimes through feeling, sometimes through intellection . . . When his intellect and mind are disconnected from the feeling of divinity, he needs to utilize this primary faith which was inherited from Abraham who is the head of the faithful. Through this faith he merits to sustain [the world]."

99 See, for example, in *Toldot Ya'akov Yosef*, 1:124c, "I heard from my teacher [the Besht] [a reading of] (Genesis 44:18), *Then Judah went up to him and said, 'Please, my lord, let your servant appeal to my lord, do not be impatient with your servant, you who are equal to Pharaoh.'* It states in BT Berakhot (32a), 'One should always organize one's praises to God and only then pray.' In BT Avodah Zara (7b) we have a statement that implies the opposite. Our teacher explained it thus: It is written in Ramban [Nahmanides] that

the spiritual force of an individual is inextricably intertwined with his creative output and no possibility exists of deciphering or redeeming the holiness that is embedded in its defiled source. Any such attempt is doomed to failure. To underscore this notion Areleh offers an auto biographical confession:

> Now I will write, with God's help, certain specifics about guarding this "precious stone" [primary faith]. First of all, the most important element of guarding is not to have any contact with heretics and sectarians [*minim*]. Also, to avoid contact with those who are weak in faith, God forbid.[100] Many times I had personal dealings with these groups, my intention being to return them to truth and to nullify their defiled opinions. After a time, I felt a "cooling" in my own faith, may the Merciful protect us . . .[101]

The assumption that contact with wickedness (or, in our case, modernity) will implant seeds of evil even into the believer is a fundamental precept in Areleh's thinking. He cites various well-known ḥasidic traditions where the Ba'al Shem Tov "saw a vessel and was able to ascertain all of the thoughts that went into the making of that vessel. Also, all of the actions of the artisan of that vessel."[102] He utilizes this correlation between actor and

---

the power of the actor remains in the result of his action. The creation is engulfed in many garments [*livushim*], one on top of the other. A spark of holiness from God exists in all types of pain. However, [this spark] is engulfed in many layers." Cf. The Maggid of Mezritch, *Maggid Devarav le-Ya'akov* #122, 200, in the Schatz-Uffenheimer edition. It is noteworthy that both early sources use this idea to speak about the divinity in the material world. Areleh adopts this position to argue that the evil remains in the work of the wicked.

100 Compare this with Maimonides' *Mishneh Torah*, "Laws of Ethical Dispositions" 6:1, "The way of a man is to be drawn after the opinions and actions of his neighbors and friends and the behavior of the people in his community. Therefore, it is necessary to have contact with *ẓaddikim* and to constantly be in close proximity to sages in order to learn from their actions. One should distance oneself from the evil ones who walk in darkness in order not to learn from their actions." There is a substantive difference between Maimonides' behavioristic formulation as the more ontological formulation of Areleh. Maimonides is making an observation about human behavior, whereas Areleh is implying that the evil element inherent in the opinions of the wicked will defile and threaten the core of faith within any individual who contemplates these opinions. Maimonides, as is known, spent a great deal of time in the study of Greek philosophy and used extraneous modes of thinking in his interpretation of Judaism. Such activity would be anathema for Areleh.

101 *Shomer Emunim* 64a.

102 See also *Shomer Emunim* 42a, b; R. Yizḥak Isaac Yehiel of Komarno's commentary on *Ethics of the Fathers, Noẓer Ḥesed* (Jerusalem, 1982), #9, 117; and R. Yizhak Isaac Yehiel of Komarno, *Hekhel ha-Berakhah* (Lemberg, 1869), 1:238a.

action to render prohibitions against any interaction with secular society, noting, for example, that politics (*politik*) has the same numerical value as Amalek, the embodiment of evil in Jewish tradition.[103] Any opinion must be evaluated according to the status of the individual who expresses it, as what appears to be legitimate may contain hidden seeds of evil.[104]

> Therefore, if a wicked person writes a book, the reader of this book will be damaged by the evil power of that person. The students of the Besht warned us not to read any book whose author is not known. If his [the author's] faith in God is not strong it will be, God forbid, like poison to the soul who reads it, even if it contains wondrous casuistry [*pilpul*] and words of Torah and *mussar*.[105]

Although this idea is not uncommon in ḥasidic and non-ḥasidic ultra-Orthodox Judaism, it is used in a specific way by Areleh. The damage caused is the defilement of the "faith of knowledge" mentioned earlier. This secondary intellectual faith, already weakened by the episode of the Golden Calf, is by its nature susceptible to impurity and distortion. That means that the intellect, and thus the faith that is founded on the intellect, can be seduced by the heresy that is necessarily contained within the creative product of the heretic or weak of faith. Therefore, his warning not only applies to ingesting information through study but even to involvement in the political process, which would make one dependent in some manner on the transgressors.

His projection for survival has two mutually dependent components. First, to avoid contact with the all-pervasive evil by refraining from any activity which would put one in physical or intellectual contact with it.[106] Second,

---

103 *Shomer Emunim* 64a.

104 *Shomer Emunim* 68a. Areleh brings a legend in the name of R. Elimelekh of Lyzensk (1717–1786). It is reported that R. Elimelekh was attempting to find a tutor for his sons. He found an able individual, who began teaching. Soon, R. Elimelekh's sons began complaining that they didn't like the tutor and refused to learn from him. R. Elimelekh questioned the tutor about his teachers from his youth until he discovered that one of his teachers "held beliefs from 'outside books' [*sefarim ḥiẓonim*]." R. Elimelekh addressed the tutor, "Know my son, this is the reason that my sons do not want to learn from you. Your teacher who taught you [in your youth] held these beliefs and embedded this certain portion of wickedness in you when you were a child. Even though you have corrected [them] with your actions, that portion of evil which you received as a child has not been entirely uprooted. This is why my sons refuse to learn from you, from their great holiness not from their bad attitude, God forbid."

105 *Shomer Emunim* 67b, 68a. Cf. R. Zechariah Mendel of Ruslav, *Darkhei Ẓedek* (Lvov, 1796), #71.

106 Cf. R. Zvi Elimelekh Shapira of Dinov, *Derekh Pekudekha* (Lvov, 1851), seventh introduction, #5. R. Zvi Elimelekh uses this notion in reference to thoughts which

to protect the "precious jewel" of primary faith by covering oneself, both physically and spiritually, in garments of protection. Guarding (*shemirah*) becomes the behavioral counterpart and externalization of faith (*emunah*).

> This is what the Torah commanded, *Guard yourselves and guard your souls,*[107] *so that you do not forget the things that you saw with your own eyes and so that they do not fade from your mind as long as you live. And make them known to your children and your children's children* . . . (Deut. 40:4, 5). God's command concerning this guarding is that one should guard *emunah* so that we should not forget what our eyes saw at *Matan Torah*. This is what the verse is trying to convey. . .[108]

The plain-sense meaning of the verse is that the object to be guarded is the body of commandments, the Law. Areleh takes it to mean something quite different. Guarding, which he views as a central motif of divine worship,[109] beckons the already defiled "faith of reason" to move back into itself and simultaneously protect the still untainted primary faith from any contact with the outside world. The term "guarding" (*shemirah*), which in biblical and rabbinic parlance is accomplished by means of "fulfilling" (*kiyyum*), receives another nuance in Areleh's formulation. He views guarding as protecting, safeguarding the "precious jewel" of faith from the demonic forces of modernity which seek to distort it and seduce it, as the serpent seduced Eve in the Garden (Genesis 3:1–6) and as Esau attempted to seduce his father Isaac on his deathbed (Genesis 27:1–3).[110] In a sense, Areleh's inter-

---

would require repentance. "Therefore, it was commanded, *Do not go after your heart [desires]*. This means when, God forbid, an inappropriate thought arises [in your mind] one must strive to fulfill the commandment, do not go after your desires, i.e., one must try to push this thought from his mind. [However] Only when one recognizes the inappropriate nature of this thought can one fulfill the commandment, *do not go after your desires* . . ."

107 I have intentionally departed from the more conventional translation of this verse (*New JPS Tanakh*), which reads, *Take utmost care and watch yourselves scrupulously*. This translation renders *nafshekha* as emphatic and not referring to another object (i.e., the soul as opposed to the self). Areleh requires the distinction between self and soul as it fits into his dichotomy between "faith of reason" (self) and "primary faith" (soul). As he reads the verse, the commandment is to guard both elements of faith, hence "self" and "soul."

108 *Shomer Emunim* 67b.

109 For an in-depth analysis of this, see his *Shulḥan ha-Tahor*, "Essay on Modesty," 35b–45b. This topic requires a more detailed analysis which is beyond the scope of this chapter.

110 See Rashi *ad loc*. He cites the rabbinic presentation of a fictitious dialogue between Esau and Isaac where Esau attempts to deceive his father by asking what appear to be sincere questions but what are in reality questions of deception.

pretation of guarding as retreating yields the opposite result of the rabbinic formulation of guarding as fulfilling. The latter manifests itself as an outwardly performed act while the former means refraining from (inter) action in order to protect the pristine jewel of faith from external defilement.

For Areleh, exile in general and modernity in particular are due to the loss of memory. Loss of memory is the result of an extreme state of divine concealment (*hester panim*), the concealment of concealment (*hester betokh hester*). In its rabbinic usage this state of severe exile becomes manifest in two instances in biblical literature: The Israelites in Egypt before the appearance of Moses and the Jews in Shushan before the unfolding of their redemption in the Book of Esther. In both cases, the determining factor was that the victims of this loss of memory were unable to recognize their own deficiency. The irony behind both biblical instances as well as Areleh's depiction of his generation is that this darkened state is viewed as the necessary prelude to redemption.[111] Areleh uses this rabbinic model and integrates it into his system of thought. The loss of memory for Areleh is the inability to connect the Torah with the primary faith which lies at its core. Or, to evoke the Ba'al Shem Tov's categories mentioned earlier, the inability to connect the Torah of Moses with the Torah of God.[112] It does not necessarily mean that the Torah has been abandoned, although that may also be the case, but that it has been severed from its source and thus becomes the subject to modern analysis. The double sense of concealment in the midst of concealment (*hester betokh hester*) is interpreted as "the concealment of the presence of God [*panim*] and the concealment of faith [*emunah*]. Therefore, it is written, *I* [*anokhi*] *will hide* [*hastir astir*] *my face on that day* . . . The concealment of faith is hinted at in the word 'I' [*anokhi*]."[113] This concealed faith is the absence of the primary faith (*emunah peshutah*) transmitted directly to the Israelites through the first two commandments (*I* [*anokhi*] *am the Lord your God* . . .). The elimination of this primary faith leaves the body of Torah as fodder for the modern mind, where it will be severed from its sacred covenantal core.

Loss of memory as the double-layered nature of divine absence leads to Areleh's innovative interpretation of the divine presence in exile (*Shekhinah*

111 In rabbinic literature, this is exhibited in numerous ways. See, for example, Rabbi Akiva's response to the mourning of the destruction in BT Makkot 24b and the assertion that the Messiah is born on the day of the destruction in Lamentations Rabbah 1:15.

112 See above, n. 81.

113 *Shomer Emunim* 93b.

be-galut).[114] The overarching rabbinic motif views this phenomenon in an optimistic light, i.e., that the *Shekhinah* accompanies the people into exile and consequently suffers along with the exiled nation.[115] Divine exile enables the covenant to be maintained by a shared suffering, one which will eventually lead to return and redemption.

The exile of the *Shekhinah* became a popular model in early ḥasidic literature.[116] Aside from its more conventional usages, it was utilized in Ḥasidism as a motif to view the sacred nature of the travels of the itinerant preachers as following the exiled *Shekhinah* and redeeming her, as it were, by acts of kindness and words of Torah.[117] Areleh offers yet another ḥasidic reading which views the exile of Torah as the exiled *Shekhinah* who has become victim to the heretical and demonic clutches of the modern mind.

> Therefore, it is incumbent [upon us] to study the wisdom of God [*da'at elokut*]. The purpose is in order to guard and fulfill it. The study of kabbalah and the other forms of knowledge which emerge from the devotional [lit. sacred] life are also necessary. However, [remember] it is possible to be an empty hole void of divine wisdom, fear of God; this is all too easy. We now bear witness to the fact that our holy wisdom has been tossed to the trash . . . because of our many sins. As we have learned from our holy masters, this is what is meant by the *Shekhinah* in exile. Oh, the falseness and distortion that our eyes see. There is no one to speak to because our words will not enter those who are buried and lost in fraudulence.

---

114 Rabbinic literature is replete with sources referring to this idea, beginning with the departure of the *Shekhinah* after Adam's sin until the exile of the *Shekhinah* in Temple Worship. Cf. *Avot de-Rebbe Natan*, a, 34, 102; *Pesikta de-Rav Kahana*, Mandelbaum ed., 234; BT Rosh ha-Shanah 31a. For a listing and analysis of these and other sources, see E. Urbach, *The Sages* (Jerusalem: Magnes Press, 1979), 50–65; and I. Abelson, *The Immanence of God in Rabbinic Literature* (London: Macmillan, 1912).

115 See, for example, in BT Megillah 29b, *Sifrei Numbers* #84, and Numbers Rabbah, 7.

116 For some examples, see *Toldot Ya'akov Yosef*, 1:129b; R. Dov Baer, the Maggid of Mezritch, *Maggid Devarav le-Ya'akov*, ed. R. Schatz-Uffenheimer (Jerusalem, 1990), #172, 270–72; and Ze'ev Wolf of Zhitomir, *Or ha-Me'ir* (Jerusalem, 1995), 2:207, 298. For a comprehensive study of the development of this idea in rabbinic, philosophic, and kabbalistic literature, see G. Scholem, "The Feminine Element in Divinity," in *On the Mystical Shape of the Godhead*, trans. J. Neugroschel (New York: Schocken, 1991), 140–96.

117 See M. Piekarz, "The Messianic Idea in the Beginnings of Ḥasidim" [Hebrew], in *The Messianic Idea in Jewish Thought: A Study Conference in Honor of the 80th Birthday of Gershom Scholem* (Jerusalem, 1982), 241–42. This idea has recently been developed further by E. R. Wolfson in "Walking as a Sacred Duty: Theological Transformation of Social Reality in Early Ḥasidism," in *Along the Path*, 91, 92.

The *Shekhinah*, viewed as the Torah, has become the object of abuse and torture by its modern interpreters, emerging from the double-layered loss of memory mentioned above. This loss of memory, defined as the concealed state of primary faith which is the root of Torah, itself exiles the Torah. Redeeming the Torah (and redeeming the *Shekhinah*) comes about by 1) the study of Torah connected to primary faith—the synthetic rather than the analytic approach, and 2) redeeming the already defiled faith of reason by moving inward, thereby allowing it to be purified by the untainted pristine primary faith of Abraham, transmitted at Sinai as *I am the Lord your God . . .* The fate of the defiled is not his concern as their world is beyond repair, being "buried and lost in fraudulence."

In sum, Areleh presents an elaborate framework which serves as his basis for an inward piety which may be labeled "redemption by retreat." Modernity is seen as the fiftieth level of defilement after which redemption will emerge.[118] However, it is only those who protect the core rather than influence the many that aid in this inevitable but undetermined process. According to his theory, the demonic seduction of modernity is the force which severs God's word from the human experience of the divine and therefore must be simultaneously opposed and avoided at all cost. The popular reductionist rendition of this ideology as a severe and uncompromising critique of modernity does not do justice, in my view, to the nuanced and highly sophisticated formulation of its creator. This brief look at the ideological and exegetical underpinnings of this unique contemporary Jewish ultra-Orthodox figure yields, I believe, a fascinating portrait of one man's battle for purity in what he determined was a defiled yet ultimately redeemable world.

118 See *Shomer Emunim* 101a/b in the name of *Asirit ha-Afah*, R. Yizhak Isaac Yehiel of Komarno's commentary to *Sifra ba-Midbar* (Lemberg, 1848), ch. 3, #6.

Chapter 7

The Holocaust as Inverted Miracle: R. Shalom Noah Barzofsky of Slonim on the Divine Nature of Radical Evil

> "This trauma [of the Holocaust] should have produced some change in Jewish life. We felt that some change must come—new books should be written in a different way; a new theology should be created; a new image of Jew and of man should at least be sought for."
>
> —Elie Wiesel, *Conservative Magazine*, 1967

In 1966 the young Jewish theologian Richard Rubenstein published *After Auschwitz: Radical Theology and Contemporary Judaism*, a book that would simultaneously become one of the most maligned as well as important statements in post-Holocaust theology.[1] Although it is often known for its "death-of-God" theology, Rubenstein's early work asks the question that became the *sine qua non* of contemporary Jewish thought: Can covenantal theology bear the weight of Auschwitz? That is, can we successfully place the Holocaust within the biblical and rabbinic paradigm of reward and punishment or the theodicy of Job? Can we apply the prophetic rebuke of Israel during the fall of the First Commonwealth and the rabbinic justification for God's destroying the Second Temple to the war against the Jews in the

1 R. Rubenstein, *After Auschwitz: Radical Theology and Contemporary Judaism* (New York: Bobbs-Merrill, 1966). The expanded and revised second edition was published as *After Auschwitz: History, Theology and Contemporary Judaism* (Baltimore, MD: Johns Hopkins University Press, 1992).

twentieth century?[2] Put differently, is there a categorical difference between evil and radical evil?[3] While the former may be an instance of divine reciprocity founded on the principle of the covenant in the Hebrew Bible, is the latter a rupture which subverts the possibility of a covenantal theology?[4]

This chapter will address the broader question of spiritual authority as it relates to the ways in which sages, here a ḥasidic master in the latter half of the twentieth century, take upon themselves the authority to interpret historical events in ways that subvert and then reconstruct conventional notions of the covenant. That is, what is at stake in creating a new category, a category I will call "meta-covenantal" divine action, as a way of

---

2 This is not to say that rabbinic Judaism is bound to a simplistic theodicy. The rabbis express certain anti-theodicy positions that attenuate their overall commitment to covenantal theology. See Z. Braiterman, *(God) After Auschwitz* (Princeton, NJ: Princeton University Press, 1998), 35–59. On a recent penetrating examination of theodicy through commentaries to Job, see R. Eisen, *The Book of Job in Medieval Jewish Philosophy* (Oxford, UK: Oxford University Press, 2004). Cf. B. Lang, "Evil, Suffering and the Holocaust," in *The Cambridge Companion to Modern Jewish Philosophy*, ed. M. Morgan and P. Gordon (Cambridge, UK: Cambridge University Press, 2007), 277–99, esp. 278–85.

3 The distinction between evil and radical evil is a Kantian one deployed in a provocative way by Hannah Arendt in *Eichmann in Jerusalem*. Arendt argued that, in fact, almost all "historical" evil, including the evil perpetrated by Eichmann, was banal and not radical in that it was not the consequence of a full reflection of the character and consequences of the act. I am using the term in a different manner in an attempt to distinguish between acts that can be justified through the covenant and those which cannot. However, I am quite sympathetic to Eliezer Berkowitz's comment in *Faith after the Holocaust* that, experientially, the murder of one child, one human being, is as egregious as the murder of six million.

4 Rubenstein was maligned for his use of the term "death of God" as a Jewish theology. Most recently see S. T. Katz, "The Issue of Confirmation and Disconfirmation in Jewish Thought After the Shoah," in *The Impact of the Holocaust on Jewish Theology*, ed. S. T. Katz (New York: NYU Press, 2005), 17–18. Katz argues that Rubenstein's claim of the death of God is not verifiable because it is based on an empirical case determined by the Holocaust. But Rubenstein does not make an "empirical" argument at all. Rubenstein writes, "The vitality of death-of-God theology is rooted in the fact that it has faced more openly than any other contemporary movement the truth of the divine-human encounter in our times. In truth the divine-human encounter is totally non-existent" (*After Auschwitz*, 2nd ed., 250). Lest one think Rubenstein is making an "empirical" claim, he writes later on the same page, "I should like to suggest that, since this information has strictly phenomenological import, *we ought to formulate it in the viewpoint of the observer*. It is more precise that we live in the time of the death of God than to declare 'God is dead.' *The death of God is a cultural fact. We shall never know whether it is more than that* [my emphasis]." Rubenstein is making a phenomenological claim and never argues it is empirical. For him, what is relevant is the *experience* of the Holocaust and not simply its factuality.

acknowledging how a historical event (the Holocaust) cannot conform to a previous model of covenant, yet cannot alter that covenant either?[5] While there are no overtly practical (i.e., halakhic) implications in this move, I suggest there are potentially some very significant theological consequences, especially when one suggests, as Barzofsky does, that the theological work done by this event is the final absorption of messianic suffering which has held the Jews in check for over two thousand years. In some way this is as radical, perhaps even more so, than messianic claims which have been made throughout Jewish history. Barzofsky is not arguing for the advent of the Messiah (as did thinkers such as David Reuveni, Solomon Molkho, Nathan of Gaza, Abraham ha-Kohen Kook, and Menahem Mendel Schneersohn of Lubavitch, among many others) but for a new period of exilic Judaism now cleansed of the messianic suffering (*ḥevlei mashiaḥ*) that has plagued Israel for most of its exilic history. The potentially radical implications I will discuss below suggest a new approach to Judaism in light of a new paradigm, one that is no longer founded on the world's resistance embodied in the divine decree of messianic suffering. The audacity to make such an assertion, even by implication, in an ultra-traditional context, especially when based on the horrific death of six million Jews, marks Barzofsky as a spiritual leader worthy of attention.

I

Much of post-Holocaust theology subsequent to Richard Rubenstein's *After Auschwitz* relates in some way to its radical thesis that the Holocaust can only make sense if we erase the covenantal theology of traditional Judaism and reconfigure our understanding of God and human power.[6] Amos

---

5 It is significant to note that Barzofsky never openly states that the Holocaust cannot fit into the covenant nor does he offer any suggestion as to why that would be the case. (Is it the pure enormity of the event? Or its historical uniqueness?) However, his entire treatise is founded on the principle that we need another category to bear its weight. Whereas progressive post-Holocaust theologians either view the covenant as broken (Rubenstein) or in need of revision (Fackenheim, Berkowitz, Greenberg), Barzofsky offers a new covenantal category which he believes can bear the weight of the Holocaust and, more than that, do some important theological work toward redemption.

6 The influence of Mordecai Kaplan on Rubenstein is well known. Kaplan did not write a great deal about the Holocaust. However, we see his influence on Rubenstein in a short comment Kaplan made in his *The Religion of Ethical Nationhood* (London: Macmillan, 1970), 12, "In such books as *The Meaning of God in Modern Jewish Religion* and *Judaism without Supernaturalism*, this author [i.e., Kaplan] has expounded a new theology

Funkenstein understands it this way: "To the most courageous among recent theologians, the very meaninglessness of the Holocaust constitutes its theological meaning. To lose faith in the face of the Holocaust is itself, they say, a manner of faith, a positive religious act."[7] Following Funkenstein's reading, for Rubenstein to find "meaning" in the Holocaust within the traditional contours of the covenant would be an act of "bad faith" since it would require us to view Hitler as a messenger of God and thus undermine the covenantal notion of God's relationship to Israel.[8]

In some way, Rubenstein's thesis is an adaptation of Christian "death-of-God" theologians, most significantly Thomas Altizer, who argued that God's greatest gift to humanity was God's disappearance (emptying Himself of His own being through the crucifixion) in order for humanity to flourish.[9] This "atheistic Christianity" was not precipitated by any one historical event. Rather, the introduction of secularism and humanism as theological catego-

---

which confronts the main challenge of the Holocaust, the problem of evil." Referring to his own theological work, Kaplan suggests that while he did not write specifically on the Holocaust, his whole project of Reconstructionism (even though it began before the Holocaust) relates precisely to this human and Jewish tragedy and the theological problems it raises about Jewish existence. Cf. Kaplan, *The Religion of Ethical Nationhood*, 202, "Two spiritual eruptions of volcanic dimension took place in Jewish life during the twentieth century: the Holocaust of the gas chambers and the establishment of the State of Israel. The first rendered the traditional idea of God untenable; the second rendered the traditional conception of normative Judaism as limited to the Land of Israel unacceptable."

7 A. Funkenstein, "Theological Responses to the Holocaust," in his *Perceptions of Jewish History* (Berkeley: University of California Press, 1993), 329.

8 This would be true, it is argued, even in light of Ezekiel 38 and other prophetic texts that predict God's wrath on Israel, because for most post-Holocaust theologians the Holocaust is *sui generis* and thus not simply an extension of these prophetic predictions. I am not suggesting that Rubenstein was the first to venture into the virgin territory of post-Holocaust theology in 1966. In fact, Rubenstein wrote numerous papers as early as 1961 relating to the Holocaust. Ignaz Maybaum published *The Face of God after Auschwitz* in 1965 in the Netherlands, a book largely ignored by American Jewish thinkers. And Emil Fackenheim's first essays on the Holocaust pre-date his early work *God's Presence in History*. However, it is likely that the theological thinking about the Holocaust before 1966 was not the result of a cohesive communal discourse but rather isolated thinkers working independently. In some sense, after the appearance of *After Auschwitz* these independent voices begin to cohere into a common, albeit not harmonious, discourse. I want to thank my colleague Michael Morgan for these insights.

9 See, for example, T. J. J. Altizer, *The Gospel of Christian Atheism* (Philadelphia: Westminster Press, 1966). For Rubenstein's assessment of Altizer, see Rubenstein, "Thomas Altizer's Apocalypse," in *The Theology of Thomas Altizer: Critique and Response*, ed. John Cobb (Philadelphia: Westminster Press, 1970); and *After Auschwitz*, 2nd ed., 249–55.

ries among radical Christian thinkers in post-war America, inspired, in part, by Paul Tillich, coupled with Altizer's thesis about the crucifixion and the disappearance of God, served as the basis for a radical theological revisioning.[10]

Rubenstein adopts this model as a theological response to a historical event of meta-historical proportions. For Rubenstein "death-of-God" theology is not based on any empirical datum but is a phenomenological construct, an attempt to save Judaism from hopeless apologetics or obsolescence, both of which he believes are inevitable when trying to theologically conform the Holocaust into a covenantal framework. Yet his adaptation is not to celebrate the liberation of the human from the divine, as Altizer does, but rather to view the "death of God" as a tragic description of the human condition after the Holocaust—a description in which the frailty of the human being is a mirror image of the frailty of God.[11] Moreover, Rubenstein never made the blanket assertion, as did Nietzsche and Hegel before him, that "God is dead," even though he may mean something quite similar to both.[12] He writes (in the first edition of *After Auschwitz*): "No man can really say that God is dead. How can we know that? Nevertheless, I am compelled to say that we live in the time of the death of God. This is more a statement about man and his culture than about God. The death of God is a cultural fact [. . .] When I say we live in the time of the death of God, I mean that the thread uniting God and man, heaven and earth, has been broken."[13] This broken thread, he asserts, is the result of not being

---

10 For an argument confirming the death-of-God theology as an extension of Christianity but utterly incompatible with Judaism, see E. Berkowitz, *Faith after the Holocaust* (New York: Ktav, 1973), 50–63. The question of atheistic theology was largely born from Martin Heidegger's ontology, adapted by his more theological disciples (e.g., Tillich, Bultmann), and was not lost on Jewish thinkers even before Heidegger. See, for example, Franz Rosenzweig's 1914 essay, "Atheistic Theology," in *Franz Rosenzweig: Philosophical and Theological Writings*, ed. and trans. P. W. Franks and M. Morgan (Indianapolis, IN: Hackett, 2000), 10–24.

11 Rubenstein distanced himself even further from his 1966 position in the 1992 second edition of *After Auschwitz*, xii. For a sensitive and compelling rereading of Rubenstein, see Braiterman, *(God) After Auschwitz*, 87–111.

12 It is, of course, true that neither Hegel nor Nietzsche used this phrase to make an empirical claim. Both, in fact, probably adopted it from Luther, who used it as a reference to Jesus before the resurrection. In this case, Rubenstein is using this term in a way similar to how Nietzsche used it in his *Thus Spoke Zarathustra*. Hegel's use of the term in his *Phenomenology of Spirit* applies it to "the unhappy consciousness" in contrast to *Geist* or the divine as it exists in the world. I want to thank my colleague Paul Eisenberg for some clarification on this matter.

13 Rubenstein, *After Auschwitz*, 1st ed., 151–52. Cf. R. L. Rubenstein and J. K. Roth, eds., *Approaches to Auschwitz: The Holocaust and its Legacy*, rev. ed. (Louisville, KY: Westminster John Knox Press, 2003), 342.

able to make theological sense of the Holocaust from the perspective of covenantal theology. Post-Holocaust theologians following Rubenstein (and post-Holocaust theology in its early stages was for the most part a critical response to Rubenstein) largely focus on the notion of covenant—its frailty and the possibility of its repair.

Post-Holocaust theologians, such as Emil Fackenheim, Irving Greenberg, and Eliezer Berkowitz, among many others, struggled to make theological sense of the Holocaust, that is, radical evil, through attenuated covenantal theologies.[14] Each posits that the Holocaust is unprecedented (theologically, historically, or both) and hence requires reassessment of the covenant but not its abolition.[15] Viewing Rubenstein's thesis as the end of covenantal Judaism, each theologian claims to salvage the covenant

---

14 For Fackenheim, see *God's Presence in History* (New York: Harper & Row, 1972), and *The Jewish Return Into History: Reflections in the Age of Auschwitz and a New Jerusalem* (New York: Schocken, 1978). Cf. Michael Morgan's thoughtful rendition of Fackenheim in Morgan, *Beyond Auschwitz: Post-Holocaust Jewish Thought in America* (Oxford, UK: Oxford University Press, 2001), 155–95. For Greenberg see, for example, "Cloud of Smoke, Pillar of Fire: Christianity and Modernity after the Holocaust," in *Auschwitz: Beginning of a New Era?*, ed. E. Fleishner (New York: Ktav, 1977), 1–55; "Judaism and History: Historical Events and Religious Change," in *Ancient Roots and Modern Meanings*, ed. J. V. Diller (New York: Bloch, 1978), 43–63; "The Third Great Cycle of Jewish History," *Perspectives* (September, 1981). For Berkowitz, see *Faith after the Holocaust* and *With God in Hell: Jerusalem in the Ghettos and Death Camps* (New York: Sanhedrin Press, 1979).

15 For a concise definition of the uniqueness of the Holocaust in Fackenheim, see his *To Mend the World* (Bloomington: Indiana University Press, 1994), 11–13. Katz rightly claims that "[. . .] the Fackenheim who hears 'a commanding voice from Auschwitz' is the Fackenheim who already stands within the covenantal affirmation (S. T. Katz, "The Issue of Confirmation," 21). Berkowitz's position is more complicated. On the one hand, he denies that Auschwitz is theologically "unique." For example, in *Faith and the Holocaust*, 90, he writes: "From the point of view of the problem, we have had innumerable Auschwitzes [. . .] While the consequences of the second destruction of the Temple have been more grievous than that of any of the other tragedies, it is of course true that in magnitude of human suffering and degradation nothing equals the tragedy of the German death camps. Yet the problem of faith of the survivors of any of those catastrophes was not different from the problem which confronts us in our days." On the other hand, he cannot support the ultra-Orthodox position that the Holocaust conforms to any traditional theodicy: "[. . .] looking at the entire course of Jewish history, the idea that all this has befallen us because of our sins is an utterly unwarranted exaggeration. There is suffering because of sins; but that all suffering is due to it is simply not true. The idea that the Jewish martyrology through the ages can be explained as divine judgment is obscene. Nor do we for a single moment entertain the thought that what happened to European Jewry in our generation was divine punishment for sins committed by them. It was injustice absolute; injustice countenanced by God" (*Faith After the Holocaust*, 94).

without arguing that Hitler was simply a tool of God (something that, within a covenantal framework, all must confront, yet none can accept).[16] Amos Funkenstein puts it this way: "Jewish theologians [. . .] such as Emil Fackenheim or E. Berkowitz, admit that they can see no theological rationale to the Holocaust. The Holocaust is incomprehensible, they say, and defies all theodicies. But they do find a theological meaning in the survival of the nation and the rebirth of the State. In both they find a confirmation of the divine presence and a promise to preserve Israel."[17] That is, for most if not all post-Holocaust theologians, the covenant may be fractured but it is not broken, the Jewish State being the sign of its survival. The creation of the Jewish State may be the very condition of post-Holocaust theology after Rubenstein. According to Funkenstein's reading, in these thinkers the metaphysical foundation necessary for (covenantal) theodicy is replaced by the socio-political foundation of national survival. Whether one agrees or disagrees with Funkenstein, his observation regarding the paradigmatic shift from metaphysics to socio-political analysis speaks to the ways in which these post-Holocaust theologians reject both Rubenstein's "atheistic" theology and the *ḥaredi* responses that the Holocaust can be, and must be, viewed solely through a traditional covenantal framework.

Ultra-Orthodox responses to the Holocaust, during and after the war, are less threatened by the event and more able, given that community's theological commitments and disdain for modernity, to offer more conventional, if provocative, assessments of the Holocaust and its message for the future.[18] These responses fall into at least three categories: (1) those who view the

16 Rubenstein first made this assertion in his contribution to a symposium on "The Conditions of Jewish Belief" in *Commentary Magazine* in 1966: "It [Judaism] has interpreted every major catastrophe in Jewish history as God's punishment of a sinful Israel. I fail to see how this position can be maintained without regarding Hitler and the SS as instruments of God's will." This formulation can be found in Rubenstein, *After Auschwitz*, 1st ed., 144–53. Katz puts it this way: "Fackenheim, like Richard Rubenstein and most other 'Holocaust theologians,' categorically rejects any attempt to give a casual explanation of the Holocaust in terms of any answer borrowing from traditional theodicy. Auschwitz is not a punishment for sin; it is not divine judgment; it is not moral education *a la* Job [. . .]" (Katz, "The Issue of Confirmation," 20). On Berkowitz's explicit response to Rubenstein, see Berkowitz, *Faith after the Holocaust*, 50–66.

17 Funkenstein, "Theological Responses to the Holocaust," 310, 311.

18 Most recently see S. T. Katz, S. Biderman, and G. Greenberg, eds., *Wrestling with God: Jewish Theological Responses during and after the Holocaust* (Oxford, UK: Oxford University Press, 2007). The volume contains a series of translations, published in English for the first time, of many of the major *ḥaredi* responses to the Holocaust before, during, and after the war. These responses have a myriad of classical sources on which to build their position. For example, R. Ammi's oft-cited statement in BT Shabbat 55a: "There is no death without sin and no suffering without transgression."

Holocaust as divine punishment for secularism, specifically Zionism (e.g., Elhanan Wasserman, Yoel Teitelbaum, and Yosef Yizhak Schneersohn);[19] (2) those who view the Holocaust as punishment for the Jews' unwillingness to leave Europe and immigrate to Palestine after the Balfour Declaration in 1917 (e.g., Ya'akov Moshe Harlap, Zvi Yehuda Kook, Yissachar Shlomo Teichthal, and Mordecai Yehoshua Attiah);[20] (3) those who view the Holocaust as just deserts for the "sinners" (secularists, Zionists) but cannot accept any theodicy justifying the death of the righteous. That is, the covenant *can* withstand the Holocaust as punitive for the "sinners" but *not* for

---

This is cited and affirmed (with some caveats) by Maimonides in *The Guide for the Perplexed* 3:17.

19 See G. Greenberg, "Elhanan Wasserman's Response to the Growing Catastrophe in Europe," *The Journal of Jewish Thought and Philosophy* 10 (2000), 171–204; Greenberg, "Faith, Ethics and the Holocaust: Orthodox Theological Responses to Kristallnacht: Chaim Ozer Grodzensky and Elhanon Wasserman," *Holocaust and Genocide Studies* 3 (1988), 431–41. Cf. E. Schweid, *Bein Ḥurban le-Yeshu'ah* (Tel Aviv, 1994), 15–38. On R. Yosef Yizhak Schneersohn see his "Four Proclamations," in *Wrestling with God*, 172–90, and Schweid, *Bein Ḥurban*, 39–64. Schweid argues, for example (34), that R. Teitelbaum did not find the Holocaust a theological challenge at all. What he found a challenge was the establishment of a secular Jewish State after the Holocaust.

20 On Teichthal, see *Eim ha-Banim Semeikhah* (Israel, 1963). On Attiah, see Greenberg, "Mordekhai Yeshua Atiyah's Kabbalistic Response to the Holocaust" (forthcoming). I want to thank Gershon Greenberg for making this essay available to me. For Ya'akov Moshe Harlap's position see his *Mei Merom: Mi-maynei ha-yeshu'ah*; G. Greenberg, "The Holocaust Apocalypse of Ya'akov Moshe Harlap," *Jewish Studies* 41 (2002), 57–66; and D. Michman "*Historiyah u-ge'ulah: Bituyim li-meshiḥiyut Yehudit Ortodoksit be-tom Milḥemet ha-Olam ha-Sheniyah*," in *The Holocaust in Jewish History: Historiography, Consciousness, Interpretations*, ed. Michman (Jerusalem: Yad Vashem, 2005). 181–210. For Zvi Yehuda Kook, see Z. Y. Kook, *Discourse of Rabbi Zvi Yehuda Kook, Tazri'a-Meẓora, Yom ha-Shoah*, ed. S. Aviner (Jerusalem, n. d.). Cf. D. Solomon, *Torat Ereẓ Yisrael: The Teaching of Rabbi Zvi Yehuda Kook* [Hebrew] (Jerusalem, 1991), ch. 10. Another important religious Zionist position that challenges Z. Y. Kook's use of his father's teachings to explain the Holocaust is that of Rabbi Yehuda Amital. See his *Ha-Ma'alot mi-Ma'amakim* (Jerusalem and Alon Shevut, 1974); Amital, "Confronting the Holocaust as a Religious and Historical Phenomenon" [Hebrew], *Alon Shevut Bogrim* 12 (1999), 45–54, and translated in M. Maya, *Olam Banuy ve-Ḥarev u-Banuy* (Alon Shevut, 2002). In English, see M. Maya, *A World Built, Destroyed and Rebuilt*, trans. K. Fish (Jersey City, NJ: Ktav, 2004). On the comparison of Zvi Yehuda Kook and Yehuda Amital, see Maya, *A World Built*, 66–74. In general, see A. Brill, "Worlds Destroyed, Worlds Rebuilt: The Religious Thought of Rabbi Yehuda Amital," *Edah Journal* 5 (2006). The notion of the Holocaust as being the punishment or consequence of Jews' attachment to the Diaspora does not only exist among religious Zionists but secular Zionists as well. See, for example, A. Eisen, *Galut: Modern Jewish Reflections of Homelessness and Homecoming* (Bloomington: Indiana University Press, 1986), 154, 155. Cf. M. Giuliani, *Theological Implications of the Shoah* (New York: Peter Lang, 2002), 195–206.

the righteous. For them, silence is the only response (e.g., Shlomo Zalman Unsdorfer, Shlomo Zalman Ehrenreich).[21] In each case, historical reality more or less aligns itself with a theological/covenantal category which justifies divine retribution or suffering as a necessary dimension of *tikkun*.[22] While for at least some of these thinkers (e.g., Unsdorfer and Ehrenreich) the Holocaust does present a theological dilemma, it does not present a theological crisis.[23] A full-blown theological crisis only emerges when two conditions are met simultaneously: first, the belief that the Holocaust was an unprecedented event in human/Jewish history; and second, that this unprecedented event must not irrevocably rupture the covenantal framework established in the Hebrew Bible.[24] The crisis is born from the ostensible incompatibility of these claims. If the event is unprecedented (that is, unique) how can it be interpreted solely within the theological parameters of the covenant? One response is that the covenant is a theological and not a historical category. Hence, to claim that the Holocaust can be a historical *novum* does not necessarily speak to its theological uniqueness.[25] It could be, perhaps, a historical manifestation of an ontological truth never before revealed. Following this reasoning, the historical uniqueness may

21 See G. Greenberg, "Shlomo Zalman Unsdorfer: With God through the Holocaust," *Yad Vashem Studies* 31 (2003), 61–94. For Ehrenreich's position, see G. Greenberg, "Shlomo Zalman Ehrenreich's Religious Response to the Holocaust," *Studia Judaica* 9 (2000), 65–93; *Wrestling with God*, 61–72. For yet another approach that pits history vs. meta-history, see I. Breuer, *Moriah* (Jerusalem, 1954), selections translated by G. Greenberg in *Wresting with God*, 111–19. Cf. A. Mittleman, *Between Kant and Kabbala* (Albany: SUNY Press, 1990), 162. Also see Yehuda Amital's somewhat unconventional rendering of the Holocaust within an Orthodox/Zionist framework. His work on this topic is examined and analyzed in Maya, *Olam Banuy*, 14–22.

22 See, for example, the comment in A. Ravitzky, *Ḥeirut al ha-Luḥot* (Tel Aviv: Am Oved, 1999), 109–10.

23 There are many passages that one can use to view the Holocaust within covenantal theology. For a salient example see Jeremiah 32:26–30.

24 The question of uniqueness is a vexing one and the subject of much debate. For example, see S. T. Katz, "Defining the Uniqueness of the Holocaust: Preliminary Clarifications and Disclaimers," in his *Historicism, the Holocaust, and Zionism* (New York: NYU Press, 1992), 162, 192. For our *ḥaredi* thinkers, the question of uniqueness does not enter into Katz's analysis of the moral, phenomenological, logical, and historical notion of the term. Rather, for them the question is more straightforward: can God introduce an event in the history of Israel that would rupture the covenant and require Jews to radically rethink the feasibility of that covenant for the future? That is, can an event make traditional approaches to both theodicy and anti-theodicy obsolete? In almost all cases, the *ḥaredi* response is an emphatic "no," although I will argue that Barzofsky moves quite close to agreeing in principle with Rubenstein's initial claim, while offering a meta-covenantal and not a non-covenantal solution.

25 See S. T. Katz, "Defining the Uniqueness," 163–64.

give rise, or make manifest, a new dimension of the covenant, for example, Fackenheim's "commanding voice of Auschwitz" or Irving Greenberg's notion of a new "voluntaristic covenant."[26] The covenant can be renewed but it must remain intact: this is the general response to Rubenstein's more radical assessment among post-Holocaust theologians.

In this chapter I analyze a *ḥaredi* post-Holocaust theology that has gotten little attention in the scholarly world.[27] In the 1970s and 1980s Rabbi Shalom Noah Barzofsky (1911- 2000), the grand rabbi of the Slonim ḥasidic dynasty and author of the popular multi-volume *Netivot Shalom* commentary on the Pentateuch and Festivals, wrote a series of essays dealing with the Holocaust that were subsequently, in 1987/88, collected and published in a small book entitled *Ha-Hareigah Alekha*.[28] While this work is a collection of material published elsewhere, it presents a fairly consistent, albeit not monolithic, picture of his understanding of the Holocaust in light of traditional covenantal categories.[29] I will argue that upon close examination Barzofsky fundamentally parts ways with his *ḥaredi* colleagues and comes quite close to Rubenstein's initial claim of the Holocaust as standing outside any covenantal framework. His conclusions are obviously different from Rubenstein's, but in some way Barzofsky cuts what may be a new position whereby the covenant forged at Sinai cannot include an event such as the Holocaust, that is, there is room for evil (the destruction of the Temples, the Crusades, etc.) but no room for radical evil (the Holocaust). The reason is not because God is "dead" (Rubenstein) or "concealed" (Berkowitz) but because the event itself is not "historical" in any covenantal sense and thus its very existence lies beyond the reciprocal relationship between God and Israel. By being not "historical" I do not mean that it did not happen.

---

26 See S. T. Katz, "The Issue of Confirmation," 21, and Fackenheim, *Quest for Past and Future* (Boston, MA: Beacon Press, 1963), 10.

27 For a preliminary discussion on Barzofsky on the Holocaust, see G. Greenberg, "Ultra-Orthodox Jewish Thought about the Holocaust since World War II," in *The Impact of the Holocaust on Jewish Theology*, 145–47.

28 The book was conceived by Shmuel Azreil Schwartzman, a Holocaust survivor who decided to publish Barzofsky's essay, "*Al ha-Hashmadah ve-ha-Ḥurban*," an introduction to a larger work, *Zikhron Kodesh*. This essay was written around 1970. Schwartzman then collected various other chapters and essays related to the Holocaust by Barzofsky and published them together as *Ha-Hareigah Alekha* (referred to in this chapter as *HA*) in 1987. For a general portrait of Barzofsky, see A. Nadler, "*Ha-Sinteza ba-Ḥasidut Slonim: Bein Ḥasidut le-Limmud Torah be Nusaḥ ha-Mitnagdim*," in *Yeshivot u-Vatei Midrashot*, ed. I. Etkes (Jerusalem, 2006), 395–415.

29 Barzofsky's approach is dealt with briefly in G. Greenberg, "Ultra-Orthodox Reflections on the Holocaust: 1945 to the Present," in *Contemporary Responses to the Holocaust*, ed. K. Kweit and J. Matthaus (Westport, CT: Greenwood, 2004), 87–89.

Rather, I mean that it is not an event that can square with Israel's notion of history as covenant. That is, for one who exists within a strong covenantal framework, all history is covenantal history and thus anything that happens to the Jews outside the covenantal framework is simply not "historical." More strongly, perhaps, nothing can happen outside that covenantal framework. Yet Barzofsky claims that, in fact, the Holocaust *did* happen outside that framework. This is where he begins.

While there are many prophetic texts which can be deployed to illustrate the relationship between Israel, covenant, and history, Maimonides, in his *Mishneh Torah*, expresses this link most succinctly and unambiguously:

> It is a positive commandment to cry out and blow trumpets (Numbers 10:9) in response to all catastrophes that affect the community [. . .] This is the way of repentance. When catastrophe comes and [the Jews] cry out [. . .] it will become known that this catastrophe is the result of Israel's sinful ways [*ma'aseihem ha-ra'im*] as it is written, *It is your iniquities that have diverted these things, your sins have withheld the bounty from you* (Jeremiah 2:25). This will cause the catastrophe to depart from their midst.
>
> However, if they do not cry out and blow [trumpets] and say instead: "This thing that has happened to us is natural and this catastrophe is coincidental," this is an expression of hostility [toward God] [*derekh akhzariyut*]. It will cause them to remain attached to their sinful ways. This will also perpetuate this catastrophe and bring in its wake others. This is written in the Torah: [. . .] *if you remain hostile to me* [*ve-halakhtem iti be-keri*] *I will act against you in wrathful hostility* [. . .] (Leviticus 26:27, 28). This means, I will bring catastrophe upon you in order that you repent. And if you say: "This is coincidence [*keri*]," I will increase [my] anger on this [so-called] coincidence.[30]

This comment clearly emphasizes the link between history and covenant. As most *ḥaredi* responses indicate, historical catastrophe viewed through the covenant must include a guilty party (some or all of Israel) without whom the catastrophe has no covenantal anchor. Progressive responses to the Holocaust (Fackenheim, Berkowitz, Greenberg, et al.) also view the event as part of the covenant, although they deny, sometimes vehemently, the existence of any guilty party. Rubenstein seems to reject this link entirely, viewing the Holocaust as the event that subverts

30 Moses Maimonides, *Mishneh Torah*, "Laws of Fasting," 1:2–3. For a ḥasidic rendering of this passage in Maimonides that supports its basic premise, see R. Ya'akov Yosef of Polonnoye, *Toldot Ya'akov Yosef* (Jerusalem, 1973), 2:444b.

the traditional notion of the God–Israel relationship. As we will presently see, Barzofsky comes quite close to Rubenstein in viewing this event as outside our normative notion of covenant (i.e., reciprocity), but suggests a meta-covenantal category I have called "radical evil" that enables God to bring about catastrophe outside the covenantal matrix of "reward and punishment," making the Holocaust necessary (or inevitable) and Israel guiltless.[31] And yet, this non-punitive divine action outside the covenant does not undermine it but, like miracles, confirms the covenantal framework by absorbing the rabbinic category of messianic suffering or *ḥevlei mashiaḥ*, another meta-covenantal component in Israel's relationship to God.

II

I must begin with the caveat that I do not advocate Barzofsky's notion of the Holocaust as meta-covenantal and thus as an inevitable act of God. Such an assertion can only sound blasphemous confronted with the utter human horror of such an evil event in human history. Even though Barzofsky's position places no guilt on any Jewish community or ideology (as such it is meta-covenantal or "simply" a divine decree) and consequently circumvents the even more problematic positions of many other ultra-Orthodox responses, his theologizing about such a human tragedy can only sound trivializing. Yet it is significant to note that Barzofsky, like many of his ultra-Orthodox compatriots, lives in an ideational world deeply committed to the idea of history having a theological foundation, most particularly the history of the Jews. As such, all events involve divine intervention; nothing is simply given over to the realm of the human, even if the divine act is *not* to intervene. Hence, Barzofsky cannot abide by Irving Greenberg's maxim that we cannot say anything about the Holocaust that "we would not say in the presence of burning children." Rather, Barzofsky *must* fit this horror, with all its human suffering, into a theological framework that can square

31 While it may be the case that reciprocity is the foundation of rabbinic theories of the covenant, there are some noteworthy exceptions in the rabbinic corpus. The most oft-cited is the dialogue between Moses and God when God shows Moses Rabbi Akiva's flesh being sold in the marketplace (after R. Akiva's martyrdom). When Moses sees this he asks God, "Is this the Torah and this its reward?," challenging the very foundation of reciprocity promised by God. God responds, "Quiet! This is how I wanted it to be" (see BT Menahot 29b). Another challenge to the reciprocal nature of the covenant can be found in R. Kalonymus Kalman Shapira of Piaseczno in his *Eish Kodesh*, 45 and 47.

with the notion of covenant. Yet, as we will presently see, doing so must first undermine a more conventional notion of covenantal reciprocity that leads many of his colleagues to place the blame on a particular party. Nor can he side with the responses to Rubenstein, which heroically try to save the covenant even as they alter its contours.

Barzofsky works with a notion already present in Fackenheim and others that there is an ontological difference between evil and radical evil (a category first suggested by Kant); only the latter is exemplified in the Holocaust. Evil is a consequence of free will; it is covenantal and thus punitive. Evil generally becomes manifest in Israel when they abrogate the covenant, although Job provides the important exception that proves the rule and thus becomes the central text of Jewish theodicy. Covenantal theology works under the general assumption that human beings (more specifically, Jews) can mostly avert, nullify, and rectify evil by means of repentance and good works. In this sense evil is natural in that it may be explained through the logic of reciprocity (*middah ke-neged middah*) and covenantal promise.[32] This evil can also include the theodicy of Job (suffering as moral education) and the rabbinic notion of *yesurin shel ahavah*, even as both require a more nuanced understanding of reciprocity.

There is, however, another dimension some post-Holocaust theologians call radical evil. Barzofsky, although he obviously never uses this term, argues by implication that radical evil is an unnatural event (*lo tivi*). For Barzofsky it is, I suggest, an inverted miracle.[33] For him radical evil is embedded in the fabric of creation, ironically reminiscent of Maimonides' provocative notion of miracle in his attempt to present it as simultaneously natural and supernatural.[34] Like a miracle, radical evil is part of the meta-covenantal relationship between God and Israel and not a consequence of covenantal reciprocity or

32 See, for example, as described in Schweid, *Bein Ḥurban*, 42.

33 The notion of the Holocaust as an act of divine intervention that is not a punishment also plays a role in the Holocaust theology of I. Maybaum in his *The Face of God After Auschwitz*. Maybaum posits the Holocaust was an act of collective sacrifice, using the model of the crucifixion. Maybaum, a Reform rabbi, held the Holocaust was about God's destroying the remnants of the Middle Ages in order to bring the world fully into the modern era. In some ways both he and Barzofsky want to view the Holocaust as playing a role in furthering society (or the Jewish people) without seeing it as punishment, albeit Maybaum obviously uses categories and terminology that Barzofsky would reject.

34 See H. Kasher, "Biblical Miracles and the Universality of Natural Laws: Maimonides' Three Methods of Harmonization," *Journal of Jewish Thought and Philosophy* 8 (1998): 25–52; Z. Langerman, "Maimonides and Miracles: The Growth of a (dis) Belief, *Jewish History* 10 (2004): 147–72; and A. Reines, "Maimonides and Miracles," *HUCA* 45 (1974), 243–85.

moral education. Radical evil is a divine decree, not punitive but a necessary part of the unfolding of creation.[35] In some way, this reflects the anti-theodicy position of classical Kabbalah, from the Zohar through Sabbateanism, that the demonic simply must unfold and have its day before being overcome and destroyed by the forces of redemption.[36] This comes to light most prominently in Lurianic Kabbalah where "divine rupture" (*shevirat ha-keilim*) and subsequently a broken world (*olam ha-nekudim*) create a cosmic condition that almost requires the periodic domination of evil, not as a consequence of sin but as a necessary part of the process of repair (*tikkun*).

Barzofsky's analysis is more empirically rooted than Luria's, and consequently his description of radical evil is more tangible and less mythic:

> In light of this we should see that the horrific Holocaust that occurred between 1940–1945 when six million Jews of the elite of the people were martyred before the whole world and there was no power [lit. kings] to stop the powers of destruction. It is clear that this horrific occurrence was embedded in the list of occurrences in creation, without which the world could not exist.[37]

This notion of (radical) evil written into creation is likely adapted from the MaHaRaL of Prague's *Be'er ha-Golah*. Yet Barzofsky differs from the MaHaRaL's more general theodicy by distinguishing between evil which is punitive and radical evil which is not. That is, the MaHaRaL may be arguing that all evil is written into creation, yet its manifestation is dependent on Israel's behavior. This is quite different from arguing, as Barzofsky does, that the radical evil written into creation is unnatural or perhaps unhistorical and therefore by definition necessary and not contingent. It must become manifest for creation to take its natural course.[38] Or, perhaps, its "unnaturalness" is its being part of the necessary course of creation's unfolding.

---

35 On silence as a response to the unnaturalness of the event, see *HA*, 11, 33. On silence more generally as a trope of response see N. Seidman, *Faithful Renderings: Jewish/Christian Difference and the Politics of Translation* (Chicago: University of Chicago Press, 2006), 199–242.

36 For anti-theodicy in the biblical and rabbinic tradition see Braiterman, *(God) After Auschwitz*, 35–59.

37 *HA*, 13: באור דברים עלינו לראות את השואה שפקדתנו בשנים ת"ש תש"ה כאשר ששה מיליוני יהודים מבחירי האומה נהרגו על קידוש ה' קבל עולם ומלואו ואין מלכים ועוצר ביד מלאכי החבלה כי בדי הדבר שמאורע איום זה קבועה היה בלוח המאורעות שבראשית אשר בלעדיהם אין קיום לעולם

38 There are other *ḥaredi* writers who argue against the Holocaust being the consequence of any particular sin. For example, Tsimerman suggests that it was the consequence of a general failure of Jews to live up to their covenantal responsibilities and not the result of any individual or collective transgression. But even here, Tsimerman must view

The unnatural status of radical evil is worth some attention. By unnatural (*lo tivi*) I take Barzofsky to mean an event outside covenantal reciprocity. Such a position may reflect some of the later sermons of submission by Kalonymus Kalman Shapira of Piaseczno collected in his *Eish Kodesh*.[39] As a wartime and not a post-war response, Shapira had no language to create meaning from his dark reality. As I read him, quite late in his life (by the end of 1941 and early 1942; the last sermon included in *Eish Kodesh* was delivered in July, 1942) Shapira reached a breaking point where he could no longer square the events unfolding before his eyes as anything that could be justified as punitive. He thus moved from a theological dilemma to the precipice of a theological crisis, although there was no time left for Shapira to articulate how such a crisis could be resolved. All he could do was prepare his community for collective martyrdom, a trope that dominates many of the sermons in *Eish Kodesh*, especially after 1940. As an aside, it has not been adequately examined how Shapira's late sermons in some sense initiate the trajectory of crisis that finds a new voice in Rubenstein and, differently, in Barzofsky's post-Holocaust thinking.

Be that as it may, while other post-Holocaust theologians have made the distinction between evil and radical evil, to my knowledge, few draw this distinction as an example of a natural (evil) versus unnatural (radical evil) event. In most cases, radical evil remains an expression of egregious human action.[40] Barzofsky offers a more theologically challenging definition. For him, radical evil is that which is not a product of human action at all but an

---

the Holocaust in some kind of diffuse covenantal framework. See Greenberg, "Ultra-Orthodox Reflections," 95.

39 See R. Kalonymus Kalman Shapira, *Eish Kodesh* (Jerusalem, 1960), now in English with notes as *Sacred Fire: Torah from the Years of Fury 1939–1942*, trans. and ann. J. H. Worch (Northvale, NJ: Jason Aronson, 2002). Cf. N. Polen, *The Holy Fire* (Northvale, NJ: Jason Aronson, 1994); and M. Piekarz, *Polish Ḥasidism: Ideological Trends between the Two Wars and in the Shoah [Hebrew]* (Jerusalem: Bialik Institute, 1990), 373–411. For another similar position, albeit not as radical, see the two letters by Hirsch Melekh Talmud, a student of Me'ir Shapira, director of the famous Yeshivah Hokhmei Lublin. For an analysis of the two letters and Talmud's war-time response to the horrific events unfolding before his eyes see G. Greenberg, "The Theological Letters of Rabbi Talmud of Lublin (Summer–Fall, 1942)," in *United States Holocaust Memorial Museum Ghettos 1939–1945: New Research and Perspectives on Definition, Daily Life, and Survival, Symposium Presentations*. I want to thank my student Barbara Krawcowicz for bringing this to my attention and Gershon Greenberg for providing me with copies of Talmud's letters. Most recently see Z. Leshem, "Between Messianism and Prophecy: Ḥasidism According to the Admor of Piaseczno" [Hebrew] (PhD diss., Bar Ilan University, 2007).

40 For example, see S. Rosenberg, *Good and Evil in Jewish Thought* [Hebrew] (Tel Aviv, 1985), 83–84. Cf. J. Turner, "Philosophical and Midrashic Thinking on the Fateful Events of Jewish History," in *The Impact of the Holocaust on Jewish Theology*, 62–64.

unnatural (and, in this case, necessary) manifestation of divine will. After a lengthy digression asking how such an event could have occurred among human beings, he concludes:

> For every specific question, every detail and act, there are answers and theories even if in the end these answers are not acceptable. Everyone who considers the larger picture in all its breadth will see and feel that the whole catastrophe was completely unnatural and [thus] solely a divine decree.[41]

As I read him, Barzofsky is turning the theological challenge of the Holocaust on its head. The radical evil of the Holocaust should not question God's place in the event (Rubenstein), but rather its unnatural status, as with miracles, is proof of its divine source. Unlike Rubenstein, the God who performs such evil, or allows it to occur, is not a God without a covenant. According to Barzofsky, radical evil as opposed to evil is not a covenantal act at all and, as such, cannot rupture or even threaten the covenant. Rather, for him the Holocaust is an inverted miracle: instead of saving Israel from catastrophe, not as reward but as divine decree, the Holocaust brings unnatural disaster upon Israel in order to complete the required state of messianic suffering and move history to its next phase. Although I write these words with trepidation, for Barzofsky, if God can arrange a miracle to save Israel *from* destruction (the parting of the Sea of Reeds) God can also, or perhaps *will* also, design the inversion of a miracle to bring Israel to the brink *of* destruction (the Holocaust). Or, put another way, to be the recipient of a miracle means, by definition, to also be the potential recipient of its inversion.

The biblical example Barzofsky invokes juxtaposes the concept of miracle and the Holocaust. He argues that the Holocaust was an extension of the decree on Purim.[42] According to the rabbis, the Jews in Shushan were saved from destruction by means of a "concealed miracle" manifest through the king's allowing them to preempt his decree to destroy them (Esther 8:11–14). Accepting the rabbinic premise that God was, in fact, ever-present in *Megillat Esther* (based on the observation that it is the only book in the

---

41 *HA*, 12: אמנם לכל שאלה לחוד לכל פרט ומקרה בפני עצמו יש תירוצים והסברים לרוב אף כי בסופו של דבר אין להם מקבלים על הדעת –ברם בכל מי שמתבונן בתמונה כללית על מלוא היקפה רואה בעליל ומרגיש שכל היקף האסון היה לגמרי טבעי אלא גזירה מלפהי ית'

42 R. Yosef Yizhak Schneersohn also uses Purim as a motif to discuss the Holocaust, but Schneersohn offers a different rendition of the biblical story and its relevance to the Holocaust. He views it very much within a covenantal framework, while Barzofsky uses Purim precisely to illustrate a meta-covenantal decree. See Yosef Yizhak Schneersohn, *Sefer Siḥot* (Brooklyn, NY, 1953); and Schweid, *Bein Ḥurban*, 41–42.

Hebrew Bible where God is not mentioned), Barzofsky suggests that the decree against the Jews in Shushan was not the act of a wicked king but a divine decree, a necessary act of suffering, perhaps part of messianic suffering (*ḥevlei mashiaḥ*), that never materialized. The conclusion of the Book of Esther, the Jews' victory over the Persians, was not the nullification of this divine decree but only its postponement.

The divine decree was not nullified but only postponed to a later time.[43]

> As is brought by the righteous ones, in the days of Mordecai there was a divine decree to *obliterate all the Jews, from youth to old age, babies and women* (Esther 3:13).[44] When this decree was nullified [in the days of Mordecai and Esther] the nullification was not complete but only postponed to a later time. In the generation of the Shoah, this decree was fulfilled that in every generation the commandment of martyrdom would be fulfilled.[45]

Here Barzofsky uses the rabbinic notion that the anonymous reference to the "king" in the Book of Esther is always a reference to God, in order to claim that the king's decree to destroy the Jews was, in fact, a divine decree that could not be nullified, only postponed. He continues that while generations of scholars were able, through the power of their Torah studies, "to continue to postpone this decree of destruction," its fulfillment was

---

43 *HA*, 14: כי לא נתבטלה הגזירה מכל וכל נחדתה לעת מאוחרת יותר

44 Barzofsky may mean two distinct things with this reference. First, he seems to imply that the modern genocidal plans of the 1940s have a biblical referent in the divine decree spoken by God in the Book of Esther. The rabbinic tradition posits that every time "king" is mentioned there anonymously, it refers to God, as we see in Esther 3:12. Thus the decree to destroy all the Jews on Purim is a divine decree and does not originate with either King Ahasuerus or Haman. Second, I think his use of Esther alludes to the rabbinic notion of Purim being the true origin of the covenant, as it is only then (and not at Sinai) that the Israelites/Jews received the covenant voluntarily. See BT Shabbat 88a. On this reading, the pre-history of the covenant begins with the "unnatural" miracle of the parting of the Sea of Reeds, but its true history begins in an "unnatural" decree of destruction, or collective martyrdom, on Purim. This decree is averted yet not erased. Here the notion that in Esther the king cannot, in fact, erase his decree, thus allowing the Jews to defend themselves, speaks to Barzofsky's notion that the decree on Purim cannot be erased but is postponed until the Holocaust. Connecting the Holocaust to the trajectory of evil from Pharaoh to Haman was also evoked in the Adolph Eichmann trial in Jerusalem. See, for example, Hannah Arendt's comments in "The Eichmann Trial and the Germans: A Conversion with Thilo Koch," in *The Jewish Writings: Hannah Arendt*, ed. J. Kohn and R. Feldman (New York: Schocken, 2007), 488.

45 *HA*, 27: וכדאיתא מצדיקי אמת שבימי מרדכי כבר היה גזר הדיו להשמיד להרוג ולאבד את כל היה היהודים מנער ועד זקן טף ונשים – וכשנתבטלה הגזירה זה היה רק בב"ת דוחין את הגזרות שלא נתבטלה לגמרי אלא נדתה לאחד זמן –בדור של השואה נתקיימה הגזרה הזאת שכל הדור קיים מצות קידוש השם

inevitable.[46] The purpose of the decree, he surmises, was to enable Israel to collectively fulfill the *miẓvah* of martyrdom (*kiddush ha-shem*) as a way to complete the decree of messianic suffering (*ḥevlei mashiaḥ*). The connection to Purim is interesting here because the order of the king to destroy Israel on Purim is one of the few biblical instances where an edict against the Jews is not interpreted as punitive.[47] I would suggest, then, that for Barzofsky the non-punitive nature of tragedy is what defines "unnatural" and thus radical evil.[48]

Another way Barzofsky exhibits this approach is through an empirical analysis of the generation following the Holocaust. The Holocaust is described in this text as the unnatural event that absorbs the entire category of messianic suffering (*ḥevlei mashiaḥ*).[49] Until this point Israel lived within two distinct paradigms: the first was the covenantal model of reward and punishment; the second the ever-present *ḥevlei mashiaḥ*, for Barzofsky a non-punitive decree of pre-messianic suffering that could, at times, be muted or postponed but not erased through human intervention. The former defined Israel's reciprocal relationship to God; the latter served as a slow and painful process of purifying Israel's collective soul in preparation for redemption. For Barzofsky, all Jewish history is covenantal history, a combination of reciprocity (reward and punishment) and the process of *ḥevlei mashiaḥ*. The Holocaust is posited as an unnatural event, an expression of a one-time collective act of martyrdom, absorbing the second category, freeing Israel from the burden of the non-punitive suffering of *ḥevlei mashiaḥ*.[50]

His evidence to support this claim is not, as one might think, the emergence of the Jewish State. This is because for Barzofsky *ḥevlei mashiaḥ* is

46 On the notion of the study of Torah as averting (postponing) the Amalekite attack on Israel, see BT Bekhorot s.b. A similar tack is taken by R. Yosef Yizhak Schneersohn. See Schweid, *Bein Ḥurban*, 52.

47 The rabbis, obviously troubled by the absence of any overt Israelite "sin" that would justify the king's decree against them, construct different ways in which the Jews transgressed, making this decree punitive and thus covenantal.

48 Isaac Breuer also makes a connection between Purim and the Holocaust. Asking why did God not perform the miracle of Purim and save the Jews from the Nazis? See his *Naḥliel* (Jerusalem 1982), 381; and Mittleman, *Between Kant and Kabbala*, 162.

49 See, for example, BT Pesahim 118a and Sanhedrin 98b. In most rabbinic descriptions of this term, acts of piety and repentance can nullify these "birth pangs." Barzofsky seems to define this phenomenon in a different manner.

50 See *HA*, 24. On various ways of understanding *kiddush ha-shem* and the Holocaust see Berkowitz, *Faith after the Holocaust*, 76–85. On the Holocaust as the end of *ḥevlei mashiaḥ* see E. Dessler, *Mikhtav me-Eliyahu* (Jerusalem, 1994), 1:209–11. Cf. Schweid, *Bein Ḥurban*, 160.

not followed by the culmination of exile.[51] The completion of *ḥevlei mashiaḥ* inaugurates another phase of pre-messianic exile that completes the purification process which cannot be achieved under the shadow of messianic suffering.[52] The progressive status of a postexilic Judaism is firstly that the Jewish people are now situated in Israel and America, two locales that provide optimal conditions for Torah study—the first being a pluralistic society, the second a Jewish society. Secondly, this posttraumatic period of Judaism is exhibited in the *ba'al teshuvah* phenomenon that he views as "unnatural" and thus miraculous.[53]

> According to what was said [above], the tragic number of six million holy souls that were bound on the altar of his holy name may tell us something about the wondrous events of our generation. We see with our eyes what no imaginative soul would ever have thought possible before our generation. Completely unexpectedly a wondrous generation of Torah and devotion arose. Halls of Torah have blossomed and the study of Torah has attained a very high level. With this, Ḥasidism is thriving in all its beauty. In addition, [we see] the wondrous *teshuvah* movement, the likes of which we have never heard of in any generation. The question arises by itself, who bequeathed all this to us? With whose strength has this generation grown? Even in previous generations we were not successful in raising such a generation, so how did this occur? It is surely the case that there is no natural explanation. It is, rather, God alone, "I am God alone, in my honor and My essence," I brought forth this generation [. . .][54]

The apparent causal link here between "the tragic number of six million holy souls that were bound on the altar of his holy name" and the illogical and thus "miraculous" nature of the proliferation of Torah, especially newly

---

51 On this see my "In Search of a Critical Voice in the Jewish Diaspora: Homelessness and Home in Edward Said and Shalom Noah Barzofsky's *Netivot Shalom*," *Jewish Social Studies* 12 (2006): 193–227.

52 *HA*, 46–63.

53 This is similar to the position of Yosef Yizhak Schneersohn. See Schweid, *Bein Ḥurban*, 61.

54 *HA*, 28: וע"פ האומר הרי המספר הנורא והאיום של ששה מיליונים כולם קדושים שנעקבו על מזבח על קדושת שמו יש בו אולי להאיר קצת את התופעה המופלה של דורנו שבעינינו אנו רואה גילויים כאלו ששום בעל דמיון וחזיון לא העז להעלותם ברעיובו לפני שנות דור. לפתע קם וצמח דור מופלא כל כח דור של תורה ודקדוק מצות –אהלי התורה פורחים ולימוד התורה בהם הוא ברמה גבוהה ביותר ויחד עם זה היכלי חסידות משגשגים במלא תפארתם וכמו כן תנועת התשובה המופלאה והמדהימה שלא שמענו כעין זה בשום דבר. והלוא מאילה נשאלת השאלה מי ילד לנו את כל אלה מי שבכוחו לטפח ולגדל דור שכזה שגם בדורו שלפנינו לא חצליחו להקים דורות כאלה מכח מה **צמח** דור שכזה. ובוודאי שאין לך שום הסבר טבעי אלא שהקב"ה לבדו **אני** ה' בכבודי ובעצמי **טיפח** וריבה הדור הזה [. . .]

religious Jews (*ba'alei teshuvah*) in the generation following the Holocaust, is quite striking. On the very next page he makes this connection even more explicit by suggesting that the illogicality of a return to Torah in the generation following the Holocaust might (must?) mean that these lofty new souls are the reincarnated return of the generation of martyrs.

> In this we can understand the wondrous phenomenon of *ba'alei teshuvah* in our generation. This also has no natural explanation. That is, how so many who stood on the pinnacle of secular life abandoned their stature and honor in order to become absorbed in their divine inheritance through the wonders and greatness and dedication. Those glowing souls that were murdered to sanctify the divine name [in the Shoah] were sent again to this world. And these souls are, in truth, [even] greater and come with opened eyes and thus they see differently and hear differently. As a result, this generation is ripe for greatness and can create what was not created in previous generations. Despite the utter darkness that rules on one side on the other side there is a very great light.[55]

Barzofsky suggests here that the collective choice of a younger generation to be more religious than their parents, especially after an event challenging the faith of even the most devout, is counterintuitive and as such a miraculous phenomenon which mirrors the special nature (or "un-nature") of the Holocaust (hence his use of the term "unnatural," *lo tivi*, and "sacrifice," *mesirat nefesh*, to describe both phenomena). The vocation of the next generation, whose collective *miẓvah* is Torah study, is a double burden. Like any generation, it must continue the work of the generation which preceded it. However, since much of that generation perished as martyrs, this is impossible.[56] In this sense, the post-Holocaust generation is severed from any real sense of continuity. Therefore, this next generation must reconstruct its predecessors as well as move beyond them.[57]

---

55 *HA*, 29: ובזה יש להבין את התופעה המופלאה של בעלי תשובה בדורנו שגם כן אין לא הסבר טבעי אך זה שרבים רבים, ומהם שעמדו ברום פסגת החיים החילוניים, זונחים את כל מעמד והכבוד כדי לבא ולהסתפח בנמחלת ה' תוך גילוים מופלאים של גדלות ומסירת נפש. שכאמור אלו נשמות לוהטות שכבר נהרגו על קידוש השם ונשלתו עוד פעם לעולם הזה, ונשמות אלה הן באמת יותר גדולות וממלא עינים פקוחות והם רואים אחרת ושומעים אחרת. ולאור זה הרי הדור מסוגל לגדלות ולנוצרות מה שבאמת לא היה בדורות קודמים, ולמרות החשך והאפלה השוררים מצד אחד הרי מאירך גיסא האור גדול מאוד

56 I think here he may be referring to survivors as well. That is, even those who physically survived the Holocaust were unable as a generation to do the progressive work necessary to move beyond the *miẓvah* of martyrdom/*kiddush ha-shem*.

57 For another rendering of the responsibilities of the post-Holocaust generation in terms of reconstructing a Torah society, see Dessler, *Mikhtav me-Eliyahu*, 1:70–71. Dessler differs from Barzofsky in that he begins his essay by stating definitively that

Success in this endeavor is possible for two reasons. First, because the post-Holocaust generation, which voluntarily rejected secularism and returned to Torah (which he considers in itself unfathomable), is viewed as a collective reincarnation of the generation of martyrs.[58] Second, the post-Holocaust generation is the first generation to no longer live in the shadow of *ḥevlei mashiaḥ*. Liberated from the burden of a divine decree consistently curtailing Israel's ability to flourish in an unhindered manner (this would include the world's willingness to allow for the proliferation of Torah study and practice), this generation can fulfill the remainder of the pre-messianic requirements through a renewal of an integrated Judaism guided by the dictates of sages in previous generations.

This approach is quite novel coming from a ḥasidic master seemingly wed to the doctrine of the "descent of the generations" (*yeridat ha-dorot*). To posit, as he does, that the post-Holocaust secular Jews who return to Torah are as great, or greater, than the deeply educated and pious Jews of pre-war Europe is noteworthy.[59] I would suggest that this supposition rests on the notion that the Holocaust absorbed the remnants of the decree of the pre-messianic suffering, enabling these returning souls to "see and hear differently," rationalizing their otherwise counterintuitive choice to abandon the comforts and rewards of a secular life for a life of Torah. The notion of collective or generational reincarnation is not foreign to the Jewish mystical tradition—it is, in fact, quite common in Lurianic exegesis, which links the generations of Babel, the Flood, and the Exodus—but its use here as a way of explaining the Holocaust as a catalyst for the proliferation of Torah values is striking.

One of the more intriguing and potentially far-reaching dimensions of viewing the Holocaust as an inverted miracle, erasing the ominous decree of *ḥevlei mashiaḥ*, is that it would appear to be an event which cannot, by

---

the generation lost in the Holocaust was superior to the post-Holocaust generation, a notion Barzofsky challenges through the deployment of *gilgul neshamot*. Cf. Schweid, *Bein Ḥurban*, 156–58.

58 The notion of reincarnation as a motif through which to understand the positive nature of the Holocaust as an act of purification exists in the work of Hayyim Yisrael Tsimerman. See his *Tamim Pa'alo* (Tel Aviv, 1947) and G. Greenberg, "*Tamim Pa'alo:* Tsimerman's Absolutist Explanation of the Holocaust," *God's Name: Religion and Genocide in the Twentieth Century*, ed. O. Bartov and P. Mack (Oxford, UK: Oxford University Press, 2001), xxx.

59 This, of course, has a rabbinic referent. See *Yalkut Shimoni* on Genesis 2, no. 20, 7b, in standard editions.

definition, be repeated.[60] While Barzofsky never draws this conclusion, it is a plausible extension of his thinking that the proliferation of radical evil during the Holocaust did, in fact, absorb the remaining oppressive forces linked to *ḥevlei mashiaḥ*. If we see the Holocaust, as he does, as a divine decree standing outside any covenantal framework (yet it does not destroy the covenant) whose function was to absorb the residual suffering resulting from *ḥevlei mashiaḥ* in a one-time act of collective martyrdom, another Holocaust would be historically impossible because it would be theologically unnecessary. This is because for Barzofsky, as opposed to Rubenstein and other post-Holocaust theologians, the covenant survived the Holocaust intact even though the Holocaust was a meta-covenantal event. That is, Barzofsky seems to hold that the Holocaust was not a consequence of covenantal reciprocity, yet not an abrogation of it either. It was, rather, an "unnatural" though necessary event (similar to a miracle) which served a larger covenantal purpose. For him, the Holocaust absorbed all remaining dimensions of *ḥevlei mashiaḥ*, thus erasing the divine decision of non-punitive Jewish suffering. Since the Holocaust was neither the result of Israel's transgression nor purely the expression of human (radical) evil, it has the status of a unique event similar to Maimonides' interpretation of the parting of the Sea of Reeds. As Maimonides argues that many biblical miracles are one-time events written into the fabric of creation, could Barzofsky be saying the same thing about the Holocaust?

In contrast, if we view the Holocaust as standing outside any covenantal framework, with the power to undermine the covenant (Rubenstein), it can surely happen again: Rubenstein's God is not a supernatural/covenantal God who protects Israel. Therefore, theoretically, there is nothing to stop human beings from repeating such radically evil actions. In short, for Rubenstein, among some other post-Holocaust theologians, the Holocaust was a human and not a divine occurrence.[61] As such, it could surely be repeated by the same token that all barbaric acts of humanity can be repeated.

---

60 The threat of another Holocaust permeates Zionism and contemporary Judaism more generally. For an analysis of this phenomenon and the dangers that underlie living in such a state of impending doom see A. Burg, *Defeating Hitler* [Hebrew] (Jerusalem: Yediot, 2007), esp. 39–40. The cry "Never Again!" that was also the title of Meir Kahane's 1971 book advocating Jewish militancy in America became a common, perhaps dominant, trope in post-war Judaism. According to my rendering of Barzofsky's theological analysis he seems to imply (he never says so explicitly) that the very conditions of messianic suffering which created the Holocaust have been erased as a result of the tragedy in question.

61 Here it is important to note another response to the Holocaust which has not received enough attention. In a lecture originally given in German in 1984, developed from

Barzofsky's metaphysical commitments could never admit such divine limitation. For him the event had to be divinely influenced. Given that for Barzofsky God's actions can be both miraculous and radically evil (the latter being the inversion of the former) they are not limited to the covenantal model of reciprocity. Radical evil can be both divine as well as unique, that is, an act of God which is, by definition, a one-time event. These implications in terms of postHolocaust Jewish thinking and living, theologically and politically, merit further exploration.

By this I mean to say that the logic of Barzofsky's position suggests that while both anti-Semitism and anti-Judaism (sometimes taking the form of anti-Israelism) can and will remain in the future, some kind of release of theological resistance has occurred, embodied in *ḥevlei mashiaḥ*, which preceded the Holocaust. The proof of such an assertion, of course, can never be determined. However, my question is: if we assert that some paradigmatic shift has taken place as a result of the Holocaust, that is, if (and here I speak with fear and trembling) we say, following Barzofsky, that the Holocaust has done theological work which brings the world closer to redemption by absorbing the remnants of the pre-messianic suffering of the Jews, what kind of Judaism should, or could, be produced in its wake?[62] Since the history of anti-Judaism is as long as the history of Judaism (if we understand this to mean the advent of rabbinic Judaism in late Antiquity) Judaism has always developed, in part, in light of, and in

an earlier English paper published in 1968, Hans Jonas argues in favor of a (self) limited notion of divinity to the effect that God not only did not but could not prevent the human evil perpetrated in the Holocaust. See Jonas, "The Concept of God After Auschwitz," in his *Morality and Mortality: A Search for the Good After Auschwitz* (Evanston, IL: Northwestern University Press, 1996), 131–43. Jonas deploys the Lurianic concept of *ẓimẓum* or divine contraction/limitation as a tool to posit God's self-limiting when it comes to human behavior. Jonas is not the first to use these Lurianic categories to explain the Holocaust. In 1965 (a year before the first edition of *After Auschwitz*) Rubenstein wrote an autobiographical essay in a volume edited by Ira Eisenstein (Mordecai Kaplan's son-in-law) entitled *The Varieties of Jewish Belief* (New York: Reconstructionist Press, 1966), where he writes about the kabbalistic ideas of creation as a response to his confrontation with the Holocaust. This is cited by Michael Morgan in *Beyond Auschwitz*, 91.

62 In *HA*, Barzofsky suggests that the free reign of Torah study, Jewish practice, and the proliferation of Torah values is the formula needed to move this stage to the final redemptive one. I am using Barzofsky's rendering of the Holocaust and asking a series of questions that would be, for him, unacceptable. Nevertheless, given the quite radical assertion he makes about the end of pre-messianic suffering, which I translate as the loosening of the resistance of the world against Jews and Judaism, I suggest my questions are not totally outside the realm of his worldview as articulated here.

spite of, resistance.[63] But what if the barrier of resistance is removed; what if some of the protective measures to prevent Jews from engaging fully in the world (some of which have become part of *halakhah*) no longer conform to the reality Jews live in? This is not to advocate the dissolution of Judaism. Far from it. Rather, it is to suggest some new thinking may be required in order to enable Judaism to be more open to the world, more embracing of a world which, on Barzofsky's reading, no longer serves as the arbiter of *ḥevlei mashiaḥ*. I write this knowing full well that Jews still face many obstacles and that anti-Semitism has far from disappeared from the global landscape. However, if we maintain, as many do, that the opposition to Jews and Judaism today is simply an extension of what preceded the Holocaust, and that the Holocaust should teach Jews to be even more distrustful of the world around them, the Holocaust can have little distinctive theological import. This assertion, although it conforms to human beings' innate fear of one another, cannot be proven any more than Barzofsky's more theological, and admittedly more speculative suggestion.[64] But if we take seriously Barzofsky's reading that, while hatred has not abated, the "big one" has already occurred, what new contours of Jewish creativity become possible?

Conclusion

Unlike almost all of his *ḥaredi* contemporaries, Barzofsky acknowledges the Holocaust as a unique event which requires a new rendering of our understanding of the covenant.[65] He also views the Holocaust as an event that absorbed the remaining dimension of *ḥevlei mashiaḥ* as a radical shift in Jewish history. Without being explicitly aware of Rubenstein's post-Holocaust theology, Barzofsky acknowledges the credibility of at least part of Rubenstein's claim, although he would surely disagree with his conclusions.[66] Unlike the many modern respondents to Rubenstein, Barzofsky

63 I find Daniel Boyarin's thesis about the twin-birth of Judaism and Christianity quite compelling. See Boyarin, *Border Lines: The Partition of Judeao-Christianity* (Philadelphia: University of Pennsylvania Press, 2004).

64 One recent, if quite extreme and, in my view, bizarre example of this type of thinking can be found in Ruth Wisse's *Jews and Power* (New York: Schocken, 2007).

65 He mentions this uniqueness numerous times in *HA*. For example, see 12, 31, 35, 52, 69.

66 There is no way to know for certain whether, in fact, Barzofsky had any knowledge of the post-Holocaust debate in America. He spent almost all of his adult life in Jerusalem in a community that was largely protected from this discourse. After the publication

does not think the covenant has to be reassessed, changed, or reframed in light of the Holocaust, and he surely rejects Rubenstein's conclusion that it must be radically reconstructed. He also outright rejects the ultra-Orthodox claim that the Holocaust was a punishment for sin.

In one sense, Barzofsky is more conservative than Rubenstein's critics, yet in another sense he is far more radical. His conservatism is manifest in his maintaining the covenantal parameters of tradition by interpreting this unique event as meta-covenantal, that is, what I have called an inverted miracle that is not punitive but, like *ḥevlei mashiaḥ*, supports the larger covenantal program.[67]

The necessity, or perhaps inevitability, of the Holocaust as Barzofsky construes it should not be linked to Zvi Yehuda Kook or Yosef Yizhak Schneersohn's notion of the Holocaust as "divine surgery" directed toward emptying the Jews from Europe or with Ignaz Maybaum's equally problematic idea (from my perspective) that the Holocaust was an act of providential divine intervention to destroy "all that was medieval in Europe."[68] Kook's position is covenantal in still being punitive, i.e., God had to destroy European Jewry and end Jewish exile because the Jews did not do so voluntarily after the Balfour Declaration in 1917. Kook's contention is almost identical in structure to Elhanan Wassermann's except that Kook changes the guilty party.

Reform Jewish theologian Ignaz Maybaum held that the victims of the Holocaust were "sacrificial offerings." He likens the destruction of "God's chosen" to martyrs who embody the true nature of the crucifixion that Christianity had distorted.[69] According to Maybaum, Christianity made

---

of *Netivot Shalom* he became popular with modern Jews and *ba'alei teshuvah*, many of whom visited him frequently. Even with that caveat I would doubt he had much, if any, knowledge of post-Holocaust theology. In general, see Nadler, "*Ha-Sinteza ba-Ḥasidut Slonim*." I would conjecture, however, that his use of the *ba'al teshuvah* phenomenon as an example of how the Holocaust released the Jews from the resistance of messianic suffering and enabled Torah study to flourish in places from which it had previously been absent may be a product of his exposure to these individuals through the popularity of his *Netivot Shalom*.

67 For a possible precedent for such a response see *Toldot Ya'akov Yosef*, 1:413: "[. . .] one who knows his creator and recognizes his origins knows that everything flows providentially from God. [For such a person] there is no place to hate his neighbor [*ḥavero*]. Even if his neighbor acts toward him with malevolence *she'asah lo ra*), the evil is not coming from him, he is just a stick in the hand of the striker."

68 Rubenstein and Roth, eds., *Approaches to Auschwitz*, 336.

69 Maybaum is hardly original here. Comparing the oppression of Jews throughout history to Jesus and his crucifixion was popular in the nineteenth and twentieth centuries among both Jews and Christians. One finds this in Reform theologians such as Isaac

Jesus into a "glorified persecuted tragic hero and obscured the fact that he was a Jew hanging on a Roman gallows."[70] He suggested, in short, that the Holocaust was a consequence of God's action, but not punitive. He writes: "the Jews died an innocent death; they died because of the sins of others [. . .] Jewish martyrdom explains the meaning which the Cross can bear better than medieval Christian dogma ever did."[71] And yet, "eighteen years after the end of the era of Auschwitz, the welcome to a new era inspires us with hope and joy."[72] Maybaum's notion of martyrdom as a (necessary?) transition to a new era, one that does not alter the covenant but affirms it by moving us beyond the Middle Ages to the next phase, shares some structural similarities to Barzofsky's notion of the Holocaust absorbing the last remnants of *ḥevlei mashiaḥ*, after which Israel can move forward through the proliferation of Torah study, without the fear of non-punitive punishment. But, of course, the differences are greater than the similarities.

As suggested by Richard Rubenstein and John Roth, it appears that Maybaum's interests were primarily pedagogical. As a Reform rabbi writing in post-war Europe, he believed that if the Holocaust could not be squared with the covenant, "Judaism's status [would be] reduced to that of a particular community's socially constructed religion." In other words, without some covenantal explanation of the Holocaust, Judaism would become Rubenstein's post-Holocaust Reconstructionism.[73] In this sense, Maybaum may have felt it necessary to justify the covenant after the Holocaust to a Christian audience as much as to a Jewish one by arguing that Jewish martyrdom in the Holocaust embodied the true nature of Jesus' death, not as a Christ figure but as an innocent sufferer who died for others at the hands of barbarians. In other words, the Jews in the Holocaust fulfilled Christianity's original intent better than Christianity ever did.

Mayer Wise, Kaufmann Kohler, and Emile Hirsch, in the "Crucifix Question" between S. Ansky and Chaim Zhitlovsky and among Christians, such as in Frank Little's *The Crucifixion of the Jews* on the Jews and the Holocaust. After the Holocaust, many Jewish theologians and writers ceased comparing Jesus' experience to the fate of the Jews, but some, like Sholem Asch, continued writing about Jesus and Jews even after WWII. A new phase of appropriations of Jesus emerged in America in the 1970s. On some of these issues, see G. L. Berlin, *Defending the Faith: Nineteenth-Century American Jewish Writings on Christianity and Jesus* (Albany: SUNY Press, 1989); and M. Hoffman, *From Rebel to Rabbi: Reclaiming Jesus and the Making of Modern Jewish Culture* (Stanford: Stanford University Press, 2007), 61–205.

70 I. Maybaum, "The Tragedy of Auschwitz," in *Ignaz Maybaum: A Reader*, ed. N. de Lange (New York: Berghahn Books, 2001), 161.

71 Ibid., 165.

72 Ibid., 165.

73 Ibid., 337.

In another sense Barzofsky's position is more radical than that of Rubenstein's respondents because, as an inverted miracle, the Holocaust need not, and perhaps cannot, recur. This opens the possibility of a new Jewish stance toward living in a post-Holocaust era, a new orientation toward the gentile "other," and an agenda for a new historical epoch regarding the Jews' role in the world.[74] As a ḥasidic master ensconced in an ultra-Orthodox community in Jerusalem, Barzofsky was not likely to entertain such progressive alternatives. Yet, I argued here that embedded in his innovative and sometimes daring reading of the horrible tragedy of the Holocaust, there are seeds of a new approach to post-Holocaust Judaism.

In one sense, perhaps, Barzofsky's (post) Holocaust theology (if one can call it that) creates the conditions for openness to a world that was previously unacceptable from the perch of ultra-Orthodoxy (if this is true, he would agree with Maybaum). Barzofsky might disagree with this, but given my reading of his writings on this topic, his work at least suggests such a position.[75] The implications of all this remain to be investigated, but if I am correct in maintaining that in Barzofsky's analysis the Holocaust can be construed as an inverted miracle, new vistas of post-Holocaust theology await exploration.

74 The use of the Holocaust as an anchor of Jewish identity and a means to justify Jewish behavior has been studied by many. Most recently, Avraham Burg's provocative *Defeating Hitler* makes a strong case claiming Israel's obsession with the Holocaust is undermining its moral foundation and disabling Israelis from entering the global community. A more sober assessment of the reception of the Holocaust in America can be found in P. Novick, *The Holocaust in American Life* (New York: Houghton Mifflin Harcourt, 2000).

75 See my "Jewish Renewal and the Holocaust: A Theological Response," *Tikkun Magazine* (March/April, 2006): 59–62, 68.

Chapter 8

The Divine/Human Messiah and Religious Deviance: Rethinking Ḥabad Messianism

"When Kabbalah came, it made of God a human; when Ḥasidism came, it made of the human a God."
—Rashbatz[*]

"[The Jew] is not an independent being; rather, all of his existence is the existence of the Holy One, Blessed be He!"
—R. Menahem Mendel Schneerson, *Hitva'aduyot Tashmav* (5746), 515

כי חלק ה׳ עמו (דברים ל״ב ט) א ייד איז א שטיקל גט
—R. Zalman Schachter-Shalomi, *Yishmaru Da'at*, 44

In March, 1970 Gershom Scholem delivered "The Neutralization of the Messianic Idea in Early Ḥasidism," the first Joseph Weiss Memorial Lecture, established to honor Scholem's student who had tragically taken his own life in August the previous year. Scholem had a complicated relationship with Weiss, though he spoke of him at the beginning of the lecture as "in many ways the closest of my pupils."[1] Weiss studied the radical strains of Ḥasidism, specifically Nahman of Bratslav, the subject of his dissertation, which Scholem

---

[*] This was communicated orally to Zalman Schachter-Shalomi in the name of Rashbatz, a teacher in adolescence of Joseph Isaac Schneersohn, the sixth Lubavitcher Rebbe and father-in-law of Menahem Mendel Schneerson. Cited in Schachter-Shalomi, *Wrapped in a Holy Flame: Teachings and Tales of the Ḥasidic Masters* (San Francisco: Jossey-Bass, 2003), 133.

1 Gershom Scholem, "The Neutralization of the Messianic Idea in Early Ḥasidism," *Journal of Jewish Studies* 20 (1969): 25–55; reprinted in Scholem, *The Messianic Idea in Judaism: And Other Essays on Jewish Spirituality* (New York: Schocken, 1971), 176–202. Throughout this chapter I cite from the reprinted version. The correspondence between Scholem and Weiss illustrates the closeness and complexity of their relationship. See

famously rejected.[2] While in principle Scholem's March, 1970 lecture may have been inspired by the messianism of Nahman and its treatment by Weiss, it was more likely a response to Martin Buber's claim that Ḥasidism has basically erased the messianic idea from its worldview.[3] Scholem responded that such a claim is not substantiated in Ḥasidism's homiletic literature. Yet, he argued, Ḥasidism did in fact defang the messianic idea by internalizing collective exile as personal alienation from God and using *deveikut* (cleaving to God) as an experience of "self-redemption," personalizing the messianic idea and severing it from its collective roots.[4] "What formerly had occurred on an ontological level was now repeated on an anthropological one," he declared.[5] More generally, Scholem argued that after Sabbateanism, there were essentially three ways open to Kabbalah. He spoke of the third one thus:

> Finally, there was a third way, and that is the one which Ḥasidism took, particularly during its classical period. . . . Ḥasidism represents an attempt

---

Gershom Scholem and Joseph Weiss: Halifat Mikhtavim 1948–1964, ed. Noam Zadoff (Jerusalem: Carmel, 2012).

2 See Scholem's letter to Weiss, March 27, 1951, in *Gershom Scholem and Joseph Weiss: Halifat Mikhtavim 1948–1964*, letter 15, 58–59. Cf. the letter from Weiss to Scholem, letter 59, 147–48.

3 See Scholem, "Martin Buber's Interpretation of Ḥasidism," in *The Messianic Idea in Judaism*, 227–50. Buber is in no way speaking out against messianism. In fact, in his "Three Lectures on Judaism" (1920), he writes, "Messianism is Judaism's most profoundly original idea." See Buber, *On Judaism* (New York: Schocken, 1967), 50. Buber defines ḥasidic messianism as "a messianism of continuity." See Buber, *Two Types of Faith* (New York: Harper, 1961), 78. On Buber's messianism more generally, see Jacob Taubes, "Martin Buber and the Philosophy of History" (1963), in Taubes, *From Cult to Culture*, ed. Amir Engel and Charlotte Fonrobert (Stanford, CA: Stanford University Press, 2010), 10–27.

4 See Rivka Shatz, "Self-Redemption in Ḥasidic Thought," in *Types of Redemption*, ed. R. J. Zwi Werblowsky and C. Jouco Bleeker (Leiden: Brill, 1970). Scholem distinguishes between redemption on the public stage of history, which he deems "Jewish," and the internalization of redemption in the soul, which he deems "Christian." On this reading, Ḥasidism, even on Scholem's terms, is a kind of "Christianization" of Judaism. See Scholem, *The Messianic Idea in Judaism*, 1. The same could be said of the internalization of messianism in modern Jewish thinkers such as Hermann Cohen. See Kenneth Seeskin, *Jewish Messianic Thoughts in an Age of Despair* (Cambridge, UK: Cambridge University Press, 2012), 64–65. For a critique of Scholem's binary reading, see Jacob Taubes, "The Price of Messianism," in Taubes, *From Cult to Culture*, 3–9.

5 Scholem, "The Neutralization," 186–87. For another view on this locution, see Elliot R. Wolfson, "Revealing and Re/veiling: Menahem Mendel Schneerson's Messianic Secret," *Kabbalah: Journal for the Study of Jewish Mystical Texts* 26 (2012): 69. For a critique of Scholem's essay, see Mendel Piekarz, "The Messianic Idea in Early Ḥasidism according to Homiletic and Mussar Literature" [Hebrew], in *The Messianic Idea in Jewish Thought*, ed. Shmuel Reem (Jerusalem: Israeli Academy of the Science and Humanities, 1982), 237–53.

> to preserve those elements of Kabbalism which were capable of evoking a popular response, but stripped of the Messianic flavor to which they owed their chief success during the preceding period. That seems to me the main point. Ḥasidism tried to eliminate the element of messianic—with its dazzling but highly dangerous amalgamation of mysticism and the apocalyptic mood—without renouncing the popular appeal of Kabbalism.[6]

Scholem viewed Ḥasidism as a reaction against Sabbateanism that used kabbalistic ideas to upset the messianic fervor. "Ḥasidism, without changing the outward façade of Lurianic teaching and terminology, introduced such subtle but effective changes as would eliminate the Messianic meaning of the central doctrine of *tikkun* or at least defer it to a remote stage, where it became again a matter of utopianism without immediate impact."[7]

Given the seemingly overt messianism of the contemporary Ḥabad ḥasidic movement, cresting with the death of their erstwhile rebbe/Messiah, Menahem Mendel Schneerson, in the summer of 1994, it seems hard to take Scholem's thesis seriously.[8] In what follows I offer one reading of how Ḥabad messianism is both a natural product of Ḥabad's metaphysics and an adaptation of Ḥasidism's "neutralization" of messianism that Scholem and many of his students claimed was Ḥasidism's great innovation. In my conclusion I suggest that even given the ostensible eruption of messianic fervor surrounding Ḥabad and its rebbe, Scholem's "neutralization" thesis may still hold.

The Construction of the Messiah

The most startling dimension of Ḥabad messianism is not the claim that the Ḥabad rebbe, Menahem Mendel Schneerson, was the long-awaited Messiah, but rather the ways in which Schneerson was understood as the Messiah before and after his death. Given the messianic claims that surrounded his personage, the theological implications embedded in the paradoxical phenomenon of a Jewish Messiah who dies (or was occluded) before fulfilling his mission cannot be underestimated, even as I will show

6 Scholem, "The Neutralization," 180.

7 Ibid., 185. For another view on Ḥasidism and messianism, see Mor Altshuler, *The Messianic Secret of Ḥasidism* (Leiden: Brill, 2006).

8 For the most comprehensive and significant work on Menahem Mendel Schneerson, see Elliot R. Wolfson, *Open Secret: Postmessianic Messianism and the Mystical Revision of Menahem Mendel Schneerson* (New York: Columbia University Press, 2009).

they are not unique. The claim that for some, perhaps many, Schneerson remains the Messiah argues that we are not living on the cusp of the messianic era but rather deeply inside it.[9]

Contemporary Ḥabad messianism is based less on what Schneerson thought about himself (about which there is unresolvable disagreement) than on how he is perceived by his disciples, before and after his death, and on how his movement interpreted his stature.[10] While my focus will be on the messianic wing of the movement, I also implicate the more agnostic wing. Contemporary Ḥabad has become so invested in the messianic status of their rebbe that openly denying that status arguably takes one outside the movement.[11] My focus in this chapter is on how Schneerson is perceived by his disciples as a super- or transhuman figure (a *ẓaddik gamur*), infallible, even a divine being, and how his messiahship is constructed on these foundations. The question of his death is, in my view, simply an articulation of his superhuman stature.[12] As superhuman, he could not die in any conventional way, hence his "death" must be

---

9 See, e.g., Wolfson, "Revealing and Re/veiling," 28–29. Ḥabad's claim that they are living *in* the messianic era is not without precedent in Judaism. See, e.g., Cyrus described as God's "anointed" in Isaiah 45 and the comments about Simon the Hasmonean in 1 Maccabees 14:4–15.

10 See Wolfson, *Open Secret*, 28–65; Yizhak Kraus, *The Seventh: Messianism in the Last Generation of Habad* [Hebrew] (Tel Aviv: Yediot Aharonot, 2007); Joseph Dan, *Modern Jewish Messianism: From Safed to Brooklyn* [Hebrew] (Tel Aviv: Ministry of Defense, 1999); Simon Dein, *Lubavitcher Messianism: What Really Happens When Prophecy Fails?* (New York: Continuum, 2011), 53–55; Michael Kravel-Tovi and Yoram Bilu, "The Work of the Present: Constructing Messianic Temporality in the Wake of Failed Prophecy among Ḥabad Ḥasidim," *American Ethnologist* 35, no. 2 (Feb. 2008): 64–80; Samuel Heilman and Menachem Friedman, *The Rebbe: The Life and Afterlife of Menachem Mendel Schneerson* (Princeton, NJ: Princeton University Press, 2010); and Aviezer Ravitsky, "The Lubavitch Messianic Movement: Between Conservatism and Messianism," in Ravitzky, *Messianism, Zionism, and Religious Radicalism*, trans. Michael Swirsky and Jonathan Chipman (Chicago: University of Chicago Press, 1996), 181–206.

11 See Tomer Persico, "Ḥabad's Lost Messiah," *Azure* 38 (Fall, 2009): 82–127; and Dein, *Lubavitcher Messianism*, 24.

12 For scholarly assessments of Schneerson's death and its implications for Ḥabad messianism, see Yoram Bilu, "'With Us More Than Ever': Making the Late Rabbi Present in Messianic Ḥabad" [Hebrew], in *Leadership and Authority in the Ultra-Orthodox Community: New Perspectives*, ed. Kimmy Caplan and Nurit Stadler (Tel Aviv: Van Leer Institute and Hakibbutz Hameuchad, 2009), 186–209; Michal Kravel-Tovi, "To See the Invisible Messiah: Messianic Socialization in the Wake of a Failed Prophecy in Ḥabad," *Religion* 39, no. 3 (2009): 248–60; Heilman and Friedman, *The Rebbe*, 197–247; and Persico, "Ḥabad's Lost Messiah." The notion of the Messiah as preexistent can be found in the Christian Bible in Hebrews 1–4 and John 1:1–18. A similar idea can be found in later talmudic literature (e.g., BT Nedarim 39b; Pesahim 5a, 54b), but there is no

interpreted through the prism of those divinized creatures (Enoch and Elijah) as articulated in ancient Israelite and later kabbalistic (including Sabbatean) literature.[13]

I am in agreement with the detailed analysis of Ḥabad messianism as described in Elliot Wolfson's *Open Secret: Postmessianic Messianism and the Mystical Revision*. There Wolfson argues that "the image of the personal Messiah may have been utilized theoretically to liberate one from the belief in the personal Messiah."[14] Or, in a more Kafkaesque register, the personal Messiah comes to tell us that there is no personal Messiah. The secret revealed is that there is no secret. For Wolfson, Ḥabad messianism constitutes a kabbalistic *coincidentia oppositorium*, a notion that opens up the possibility of "the infinite expanse in an infinitesimal point," enabling the corporeal and incorporeal to exist in a state of "being together."[15] I cannot delve here into the complicated argument Wolfson presents in *Open Secret*. However, it is significant to note that his argument suggests that the claims made by many disciples regarding Schneerson's messianic quasi-divine status (an issue Wolfson does not deal with extensively) are a direct product of Ḥabad's acosmic metaphysical assumptions regarding the ultimate collapsing of the barrier between the divine and the world. Wolfson suggests the term "apophatic panenthism" to define the distinctive way Ḥabad has rendered the kabbalistic relationship of the divine to the world. On the point of *coincidentia oppositorium* and its relationship to the status of Schneerson as "dead," Simon Dein notes, "Ḥabad understands the world in each of these ways simultaneously; as both an illusory manifestation of a concealed divine essence and as the one true actualized existence. Through these teachings, it is possible to understand how some Lubavitch followers held Rabbi Schneerson to be both revealed and concealed after his death."[16] To these followers,

---

particular person ascribed that preexistent status. The preexistence of the Son of Man is also explicit in 1 Enoch 48:3.

13 The question of the death of an ostensible Messiah in Judaism exists long after the overcoming of death in the Christ event in the Christian Bible. Similar questions were asked about Shabbatai Zevi. See, e.g., Gershom Scholem, *Sabbatai Sevi: The Mystical Messiah* (Princeton, NJ: Princeton University Press, 1973), 918–19; Isaiah Tishby, "Letters of R. Meir Rofe to R. Abraham Rovigo from the Years 1675–1680" [Hebrew], *Sefunot* 3–4 (1960): 71–130; and Nathaniel Riemer, "The Mystery of Adam, David, Messiah: Reincarnations of the Messianic Soul in 'Beer Sheva' (Seven Wells) by R. Beer Perlhefter," *Kabbalah: Journal for the Study of Jewish Mystical Texts* 26 (2012): 120.

14 Wolfson, *Open Secret*, 273. Cf. Wolfson, "Revealing and Re/veiling," 64–65, 92–93.

15 Wolfson, "Revealing and Re/veiling," 52. Cf. Wolfson, *Open Secret*, 92–93.

16 Dein, *Lubavitcher Messianism*, 32. Kenneth Seeskin pointed out to me the distinction between rationality and mythology, the former of which is Maimonidean and must be

Schneerson's concealment (*histalkus*) depends on his having in some real sense transcended his humanity and thus achieved a "being-together" with the divine that renders his death impossible. In my view, Wolfson's analysis illustrates that this claim is a practical application of Ḥabad's basic metaphysical assumptions.

In one sense, the messiah portrayed in Ḥabad's messianism is the individual embodiment of a universal messianic trajectory. This messiah joins the collective messianism of pre-ḥasidic, i.e., Lurianic doctrine, with the "neutralization" Scholem claimed Ḥasidism had achieved. In Ḥabad, Schneerson's "being-together" with the divine (to borrow Wolfson's locution), both bodily and spiritually, is nothing more than a prelude and microcosm of what will unfold collectively in the future.

My analysis will be divided into two parts. In the first part, I offer a reading of the complete *ẓaddik* (*ẓaddik gamur*) in *Sefer ha-Tanya*, the early Ḥabad text and cornerstone of its subsequent metaphysics. I suggest that the *Tanya* extends earlier kabbalistic and ḥasidic renderings of the *ẓaddik* and serves as a precedent for contemporary Ḥabad messianism.[17]

In the second part of my analysis, I suggest that while the notion of a divinized leader may be foreign to rabbinic Judaism (as refracted through post-rabbinic rabbinism and later early modern Orthodoxy), it has strong precedent in pre-rabbinic Judaism/Israelite religion. Late biblical and intertestamental messianisms, some of which posited the divine nature of the Messiah, including precepts for worshiping him, were largely rejected by the talmudic sages but may have informed some early Christologies and may have survived in altered states in early mystical Jewish traditions. I am not making a historical claim that contemporary Ḥabad is drawing from these pre-rabbinic sources, but rather suggesting some structural analogies that may help us further understand the metaphysical assumptions underlying Ḥabad's historical messianic claims.

Admittedly, the very different cultural and religious contexts of late antiquity and modernity make any such comparison challenging. The

---

retained as the messianic template to avoid the heretical conclusion that, I submit, is precisely what Ḥabad provides. See Seeskin, *Jewish Messianic Thoughts in an Age of Despair*, 3–26.

17 The notion of the *ẓaddik gamur* is not new in Ḥabad or Ḥasidism more generally. The notion exists in sixteenth-century Kabbalah of the Lurianic fraternity. See, e.g., in Menahem Kallus, "The Theurgy of Prayer in Lurianic Kabbalah" (PhD diss., Hebrew University, 2002), 368, on the notion of "first order" *ẓaddikim* in Lurianic literature. Cf. Jonathan Garb, "The Cult of Saints in Lurianic Kabbalah," *Jewish Quarterly Review* 98, no. 2 (Spring, 2008): 221.

ancient world, within and without Israelite society, divinized emperors and considered the divine and the world separated by a permeable barrier. And yet, even as Greek philosophy became monotheized in the early Middle Ages, remnants of permeable boundaries remained, not only in Christianity, which considered such boundary crossing part of its doctrinal commitments, but also in certain strains of medieval Kabbalah. Given the metaphysical descriptions of messianic mystical leaders in kabbalism, the use of superhuman categories to describe biblical figures in Kabbalah and later in ḥasidic exegesis, and the integration of the *ẓaddik* as a metaphysical category in Ḥabad Ḥasidism, the notion of a superhuman Messiah sharing dimensions of divine infinitude is not an unreasonable leap, even in a world where such traversing of the divine/human divide is not as culturally normative.[18]

Is the *Ẓaddik Gamur* a Divinized Human?

One of the salient features of Ḥabad literature is the way it turns the largely exegetical nature of early Ḥasidism into its own distinct neo-kabbalistic metaphysics. While there are numerous examples of ḥasidic masters and schools that are heavily kabbalistic in the classical sense, Ḥabad distinctively develops its own metaphysical system. This system, built on the Zohar and its Lurianic interpretation, is deployed to describe the relationship between the material

18 Perhaps the most compelling comparison to date is Joel Marcus, "The Once and Future Messiah in Early Christianity and Ḥabad," *New Testament Studies* 47, no. 3 (2001): 381–401. Cf. Dein, *Lubavitcher Messianism*, 122–38. The foundations of this story are not solely discussions of the status of the *ẓaddik* or rebbe in Ḥabad Ḥasidism, but are also the entire superstructure of Ḥabad's mystical vision. See, e.g., Rachel Elior, *The Paradoxical Ascent to God: The Kabbalistic Theosophy of Habad Ḥasidism* (Albany: SUNY Press, 1993), 104: Ḥabad Ḥasidism includes "a complex dialectical structure [that] corresponds to the dynamic of concealment and manifestation, coming into being and self-annihilation, stripping away and concretization, emanation and withdrawal, infusing and removal, or to the dynamics of the unity of opposites." This orientation arguably lends itself to a complex (re)reconstruction of the divine/human relationship. The "stripping away of corporeality" as an ontological and not symbolic (or metaphoric) idea is quite reminiscent of Christian notions of theosis and, parenthetically, of Islamic notions of the occultation of the Mahdi in Isma'ili, Shi'ite, and Sufi literature. See, e.g., Mohammad Ali Amir-Moezzi, *The Divine Guide in Early Shi'ism* (Albany: SUNY Press, 1994), 99–132; and Henri Corbin, "Divine Epiphany and Spiritual Birth in Ismailian Gnosis," in his *Cyclical Time and Ismaili Gnosis* (London: Kegan Paul, 1983), 59–150.

and spiritual realm and the nature and purpose of divine worship.[19] In contemporary Ḥabad, much of this system focuses on messianism in general and Rabbi Menahem Mendel Schneerson as Messiah in particular. I suggest that the precedent for this current focus is the broader discussion of the *ẓaddik* in early Ḥabad.[20] Ḥabad transforms the early ḥasidic populist notion of the *ẓaddik* as healer, miracle worker, and shaman. This transformation is influenced in part by the metaphysical inclination of Dov Baer of Mezritch, the teacher of Shneur Zalman of Liady.[21] That is, early Ḥabad literature such as *Sefer ha-Tanya* is more interested in the nature of the *ẓaddik*—one could say the metaphysical construction of the *ẓaddik*—than in his social function.[22] Given contemporary Ḥabad's seemingly uncharacteristic focus on active messianism, captured in the adage of the sixth rebbe, Joseph Isaac Schneersohn, "*Le-alter le-teshuvah le-alter le-ge'ulah!*" ("Repent immediately and redemption will come immediately!"—an adage ostensibly betraying Ḥabad's "neutralization"), it is noteworthy that early Ḥabad seemed quite uninterested in the zaddikism that was in full swing in Polish and Galician Ḥasidism during the same period.[23] The *Tanya* speaks at great length about the *ẓaddik* but does not connect him to the Messiah nor focus on any particular *ẓaddik*. It is my contention, however, that the template of the *ẓaddik* introduced in the *Tanya* sets the precedent for the conflation of rebbe and Messiah in contemporary

---

19 On some of the other ḥasidic schools that are heavily kabbalistic, see Louis Jacobs, *Turn Aside from Evil and Do Good: An Introduction and Way to the Tree of Life* (London: Littman Library of Jewish Civilization, 1997); Moshe Idel, *Ḥasidism: Between Ecstasy and Magic* (Albany: SUNY Press, 1995), 31–145; Menahem Kallus, "The Relationship of the Baal Shem Tov to the Practice of Lurianic Kavvanot in Light of his Comments on the *Siddur Rashkov*," *Kabbalah: Journal for the Study of Jewish Mystical Texts* 2 (1997): 151–68.

20 The connection between the Messiah and the notion of superhumanity (however defined) has a long history in Kabbalah, from Abulafia to Shabbatai Zevi, Cordozo, and others. See Idel, *Ben: Sonship and Jewish Mysticism* (London: Continuum, 2007), 597.

21 For the relationship to shamanism and the *ẓaddik*, see Alan Brill, "The Spiritual World of a Master of Awe: Divine Vitality, Theosis and Healing in the Degel Mahane Ephraim," *Jewish Studies Quarterly* 8, no. 1 (2001): 27–65; and Jonathan Garb, *Shamanic Trance in Modern Kabbalah* (Chicago: University of Chicago Press, 2011), 99–118.

22 On the social function of the *ẓaddik*, see Immanuel Etkes, "The Zaddik: The Interrelationship between Religious Doctrine and Social Organization," in *Ḥasidism Reappraised*, ed. Ada Rapoport-Albert (London: Littman Library of Jewish Civilization, 1998), 159–67.

23 The seventh rebbe, Menahem Mendel Schneerson, added the emphasis *Moshiaḥ akhshav, teikef u-miyyad mamash* (Messiah now, immediately, literally!).

Ḥabad.[24] The potential of the superhumanity of a perfected human, described exegetically in Ḥabad teaching below, is concretized in the category of the *ẓaddik gamur*, who has transcended the limits of human nature.[25]

The concept of the *ẓaddik gamur*, which may inform contemporary Ḥabad messianism, is one of the fundamental concepts in Ḥabad metaphysics and psychology, especially in the *Tanya*. In chapter 1, Shneur Zalman of Liady, citing both Vital's *Sha'arei Kedushah* and *Eiẓ Ḥayyim*,[26] argues that both the *ẓaddik* (righteous person) and *rasha* (evil person) contain two souls, one that is embedded in the material world and thus limited by the body, and one that is divine. This divine soul is described in the verse "a portion of the supernal God" (Job 31:2)—that is, a soul not limited by corporeality.[27] In a quasi-Gnostic register, Shneur Zalman (following Luria) defines humanness as the limitation of the divine soul by the corporeal soul, itself limited by being inextricably bound to the physical body and its innate desire.[28] Thus the human has "divine" potential that is only intermittently manifested due to its inability to liberate itself permanently from its corporeal counterpart.

---

24 On the distinct dimension of contemporary Ḥabad in terms of ḥasidic messianism more generally, see Joseph Dan, "The Dual Nature of Ḥasidic Messianism," in *Hesed Ve-Emet: Studies in Honor of Ernest S. Frerichs*, ed. Jodi Magness and Seymour Gitin (Atlanta, GA: Scholars Press, 1998), 391–407.

25 But see Dan, "The Dual Nature of Ḥasidic Messianism," 405–406: "The scholar is willing to accept that Christians believe that there was a man who was the embodiment of God. And, that the believers in Sabbatai Zevi and Jacob Frank also believed in that. But regarding Ḥasidim, many of whom live among us, and today represent us in the Knesset and in Jerusalem, to say that they believe the *ẓaddik* is God, this is impossible to accept. It is possible to understand that some Lubavitch Ḥasidim who have become so enthused that they have lost their sense believe in such a thing, but this group is insignificant in number" (my translation). This seems odd. To say that people who function in the mainstream of a community simply cannot hold beliefs that are anathema to that community is not, in my view, an argument. In fact, the opposite is the core of David Berger's argument in *The Rebbe, The Messiah, and the Scandal of Orthodox Indifference* (London: Littman Library of Jewish Civilization, 2001).

26 See Hayyim Vital, *Sha'arei Kedushah*, part 1, gate 2 (end); *Eiẓ Ḥayyim*, 50:2.

27 On this see Elijah de Vidas, *Reishit Ḥokhmah* (The Gate of Love), ed. Aharon Kotler (Jerusalem, 1984), ch. 3, 386–87; and Moshe Idel, *Kabbalah: New Perspectives* (New Haven, CT: Yale University Press, 1988), 64–65.

28 The *Tanya* presents an abbreviated version of Luria's idea in *Eiẓ Ḥayyim*, 50:2. Luria suggests that the "animal soul" contains the four elements of materiality that are doubled to eight—four parts good inclination and four parts evil inclination. Therefore, the very experience of being human is driven from this "animal soul." The "divine soul" is embedded in this animal soul and thus unable to function independently. In the *Tanya*, the sign of a *ẓaddik gamur* is one who has severed his divine soul from the confines of his animal soul by transforming the fours parts of the evil inclination into the good. Luria makes no such assessment in his discussion.

In chapter 1 of the *Tanya*, the *ẓaddik* is mentioned generically, without distinction.[29] It appears that the *ẓaddik* here refers to the incomplete (or unfulfilled) *ẓaddik* who still battles with the challenges of corporeality—that is, one who is still capable of sin, is fallible, and dies. Put differently, the *ẓaddik* in chapter 1 of the *Tanya* is a human being.

> Every Israelite, whether a *ẓaddik* or a *rasha*, has two souls, as it is written *and the souls I made* (Isaiah 57:16).[30] There are two souls, one soul from the side of the demonic that is enveloped in the blood of the human in order to sustain the body, as it is written, *the soul [life] of the flesh is in the blood* (Leviticus 17:11).[31] This houses all the corporeal attributes from the four foundations of corporeality. . . . The second soul in the Israelite is *a portion of God* (Job 31:2) literally [*mamash!*], as it says, *and He blew into his mouth the soul of life* [*nishmat ḥayyim*] (Genesis 2:7).[32]

This is not simply a structural comment but a phenomenological one as well. The *ẓaddik*, like all others, contains these two souls and is thus limited in his ability to actualize his divine nature consistently. In chapter 10, the distinction in chapter 1 is applied to the *ẓaddik gamur*:

> The *ẓaddik gamur* is one who transforms his evil to good, as it is thus called "a *ẓaddik* who owns his good" [*ẓaddik ve-tov lo*]. This occurs by means of removing the "soiled garments" from evil completely—that is, he will hate the pleasures of the world which people enjoy in order to satisfy corporeal desire alone and not to worship God, since those pleasures are drawn from the side of the demonic. The *ẓaddik gamur* will [naturally] despise all that stems from the demonic due to his love of God and his holiness.[33]

We are introduced here to the *ẓaddik gamur* as one who turns his evil nature to good, who completely disrobes from his soiled garments (his corporeal limitations), and who is disgusted by material pleasures because he

29 There is a distinction made earlier in this chapter between the complete and incomplete *ẓaddik*, drawing from BT Berakhot 7a, but this is largely descriptive.

30 The more contextual translation would read, "Also create the breath of life." See the *JPS Hebrew-English Tanakh* (Philadelphia: Jewish Publication Society, 1999). I translate the verse above in the context of how it is being deployed as a proof-text for the notion of two souls, since the term *neshamot* is the plural form of "soul" (*neshamah*).

31 The notion of the "animal soul" is rooted in Ecclesiastes 3:21 and is developed in detail in *Zohar Ḥadash* on Ruth, 65a–b. Cf. Zohar 1.69b and 3.33b. *Eiẓ Ḥayyim*, 49:3, 50:2.

32 *Sefer ha-Tanya*, chs. 1 and 2, 5b, 6a. All translations are mine. For a similar description a bit earlier, see Ya'akov Yosef of Polonnoye, *Toledot Ya'akov Yosef* (1782), 1:239b, 240a.

33 *Sefer ha-Tanya*, ch. 10, 14b, 15a.

is no longer limited by human desire (his divine soul is no longer embedded in, or limited by, his corporeal soul). These principles have roots at least as far back as the Zohar.[34] In the Zohar, we read that the *ẓaddik gamur* simply has no evil inclination, although the Zohar never elaborates what this means.[35] In the *Tanya*, I would translate this state as one of theosis (at least as it is adopted by Eastern Orthodox Christianity), whereby a human being becomes a divine being while still maintaining the shell of their humanity.[36]

This is better illustrated by a clever turn of phrase later in the same chapter. Commenting on a passage from the Babylonian Talmud, Sanhedrin 97b, "I have seen the elite [*benei aliyah*] and they are few," Shimon bar Yohai (Rashbi), speaking about his illuminati, teaches that they, and only they, are *benei aliyah*. Shneur Zalman transposes Rashbi's comment about his disciples to a description of the *ẓaddik gamur*. In the *Tanya*, *benei aliyah* now means "those who invert evil (in themselves) and elevate it to holiness."[37]

34 This is likely drawn from *Sha'arei Kedushah*, cited above, where we read, "When one overcomes his evil inclination and excises all the corporeal traits through heroic means and fulfills Torah and *miẓvot*, he is called a *ẓaddik gamur* and fearer of heaven. . . . If he continues in that manner he can excise all of those corporeal traits completely until he no longer has any corporeal desire whatsoever. He will absorb the spiritual traits such that he will no longer have to do battle with the evil inclination. His body and foundational soul will be cleansed from all manner of materiality." Cf. Moshe Idel, "By purifying one's soul, or actualizing one's intellect, the mystic escapes the domain of limitation and multiplicity and becomes similar to the upper spiritual world." See Idel, "Universalization and Integration: Two Conceptions of Mystical Union in Jewish Mysticism," in *Mystical Union and Monotheistic Faith: An Ecumenical Dialogue*, ed. Moshe Idel and Bernard McGinn (New York: Macmillan, 1989), 51.

35 See, e.g., Zohar 2.117b, 3.213a.

36 On the concept of theosis in the Eastern Orthodox Church, see Georgios Mantzaridis, *The Deification of Man: St. Gregory Palamas and the Orthodox Tradition* (Crestwood, NY: St. Vladimir's Seminary, 1984), 15, 29, 31. On the extent to which this notion of the deification of man has become the backbone of Orthodox doctrine, see Jules Gross, *La divinization du chrétien d'après les Pères grecs: Contribution historique à la doctrine de la grâce* (Paris: Lecoffre, 1938). See also Vigen Guroian, *Incarnate Love: Essays in Orthodox Ethics* (Notre Dame: University of Notre Dame Press, 1987). For more on this from a ḥasidic perspective, see my "Ethics Disentangled from the Law: Incarnation, the Universal, and Ḥasidic Ethics," *Kabbalah: Journal for the Study of Jewish Mystical Texts* 15 (2006): 31–76. Cf. Idel, *Ben*, 552.

37 *Sefer ha-Tanya*, ch. 10, 15a. The notion of a human reaching the place where they simply cannot sin is also found in Ya'akov Koppel (Lipshitz) (d. 1740), *Sha'arei Gan Eden* (1801; Brooklyn: Karetz, 1994), which was an enormously popular work among early *ḥasidim*. See *Sha'arei Gan Eden*, "*Derekh Emet*," opening 4, path 5, 33a. Referring to the five levels of the cosmic soul, Koppel writes, "One who reaches the level of the *nefesh* can certainly sin, but one who reaches the level of *ḥayye* and certainly the *yeḥidah* cannot sin because in him the four letters of the divine name (YHVH) are complete and he becomes a chariot for the name [of YHVH]." For an analysis of Koppel, see Isaiah

Tying this back to the chapter 1 comment about the incomplete *ẓaddik* as containing two souls, this description of the *ẓaddik gamur* suggests that he has shed himself of the limitation of his corporeal soul. It is not that the divine soul of the *ẓaddik gamur* is different from others (though he may be loftier). Rather, the *ẓaddik gamur* is one whose divine soul is no longer limited by his corporeal soul. He has no *yeẓer ha-ra* and no *yeẓer tov* (evil inclination and good inclination, both of which are characteristics of the corporeal soul, in Lurianic Kabbalah).[38] This Jewish definition of (a permanent state of) theosis yields a divinized being who is unable to sin, infallible (i.e., not susceptible to human error), and perhaps unable to die in any conventional way because he has already shed the material garments that constitute his mortality. In this sense the *ẓaddik gamur* is the human embodiment of the ḥasidic notion of *dirah be-takhtonim* (God's dwelling place on earth). In short, a theology that acknowledges "theosis" as a working category can easily adopt a notion of "apotheosis," whereby a person does not die because he has transcended his humanness in life.[39]

A final comment is made about the *ẓaddik gamur* in *Tanya* chapter 35. Here, Shneur Zalman addresses by implication the danger inherent in collapsing any distinction between theosis and apotheosis:

> The soul of a person, even of a *ẓaddik gamur*, should serve God with awe, love, and enjoyment. Even [for the *ẓaddik gamur*] existence is not nullified completely nor is he taken up literally in the light of God to become one [with it]. Rather, he remains an independent being who loves and fears God. . . . Concerning the dwelling of the *Shekhinah*: this is the full disclosure of God

Tishby, "Between Sabbateanism and Ḥasidism: The Sabbateanism of the Kabbalist R. Yaakov Koppel Lipshitz of Mezritch" [Hebrew], in Tishby, *Netivei Emunah u-Minut* (Jerusalem: Magnes, 1982), 204–26; and my "Early Ḥasidism and the Metaphysics of *Malkhut*: *Malkhut* as *Eyn Sof* in the Writings of Ya'akov Koppel of Mezritch," *Kabbalah: Journal for the Study of Jewish Mystical Texts* 27 (2012): 245–67.

38 Such an idea is not foreign to the rabbis either. See, e.g., the discussion about the boundaries required to prevent physical contact between a man and a woman who is not his wife. See BT Shabbat 13a regarding Ulla and Tosefot s.v. "*upliga*."

39 For a medieval precedent to this way of thinking, see Isaac of Acre, *Me'irat Einayim*, ed. Amos Goldreich (Jerusalem: Hebrew University Press, 1984), 222. Cf. Moshe Idel, *Kabbalah and Eros* (New Haven: Yale University Press, 2005), 158. A similar locution appears in Nathan of Gaza, as quoted by Scholem: "Real faith is the belief that the Messiah will reach the greatness of pure divinity (*elohut gamur*) close to emanation (*azilut*). This is the whole notion of the Messiah. If this does not transpire, he is not the Messiah even if he does all the miracles and wonders in the world." See Gershom Scholem, "New Sabbatean Documents from the Book *To'eh Ruah*" [Hebrew], *Zion* 7 (1942): 188. Cf. Chaim Wirszubski, *Bein ha-Shitim: Kabbalah, Kabbalat Nozrit, Shabta'ut*, ed. Moshe Idel (Jerusalem: Magnes Press, 1990), 243–44.

> and the light of *ein sof* in a particular thing. We would say that this thing becomes absorbed in the light of God and is nullified completely. At that moment the Oneness of God fully dwells there. However, anything whose existence is not nullified cannot house the full disclosure [of God]. Even the *ẓaddik gamur*, who is bound to God with great love, a God whom no thought can fathom. . . . This love is "existent" [*yeish*] and not "infinite" [*efes*]. The light of God is not fully disclosed in him except through the performance of *miẓvot*, which are the will and wisdom of God literally with no concealment.[40]

Shneur Zalman describes the *ẓaddik gamur* as one who has overcome his corporeal soul but whose materiality remains intact. That is, he has not been "taken up" or liberated from his corporeal existence (like Enoch or Elijah). Therefore the *ẓaddik gamur* exists in a state of (permanent?) theosis whereby his physicality does not limit his divine nature, and thus he is still obligated to perform *miẓvot*.[41] Later in this chapter, Shneur Zalman discusses how *miẓvot* draw down the light of God into one's physical existence and transform the evil in the corporeal soul to good.[42] I do not think this part of the chapter relates to the *ẓaddik gamur*, who no longer needs to transform the evil, since it has already been transformed.[43] The obliga-

40 *Sefer ha-Tanya*, ch. 35, 44a–45a. Cf. Menahem Mendel Schneerson, *Torat Menahem* (Brooklyn: Lahak Hanochos, 2008) vol. 1, 193 and vol. 3, part 2, 278.

41 Even though the *ẓaddik gamur* remains obligated to the *miẓvot*, the nature of his obligation differs from the obligation of one for whom the *miẓvot* still serve to perfect his body and soul. For an interesting take on this question, see Moshe Elyakum Beri'ah of Kuznitz, *Be'er Moshe* (Tel Aviv, n.d.), 127c, cited and discussed in Moshe Idel, *Enchanted Chains: Techniques and Rituals in Jewish Mysticism* (Los Angeles: Cherub, 2005), 70–71. For a discussion of the nature of *miẓvot* for someone who has already transcended them, see my *Ḥasidism on the Margin: Reconciliation, Antinomianism, and Messianism in Izbica and Radzin Ḥasidism* (Madison: University of Wisconsin Press, 2003), 216–39.

42 The notion of being man and not God yet also divine is iterated by the Sabbatean Abraham Miguel Cardozo, who describes the Messiah as one who "will be a man but not God, even if he will be greater than Adam." Cardozo is cited in Scholem, *Sources and Texts Concerning the History of Sabbateanism and Its Metamorphoses* [Hebrew] (Jerusalem: Mosad Bialik, 1974), 288; and Idel, *Ben*, 464.

43 We have other examples where the *ẓaddik* is viewed as one who no longer needs to perform *miẓvot* even as he may continue to do so. For example, Hayyim of Chernovitz's *Sidduro shel Shabbat* tells us: "One who has left the bounds of humanity can fulfill no *miẓvah* and can study no Torah because he has already transcended the human condition. This is why God put it into our nature to be cut off and fall back from too much love. Then he will be able to fulfill the Torah." See *Sidduro Shel Shabbat* (Jerusalem, 1960), 81a–b. Cf. Arthur Green, *Devotion and Commandment: The Faith of Abraham in the Ḥasidic Imagination* (Cincinnati: Hebrew Union College Press, 1989), 87 and note 103; and Idel, *Ben*, 566. Another example can be found in Gershon Henokh

tory nature of the *miẓvot* for the *ẓaddik gamur* is no longer utilitarian in a Maimonidean sense—it does not perfect the body or the soul. Rather, it serves as a pure manifestation of divine will in a person liberated from his human limitations but not yet liberated from his physical existence.

A few questions can now be asked. First, considering that the *Tanya* is subtitled "the book for intermediates [*beinonim*]," are we to surmise that the category of the *ẓaddik gamur* is purely theoretical?[44] That is, did Shneur Zalman believe there were such people? Did Menahem Mendel Schneerson believe it? Second, is the *ẓaddik gamur* a transitory state that we all can experience—that is, is it an interpretation of ḥasidic *deveikut*, or is it a state where the limitations of humanness are permanently discarded while physicality remains?[45] To my knowledge, the *Tanya* never directly answers these questions or designates any person as a *ẓaddik gamur*. But my focus is not on Shneur Zalman or the *Tanya*. Rather, I am examining Ḥabad's description of its rebbe as a superhuman Messiah and wondering if the superhuman attributions of Schneerson are in fact drawn from this early description of the *ẓaddik gamur*. In short, is Schneerson considered a *ẓaddik gamur* by his disciples? If so, the many descriptions of him (built on his own descriptions of Moses) as infallible and quasi-immortal make more sense.[46] The claims are not only descriptive but metaphysical and, like Incarnation in Christianity, become the centerpiece of contemporary Ḥabad religiosity.[47]

---

of Radzin's notion of the messianic figure for whom *miẓvot* serve only to connect to the collective and are no longer needed to perfect the Messiah's soul. See my *Ḥasidism on the Margin*, 205–48.

44 See, e.g., Rashi on BT Berakhot 61b, s.v. "*im atah min ha-beinonim*."

45 The transitory nature of the term seems to exist in the Talmud. For some examples, see BT Ketubot 105b; BT Kiddushin 40b, 49b; PT Peah 5:1. The *Tanya* appears to present a structural model that does not conform to the more colloquial notion of *ẓaddik gamur* as it is used in halakhic literature. The relationship between theosis and *deveikut*, a unitive mystical experience, is complicated. See Idel, *Kabbalah: New Perspectives*, 66–67, citing Menahem Nahum of Chernobyl's *Me'or Einayim*.

46 The notion of Moses as a Messiah who is at once divine and human has precedent in the Israelite religion. See Wayne Meeks, "Moses as God and King," in *Religions in Antiquity: Essays in Memory of Erwin Ramsdell Goodenough*, ed. Jacob Neusner (Leiden: Brill, 1968), 354–71.

47 The kabbalistic notion of the incarnation of the Messiah is rooted in the depiction by Shimon bar Yohai in the Zohar. See Yehuda Liebes, "Messiah of the Zohar" [Hebrew]), in *The Messianic Idea in Jewish Thought*, ed. Shmuel Reem (Jerusalem: Israel Academy of Science and Humanities, 1982), 87–234. This idea also becomes prominent in Sabbatean thought and appears in *Ẓaddik Yesod Olam*, thought to be a Lurianic commentary on the book of Ruth that is actually a Sabbatean tract likely written by Leibel Proznitz. It is still printed as a supplement to most editions of Luria's *Sha'ar ha-Yiḥudim*. See Yehuda Liebes, "*Ẓaddik Yesod Olam*: Sabbatean Myth" [Hebrew],

For Schneerson, the *ẓaddik gamur* was *not* simply a theoretical category. It describes the personality of the Messiah. He writes, "Moses brought forth the disclosure of the Messiah. And Moses was certainly a *ẓaddik gamur* from his very essence."[48] The notion of Schneerson as a *ẓaddik gamur* finds later expression in the claim that he had "totally nullified his [corporeal] existence," a common assertion describing his spiritual stature and his similarity to Moses.[49] The complete nullification of his corporeal existence (in line with *Tanya*, ch. 35)—that is, the liberation of his divine soul from the confines of his corporeal soul—would lean in the direction of a permanent *ẓaddik gamur* status, according to my understanding of the *Tanya*.[50]

This status is suggested by Schneerson himself in volume 2 of *Likkutei Siḥot*, where he writes about a description of the Rashbi in the Zohar.[51] Provocatively, Zohar 2.38a asks about Exodus 34:23, "Three times a year all your males shall appear before the face of God," "Who is the face of God?" The Zohar answers its own question: the face of God is Rabbi Shimon bar

---

in Liebes, *Sod ha-Emunah ha-Shabta'it* (Jerusalem: Bialik Institute, 1995), 62 and 69. For two other attempts to link Ḥabad to incarnation, see 311–14 of Barbara Redman, "One God: Toward a Rapprochement of Orthodox Judaism and Christianity," *Journal of Ecumenical Studies* 31, nos. 3–4 (Summer–Fall, 1994): 307–31; and Alon Goshen-Gottstein, "Judaisms and Incarnational Theologies: Mapping Out the Parameters of Dialogue," *Journal of Ecumenical Studies* 39, nos. 3–4 (2002): 219–47.

48 Schneershon, *Torat Menaḥem*, vol. 3, part 2, 51. Cf. *Torat Menaḥem*, vol. 9, part 3, 34, where Schneerson alludes to Abraham being a *ẓaddik gamur* as well.

49 See Yizhak Ginsburgh, "Thoughts before the Yahrzeit of Our Holy Messiah—The Holy Day 3 Tammuz" [Hebrew], *Beis Moshiaḥ* 41 (June, 1995): 13; Shalom Dov Wolpo, "'Comfort Ye, Comfort Ye, My People'—Double Comfort" [Hebrew], *Kfar Ḥabad* (5743): 6–7; and Berger, *The Rebbe, the Messiah, and the Scandal of Orthodox Indifference*, 25, 30.

50 A similar though not identical description of Moses can be found in Ya'akov Moshe Harlap's *Mei Marom on Numbers* (Israel, 1997), 166: "We find that, regarding Moses, the *Shekhinah* spoke from his throat: *Moses spoke and God answered in a voice* (Exodus 19:19). That is, the voice went from his mouth without his lips moving. It states that Moses was disabled with his mouth and tongue to teach us that the *Shekhinah* was speaking and not him. However, afterward, when Moses reached the stature of *These are the things Moses spoke*, he became so elevated and holy that even his lips were part of the power of God. His body was elevated to the level (*beḥinat*) of the *Shekhinah*! And this is what it means that *Moses spoke on his own accord*. It was not only that the *Shekhinah* spoke in his throat but rather the *Shekhinah* was also in his mouth." Cf. *Mei Marom* to Deuteronomy 1: "Moses had elevated himself to the place of 'all is for God,' until there was no need to prophecy because everything [in him] was prophecy. This was different than before when the word [of God] was in his mouth but it was according to reason [*da'at*]. Now he became so elevated that he lost his essence completely and everything he spoke was the word of God." See Hayyim of Volozhin, *Nefesh ha-Ḥayyim* 3:14, for the possible roots of this idea.

51 Schneerson, *Likkutei Siḥot*, 2:444.

Yohai, and only the pure males (those who are the elite) merit to be seen before him. (For "pure," we read a play on the phrase "all your males" [*kol zakhurkha*] that means "the male of males"—the male of males will be seen before the face of God.[52]) Schneerson describes this face of God as an example of the *ẓaddik gamur*, one who has been liberated from the limitations of conventional human existence. Joseph Isaac Schneersohn, Schneerson's father-in-law and the sixth Lubavitcher Rebbe, makes a starker suggestion by commenting that since he (Rashbi/*ẓaddik gamur*) has no human existence whatsoever, it is fitting to call him God (*Adon ha-Shem*). Why? Because that description applies to the "divinity within him," says Joseph Isaac, which, I would add, referring back to the *Tanya* cited above, is now unhampered by the material dimension of the corporeal soul. The divine soul ("the portion of God above") is fully realized in the human, thus effacing the human, only when unencumbered by the corporeal soul.[53]

I will briefly treat the question of Schneerson's death. It has been argued that to acknowledge Schneerson's death would disqualify him as the long-anticipated Jewish Messiah.[54] Some liken the notion of the dead Messiah to Christianity, but this is, in my view, an error. Christianity has no dead Messiah—it has a resurrected Messiah. As Paul made clear, Christianity rests on the belief in Jesus's resurrection as an overcoming of death (1 Corinthians 15:1, 15:11; Romans 1:4).[55] Jesus did indeed die on the cross at Calvary, for if not, he could not have been resurrected. It was only by dying that Jesus could overcome death. The claim that Schneerson

---

52 See "Yedid Nefesh" to Zohar 2.38a in Yechiel Avraham Bar Lev, *Sefer ha-Zohar im Bi'ur Yedid Nefesh* (Petah Tikva, Israel, 1994), 5:190–91. I also thank Nathaniel Berman for clarification of this passage. On the notion of the illuminati as having "the face of the *Shekhinah*," see 104 of Yehuda Liebes, "Zohar and Eros" [Hebrew], *Alpayyim* 9 (1994): 67–119; Elliot R. Wolfson, *Through a Speculum That Shines: Vision and Imagination in Medieval Jewish Mysticism* (Princeton, NJ: Princeton University Press, 1994), 368; Melila Hellner-Eshed, *A River Shines Forth from Eden* [Hebrew] (Tel Aviv: Am Oved, 2005), 45; and the discussion in Eitan Fishbane, "The Scent of a Rose: Drama, Fiction, and Narrative Form in the Zohar," *Prooftexts* 29, no. 3 (2009): 324–61.

53 The notion of Moshe being called "the face of God" exists in a thirteenth-century Castilian text by Shema'yah ben Issac ha-Levi entitled *Sefer Seror ha-Ḥayyim*, ms. Leiden, Warner 24, folio 199a–b, cited in Moshe Idel, *Enchanted Chains*, 87–88: "And the face of Moshe was like the face of God, blessed be He, and understand that before the birth of Moshe the essence of the name YHWH was not known." See the comments on this by Goshen-Gottstein, "Judaisms and Incarnational Theologies," 236–37.

54 See the discussion in Berger, *The Rebbe, the Messiah, and the Scandal of Orthodox Indifference*, 80–94.

55 Cf. Martin Buber, *Two Types of Faith*, trans. Norman P. Goldhawk (New York: Collier, 1951), 98–99.

did not die—or did not die in the way humans die—is something else.[56] This claim, one that I think is rooted in the doctrine of the *ẓaddik gamur*, is closer to the idea stated in the Qur'an, 4:156–57: the Jews did not kill Jesus, nor did he die on the cross, but rather "God raised him up to Himself." The claim resembles too the Shi'ite and Isma'ili notion of the occultation or disappearance of the Mahdi, or twelfth Imam, who will remain concealed until the end-time.[57] The idea of an undying holy person also became popular in Sabbatean doctrine and was included in crypto-Sabbatean texts such as *Ẓaddik Yesod Olam*, which continues to be printed as an authentic Lurianic text.[58] The root of the idea likely lies in Deutero-Isaiah (Isaiah 52:14, 53:11).

The notion that Schneerson did not die is buttressed by a plethora of sources in classical Jewish literature concerning Enoch, Elijah, and Jacob (even, in one case, Moses). These sources report that these figures—seven in all, according to the Talmud—did not die but instead experienced varying

56 See, e.g., Shalom Dov Wolpo's *Ha-Nisayon ha-Aḥaron* (Keriyat Gat: Shalom Dov Wolpo, 1994). The notion that Judaism before Christianity has no notion of a resurrected Messiah is often cited as a distinguishing mark separating Judaism from Christianity. See, e.g., Paula Fredriksen, *Jesus of Nazareth, King of the Jews: A Jewish Life and the Emergence of Christianity* (New York, Vintage, 1999), 126.

57 See Mohammad Ali Amir-Moezzi, *The Divine Guide in Early Shi'ism: The Sources of Esotericism in Islam*, trans. David Streight (Albany: SUNY Press, 1994); Abdulaziz Abdulhussein Sachendina, *The Just Ruler in Shi'ite Islam: The Comprehensive Jurist in Imamite Jurisprudence* (New York: Oxford University Press, 1988), 237–45; Moojan Momen, *An Introduction to Shi'i Islam* (New Haven, CT: Yale University Press, 1985), 161–71; Riffat Hassan, "Messianism and Islam," *Journal of Ecumenical Studies* 22, no. 2 (Spring, 1985): 261–91; and Henry Corbin, *Cyclical Time and Ismaili Gnosis* (London: Kegan Paul, 1983), 117–30. Most importantly, see Shahzad Bashir, *Messianic Hopes and Mystical Visions: The Nūrbakhshīya between Medieval and Modern Islam* (Columbia: University of South Carolina Press, 2003), esp. 3–28, 76–108. The parallels between Ḥabad's rendering of their rebbe's "death" and the occultation of the Mahdi are quite rich and will, I hope, be the topic of another essay. The phenomenological connection between the Mahdi and Schneerson as Messiah may have a historical link in the relationship between Sabbatean messianism and Isma'ilan theology. See Israel Friedlander, "Jewish-Arabic Studies: Shiitic Elements in Jewish Sectarianism," *Jewish Quarterly Review*, n.s., 2 (1912): 492–96, 514–16; Scholem, *Sabbatai Sevi*, 901–13; Paul Fenton, "Shabbetay Sebi and His Muslim Contemporary Muhammad an-Niyazi," in *Approaches to Judaism in Medieval Times*, vol. 3, ed. David R. Blumenthal (Atlanta: Scholars Press, 1988), 81–88; and Betsal'el Na'or, *Post-Sabbatian Sabbatianism: Study of an Underground Messianic Movement* (New York: Orot, 1999), 14–20.

58 More generally, see Scholem, *Sabbatai Ẓevi: The Mystical Messiah* [Hebrew] (Tel Aviv: Am Oved, 1957), 792. On the notion of occultation in crypto-Sabbatean texts, see Liebes, "*Ẓaddik Yesod Olam*," 67. Cf. Chaim Wirszubski, *Bein ha-Shitim*, 245, citing Nathan of Gaza.

states of apotheosis.[59] And yet with the death of every one of these figures, except Enoch and Elijah, mourners acted as if the figure in question were dead: they buried the figure (except Moses), eulogized him, and so on. If we want to get a sense of what Schneerson thought about this issue, we need to explore whether he thought a *ẓaddik gamur* dies and, if so, what the nature of his death is.[60]

I have found one source (I am sure there are many more) that makes the explicit claim that the *ẓaddik gamur* indeed dies: "'With the kick of the serpent.'[61] [This describes the death] of very great *ẓaddikim*. The reason they die is solely due to the sin of the Tree of Knowledge. Therefore, even *ẓaddikim gamurim* have a sense of themselves [as independent beings], as is known, 'even a *ẓaddik gamur* should serve God with awe, love, and enjoyment, as his existence is not nullified completely . . . (*Tanya*, ch. 35).'"[62] As I understand this somewhat oblique comment, Schneerson is suggesting that *ẓaddikim gamurim* surely die.[63] Their death is like one who did not sin, as described in the Talmud. Citing the passage from the *Tanya* discussed above, he suggests that since the *ẓaddik gamur* still retains a physical existence, even in a perfected state, that existence must expire. However, the nature of that expiration is different from the death of those who are not *ẓaddikim gamurim*.

For those who are fully human, death is the separation of the soul from the body and the liberation of the divine soul from the corporeal soul. This separation (in Hebrew, *petirah*, or "separation," is the euphemism for death)

59 On Enoch, see Genesis 5:22, 5:24. On Elijah, see 2 Kings 2:11; in general see BT Bava Batra 121b. On Jacob, see Genesis 49:33 and BT Ta'anit 5b. For a discussion of these and many other sources see Gil Student, "Is the Rebbe Alive?," in *Can the Rebbe Be Moshiah: Proofs from Gemara, Midrash, and Rambam* (Boca Raton, FL: Universal, 2002), 24–45. Cf. Berger, *The Rebbe, the Messiah, and the Scandal of Orthodox Indifference*, 18–31.

60 Therefore I think the whole issue about resurrection is not central here. Much has been written in contemporary Ḥabad about the legitimacy of a Jewish Messiah who dies and is resurrected. The most comprehensive treatment can be found in Wolpo's *Ha-Nisayon ha-Aḥaron*.

61 This is an expression used to describe those who died without sin. See BT Shabbat 55b; Baba Batra 17a. It is used quite often in the Lurianic discussions about *gilgul*. See *Sha'ar ha-Gilgulim*, introduction, 23 and 38.

62 Schneerson, *Torat Menaḥem*, vol. 4, part 1, 334. The notion that the righteous without sin die as a result of Adam's sin is a prominent feature in the Zohar and later in Lurianic Kabbalah and points to a notion of original sin in Judaism. On this, see my *From Metaphysics to Midrash: Myth, History, and the Interpretation of Scripture in Lurianic Kabbala* (Bloomington: Indiana University Press, 2008), 34–74.

63 In this sense they do not transcend the biblical comments about human mortality, e.g., Genesis 6:3; Psalm 90:10; and Ecclesiastes 6:6. But their relationship to their bodies is different from the relationship of those who have not reached the same state of purification.

is understood as a liberating experience in that the divine soul can return to its source while the corporeal soul undergoes its postmortem purifications. The death of the *ẓaddik gamur* is different because his divine soul is not limited by his corporeal soul even during his physical existence. Moreover, his corporeal soul (*nefesh behamit*) that contains both the good inclination and the drive to sin has already been transformed during his life and thus there is no need for postmortem purification. In one sense, the *ẓaddik gamur* is "dead" during his life and thus alive in his death in that he has already transcended the limitation of what it is to be human even though he maintains a physical presence in the world. On this reading, the *ẓaddik gamur* cannot die because he accomplished what death accomplishes during his life.[64] What can happen, then, is an occultation or concealment of his physical presence (in Ḥabad nomenclature, *helem gamur*, "complete concealment") that can be reversed at some future time.[65] Thus Ḥabad messianists refer to their rebbe's *histalkus*, his disappearance or occultation.

This is not, in my view, resurrection. If we are to say that Ḥabad holds Schneerson to be a *ẓaddik gamur*—perhaps, as Messiah, the last *ẓaddik gamur*—then his death is extraordinary and his present state is one of occultation. The grave is not empty—it contains the remains of a body that the *ẓaddik gamur* had already transcended during his time on earth. Is this apotheosis? It all depends on how we define it. I prefer "occultation" as it enables one to regard the grave as full and death (as we know it) as not having occurred. I do not defend Ḥabad's claim that Schneerson did not die a conventional death, at least not *prima facie*, nor do I argue that such a claim is or is not within the parameters of "Orthodox" Judaism. Rather, I attempt to understand the theological claim within the context of Ḥabad's own metaphysical nomenclature—to view the logic of the argument on its own terms. The "legitimacy" of the claim is a sociological question beyond the scope of this chapter.

---

64 See, e.g., Ya'akov Yosef of Polonnoye, *Toledot Ya'akov Yosef*, 2:490a: "*Every soul will praise You* (Psalm 150:6). With every breath [the soul] wants to exit from the body. . . . This is not the case of one who makes his corporeality spiritual [*ḥomer, ẓura*]. This person has achieved a 'life of peace' [or a 'complete life': *ḥayyim shel shalom*]. That is, there is no longer any distinction between body and soul, corporeality has been overcome even though it continues to exist." It is noteworthy that this is built on the very last verse in Psalms, as if to say this is the telos of all human existence."

65 The notion of the occultation of the *ẓaddik* is an idea that has Jewish precedent in Sabbateanism. Perhaps more relevant to our concerns, it is an idea that was advocated by the eighteenth-century Italian kabbalist Emanuel Hai Ricci in his *Ḥashev Maḥshavot*. See Na'or, *Post-Sabbatian Sabbatianism*, 55, 177n1; and Pinchas Giller, *Shalom Shar'abi and the Kabbalists of Beit El* (New York: Oxford University Press, 2008), 101.

My point here is to assert that the most controversial aspects of the claims about Schneerson—his superhuman/divine nature, his not succumbing to death, his infallibility—are logical if we conclude that he embodies the state of the permanent *ẓaddik gamur*, as described in Ḥabad metaphysics. By linking Rashbi's comment about the *benei aliyah* as real yet limited (*ma'atim*) to the *ẓaddik gamur*, Schneerson may be hinting that the *Tanya*'s category of *ẓaddik gamur* is not merely theoretical but, in fact, a manifest reality. This is surely how many Ḥabad *ḥasidim* understand their rebbe. To employ this category to describe one person (making him a divine being, "the proof of God on earth") may deviate from Orthodox doctrine but is not without precedent in Ḥabad, and even classical kabbalistic metaphysics, the former informed as it is by the Zohar-Luria kabbalistic trajectory. Hence, an indictment of heresy against contemporary Ḥabad is, by extension, an indictment against the entire metaphysical system of Ḥabad and, perhaps, against Kabbalah more generally.

The Ancient Israelite Precedent of Ḥabad's Messianism: Worshiping a Divinized Being during the Transition from Israelite Religion to Judaism

One of the more complicated dimensions of Ḥabad's messianism is the way in which the messianist community understands how one should relate to their venerated master—in life and subsequently in death. I argue here that while the notion of a human who is also divine may not be in accord with normative Judaism as it has developed in the post-rabbinic period (Kabbalah excepted), it was indeed part of pre-rabbinic proto-Judaism. The Israelite king and the High Priest were both worshiped as quasi-divine beings in ancient Israelite religion.[66] Moreover, as we will see in cer-

66 See Margaret Barker, "The High Priest and the Worship of Jesus," in *The Jewish Roots of Christological Monotheism: Papers from the St. Andrews Conference on the Historical Origins of the Worship of Jesus*, ed. Carey C. Newman, James R. Davila, and Gladys S. Lewis (Leiden: Brill, 1999), 93–111; and more generally Margaret Barker, *The Great Angel: The Study of Israel's Second God* (London: SPCK, 1992). We also have clear evidence that Jesus was known as the High Priest in Paul's Letter to the Hebrews. See George W. E. Nickelsburg, *Ancient Judaism and Christian Origins: Diversity, Continuity, and Transformation* (Minneapolis, MN: Augsburg Fortress, 2003), 109. Cf. Morton Smith, *Clement of Alexandria and a Secret Gospel of Mark* (Cambridge, MA: Harvard University Press, 1973), 137–38; John J. Collins, "A Throne in the Heavens: Apotheosis in Pre-Christian Judaism," in *Death, Ecstasy, and Other Worldly Journeys*, ed. John J. Collins and Michael Fishbane (Albany: SUNY Press, 1995), 43–58; and Shlomo

tain intertestamental documents likely written between the third century BCE and the second century CE, the divine/human nexus in the form of a human is often described as a Messiah.[67]

I argue that the notion of Schneerson as a permanent *ẓaddik gamur*, a state that is both God and not-God, human and not-human, is not categorically different from the ancient Israelite idea, whose resonances may be embedded in the more opaque conduit of the Zohar and Lurianic tradition.[68] Admittedly, it is an ancient Israelite idea that the talmudic rabbis (at

---

Pines, "God, Divine Glory, and the Angels according to a Second-Century Theology" [Hebrew], in *The Beginning of Jewish Mysticism in Medieval Europe: Proceedings of the Second International Conference on the History of Jewish Mysticism*, ed. Joseph Dan (Jerusalem: Jewish National and University Library, 1987), 1–14. Further, Alon Goshen-Gottstein addresses the question of worship-oriented versus non-worship-oriented incarnation. See his "Judaism and Incarnational Theologies: Mapping Out the Parameters of Dialogue," *Journal of Ecumenical Studies* 39, nos. 3–4 (Summer–Fall, 2002): 238–39. He cites how Avraham Pevzner (author of *Al ha-Ẓaddikim*) argues how self-annihilation can allow Moses and Shimon bar Yohai to speak as if they were God even as they are not worshiped as divine. I am suggesting here that the late Israelite notion of the king and High Priest as worshiped beings may serve as some kind of precedent for the worship-oriented model in proto-Judaism.

67 Some of this Israelite material, e.g., 2 Baruch and 4 Ezra, is used by Paul in his Christology. See 1 Enoch 48:10. In the Christian Bible, see Matthew 19:28, 25:31; Hebrews 1:3; Revelations 3:21, 20:4. On the influence of Jewish messianism to Christology more generally, see Albert Schweitzer, *The Mysticism of Paul the Apostate* (1931; New York: Macmillan, 1955), 75–100. Cf. Collins, "A Throne in the Heavens," 50–53. Rabbinic literature also entertains this idea. See BT Hagigah 14a and Sanhedrin 38b. The apotheosis of Moses is a common trope in the intertestamental period. See Wayne Meeks, "Moses as God and King," 354–71. Richard Bauckham argues that "intermediary figures are by no means characteristic of the literature of Second Temple Judaism. They should not be the focus of a study of Second Temple monotheism." Bauckham claims that Jews in that period had a solid monotheistic belief in the uniqueness of God even as they acknowledged lesser "divine" figures as serving certain functions but not sharing in God's uniqueness. See Richard Bauckham, *God Crucified: Monotheism and Christology in the New Testament* (Grand Rapids, MI: Eerdmans, 1998), 1–22.

68 This is surely a contested position. There are many scholars, perhaps beginning with Adolph von Harnack, who argue that the doctrine of the incarnation was not endemic to Israelite religion but adopted from "Greek modes of thought." See Adolph von Harnack, *History of Dogma* (New York: Williams and Norgate, 1897), 1:218. The "son of God" was surely a term used in ancient Israelite literature, although no one is quite sure what was meant by it. For examples of such use, see Wisdom of Solomon 9:7, 18:13; Jubilees 1:24; and Psalms of Solomon 17:30, where Israel is referred to as "sons of God." In other places individuals, usually the righteous man, garner the same appellation. See Wisdom of Solomon 2:13, 2:16, 2:18; Sirach 4:10, 51:10; and Psalms of Solomon 13:8. In one rabbinic case, Hanina ben Dosa is referred to by a heavenly voice as "my son." See BT Ta'anit 24b; and Idel, *Ben*, 440–46. This does not mean

least those in Babylonia) largely rejected and Christianity partially adapted for its own Christology. Thus David Berger, in *The Rebbe, the Messiah, and the Scandal of Orthodox Indifference*, is correct in asserting that Ḥabad messianic claims are not Orthodox, if we define "Orthodoxy" as it defines itself: living inside the parameters of the rabbinic mind. But Berger is, in my view, mistaken in claiming that Ḥabad messianic claims are therefore not Jewish, if by "Jewish" we are willing to expand our definition beyond those rabbinic parameters—that is, if we are willing to challenge rabbinic hegemony and its later Orthodox interpretation.[69]

I am in agreement with those who maintain that medieval Kabbalah pushes those very boundaries, albeit in esoteric and obscure ways that are all too easily interpreted to conform to more normative Orthodox claims.[70] Ḥabad proves a good example (Sabbateanism is another example, with a different historical trajectory) of how camps inside Orthodoxy incorporate, perhaps unwittingly, kabbalistic doctrines, doctrines that were rejected yet

---

that these texts had any doctrine of incarnation like Christianity, but it does indicate that the term was quite common and could have meant different things to different authors. But see Geza Vermes, *The Changing Faces of Jesus* (New York: Penguin, 2002), 37: "No biblical or post-biblical Jewish writer ever depicted a human being literally as divine, nor did Jewish religious culture agree to accommodate the Hellenistic notions of 'son of God' and 'divine man.' The designations, common in the terminology of ruler worship in imperial Rome and in the description of charismatic personalities in Hellenism, remained taboo in Judaism." This sweeping and unequivocal statement seems odd given the use of the term "son of God" in intertestamental literature. David Blumenthal is a bit more uncertain of this absolute negation. See his "*Tselem*: Toward an Anthropomorphic Theology of Image," in *Christianity in Jewish Terms*, ed. Tikva Frymer-Kensky, et al. (Boulder, CO: Westview Press, 2000), 345–46. Cf. Irving Greenberg, "Covenantal Partners in a Postmodern World," in Greenberg, *For the Sake of Heaven and Earth: The New Encounter Between Judaism and Christianity* (Philadelphia: Jewish Publication Society, 2004), 72: "Historically, Judaism rejected what it saw as the divination of a man." For a more forceful claim, see James D. G. Dunn, *Christology in the Making* (Philadelphia: Westminster Press, 1980), 19, 22. The notion of the divine human who is not God has a history in Jewish-Christianity from the first century through the Arian controversy in the fourth century. Ebionite Jewish-Christians rejected the incarnational theology of Paul in favor of a position accepting Jesus as a human Messiah. More relevant is the doctrine of Arius (c. 250–336), which makes a sharp distinction between the father and the son, arguing that the son, while divine, is not eternal in the same sense as the father. Arius's position evoked a controversy that was only put to rest with the Council of Nicea (325 CE), which made incarnation a Christian doctrine. If one were looking for parallels between Ḥabad's messianism and Christianity's, it might be worth investigating these marginal Christianities that have largely been discredited in the Christian world but were very influential in the past.

69 For a similar view see Idel, *Ben*, 588.

70 See, e.g., the work of Yehudah Liebes and the recent work of his student Yonatan Benarosh on the Zohar and Christianity, as well as the work of Elliot R. Wolfson.

remained part of a subterranean esotericism. Such incorporation can be put to various uses; Ḥabad uses kabbalistic doctrine to justify their historical claims about Messiah.

It may be that Berger is mistaken in another regard. It is not that Ḥabad has theologically abandoned Orthodoxy. Rather, the Ḥabad "heresy" may be the use and application of earlier theological doctrines that were discarded or became subterranean. Ancient Israelite comments about the apotheosis of the High Priest or even similar zoharic comments about Shimon bar Yohai are now benign because they pose no real historical threat, even though they share many of the same theological premises with contemporary Ḥabad, who claims their rebbe is, in fact, the Messiah. These ancient Israelite and zoharic comments have been thoroughly (re)interpreted, and neutered, through a rabbinic lens.

In any event, I am not making a historical claim of influence—either between late Israelitism and Ḥabad or between late Israelitism and Kabbalah (although such historical links have been suggested by others). My claim is phenomenological or perhaps structural.[71] I am suggesting that ancient Israelite religion, both before and after its emergence in a canonized form known as rabbinic Judaism (when that happened is a matter of scholarly debate), struggled mightily trying to navigate the elusive nexus between the human (the "image of God" in Genesis 1:26) and the incorporeal God (Exodus 33:20). The complexity of this nexus is built into the very fabric of biblical monotheism.[72]

Although normative Judaism today, traditional and liberal, may present a unified front in the rejection of any overlap between the human and the divine, a more complex picture results from a close reading of pre-rabbinic Judaism, Kabbalah, Ḥasidism, and even certain strains of rabbinic

71 Here I am in total agreement with Moshe Idel when he writes, "Instead of concentrating solely on the ancient apocryphal material as historically relevant for the understanding of the Christian sonship of God, one may turn now also to other Jewish material in order to compare the two religions from a phenomenological point of view. . . . The Enochic elements that were instrumental in shaping the apotheotic vector in nascent Christianity lost their formative status, while in Jewish mysticism, whose first clear manifestations as literature coincided with this decline, the ascent of the Enochic movement as shaping important aspects of this mystical literature only started then" (*Ben*, 585). Such a phenomenological approach would not be discredited if we could claim that, in fact, early Ḥabad masters had no real access to the more overt Enochic tradition extant in Apocryphal literature. As Idel suggests, many of these themes are embedded in classical Kabbalah and thus informed the imaginations of later readers of Kabbalah (*Ben*, 597).

72 On the complexity of the term "monotheism," see Peter Hayman, "Monotheism—A Misused Word in Jewish Studies," *Journal of Jewish Studies* 42, no. 1 (1991): 1–15.

tradition, if not read exclusively through the lenses provided by Orthodoxy. This picture complicates the categorical distinctions between Judaism and Christianity that have become readily accepted.[73] This is not to argue that Jews can or should accept the viability of Christian doctrine. That is another matter entirely. It is simply to state that the criticism of Ḥabad as blurring the distinction between Judaism and Christianity may, in fact, be true but is not necessarily sufficient to argue that Ḥabad has moved beyond the boundaries of "Judaism." Those lines were quite blurry in Judaism's formative years, long before they became clear with the emergence of Jewish Orthodoxy.[74]

This blurriness is surely vexing for normative Judaism, as has been passionately shown by David Berger. Yet, as Avraham Pevzner has documented in his collection *Al ha-Ẓaddikim*, classical Jewish sources at least hint at the overlap between human and divine, albeit in theory but not in practice.[75] I want to suggest another avenue of exploration. The notion of

---

73 See, e.g., Lawrence Schiffman, "Messianism and Apocalypticism in Rabbinic Texts," in *The Cambridge History of Judaism*, vol. 4, ed. Steven T. Katz (Cambridge: Cambridge University Press, 2006), 1053–72. I want to thank Professor Schiffman for allowing me to review this chapter before its publication. Schiffman argues that the diminution of Second Temple radical messianic themes in the early rabbinic period returned in later rabbinic Judaism in Babylonia and became part of canonized Jewish messianism. This thesis underlies the work of Jacob Neusner, Marc Hirschman, and Daniel Boyarin. See *Judaisms and Their Messiahs at the Turn of the Christian Era*, ed. Jacob Neusner, William S. Green, and Ernest Frerichs (Cambridge, UK: Cambridge University Press, 1987); Neusner, *Messiah in Context: Israel's History and Destiny in Formative Judaism* (Philadelphia: Fortress, 1984); Marc Hirshman, *A Rivalry of Genius: Jewish and Christian Biblical Interpretation in Late Antiquity*, trans. Batya Stein (Albany: SUNY Press, 1996); and Daniel Boyarin, *Dying for God: Martyrdom and the Making of Christianity and Judaism* (Stanford, CA: Stanford University Press, 1999), 1–41. Traditional thinkers such as Elijah Benamozegh (1832–1900, Italy) acknowledged that the Christian notion of Jesus may be rooted in ancient Israelite or Jewish esoteric teachings that surfaced once again in medieval Kabbalah. See Idel, *Ben*, 600.

74 See Daniel Boyarin, *Border Lines: The Partition of Judaeo-Christianity* (Philadelphia: University of Pennsylvania Press, 2004), 37–88; and Daniel Boyarin, *The Jewish Gospels: The Story of the Jewish Christ* (New York: New Press, 2012).

75 Avraham Pevzner, *Al ha-Ẓaddikim* (Kfar Habad: Beit Agudat Hasidei Habad, 1991). Pevzner takes a very different approach from this chapter, committed as he is to showing the ways in which Ḥabad messianism is in concert with normative Jewish tradition. I think Berger's critique of Pevzner is largely convincing precisely because Pevzner has chosen to play on the turf of Orthodoxy and his position is thus significantly weakened. The sources Pevzner brings to bear are ambiguous and opaque enough to be read (as they have been) in ways that conform to Orthodox theology. It is significant to note that Pevzner's book was written before Schneerson's death and thus does not deal with the important question it raises. Schneerson's death is the subject of Wolpo's *Ha-Nisayon ha-Aḥaron*.

Schneerson as a human/divine being, one infallible and worthy of veneration, may be more aligned with pre-rabbinic (and thus proto-Jewish) attitudes about the human and the divine, some of which were likely adopted by early Jewish-Christians (when Christianity was still a Jewish sect) and subsequently, in revised form, became part of Christianity. Many of these attitudes appear in Apocryphal and other non-canonical texts likely written by Israelites/Jews (some of whom may also have been Christians) between the first century BCE and the end of the first century CE. This transitional phase saw the last vestiges of ancient Israelite religion (the end of the Second Temple) and the beginning of what would eventually become rabbinic Judaism. Excluded from the Jewish canon by the Pharisees and their spiritual descendants (for all kinds of reasons, some of which are unrelated to our focus), these texts did not become a part of rabbinic thinking even as some were incorporated, in revised form, in the later talmudic tradition.[76] Thus, even though these texts may not be a part of rabbinic orthodoxy, they remain an important historical window onto what Jews may have believed and how they may have practiced in this crucial transitional period. I will focus on one small aspect of this phenomenon: that human/divine beings (human and not human, God and not God) were thought to exist and were venerated and even worshiped by Israel in recognition of their divine authority.[77]

---

76 Schiffman makes much of the reintroduction of utopian and apocalyptic messianic themes into the Babylonian talmudic corpus. Issues in Second Temple messianism, such as the preexistence of the Messiah (BT Nedarim 39b; Pesahim 5a, 54b), are absent in early rabbinic messianism and reappear only in the Babylonian traditions. Schiffman sums up his findings as follows: "The only way to explain this phenomenon is that it represents the re-emergence into the light of day of religious trends that had continued to circulate among elements of the Jewish people, even if the Tannaim had tried to suppress or to limit these ideas after the twin debacles of the Great Revolt and the Bar Kochba Revolt. These Second Temple–period traditions emerged again into the light of day in amoraic literature and thereafter continued to play a role in the ongoing development of Jewish messianic and apocalyptic speculation." Schiffman, "Messianism and Apocalypticism in Rabbinic Texts," 1070. This approach is very close to my own. However, I think the "suppressed" doctrines may have continued in dehistoricized, even mythic esoteric forms in Kabbalah that have been rehistoricized and inserted into the historical realm. For information on the early period, see Jacob Neusner, "Mishnah and Messiah," in *Judaisms and Their Messiahs*, 265–82.

77 The recent discovery of what has become known as *Ḥazon Gabriel*, a stone with ink writing dated to the first century BCE, presents potentially significant evidence that Christianity may have borrowed notions used by the ancient Israelite religion of that time. While the writing on the stone requires some deciphering, Israel Knohl has argued that the stone speaks of a messianic figure who dies and is then resurrected in three days. See Israel Knohl, *The Messiah before Jesus: The Suffering Servant of the*

Regarding late antique Judaism and early Christianity, Richard Bauckham argues as follows:

> There are those [figures] who are included in the unique identity of God. These are personifications or hypostatizations of aspects of God himself, such as his Spirit, his Word, his Wisdom. . . . They are fully compatible with the absolute uniqueness of God, as understood in the Jewish monotheism of this period, and are not seen as in any way qualifying or threatening it. The second category is of figures who, though they act as servants of God, exercising some degree of delegated divine authority, are not included in God's unique identity and in no way disqualify or threaten his uniqueness. These are principle angels and exalted patriarchs. Once we take full account of the ways in which Jewish monotheism itself characterized the unique identity of God, it becomes possible to see that one category, the personifications or hypostatizations of aspects of God, falls unproblematically within it, while the other category, the principle angels and exalted patriarchs, falls (in every case but one) unproblematically outside it.[78]

If Bauckham is correct in his assessment that ancient Jewish monotheism absorbed individuals (human and otherwise) who acquired some aspect of divinity, why should we assume that this category was erased from canonical Judaism? In fact, the preexistence of the Messiah in rabbinic texts, the transcendence of human limitations via contemplation in classical Kabbalah, and the doctrine of the *ẓaddik* in Ḥasidism all seem based on this premise. While it may be true that Maimonidean rationalism and the contentious competition with Christianity have made this ancient precept problematic for contemporary Judaism, that is quite different from saying it is not "Jewish" (whatever that might mean). I suggest that we

---

Dead Sea Scrolls (Berkeley: University of California Press, 2002); and Israel Knohl, "'By Three Days, Live': Messiahs, Resurrection, and the Ascent to Heaven in *Hazon Gabriel*," *Journal of Religion* 88, no. 2 (2008): 147–58. Cf. Claudia Setzer, *Resurrection of the Body in Early Judaism and Early Christianity: Doctrine, Community, and Self-Definition* (Boston: Brill, 2004), 21–52.

78 Richard Bauckham, "The Throne of God and the Worship of Jesus," in *The Jewish Roots of Christological Monotheism*, 49. See also his more comprehensive *God Crucified*, 1–25, 17. Martin Buber, the rare scholar of both the Bible and Ḥasidism, makes some similar remarks in attempting to view Jesus in the frame of late antique Judaism. Buber suggests that the Son of Man tradition in 1 Enoch could have been Jewish reflections on Daniel and the "servant of God" traditions in Isaiah 62. In other words, Buber is open to the Son of Man as Messiah (later perhaps used by the Christian Bible) as rooted in the Jewish imagination. See Buber, *Two Types of Faith*, 102–13.

consider whether Ḥabad messianism is, in fact, another permutation of this doctrine.[79]

While there are many intertestamental texts that suggest a nexus between the human and the divine, the text that is most startling in this regard and also links this nexus to the Messiah/savior are the similitudes in 1 Enoch 37–71. Admittedly, the similitudes, or parables, in 1 Enoch are the source of considerable controversy.[80] As a composite work, 1 Enoch is generally thought to be of Israelite origin. James Charlesworth posits that most of it was likely composed in the second or first century BCE, written by Israelites/Jews in either Hebrew or Aramaic.[81] However, the similitudes in 1 Enoch were not found in the Qumran version of 1 Enoch, giving rise to Jozef Milik's thesis that these chapters may have been written in a later, post-Christian era, as late as 400 CE.[82] James Charlesworth and others contest Milik's thesis and suggest that the similitudes were written in pre-Christian Israel and that their absence in

---

79 Rationalists such as Kenneth Seeskin and Menachem Kellner lament the reintroduction of mythology into the messianic, and more broadly into Jewish discourse and practice. See, e.g., Seeskin, *Jewish Messianic Thoughts in an Age of Despair*, 172–95, and Kellner, *Maimonides' Confrontation with Mysticism* (London: Littman Library of Jewish Civilization, 2006).

80 For an overview of this literature, see M. Black, "The Messianism in the Parables of Enoch: Their Date and Contribution to Christological Origins," in *The Messiah: Developments in Earliest Judaism and Christianity: Princeton Symposium on Judaism and Christian Origins*, ed. James H. Charlesworth (Minneapolis, MN: Fortress, 1992), 145–68; Barnabas Lindars, "Re-enter the Apocalyptic Son of Man," *New Testament Studies* 22, no. 1 (1975/76): 52–72; J. H. Charlesworth, "From Jewish Messianology to Christian Christology: Some Caveats and Perspectives," in *Judaisms and Their Messiahs*, 225–64; and S. R. Scott, "The Binitarian Nature of the *Book of Similitudes*," *Journal for the Study of Pseudepigrapha* 18, no. 1 (2008): 55–78.

81 See *The Old Testament Pseudepigrapha: Apocalyptic Literature and Testaments*, vol. 1, ed. James H. Charlesworth (Garden City, NY: Doubleday, 1983), 7. Charlesworth notes that before the discovery of the fragments of 1 Enoch, he dated the similitudes as 105–64 BCE. After the discovery, he posits that the similitudes were likely a later addition to the text written sometime before the end of the first century BCE. This does not mean that they are necessarily post-Christian, but it means they certainly could be. Cf. Pierlugi Piovanelli, "'A Testimony for the Kings and the Mighty Who Possess the Earth': The Thirst for Justice and Peace in the Parables of Enoch," *Enoch and the Messiah Son of Man: Revisiting the Book of Parables*, ed. Gabriele Boccaccini (Grand Rapids, MI: Eerdmans, 2007), 363–79; and Jonas C. Greenfield and Michael E. Stone, "The Enochic Pentateuch and the Date of the Similitudes," *Harvard Theological Review* 70, nos. 1–2 (1997): 51–65.

82 See Jozef Milik, *The Books of Enoch: Aramaic Fragments of Qumrân Cave 4* (Oxford: Clarendon Press, 1976), 89–100.

the Qumran version may be for unknown reasons. M. Black summarizes this opinion as follows:

> Scholars have differed on whether the Parables were a Jewish and pre-Christian or a Jewish/Jewish Christian, but post-Christian composition, uninfluenced nor influenced by the New Testament. While one can hardly speak of an *opinio communis* or perhaps even a likelihood of one, views have certainly been hardening in favor of a basically Jewish work, composed around the turn of the millennium, c. first century B.C.E.–first century C.E.[83]

Even though Milik raises the possibility that the similitudes were post-Christian, the influence of the New Testament on the similitudes is far from conclusive.[84] It is arguably the case that even given the later date of their composition, the similitudes do not introduce any radical new doctrine but largely deploy an already common theme in pre-Christian Israelitism regarding the divine/human figure.[85] I choose to use this material because it exhibits one of the most remarkable Israelite synthesiesof the human/divine savior and offers an interesting interpretation of

---

83 Black, "Messianism in the Parables of Enoch," 161–62. Scholars who attest to this position include J. H. Charlesworth, G. Nickelsburg, M. E. Stone, D. W. Suter, J. C. Greenfield, and J. VanderKam. Charlesworth argues the documents in question are of Palestinian origin.

84 The case of 1 Enoch 70–71 may be an exception, as these chapters seem to be a later addition to the similitudes. See Black, "Messianism in the Parables of Enoch," 165–67.

85 For other divine/human figures, see the figure of Jaoel in the Apocalypse of Abraham and Metatron in 3 Enoch, who is called "the lesser YHWH." In 4 Ezra we have the depiction of the Messiah who will die and rise on clouds, an example of Jewish apotheosis during this period. See Michael Stone, "The Concept of Messiah in 4 Ezra," in *Religions in Antiquity*, 295–331. Another case may be the depiction of the apotheosis of Moses in the Exagoge of Ezekiel the Tragedian. On this, see Bauckham, *God Crucified*, 20n34. On Metatron, see Ithamar Gruenwald, *Apocalyptic and Merkavah Mysticism* (Leiden: Brill, 1980); Moshe Idel, "Enoch Is Metatron" [Hebrew], *Jerusalem Studies in Jewish Thought* 6, nos. 1–2 (1987): 151–70. In English, see Idel, "Enoch Is Metatron," *Immanuel* 24–25 (1990): 220–39; John J. Collins, "Messianism in the Maccabean Period," in *Judaisms and Their Messiahs*, 102; and *The Book of Enoch or 1 Enoch: A New English Edition*, ed. Matthew Black and James C. VanderKam (Leiden: Brill, 1985), 189. See also George W. E. Nickelsburg, *Ancient Judaism and Christian Origins*, 97–98. Cf. Nickelsburg, *Resurrection, Immortality, and Eternal Life in Intertestamental Judaism* (Cambridge, MA: Harvard University Press, 1972), 82–92; and Nickelsburg, "Salvation without and with a Messiah," in *Judaisms and Their Messiahs*, 63, where Nickelsburg mentions other clearly pre-Christian sources that share some of the assumptions of the similitudes in 1 Enoch.

the Messiah that will hopefully nuance and enrich the analysis of Ḥabad messianism.[86]

I wish to cite two texts from the Apocryphal genre, one excerpt from Josephus and then one talmudic passage (BT Yoma 69a) that may serve as a remnant of the human/divine nexus in the rabbinic corpus but is ambiguous enough to be interpreted as normative. The texts under consideration make the following two claims: first, that the notion of an incarnate being—that is, a human who embodies a revealed state of divinity—is not as foreign to ancient Israelite religion as we are led to believe; and second, that such a being merits being worshiped, not as God, but as "proof of God on earth." The overarching theme is that in ancient Israelite monotheism (and perhaps later in kabbalistic tradition), God is one but divinity is shared. Sometimes, as in 1 Enoch, this is represented as a state of apotheosis, and other times, as in the worship of the High Priest, as documented by Josephus and others, one's divinity is a result of his office.

The two Apocryphal passages germane to my argument are 1 Enoch 48:5–6 and 62:6–9. Speaking of the Son of Man as the Chosen One (a reference to Daniel 7:13—"one like a human being"), 1 Enoch writes, "All those who dwell upon the earth shall worship before him, they shall glorify, bless, and sing the name of the lord of Spirits." The object of worship here is clearly the Son of Man and not God.[87] In chapter 62 we learn more about why this human/divine being is worshiped: "For the Son of Man was concealed from the beginning, and the Most High One preserved him in the presence of His power, then he revealed him to the holy and elect ones. . . . On that day . . . those who rule the earth shall fall down before him on their faces, and worship and raise hopes in that Son of Man." The preexistence

86 See Nickelsburg, "Son of Man," in the *Anchor Bible Dictionary*, vol. 6., ed. David Noel Freedman (Doubleday: New York, 1992), 138–40. As a curious aside, the Enoch traditions and Ḥabad both grant import to the number seven as a genealogical referent. Enoch is the seventh generation from Adam, and Menahem Mendel is the seventh rebbe in the Ḥabad dynasty. The kabbalistic significance of seven is the seventh *sefirah* counting down from *ḥesed*, well-known in medieval Kabbalah. The number seven as a messianic trope also has roots in Daniel, and seven corresponds to heavenly ascent in the Second Temple period, *heikhalot* and *merkavah* literature, and Jewish magical literature. On the messianic significance of the seventh generation of Ḥabad, see Persico, "Ḥabad's Lost Messiah," 89–91 and notes.

87 On the reference in Daniel as implying a heavenly being, see Stefan Beyerle, "'One Like the Son of Man': Innuendos of a Heavenly Individual," in *Enoch and Qumran Origins: New Light on a Forgotten Connection*, ed. Gabriele Boccaccini (Grand Rapids, MI: Eerdmans, 2005), 54–58; and Matthias Albani, "The 'One Like the Son of Man' (Dan 7:13) and the Royal Ideology," in *Enoch and Qumran Origins*, 47–53.

of the Son of Man, made explicit here, attests to his divine character.[88] In another passage (46:1, alluding again to Daniel 7:13), we read that the Son of Man had a face that "was *like* that of a human being."

The notion of the divine/human "occulted" Messiah who will return to earth in the future is not unique to 1 Enoch but appears also in the Gospel of Mark. And we read in the Syriac Apocalypse of Baruch 30, "And it shall come to pass after this, when the time of the presence of the Messiah on earth has run its course, that he will return in glory to the heavens; then all who have died and have set their hopes on him will rise again. And it shall come to pass at that time that the treasuries will be opened in which is preserved the number of the souls of the righteous."[89] While the exact time and authorship of this text is not definitive (it was likely written around 70 CE), the text does exhibit a messianic notion that resonates with 1 Enoch.

The ambiguity of these passages makes it almost impossible to determine their meaning. However, at the very least it appears as if we are dealing with a tradition that acknowledges the possibility of an intermediary or lesser-divine being as savior who shares in the life of the divine. This does not necessarily imply a deitheistic or binitarian theology, but does complicate the boundary separating God from human life that becomes concretized in post-rabbinic and later Orthodox Judaism (influenced in no small part by the Maimonidean theology of radical transcendence). There is a liminality in the divine/human nexus here that is erased in post-Maimonidean monotheism yet survives in a truncated form in the kabbalistic tradition from which Ḥabad derives its intellectual and imaginative sustenance.

The next excerpt is from *The Life of Adam and Eve*, a text extant only in Greek and Latin translations but probably written in Hebrew sometime in the first century CE. It is an elaborate and often quite entertaining description of Adam and Eve's life in the Garden of Eden and contains numerous debates among them, Satan, and the heavenly hosts. The relevant passage

88 The transference of "divine judgment" from God to the Son of Man begins in 1 Enoch 61:8: "And the Lord of spirits placed the Elect One on the Throne of glory, / And he shall judge all the works of the holy ones in heaven above, / And in the balance shall their deeds be weighed." In 1 Enoch 62:8, this Son of Man is labeled the deliverer or redeemer.

89 See *The Apocryphal Old Testament*, ed. H. F. D. Sparks (Oxford: Clarendon Press, 1987), 857. Sparks argues that this text was written by a Jew "living in the difficult times following the destruction of Jerusalem in AD 70." Whether he could have *also* been a Christian, Sparks does not say. For an analysis and argument as to why this passage in 4 Ezra is not a Christian emendation, see Charlesworth, "From Jewish Messianology to Christian Christology," 243–45. On the coming, disappearance, and return of the Messiah, see also 2 Baruch 30:1.

illustrates another instance of Jews of this period acknowledging the viability of worshiping human beings who have achieved a perfected state (in this case the prelapsarian Adam). Chapters 14–15 of the Vita (Latin translation) of *The Life of Adam and Eve* describe an argument between the angel Michael and Satan. We read, from Satan's perspective:

> And Michael went out and called all the angels, saying, "Worship the image of the Lord God, as the Lord God has instructed." And Michael himself worshiped first, and called me and said, "Worship the image of God, Yahweh." And I answered, "I do not worship Adam." . . . When they heard [that I refused to worship Adam] other angels under me refused to worship him. And Michael asserted, "If you will not worship Adam, the Lord God will be wrathful to you." And I said, "If he be wrathful to me, I will set my throne above the stars of heaven and will be like the Most High. . . ."

This imaginative description about the fall of Satan rests on the figure of the prelapsarian Adam as an object of worship for the angelic world, which is commanded by God. Adam's semi-divinity melts away when he sins and becomes a mere mortal. As in the case with Enoch's "Chosen One," the whole concept of the human/Adam as worthy of worship exists only when he is in a perfected state, a state that I suggest is reflected, in a different context, in the Ḥabad rendition of the *ẓaddik gamur*. While we do not have evidence that Ḥabad renders its rebbe as having achieved a prelapsarian state, as a *ẓaddik gamur* (according to Ḥabad's definition) he has achieved a state that seems both infallible and beyond any conventional notion of sin.

My final textual example of a semi-divine human includes two readings of the meeting between Alexander and Shimon ha-Zaddik, one of the more prominent High Priests of the Second Temple. Josephus tells us of this meeting in his *Antiquities* 11.329–334. He describes the Chaldeans (called the Kutim in the Talmud) who threaten to destroy Jerusalem and kill the High Priest. To ward off this threat, Shimon, dressed in full High Priest vestments (which the Talmud suggests are not to be worn outside the Temple environs—this is the halakhic frame of the aggadic statement) goes out to greet Alexander, who is approaching the city. When Alexander sees the High Priest in full regalia, he bows down and worships him. Alexander's assistant asks, "How did it come to pass that when all others worship you, you should worship the High Priest of the Jews?" Alexander replies, "I did not worship him but that God who has honored him with his High Priesthood, for I saw this very person in a dream, in this very habit . . . when I was considering with myself how I might obtain the dominion of

Asia." The Talmud (BT Yoma 69a) gives a more dramatic version of the narrative. When Alexander sees Shimon, he descends from his horse and bows down to him. When asked why he does this, Alexander responds, "I saw the image of his face before me when I went into battle against others."

Predictably, medieval talmudic commentators such as Samuel ha-Levi Adles (MaRShA)—living totally according to the rabbinic revision of ancient Israelite theology—offer a fully orthodox version of the Shimon ha-Zaddik narrative. Adles writes that Alexander dreamt of an angelic apparition with Shimon's face that helped him in battle. Shimon's face reminded Alexander of the dream, and he realized that Shimon, as High Priest, represented, but did not embody, the one true God. The dream component is a classic rabbinic way of softening the likelihood of Alexander seeing Shimon as a divine being. My point is not to discount Adles's account but rather to suggest that if we juxtapose this admittedly ambiguous episode with the abundant intertestamental material affirming that the human in a perfected state is divine and worthy of worship and with the Zohar's identifying the face of God with Rashbi, Adles's rendition seems like a defense against what may have been, in its time, a case of ancient Jewish worship of a human being.

It has been argued that in ancient Israel the High Priest (especially in the First Temple) was viewed as a quasi-divine being and worshiped as such (this, of course, can be drawn only from descriptions of his status made many centuries later).[90] For example, Leviticus 16:17 reads, "There shall be no man [in the Tent of Meeting] when he [the High Priest] enters to make atonement." Philo, in his work *On Dreams* (2.188, 230), reads the verse "There shall be no man" as "He *shall not be a man* when he enters the Holy of Holies," a fascinating misreading that may imply a belief in the apotheosis of the High Priest in Alexandrian Jewry. Another biblical example that may point to a belief in the apotheosis of the High Priest or king at his coronation is the coronation of Solomon in 1 Chronicles 29:20–23: "David said to the whole assembly 'Now bless the Lord your God.' And the assembly blessed the Lord God of their fathers and prostrated themselves to the Lord and the king. . . . Solomon sat on God's throne as king instead of his father David, and all went well with him. All Israel accepted him."[91] Ancient civilizations often viewed sitting on (God's) throne as an act of divinization. While the ambiguity of the verse allows rabbinic and post-rabbinic interpretation to render the phrase idiomatically, given other evidence for

90 See Barker, "The High Priest and the Worship of Jesus."

91 The *JPS Tanakh* renders this idiomatically as "Solomon successfully took over the throne of the Lord." This is the trend of all rabbinic-minded interpreters. See, e.g., *Mesudot David*: "On the throne of God: that is, to enact divine judgment."

worship of people in intertestamental literature, its more literal, contextual meaning cannot be rejected out of hand. More to the point, in Ḥabad messianism, which builds on Lurianic doctrine, the Messiah embodies the highest cosmic real of *yeḥidah*, which is a late kabbalistic term of the human soul describing an aspect of the soul that fully transcends humanity.

My point in all this is to show that while Ḥabad's claims about their rebbe may indeed move beyond the confines of contemporary Orthodoxy, they are not necessarily outside the wider spectrum of Israelite and early Jewish reflection on the nexus between the human and the divine, reflections that may have been preserved in classical Kabbalah and become more overt in Ḥasidism. In some way this comes down to the elasticity of monotheism. In his essay "Monotheism—A Misused Word in Jewish Studies," Peter Hayman argues that the common idea that Jewish monotheism rejects out of hand the idea of a human/divine being who shares divine authority with God is simply false and to a large degree the result of a reconstruction of Judaism through the lens of late rabbinic polemics against Christianity and medieval rationalism, influenced by Maimonides, among many others.[92] Hayman proposes an alternative category he calls "cooperative dualism" to describe antique Israelite and later kabbalistic views of the Godhead. Hayman argues that it is precisely Kabbalah that in part preserves, in opaque form, the dualistic monotheism that ancient Israelitism may have inhabited. I will not rehearse Hayman's argument nor reproduce the many sources he brings to bear. There are, however, two points worth mentioning that are directly relevant to our discussion. First, he posits that "the fact that functionally Jews believed in the existence of two gods explains the speed with which Christianity developed so fast in the first century towards the divinization of Jesus."[93] In this I assume he means the popularity of Christianity among Jews and not Greeks. Reiterating an idea becoming more common among early Christian scholars, Hayman argues that "the ground for Christology had already been well laid in pre-Christian Judaism" and that "for most Jews [in this period] God is the sole object of worship but is not the only divine being."[94] From a different perspective, George Nickelsburg notes,

92 Hayman, "Monotheism." Cf. Alan D. Segal, *Two Powers in Heaven: Early Rabbinic Reports about Christianity and Gnosticism* (Leiden: Brill, 1977), 186–200; and Larry W. Hurtado, "What Do We Mean by 'First-Century Jewish Monotheism'?," *Society of Biblical Literature: 1993 Seminal Papers*, ed. Eugene H. Lovering (Atlanta, GA: Scholars Press, 1993), 348–54.

93 Hayman, "Monotheism," 14.

94 Ibid., 15. Cf. Nickelsburg, *Ancient Judaism*, 9–20, 120–34; Larry W. Hurdato, *One God, One Lord: Early Christian Devotion and Ancient Jewish Monotheism*, 2nd ed. (New York: Continuum, 1998), 93–124.

"The first Christians were good eschatological Jews."[95] My question is: can the same be said of contemporary Ḥabad?

Is Ḥabad Messianic?

I have argued throughout this chapter that in contemporary Ḥabad we are dealing with a new form of zaddikism. This zaddikism embodies Scholem's warning of Ḥasidism's "amalgamation of mysticism and the apocalyptic mood," except that here there seems to be a renewed interest in collective as opposed to only personal redemption.[96] When contemporary ḥasidic zaddikism cum messianism serves the immediacy of redemption—not, as usual, in response to a time of despair but in a time of unprecedented security (with the State of Israel and a largely tolerant Diaspora)—new forms of Judaism seem to rise to the surface. The question is, what has emerged? While the conflation of the vocation of rebbe and Messiah is not new, Ḥabad seems to have taken new steps in describing their rebbe in terms that appear to transgress the boundaries of normative Judaism.

A relevant sociological question is why Ḥabad's messianic claims, even after Schneerson's death, did not result in the backlash we saw in Sabbateanism. Arguably, Ḥabad's ability to make its claims and, more importantly, avoid collective condemnation exhibits the extent to which Sabbateanism today is a non-issue. David Berger's attempt to reveal Ḥabad's messianic heresy and its failure to evoke any sustained reaction against Ḥabad illustrates my point.[97] While Sabbateanism was real for Jews up through the nineteenth century, today it is at most a scholarly curiosity.[98] Strikingly, most traditional Jews not trained in universities know almost nothing about the Sabbatean heresy, interesting considering that the heresy was perhaps the most serious challenge to rabbinic hegemony in the last eight hundred years. The reason for this ignorance, I surmise, is that Sabbateanism is largely irrelevant (even as it may live on structurally in many forms of modern Judaism), and heresy more generally is an empty category in modern pluralistic Judaism. This may be why Ḥabad's messianism has been able to avoid the accusation of heresy it may in fact deserve.

---

95 Nickelsburg, *Ancient Judaism*, 194.

96 Scholem, "The Neutralization," 180.

97 Berger, *The Rebbe, the Messiah, and the Scandal of Orthodox Indifference*.

98 See, e.g., Elisheva Carlebach, *The Pursuit of Heresy: Rabbi Moses Hagiz and the Sabbatian Controversies* (New York: Columbia University Press, 1990); and Na'or, *Post-Sabbatian Sabbatianism*.

Menachem Kellner and Kenneth Seeskin offer another assessment. Seeskin writes, "The most important contribution of religion is to insist on the inviolability of the line separating the divine from the human. . . . On that score, the record of Judaism is clearly inadequate. . . . No sooner did [Maimonides] attempt to take away the magical component of ritual than Kabbalah, which may have been motivated by a reaction against Maimonides, reinstated it."[99] Thus David Berger may be correct on doctrinal grounds largely defined by an Orthodoxy formed in the eighteenth century, but sociologically he may be at least a century too late. Perhaps it was precisely Ḥasidism's "neutralization" of the messianic idea that enabled heretical sentiments unobtrusively to cross the border into Jewish normative tradition.

In this chapter I have made two arguments. First, the parameters of "normativity" in the polemical literature against Ḥabad are largely the result of contemporary Orthodoxy, a sociological phenomenon that claims exclusive rights to rabbinic Judaism.[100] Orthodoxy is, in fact, little more than a modern articulation of the medieval construction of rabbinic Judaism filtered through literature that is, to some degree, founded in part on polemical responses to both Christianity and Islam.[101] While Kabbalah and Ḥasidism, as two forms of mysticism, have become part of this Orthodox canon, their inclusion requires viewing each through interpretive schemes that soften the sometimes "heretical" edges and suit each to the norms of non-kabbalistic Judaism. This is not to say that Jewish mysticism is, by definition, non-normative. That is another discussion entirely and depends on who gets to define the normative. Rather, it is to suggest that if we dare to read some of this literature without the Orthodox lens that contemporary traditionalism provides, we may find that it may be suggestive of spiritual alternatives incompatible with modern traditionalism called Orthodox Judaism. [102]

---

99 Seeskin, *Jewish Messianic Thoughts in an Age of Despair*, 183; Kellner, *Maimonides' Confrontation with Mysticism*, 286–96.

100 See Moshe Samet, "The Beginnings of Orthodoxy," *Modern Judaism* 8, no. 3 (1988): 249–69. Regarding Orthodoxy more generally, Samet argues, "A closer examination of the phenomenon called Orthodoxy reveals that it too is a historic innovation, more a mutation than a direct continuation of the traditional Judaism from which it emerged" (249).

101 While Boyarin may be correct that Orthodoxy more formally defined begins in Late Antiquity, what we now call Orthodoxy is rabbinic Judaism filtered through medieval lenses. If this is correct, Orthodoxy is deeply polemical in the way it defines Judaism against competing monotheisms. See Boyarin, *Border Lines*, 37–73.

102 Idel, *Kabbalah and Eros*, 154.

Scholars of Kabbalah from Scholem onward have carefully navigated the tension between the rabbinic distance separating the divine and the human and the mystical goal of reducing or, in some cases, eliminating that distance. Throughout the history of Jewish mysticism, groups have approached or transgressed the human/divine boundary, either in thought or deed, or both. In some instances, such as Sabbateanism, we see a rupture, and in other instances, such as early radical Ḥasidism, we see how the boundaries themselves can be renegotiated and expanded. In any case, Orthodoxy will always, and understandably, attempt to (re)interpret canonical texts to conform to its own doctrinal norms. Given Ḥasidism's success, both socially and doctrinally, and the irrelevancy, and ignorance, of Sabbateanism, Ḥabad has been able to navigate its messianic claims in a way that thus far deflects any lasting accusations of heresy.

Second, I have argued that the fluidity between the human and the divine that emerges (problematically) in Ḥabad messianism is endemic to some strains of ancient Israelite religion and some later forms of mystical Judaism and is very much in harmony with Ḥabad's own metaphysical system. Reports of theosis, apotheosis, divination, and worshiping a human as a divine being are not foreign to late antique Israelite religion or to intertestamental proto-Judaism. And traversing the separation between the divine and the corporeal is central to Ḥabad's acosmic metaphysics. While it is surely true that early rabbinism excised, suppressed, or reinterpreted many of the problematic dimensions of its spiritual predecessors, the ancient Israelites, Jacob Neusner, Peter Schaefer, Daniel Boyarin, and Lawrence Schiffman have shown that some Second Temple messianic ideas were revived in the later rabbinic corpus and (re)interpreted in accord with "orthodox" or doctrinal principles more suited to the rabbinic imagination. My intention here is not to challenge this dimension of the rabbinic project. I want only to see it as a particular formulation of a more multivalent religiosity. My contribution is to consider these wider boundaries when attempting to understand the contemporary Ḥabad project.

Having said all this, I return to ask whether Scholem's thesis in his essay "The Neutralization of the Messianic Idea in Early Ḥasidism" is now debunked. I think not. Given all the fanfare regarding Ḥabad messianism, given David Berger's polemic against it and Jewry's largely nonplussed, even apathetic, response, I think contemporary Ḥabad may have proved Scholem's point. What Ḥabad messianism has produced is largely a "normalization" of the messianic idea. That is, people can sing, "We want *Moshiaḥ* now!" or even "Long live our master King Messiah!" (in reference to Schneerson), and yet do nothing to substantiate that proclamation. They largely live their lives as they did before; some more religious, some less. In America, at least, Ḥabad messianism has simply become another cog in the wheel of Jewish outreach, a source of Jewish pride, a logo on a T-shirt. Few people are packing their suitcases and traveling to Jerusalem to meet King Messiah. Most people couldn't care less whether Rabbi Menahem Mendel Schneerson is buried in a cemetery in Queens or hovers in an occluded state waiting to return at the proper time. They care more about leading meaningful Jewish lives, perhaps an American refraction of "self-redemption."[103] Ḥabad messianism is thus yet another example of a messianism neutralized, in this case by three factors: (1) American Jewry's comfort in the Diaspora, a place that affords them a free and meaningful Jewish life if they so desire; in other words, "We want *Moshiaḥ* now!" meets "Who needs *Moshiaḥ*?"; (2) the irrelevance of heresy in a Jewish world void of hegemony, and the erasure of Sabbateanism from collective memory; and (3) Ḥasidism's neutralization of the messianic idea by focusing on one's individual religious life, self-fashioned according to taste and inclination. Ḥabad's "mythological" messianism, heretical or not, has not brought destruction or even trauma to the Jewish people.[104] On that reading, and perhaps by traditional standards, it may not be messianic at all.

103 In fact, Schneerson's famous claim that he has done all he can do to bring the Messiah and now it is up to us to finish the job with good works is a "neutralizing" element, making the collective all about the personal. See Schneerson, *Likkutei Siḥot* 5751, part 3 (5753), 118–19.

104 See Scholem, *The Messianic Idea*, 17: "Jewish messianism is in its origin and by its nature . . . a theory of catastrophe." Wolfson offers a more poetic description: "From Schneerson's perspective, for the Messiah to be on the way means the Messiah is already present, albeit as what is still absent—therein lies the hope that cannot be disentangled from despair" ("Revealing and Re/veiling," 94).

Chapter 9

Covenantal Rupture and Broken Faith in R. Kalonymus Kalman Shapira's *Eish Kodesh*

"Is he willing to prevent evil, but not able? Then he is impotent. Is he able but not willing? Then he is malevolent. Is he both willing and able? Whence then is evil?"

—Epicurus cited by Lucretius, *De Rerum natura*

Commenting on the verse in Genesis 7:23 *And he remained Noah*, the ḥasidic master R. Ya'akov Yizhak Horowitz, known as the Seer of Lublin (1745–1814), adapting the standard reading of the verse *And Noah remained*, asked, "*And he remained Noah*? After Noah witnessed the destruction of the world, can it be he remained as he was?" In a similar vein Elie Wiesel was alleged to have said, "I understand people who lived through the Shoah who didn't believe in God before the Shoah and believed in God afterward. And I understand people who did believe in God before the Shoah and didn't believe in God afterward. What I don't understand is someone whose belief was not altered by living through the Shoah. How can it have remained the same?"[1] Both of these comments gesture to the relationship between belief (or non-belief) and experience, more pointedly between belief (or non-belief) and an experience that renders that belief (or non-belief) untenable. Events certainly stretch, test, and challenge beliefs about the world, in some cases causing us to revise our beliefs, in some cases defend then, and in some cases events

1 I would like to offer my thanks and gratitude to James Diamond, David Mayan, Daniel Reiser, and Don Seeman for their invaluable comments and suggestions. חברותה או מיתותה.

I heard this orally from someone who heard it from Wiesel but I have not found a source for this.

simply justify what we already believe. For many Jews, the Holocaust was an event that betrayed any attempt at justification according to common traditional belief in divine providence. One way to articulate this view would be to say that believing God was present in the Holocaust is blasphemy, yet to believe God was absent is heresy.[2]

There was, of course, much more reflection on these matters after the final bodies were laid to rest, after survivors began to rebuild their lives, after the fear of extinction proved false but near annihilation proved true. There were some cases of individuals, scholars, rabbis, and laypeople who did write about the implications of the events as they were happening. One case of note was the ḥasidic rabbi Kalonymus Kalman Shapira of Piaseczno (1889–1943), whose Holocaust testimony in the form of sermons from the Warsaw ghetto were collected and hidden before the destruction of the ghetto. They were subsequently found after the war and published in 1960.[3] The oddity of these sermons as a testimony of the Holocaust, as opposed to, for example, the work of Primo Levi and many others, is that Shapira never mentions the Nazis, almost never mentions current events, never even overtly mentions the deaths of his family.[4] The material is therefore somewhat of a unique testimony of the Holocaust purely through the lens of Torah from the years 1939–1942, embedded in sermons preached in Shapira's synagogue in the ghetto.[5] Noteworthy is that the sermons were dated and thus ostensibly enable us to read them in light of the events that unfolded as they were being written and delivered. I say "ostensibly" because the very recent work by Daniel Reiser,

2 Of course there are post-Holocaust theologies, such as Eliezer Berkowitz's *Faith after the Holocaust*, that present theories of *hester panim*, or God concealing his face, as a traditional theological posture that could explain God and also justify God's inactivity in the Holocaust. For more examples, see David Wolpe, "*Hester Panim* in Modern Jewish Thought," *Modern Judaism* 17, no. 1 (February, 1997): 25–56. I would suggest that, that for many Jews, rabbis, theologians, and laypeople alike, such a rabbinic category does not adequately explain the Holocaust. In some way post-Holocaust theology exists between the poles of Berkowitz's *hester panim* theory and Richard Rubenstein's covenantal rupture theory.

3 I will not rehearse the many stories about how these sermons were concealed and how they were found. This has been expertly done by Daniel Reiser in his "*Esh Kodesh*: A New Evaluation in Light of a Philological Examination of the Manuscript," *Yad Vashem Studies* 44 (2016): 66–69.

4 See Daniel Reiser, *R. Kalonymus Kalman Shapira: Derashot me-Shanot ha-Za'am* [Hebrew] (Jerusalem: Yad Vashem, 2017), 1:55.

5 We don't actually know if the written sermons, even in manuscript form, were exactly those that were preached. Shapira could have easily excised things he felt were redundant or added things he thought about later. Thanks to David Mayan for this insight.

a two-volume reworking of the texts of these sermons from manuscript with an important introduction, shows us that what we thought was a linear progression in these sermons is a far more complex exercise of editorial review and revision, what he calls a "layered approach," which undermines the linearity of the material. What Reiser proves through a close examination of the manuscript written in Shapira's own hand is that he continually returned to his work, adding, deleting, and including marginalia, errata, and notes until he gave over his materials to the *Oyneg Shabbos* archives in the winter of 1943. Some of these markings prove significant in regard to viewing the dates the sermons were initially written as definitive of Shapira's reaction to any particular event.[6]

Below I explore the question asked by both the Seer of Lublin and Elie Wiesel: whether and how a believer can sustain their previous belief in light of a world historical disaster. Or, asked in a somewhat different vein by Israeli scholar Eliezer Schweid, "How is it possible to withstand [a test of faith] when the suffering is so intense as to destroy the sole means capable of reinforcing faith in God and the Torah in the present age?"[7] Schweid argues, with others who have written on these sermons, that Shapira, given the caveat of his theological protest and the erosion of the congruity of his belief, expresses in these sermons a sustained belief in God and covenant to the very end. Schweid writes that the goal "of all the sermons was to find ways in which the faithful could maintain their faith."[8] In general this is correct. However, I will argue that there is a distinction between Shapira's public persona as it comes through in his sermons and his own struggles with faith after the Great Deportation in late summer, 1942, expressed in the last words we have from his pen, and the future audience he was writing for in these final entries.[9]

---

6 Reiser, *R. Kalonymus Kalman Shapira.*

7 Eliezer Schweid, "The Bush is Aflame—but the Bush is not Consumed," in Schweid, *From Ruin to Salvation* [Hebrew] (Tel Aviv: Hakibbutz Hameuchad, 1994), 105, and James Diamond, "The Warsaw Ghetto Rebbe: Diverting God's Gaze from a Utopian End to an Anguished Now," *Modern Judaism* 30, no. 1 (October, 2010): 299. Shapira was not the only one who lived through the Holocaust who seriously confronted the question of faith in light of it. Aside from the many works of Wiesel it is worth mentioning David Weiss Halinvi's *The Book and the Sword* (New York: Farrar, Straus & Giroux, 1996). More recently see Yishai Mevorach, *Theology of Absence: On Faith after Chaos* [Hebrew] (Tel Aviv: Reisling Books, 2016). Mevorach, a student of Rav Shagar, works through the writings of Rav Shapira and also discussed Shapira, Nahman of Bratslav, among others on the question of faith and absence in contemporary religious life.

8 Schweid, *From Ruin to Salvation*, 138.

9 This is not exactly true. We do have a note that he wrote on January 3, 1943 (the 17th of Tevet) that offers instructions to the one who finds his writings to mail them to his

Shapira's career as a ḥasidic master was, for better or worse, overshadowed by the survival and publication of these wartime sermons. He called his collection of ghetto sermons simply *Ḥiddushei Torah auf Sedros, Torah Novella from the Weekly Parshah, or Derashot me-Shanot ha-Za'am (Sermons from the Years of Fury).* They were later published under the title *Eish Kodesh* (*Holy Fire*). Before the war, Shapira was widely known as an innovative ḥasidic rebbe. During that time he wrote a trilogy on Jewish education, including educating young men for prophecy, only one volume of which was published in his lifetime.[10] Two of those volumes, *A Student's Obligation: Advice from the Rebbe of the Warsaw Ghetto* (*Ḥovot ha-Talmidim*), for young children, and very recently, *Jewish-Spiritual Growth: A Step-by-Step Guide by a Ḥasidic Master* (*Hakhsharat ha-Avreikhim*), for adolescents, have appeared in English. Another slim volume on building community, *Benei Maḥshavah Tovah (Conscious Community),* appeared in translation in 1996 and has become popular in Jewish Renewal circles.[11] A collection of earlier sermons, *Derkeh ha-Melekh (The Way of the King)*, is widely viewed as a ḥasidic classic of the period.[12] But it is his Warsaw Ghetto sermons, published as *Eish Kodesh* (appearing in English in 2000 as *Sacred Fire: Torah from the Years of Fury 1939–1942*) that has become the most popular.

The fact that these heart-wrenching sermons were dated to the years of the ghetto gives us a startling view into one man's struggle with faith, as

---

brother Isaiah in Tel Aviv. In it, he writes about his other works as well and, like the final note in November, 1942, he ends with a liturgical flourish, using the same locution that "God should save us in the blink of an eye [*ke'heref ayin*]." See below where I offer a reading of this end to his note in November, 1942. I suggest the same would apply here. While this note certainly post-dates his final insertion in *Eish Kodesh* it does not relate to the events and their significance but rather is more practical. Thus I claimed above that the final note in November, 1942 is really the last significant thing we have from him. I want to thank Daniel Reiser for pointing out this final note from January, 1943.

10 This is discussed at length in Don Seeman, "Ritual Efficacy, Ḥasidic Mysticism, and Useless Suffering in the Warsaw Ghetto," *Harvard Theological Review* 101, nos. 3–4 (2008): 465–505. Cf. Zvi Leshem, "Between Mysticism and Prophecy: Ḥasidism According to the Piaseczner Rebbe" (PhD diss., Bar Ilan University, 2008); and David Mayan, "The Call to the Self: Devotional Individuation in the Teachings of Rabbi Kalonymus Kalman Shapira of Piaseczno" (MA thesis, Hebrew College, 2017).

11 See *A Student's Obligation: Advice from the Rebbe of the Warsaw Ghetto* (*Ḥovot ha-Talmidim*), trans. M. Oddenheimer (Northvale, NJ: Jason Aronson, 1995); *Jewish-Spiritual Growth: A Step-by-Step Guide by a Ḥasidic Master, trans. Yaacov David Shulman (CreateSpace Independent Publishing, 2016); and Conscious Community, trans. Andrea Cohen Kiener (*Northvale, NJ: Jason Aronson, *1997).*

12 Shapira moved from Piaseczno to Warsaw in 1917 where he founded the *yeshivah Da'at Moshe*. In the ensuing years he travelled back and forth from Piaseczno to Warsaw, residing mostly in Warsaw. See Reiser, *Eish Kodesh*, 1:14.

the world—and, ultimately I will argue, his faith—collapsed around, and within, him. Nehemia Polen, in his *The Holy Fire* (1999), calls this book "a testament of fidelity to Torah and tradition, in the face of the enemy's efforts to destroy both."[13] Polen, whose work initiates English-language scholarship on Shapira, adeptly traces the trajectory of his struggle with the incongruence between tradition and destruction as life in the ghetto became unbearable, and ultimately, unlivable. Following him, James Diamond views the sermons through a dialectical lens, showing the ways Shapira reaches the precipice of hopelessness, and faithlessness, only to retreat back into faith, only to approach the precipice once again.[14] While each scholar who has written on Shapira has offered novel contributions to our understanding of this emotionally charged testimony to the struggle of one man with the reality of human evil and faith in God, whose behavior appears increasingly incomprehensible, all maintain Shapira died in the embrace of a belief he never abandoned. For example, while he acknowledges that Shapira's last sermons in the spring and summer of 1942 indicate a shift in his theological orientation, Polen claims that to the end Shapira remained committed to faith in a God that could not, or would not, save him. Henry Abramson does so as well, when he writes, "Did the Rebbe lose his faith in the Holocaust? Even a cursory reading of his wartime writings demonstrates the absurdity of that question. At no point does he ever despair of God's existence and omnipotence, even up to his final will and testament...."[15] Daniel Reiser makes a similar but by no means identical observation:

> Now, as his sermons are about to end, and as 'the woes continue', he tells his public that he no longer has the ability to strengthen and comfort either

---

13 Nehemia Polen, *The Holy Fire: The Teachings of Rabbi Kalonymus Kalman Shapira, the Rebbe of the Warsaw Ghetto* (Northvale, NJ: Jason Aronson, 1999), 19. Others who have written about *Eish Kodesh* include Mendel Piekarz, *Polish Ḥasidism: Ideological Trends between the Two Wars and in the Shoah* [Hebrew] (Jerusalem: Bialik Institute, 1990); Pesach Schindler, *Ḥasidic Responses to the Holocaust in Light of Ḥasidic Thought* (Brooklyn, NY: Ktav, 1990); Henry Abramson, *Torah from the Years of Wrath* (CreateSpace Independent Publishing, 2017); Itzhak Hershkowitz, "Rabbi Kalonymus Kalman Shapira, the Piasechner Rebbe: His Holocaust and Pre-Holocaust Thought" [Hebrew] (MA thesis, Bar Ilan University, 2005); Seeman, "Ritual Efficacy"; Diamond, "The Warsaw Ghetto Rebbe"; Ron Wacks, *The Flame of the Holy Fire* (2010); Erin Leib, "God in the Years of Fury: Theodicy and Anti-Theodicy in the Holocaust Writings of Rabbi Kalonymus Kalman Shapira" (PhD diss., University of Chicago, 2014); and most recently Daniel Reiser, *R. Kalonymus Kalman Shapira*, his two-volume Hebrew work on the manuscript edition of *Eish Kodesh*.

14 See Diamond, "The Warsaw Ghetto Rebbe."

15 Abramson, *Torah from the Years of Wrath*, 249.

> himself or others. Furthermore, the Rebbe admits that his exhortations no longer affect him, and he is aware that they do not have any effect on his listeners either. Lest this be misunderstood, what we observe here is not a loss of faith—the continuation of this sermon [referring to a sermon delivered on *Shabbat Zakhor*, February 28, 1942] and the ensuing sermons rule that possibility out—but extraordinary candor and a sharing of his profound agony and personal vacillations with the reader.[16]

Below I suggest that Abramson's description of what loss of faith might mean—"despair of God's existence and omnipotence"—does not negate what I call Shapira's broken faith that resulted from Shapira's realization that God will not save the Jews from the fires of Nazi evil and that nothing the Jew might have done made him deserve that fate. And while Reiser's "loss of faith" is never quite explained (i.e., what was the faith that was not lost?), I want to suggest that indeed there was a loss of faith but not its total erasure, especially in the transition between the final sermon in the summer of 1942 and the addendum from November of that year. It is worth pointing out that Shapira does end that infamous note with a classical liturgical flourish: "May God have mercy upon us, and save us from their hands, in the blink of an eye [*k'heref ayin*]." Is that not a prayer? Perhaps. But I would suggest we see it otherwise for the very fact that it undermines the note that precedes it. Rather, I see this as a classic liturgical conclusion (*ḥatimah*), a formulaic finale to the words of one who has, in effect, stopped praying, or at least stopped believing in the efficacy of his prayer, because he knows those prayers will not be answered (not unlike the fictitious Yosl Rakover, whom I discuss below, who continues to pray to God despite his acknowledging God has abandoned him). We cannot know why Shapira decided to end this very radical note, really his final comment to us, with such a formulaic liturgical conclusion. But I certainly do not think we can conclude from this that the note that precedes it does not undermine the very covenantal frame in which such liturgical formulas are operative.

My assessment of what Shapira comes to in the end respectfully moves in another direction from Polen, Abramson, Reiser, Schweid, and others.[17]

---

16 Reiser, "*Eish Kodesh*," 70. A more apologetic reading by Esther Farber in her *Hidden in Thunder: Perspectives on Faith, Halacha, and Leadership During the Holocaust*, 2 vols. (New York: Feldheim, 2007), 579–612, pushes back even harder against any notion that Shapira's faith diminished at all.

17 In his essay "Ritual Efficacy," Don Seeman does indeed address the notion of broken faith in the final sermons of Shapira. Like few others (James Diamond would be another example), Seeman entertains the real possibility that by 1942 Shapira loses something he had before, although he does not go as far as I am suggesting that for Shapira faith

My reasoning is that these scholars never quite define what they mean by faith (faith in what?) and thus the claim that Shapira's faith remained is not adequate. Most of those mentioned above do acknowledge that something changed in Shapira's faith, but what it was is not clear. Abramson suggests what was lost was not faith in God but "faith in history." "The Rebbe could no longer fit the suffering of Warsaw Jewry into his paradigm of history, which operated with the notion that persecution promoted repentance, which brought about redemption."[18] Here I side with Jacob Neusner, Yosef Yerushalmi, and Amos Funkenstein (discussed below) that in a covenantal model, at least a Jewish one, there cannot be a loss of faith in history without also a loss of faith in God. The disunion between history and God in a covenantal and providential model is, to my mind, not tenable.[19] From a classical Jewish standpoint, to distinguish between God and history, which is what Abramson suggests, is to leave the orbit of covenantal theology. This notion is shared by many others as well. For example, biblical historian Ernst Wright writes, "Biblical history is the confessional recital of the redemptive acts of God in a particular history, *because history is the chief medium of revelation*" (my emphasis).[20]

I would like to revisit these sermons in order to suggest that something *seismic* indeed shifts in Shapira's belief, in the very *possibility* of belief, as it may have existed before, even as late as 1942. I am specifically interested in his final sermon in the summer of 1942 and the brief addendum he added in November, 1942 to a previous sermon that to my mind breaks through something Shapira never quite acknowledged before—that what he and his community are experiencing, what the Jews are experiencing, has never been experienced before. This admission, apparently a final edit to his writings after he had put his pen to rest, likely a rereading of an earlier sermon after the Great Deportation, is more than a mere depressing flourish, although certainly that too; I think it breaks faith in a covenantal God and sets the stage for what would become post-Holocaust theology a few decades later. The observation that Shapira's ghetto sermons set the stage

in the covenant itself collapses. See Seeman, "Ritual Efficacy," 503–504. On Seeman's reading of the final added footnote, see "Ritual Efficacy," 494. Seeman does not read into that note as much as I do, while he does recognize its significance.

18 Abramson, *Torah from the Years of Wrath*, 251.

19 See, for example, in Neusner's *The Idea of History in Rabbinical Literature* (London and Boston: Brill, 2004) and Neusner, "Paradigmatic versus Historical Thinking: The Case of Rabbinic Judaism," *History and Theory* 36, no. 3 (1977): 353–77.

20 Wright, *God who Acts: Biblical Theology and Recital* (London: LSCM Press, 1954), 13, and Barbara Krawcowicz, "Covenantal Theodicy and Paradigmatic Thinking," p. 19 in typescript.

for post-Holocaust theology is not new; Erin Leib makes this point in her 2014 dissertation "God in the Years of Fury."[21]

Leib frames Shapira's sermons around the question of theodicy and anti-theodicy in Zachary Braiterman's study of post-Holocaust theology *God (After) Auschwitz*.[22] Braiterman claims that the engine that generates post-Holocaust theology in thinkers such as Richard Rubenstein, Eliezer Berkowitz, Irving (Yitz) Greenberg, and others largely rests on the notion of anti-theodicy, that the question of evil can no longer be an integral part of God and God's relationship to the Jewish people or the world. Braiterman defines anti-theodicy this way, "By anti-theodicy we mean any religious response to the problem of evil whose proponents refuse to justify, explain, accept as something meaningful the relationship between God and suffering."[23] For post-Holocaust theologians, the Holocaust made classical theodicy impossible. Belief in God can continue to exist but it can no longer be wed to the problem of evil. If it is believing at all it is believing "otherwise." Amos Funkenstein puts it this way: "Jewish theologians ... such as Emil Fackenheim or E. Berkowitz admit that they see no rationale to the Holocaust. The Holocaust is incomprehensible, they say, *and defies all theodicies* ... Even these diluted versions of theodicy are offensive" (emphasis added).[24] On Braiterman's reading, post-Holocaust theologians from the more traditional Berkowitz to the more progressive Rubenstein all work along the anti-theodic spectrum founded on the notion that the Holocaust was unprecedented and, as such, drove a stake into classic notions of covenantal belief. Braiterman contends that this notion "gains a larger currency in specifically religious circles only after the Holocaust."[25] Leib suggests that "*Esh Kodesh* demonstrates that, in fact, the 20th century turn toward anti-theodicy actually began during the war itself."[26] She notes, "In this final sermon, we find a turn toward anti-theodicy, a quiet but final abandonment of the project of theodicy altogether. Either God will soon respond to Jewish suffering with salvation or he will not, but either way, the attempt

21 Leib, "God in the Years of Fury."

22 "Theodicy" is a term coined by Gottfried Wilhelm Leibnitz in 1709. See his *Theodicy: Essays on the Goodness of God, the Freedom of Man, and the Origin of Evil* (La Salle, IL: Open Court, 1996). This term was criticized often by thinkers from Voltaire to William James.

23 Braiterman, *God (After) Auschwitz* (Princeton, NJ: Princeton University Press, 1998), 31.

24 Amos Funkenstein, *Perceptions of Jewish History* (Los Angeles and Berkeley: University of California Press, 1993), 310, 311.

25 Funkenstein, *Perceptions of Jewish History*, 14.

26 Leib, "God in the Years of Fury," 12.

to rationalize, reframe, or justify it is over."[27] I agree with her view here and would like to move the discussion from the metaphysical or even theological frame of theodicy to the realm of faith—what kind of God can one believe in when theodicy ceases to function? And can we label such belief as identical, or even categorically similar to, a theodic one?

The consequences of anti-theodicy are varied. As Braiterman notes, "Although it borders on blasphemy, anti-theodicy does not constitute atheism; it might even express love that human persons have for God."[28] In the final section of this chapter I will explore this insight through a reading of Zvi Kolitz's *Yosl Rakover Talks to God* and Shlomo Carlebach's story of the "Holy Hunchback" about a student of Shapira Carlebach allegedly met in Tel Aviv.[29] For now, the border where blasphemy can coexist with love for God is where I would like to place Shapira's broken faith. As opposed to Abramson, this is not a loss of faith in history; it is a loss of faith of *God* in history.[30] The God that remains, the God that can be believed in, or loved, after theodicy, after history is de-theologized, is not the same God as before theodicy crumbled with the ghetto walls or the Great Deportation. Before getting there, however, some preliminary remarks are in order.

II

Few traditionalists wrote about the Holocaust in any systematic way. And those who did record reflections of the war raging around them, did not tend to view it as an event that shattered the covenantal foundation upon which Judaism is constructed. The traditional, and ultra-traditional, mindset, it

---

27 Leib, "God in the Years of Fury," 178.

28 Braiterman, *God (After) Auschwitz*, 4.

29 The first English translation of Kolitz's story appeared in *Cross Currents* in 1994 as "Yossel Rakover's Appeal to God," trans. Jeffry V. Malow and Franz Jozef van Beeck. It was then published as *Yossel Rackover Speaks to God* (Hoboken, NJ: Ktav, 1995) and later as *Yosl Rakover Talks to God*, trans. Carol Brown Janeway (New York: Vintage Books, 2000).

30 For a theological reflection of God in relation to history on the question of the Holocaust see Emile Fackenheim, *God's Presence in History* (New York: Harper Torchbooks, 1972). In most of his post-Holocaust work Fackenheim does not engage with *Eish Kodesh*. He does discuss it in *What Is Judaism: An Interpretation for the Present Age* (New York: Summit Books, 1987, repub. Syracuse University Press, 1999), 290ff. There he thanks Nehemia Polen in the acknowledgments for introducing him to Shapira. It still remains somewhat curious that *Eish Kodesh* was printed in 1960 and Fackenheim would not have known of Shapira's work until the 1980s when he read about him in Polen.

has been argued, lives in what Jacob Neusner called "paradigmatic thinking"—a belief that all events correspond to a predetermined notion of covenant, even if that correspondence, or God's providence, may be veiled from view, for example, in a state of *hester panim* or *deus obsconditus*. Neusner believed that "paradigmatic thinking," and thus the traditional model of the covenant, became impossible with the introduction of historicism.[31] His view of "paradigmatic thinking" is that history conforms to a special model of theological cause and effect, even if not always evident, that cannot bear the weight of a historicist critique. That is, for Neusner, once history becomes the lens through which Judaism or the covenant is viewed, classical theodicy can only function as a historically contingent phenomenon and no longer an operative theological principle. Barbara Krawcowicz puts it nicely when she writes, "[For Neusner] it is the paradigm that defines and shapes reality and not the other way round. Paradigmatic thinking identifies, 'a happening not by its consequence … but by its conformity to the appropriate paradigm.'"[32] Yosef Hayim Yerushalmi sums up "paradigmatic thinking" quite neatly in his seminal book *Zakhor*, "What has occurred now is similar to the persecutions of old, and all that happened to the forefathers has happened to their descendants. Upon the former already the earlier generations composed *selihot* and narrated the events. It is all one."[33] Paradigmatic thinking offers a cyclical view of history determined by a promise made that lies beyond historical contingency. This is, of course, a play on a popular rabbinic dictum "the acts of the fathers are signs for their children."[34] We live in a world of reward and punishment not totally of our own making but not arbitrary either. "It is all one."

For post-Holocaust theologians, the Holocaust could not fit into this paradigm. More strongly, the belief that it could, for some, might itself be blasphemous (for an anti-theodician theodicy is heresy). Jewish historian Amos Funkenstein notes in his essay about the Holocaust, "To the most courageous among recent theologians, the very meaningless of the Holocaust

---

31 See Neusner, "Paradigmatic versus Historical Thinking."

32 Krawcowicz, "Covenantal Theodicy and Paradigmatic Thinking," p. 24 in typescript. I want to thank Barbara Krawcowicz for sharing the revisions of her dissertation, "Covenantal Theodicy among Haredi and Modern Jewish Thinkers During and After the Holocaust" (PhD diss., Indiana University, 2013).

33 Yosef Hayim Yerushalmi, *Zakhor* (Seattle: University of Washington Press, 1982), 50.

34 Midrash Tanhuma 9.

is itself, they say, a matter of faith, a positive religious act."[35] Believing in a covenantal God after the Holocaust was, for many, an act of "bad faith." Braiterman puts it this way: "With Auschwitz in mind, many contemporary readers are repelled by theodicies found in traditional Jewish sources."[36] Acknowledging this rupture was not solely the product of Richard Rubenstein's groundbreaking *God After Auschwitz*. Rubenstein's teacher Mordecai Kaplan, who really never wrote directly about the Holocaust, wrote obliquely in his 1970 book *The Religion of Ethical Nationhood*, "[The Holocaust] rendered the traditional idea of God untenable."[37]

All post-Holocaust theologians were deeply influenced by modernity, even though some, like Berkowitz and Greenberg, were Orthodox. Shapira, writing during the Holocaust, and thus not a post-Holocaust theologian, is nevertheless one who understood the depth of the covenantal rupture and its implications as it was happening in ways post-Holocaust theologians later developed. He may be in one way an exception to those writing during the Holocaust and in another a signpost to the impossibility of faith after such a rupture. Thus post-Holocaust theology is not dependent on modernity *per se* but can be gleaned through a stark and honest confrontation with the limitations of tradition that Shapira understood during the war. Braiterman notes that classical Jewish texts do indeed contain anti-theodic elements even as they are mostly overwhelmed by a theodicy response. Modernity may be the context that makes post-Holocaust theology permissible, even necessary, but it is not a theological *novum* as much as turning up the volume of a whisper that, in my view, already appears in the tension between Shapira's final sermon in the summer of 1942 and his addendum in November, 1942.

If Shapira is an exception, what of most other ultra-Orthodox Jews? Some, like Rabbis Yoel Teitelbaum of Satmar (saved from almost certain death in Bergen-Belsen by the Katzner transports), Yosef Yizhak of Lubavitch, and Elhanan Wasserman (who was murdered by Lithuanian collaborators of the Nazis in the summer of 1941 after he returned to Europe from America to be with his students), maintained a belief in the traditional covenant and viewed the Holocaust as punishment for Jewish secularism, including Zionism.[38] Others, such as Rabbis Zvi Yehudah Kook and Ya'akov Moshe

35 Funkenstein, *Perceptions of Jewish History* (Berkeley and Los Angeles: The University of California Press, 1993), 329.

36 Braiterman, *God (After) Auschwitz*, 30.

37 Kaplan, *The Religion of Ethical Nationhood* (New York: Macmillan, 1970) 202.

38 See Teitelbaum, *Va-yoel Moshe* (Jerusalem, 1961), 7–9. See also Menachem Keren-Krantz, "R. Joel Teitelbaum: A Biography" (PhD diss., Tel Aviv University, 2013). He stated this in other places in very explicit terms. See, for example in the journal *Ha-Me'or*, Tammuz 1958, 3–9, cited in Keren-Krantz, "R. Joel Teitelbaum," 291, where

Charlap, viewed the Holocaust as a punishment for not leaving Europe after the Balfour Declaration—that is, for rejecting Zionism.[39] Zvi Yehudah even called the Holocaust an act of "divine surgery." Each case, however different, is an exercise in "paradigmatic thinking," and as different as these views are from one another, they actually share more with each other than they do with any post-Holocaust theologian or, I would argue, with Shapira. He may have agreed with these views in one form or another at the outset of the war but by the summer of 1942, and certainly after the Great Deportation, I hope to show that he did not.

If the frame of anti-theodicy requires rupture of theodicy, on what foundations does classical theodicy rest? Here I am indebted to my graduate student Barbara Krawcowicz, whose 2013 dissertation, "Covenantal Theodicy among Haredi and Modern Jewish Thinkers During and After the Holocaust," deftly explores ultra-Orthodox responses to the Holocaust during the war.[40] Krawcowicz is the first to deploy Neusner's notion of "paradigmatic thinking" in reference to the Holocaust by treating some of the major ultra-Orthodox rabbis reflecting on the events during and immediately after the war. Krawcowicz argues that many of these figures who wrote about the Holocaust during the war, e.g., Rabbis Shlomo Zalman Ehrenreich (1862–1944), Shlomo Zalman Unsdorfer (1888–1944), and Yissakhar Teichthal (1885–1945), all of whom perished, while they did not conclude, as did many post-Holocaust theologians did afterward, that the covenant was irreparably broken, nevertheless also did not offer reasons for

---

he adds a political reason for Zionism's culpability. "Today it is known that Zionism caused the death of six million Jews. This is not only because they positioned the hearts of many in Israel with their heresy … for it is known that heresy is the cause of evil, but their very political behavior and irresponsibility was responsible for the death of millions of Jews because they believed that the establishment of a sovereign state can only come about with Jewish blood. In the Nazi tragedy there were many opportunities to save thousands of Jews … we see now from the Katzner trials that reveal only a small part of the Zionists' culpability in saving the lives of Jews." An indispensible collection of translated material from these and other traditional thinkers on the Holocaust can be found in Gershon Greenberg and Steven T. Katz, *Wresting with God: Jewish Theological Responses During and after the Holocaust* (New York: Oxford University Press, 2007). In addition, see the many essays written on a variety of ultra-Orthodox thinkers on the Holocaust by Gershon Greenberg and Eliezer Schweid, *Wrestling until Daybreak: Searching for Meaning in Thinking on the Holocaust* (Lanham, MD: University Press of America, 1994).

39 See, for example, R. Zvi Yehudah Kook, "*Ha-Shoah*," in *Siḥot R. Ẓvi Yehudah Kook: Mo'adim—Rosh ha-Shanah—Purim*, ed. Shlomo Aviner (Jerusalem: Hava Books, 2013), 264–86. For a more extensive rendering of Kookean views on the Holocaust see Shlomo Aviner, *Me'orot me-Ofel: Al ha-Shoah* (Jerusalem: Hava Books, 2010).

40 Krawcowicz, "Covenantal Theodicy among Haredi and Modern Jewish Thinkers."

the Holocaust that fit neatly into the paradigmatic thinking that, as Hayim Yerushalmi states, "It is all one." For them, the Holocaust posed a theological dilemma but not a theological crisis. Teichthal is an interesting case here because the Holocaust did evoke in him a radical shift from being a staunch anti-Zionist to one who believed that establishment of a Jewish homeland in *Ereẓ Yisrael* was indeed a priority.[41]

Krawcowicz chose not to include Shapira in her dissertation, but here I would suggest that Shapira stands somewhere between her ultra-Orthodox subjects and the modern post-Holocaust theologians. More strongly I think Shapira presages post-Holocaust theology from the very depths of its destructive fire. He chose a path none of the others dared to tread. Shapira, of course, never lived to further articulate some of his more radical notions articulated in his final sermons. At the end of the ghetto revolt in May 1943 Shapira, with many other Jews who remained in the ghetto, was deported to the Trawniki labor camp. Although we do not know for certain, it is thought that he was murdered on November 3rd, in what was known as "the Harvest Festival" (*Aktion Erntefest*) in response to violent uprisings in other camps.[42]

Considering their historical import, it is surprising that the collection of Shapira's sermons in the ghetto was not published until 1960. Even after its publication, *Eish Kodesh* remained very much within ḥasidic circles until Shlomo Carlebach and a few others discovered the work and began conveying its teachings in non-ḥasidic communities. Carlebach captured this work in his story "The Holy Hunchback," the story of a broken, elderly street cleaner Carlebach encountered in Tel Aviv who, as a child, was one of Shapira's students in his *yeshivah* in Piaseczno.

III

Daniel's Reiser's two-volume work *Derashot Me-Shanot Ha-Za'am* (*Sermons from the Years of Rage*) is more than another significant contribution to the work of R. Kalonymus Kalman Shapira. It is a piece of scholarship that potentially changes how *Eish Kodesh* is studied and understood, in part because Reiser shows mistakes, errors, and misreadings in some of the transcriptions that became the 1960 printing of *Eish Kodesh*. As I mentioned

41 See in Teichtal's *Em ha-Banim Semeiḥah* now in English as Yissakhar Shlomo Teichtal, *Em Habanim Semeichah: On Eretz Yisrael, Redemption and Unity* (Jerusalem: Urim Press, 2002).

42 Reiser, *Derashot*, 1:24, gives November 2nd as the date of his death.

above, one of the distinctive characteristics of *Eish Kodesh* is that we know when each sermon was delivered and thus can link that week with events in the ghetto, suggesting the ways in which the unfolding horror of the ghetto, including the travails of Shapira's own family, may be embedded in the sermon. Given that Shapira does not mention events in the sermons themselves, the dating is the primary way for us to view this work as a Holocaust testimony, that is, to view it as an account of the tragedy of the Warsaw Ghetto. Reiser's re-examination of the original manuscript, using new technology to make it more easily discernible, enabled him to make many corrections in the only printed edition until now (1960) and produce a corrected text that includes many significant changes. More relevant to our purposes, Reiser reproduces the manuscript, which exhibits detailed editing, deletions, redistribution of paragraphs, and addenda in the margins of many of the sermons. Analyzing the different markings, he concludes that Shapira seemed to continue to rework and edit the sermons throughout his time in the ghetto.[43] Thus he concludes, "It seems to me that, although different phases in the Rebbe's theology of suffering are discernible and have been clearly distinguished, this differentiation is not clear cut and each phrase does not constitute a paradigm in itself. One may detect, for example, a 'late' concept of suffering in the Rebbe's early sermons and an 'early' one in later sermons. Nevertheless, this does not refute the thesis that his theory was of an evolutionary nature; it merely refines it."[44] Toward the end of his English essay "*Eish Kodesh*," largely a translation from a section of his Hebrew introduction to *Derashot*, Reiser makes a slightly more definitive claim: "Given the layered nature of the entire manuscript, it is virtually impossible to attempt to date each and every sermon … Accordingly, I prefer to avoid any discourse about 'meaning' and to propose a different research approach. Instead of seeking development and meaning this views *Eish Kodesh* as a work that re-expresses the question of suffering in phenomenological terms and takes its readers on a jarring spiritual journey."[45]

In the next section I look at two texts from *Eish Kodesh*; first, Shapira's final sermon delivered on the Shabbat before Tisha b'Av (Shabbat Ḥazon) 1942 and, second, a well-known addendum added to an earlier sermon delivered on Hanukkah, 1941 that serves as the last written testimony we

43 See Reiser, *Derashot*, 2:59, 60.

44 Reiser, *Derashot*, 2:72.

45 Reiser, *Derashot*, 2:97. Cf. Seeman, "Ritual Efficacy," esp. 448–93.

have from his hand.[46] This addendum was written in November, 1942. I want to offer a "phenomenological" reading of the space between the Shabbat Ḥazon sermon and the later addendum, paying attention to how the addendum appeared in the manuscript, and suggest how the subtle shift from the Shabbat Ḥazon sermon to the addendum marks a break in Shapira's faith as he reconciled the impending doom that was about to unfold. This gestures back to Schweid's question I noted at the outset, "How is it possible to withstand [a test of faith] when the suffering is so intense as to destroy the sole means capable of reinforcing faith in God and the Torah in the present age?" Unlike Schweid, I suggest that it wasn't.

IV

Shapira's final sermon focused on the first verse of the *haftarah* Isaiah 1:1, *A vision, shown to Isaiah son of Amoz.* This first chapter in Isaiah is one of the darkest in the Prophets, as it describes the destruction of Israel in vivid and horrific terms. The final verse of the chapter, *The mighty will become tinder and his work a spark, both will burn together and no one to quench the fire* could not but catch the attention of Shapira, who lived in circumstances surrounded by fire and the righteous being relegated to hapless victims of the power of evil. The sermon revolves around the distinction between "seeing," "hearing," and "knowing." His midrashic text is from Song of Songs Rabbah 3:2, "There are ten expressions of prophecy, but which one is the most difficult? R. Eliezer said, 'A vision is the hardest,' as it says, *A cruel vision was told to me* (Isaiah 21:1)." Asking about the seeming incongruity between "seeing" and "knowing" in the verse, *I have truly* ***seen*** *the suffering of my people ... for I* ***know*** *their pain* (Exodus 3:7), Shapira likens this to a father who knows the necessity of a son's operation yet cannot bear to watch it because seeing it makes him unable to truly know that the operation is for the son's own good. That is, the experience of the pain of a loved one makes knowledge of its benefits impossible. So therefore, God says, *Now go, I am sending you to Pharaoh, take My people out of Egypt* (Exodus 3:10), as if to say, "I cannot watch, just go. . . ." The "vision" is the hardest level of prophecy because it disables any recognition of a future; it is stuck in the present moment of seeing.

46 For the Hanukkah sermon see Reiser, *Derashot*, 2:240. The addendum appears there as well. All references are to Reiser's 2017 edition.

This is one example where Diamond's dialectical approach is operative. Shapira comes to the precipice; the pain of seeing the fire of the ghetto, the degradation of the righteous, the vision that makes "knowing" impossible, makes a future impossible, makes the covenant impossible. And at that very moment Shapira digs back into Torah to grasp onto Daniel 9:18, *Open your eyes and see.* This is part of Daniel's prayer for Israel. Verses 18 and 19 read, O my God, incline Your ear and hear; open Your eyes and see our desolations, and the city which is called by Your name; for we do not present our supplications before You because of our righteous deeds, but because of Your great mercies. O Lord, hear! O Lord, forgive! O Lord, listen and act! Do not delay for Your own sake, my God, for Your city and Your people are called by Your name. Even in the moment where vision blinds knowledge of the good end, perhaps the belief in any good end, there is Daniel who beseeches God for salvation. And so Daniel's call here is answered by the final verse in the haftarah (the sages knew better, I think, to end here and not read to the end of the chapter), Zion will be redeemed with justice, and her captives with charity (Isaiah 1:27). With that Shapira put down his pen. Almost. As Reiser shows, while he did not write any more sermons, he apparently continued to revise the ones already written.

In a sermon delivered on Hanukkah, December, 1941, Shapira reflected on the liturgical insert for Hanukkah known as Al ha-Nissim, one of the earliest extant liturgies in the Jewish tradition. In general, though, the sermon is about faith (emunah) one of the more sustained sermons about faith in *Eish Kodesh*. Shapira comments that Israel's faith and Abraham's faith are categorically different because Abraham's faith "was an act of righteousness" (not being reared in faith) while Israel's faith, as inheritors of Abrahamic faith, is intrinsic to who they are ("faith is the light and holiness of God inside the Jew"). Following this he turns to his present situation. "To our chagrin, we see that even among those who have faith, there are now certain individuals whose faith has been damaged [*nifgamah ha-emunah eẓlam*]. They question God, saying, 'Why have you forsaken us? . . . why is the Torah and everything sacred being destroyed?' " Responding to this sentiment, while not denying its emotional impact, he launches into what can be viewed as a classical theodic claim preached from a moment of high anxiety and utter turmoil.

> ...[F]aith must be with one's whole being [*be-mesirat nefesh*—self sacrifice] because all mesirat nefesh comes from faith. If faith is not exercised with

> *mesirat nefesh* how can mesirat nefesh exist at all?! The notion of mesirat nefesh in faith must be operative, and even when God is concealed [ha-hester] one must believe that everything is from God and is for the good and the just and all suffering is filed with God's love for Israel ... In truth there is no room for questioning (heaven forbid). Truthfully, the sufferings we are experiencing are like those we've suffered every few hundred years ... What excuse does one have to question God and have his faith damaged by this suffering more than the Jews who suffered in the past? Why should one's faith be damaged now when it wasn't when he reads descriptions of Jewish suffering from the past? Why is it when one reads a line from the Talmud or Midrash and hears of past sufferings in Israel is his faith not damaged but now [confronting the experience on the ghetto] it is? Those who say that the suffering now has never happened before to Israel are mistaken. The destruction of the Temple and the massacre at Betar were like what we are suffering now. May God have mercy and call an end to our suffering; may God save us now, immediately, and forever.[47]

This is an impassioned and almost quintessential expression of classical Jewish theodicy, almost angry, quite atypical of Shapira's wartime sermons. So many of Shapira's sermons stress suffering and express empathy and understanding and yet here he turns into a fire-and-brimstone orator chiding his listeners, warning them not to be deluded that they are living in some unprecedented reality. While we do not know for sure, it appears this change in attitude may have been instigated by "those who say that the suffering now has never happened before." Who this refers to we do not know. In any case, I think Shapira deeply understood the theological implications of such an assertion, likely more than his listeners, and perhaps that is why he was pushing back so hard against it. The very foundations of faith that he speaks about in the beginning of the passage, the faith driven by mesirat nefesh, the faith is God's saving power, is dependent on the covenantal principle of "paradigmatic thinking," that what we are experiencing not is not a novum, that providence remains operative, that salvation is still possible. That nothing here is new, that this is our covenant, that this is the test we must pass ("every few hundred years") to maintain our place in God's love is what underlies the passion of these comments.[48] As Neusner

47 Reiser, *Derashot*, 2:173–75.

48 Diamond seems to recognize this change, even noting that after the summer of 1942 the "traditional rationale for suffering as a necessary stage in the unfolding of the divine plan [was] ... no longer viable," that is, after the Great Deportation. But he does not extend this to its natural conclusion of the end of theodicy for Shapira and its, to

puts it, "A paradigm predetermines and selects happenings in accord with a pattern possessed of its own logic and meaning, unresponsive to the illogic of happenings, whether chaotic or orderly, from the human perspective. . . . Paradigms admit to time—the spell that intervenes between this and that, the this and the that beyond defined within the paradigm" (emphasis added).[49]

As Reiser has shown us, Shapira continuously revisited and revised these sermons throughout his time in the ghetto. He writes, "The Rebbe's renunciation of certain persecutions that he had presented and his decision to delete them are crucial for our understanding of his thinking vacillations, and change of heart during the Holocaust years."[50] Sometimes he crossed out a word, leaving the word legible, sometimes he drew a line through an entire section of a sermon, sometimes he blackened a word beyond recognition and replaced it with another; in many cases he added marginalia, clarifying a point. In some cases the meaning of the original comment is altered, sometimes nuanced, but rarely is it rejected entirely.[51] In one case, in the sermon he delivered on Hanukkah, 1941, he did something quite unusual; he added an addendum (in Hebrew *haga'ah*) on the bottom of the page (not in the margins). The addendum relates back to the passage quoted about faith.

> It is only the sufferings [zarot] that were experienced until the middle of 1942 that were not unprecedented [she-hayu kevar]. But the bizarre suffering [*zarot meshunot*] and the evil bizarre deaths [*u-mitot ra'ot u-meshunot*] that were invented by these evil bizarre murderers on Israel in the middle of 1942, according to my opinion and the teachings of the sages of the chronicles of the Jewish people more generally, there were none like these before. And God should have mercy on us and save us from their hands in the blink of an eye. Erev Shabbat Kodesh 18th of Kislev 1942. The author.[52]

---

my mind, necessary and radical consequences. See Diamond, "The Warsaw Ghetto Rebbe," 4; and Seeman, "Ritual Efficacy." Cf. Seeman, "Otherwise than Meaning: On the Generosity of Ritual," *Social Analysis* 48, no. 2 (Summer, 2004): 62–67.

49 Neusner, "Paradigmatic versus Historical Thinking," 359.

50 Reiser, "*Eish Kodesh*," 91.

51 This is all laid out in detail in Reiser's Introduction to *Derashot*. In English see Reiser, "*Eish Kodesh*," 83–97. See esp. 90–91. On crossing out an entire sermon, see his sermon for *parashat kedoshim*, May 4, 1940. Reiser notes that this sermon was printed in the 1960 edition without any indication it was crossed out.

52 This translation comes from the Reiser manuscript edition in *Derashot*, 2:175. There are some differences between previous translations, e.g., J. Heshy Worch, *Sacred Fire*, 251. I tried to offer a more literal, if also perhaps more clumsy translation, in order to render a reading as close as possible to the original. For example, Worch uses the terms

The suggestion that the tragedy unfolding was both *unprecedented and unparalleled ("there were none like these before")* may seem ordinary, even obvious, to many contemporary readers. However, much of the thinking about the Holocaust, both by scholars and laypeople, and much of the way the Holocaust has been ceremonialized (e.g., establishing a national Holocaust Memorial Day, etc.), is founded on this very principle. Much of the *ḥaredi* protest against Holocaust Memorial Day is precisely based on their conviction that the Holocaust is *not* unprecedented and should thus be folded into Tisha b'Av.[53] Zvi Yehuda Kook included his reflections on the Holocaust as an extension of his sermons of the tenth of Tevet, a fast day commemorating the beginning of the siege of Jerusalem.[54] But for a ḥasidic Jew in 1942 or 1943 who lived deep within the orbit of the covenantal theology and "paradigmatic thinking" of Judaism, such a comment, even if thought, was almost never stated outright; it gestured to what would become a few decades later a radical reassessment of the Holocaust as a full-blown theological crisis and a serious challenge to the Jewish tradition. A full-blown theological crisis, in this case, emerges only when two conditions are met simultaneously: first, the belief that the Holocaust was an unprecedented event in Jewish history; and second, that this unprecedented event must irrevocably rupture the covenantal framework established in the Hebrew Bible. Shapira's comment certainly adopts the first condition and, I would argue, also gestures toward the second.

The way this addendum appears in the original manuscript, thanks to Reiser's publication of it, I think strengthens my point. Shapira could have simply crossed out the theodicy paragraph in the original Hanukkah sermon. We see in the manuscript he often does that. Or he could have softened its harshness with marginalia, which he does quite often as well. He did neither. He left this theodicy statement of covenantal theology intact and, in the note (*haga'ah*) on the bottom of the page he qualified it out of existence. The foundational notion of exercising faith through self-sacrifice (*mesirat nefesh*) by arguing that faith serves as the bedrock of all acts of *mesirat nefesh*, the belief in God's salvific promise and potential, in his mind did not survive the Great Deportation that occurred between July and September, 1942. The Shabbat Ḥazon sermon delivered July 18, 1942, was a final testament to an entire theological structure that would

---

"unprecedented" and "unparalleled" for "there were none like them before." (*lo hayu ke-motam*). I agree with Worch's reading which in some sense makes my point even more strongly, but I wanted to keep it as close to a literal rendering as possible.

53 See 2 Kings 25:1–25.

54 See Zvi Yehudah Kook, *Siḥot ha-Rav Ẓvi Yehudah: Mo'adim*, 264–86.

collapse for Shapira in the coming months. As that was his last sermon that has survived, almost nothing remains extant from him after July, 1942 aside from this addendum he added in November of that year.

One can only shudder to imagine Shapira sitting in his home during those dark months, hungry and weak, and reading through these sermons one more time only to come across his Hanukkah sermon of 1941, read his exhortation about faith and the fact that "this [suffering] happens every few hundred years," and how dare we think otherwise, and then pick up his pen, one more time, to add a few final sentences. I assume he wanted his reader to know that something changed between the autumn of 1941 and November, 1942. He did not blot out his call to faith. Rather, he contextualized it by saying it was no longer relevant. His comment in the Hanukkah sermon, "those who say that the suffering now has never happened before to Israel are mistaken," is undermined. His comment, "there are now certain individuals whose faith has been damaged," is justified. And now he counts himself among them. This is an example of a courageous admission of error in a time of crisis; and he apparently wanted his reader know he was mistaken as he left for posterity his words from Hanukkah, 1941 and November, 1942. That mistake, I suggest, was not simply an empirical admission of miscalculation but a deep theological rupture, as I read the claim of the Holocaust as an "unprecedented" event that makes "paradigmatic thinking" impossible, as Rubenstein and other post-Holocaust theologians argue as well. If we return once more to Diamond's dialectical hypothesis, I would argue that there is no stepping back from that final note in November, 1942; in other words, the dialectic is broken. This is a step off the cliff of theodicy into the abyss of anti-theodicy and, more relevant to my concerns here, a move from theodic faith to broken faith. To reiterate, I am not saying Shapira lost faith in God entirely; I think he did not. But the faith he had after November, 1942, based on the only words we have, is not the faith he had previously. It structurally cannot be, for the simple reason that he removed the very theological, and theodic, structure that made that faith possible.

What is noticeably different in Shapira's Hanukkah addendum is that his unprecedented claim does not come from historicism or secularism, or even from theology, but from a deep existential realization of the utter inability of the tradition, which was for him until those months of darkness, ironclad and indestructible, to withstand this level of radical evil. He brings no anti-theodic text, in fact no text at all, just an empirical observation with what seemed to him an obvious conclusion. Theodicy collapses and nothing exists to take its place. Disbelief was untenable. But belief as previously defined was no longer possible. God remained, but the covenant, at least as it existed previously, did not.

Taking Reiser's "layered approach" into account, I suggest that *Eish Kodesh* can be divided into three distinct but overlapping parts, not linearly defined, that loosely correspond to the period when he began his sermons in the ghetto in September, 1939 until the final recorded sermon on the Shabbat before Tisha b'Av in the summer of 1942. These three periods can be marked by three aspects of his vocation: in the first phase, Shapira functioned largely as a pastor, offering his community words of strength in times of peril. Here, he thought very much within the paradigmatic model that what Jews are facing is not categorically different than previous times of Jewish suffering. Perhaps the sermon on Hanukkah, 1941 is the quintessence of that.

In the second phase, Shapira had the ominous job of teaching his people how to die. This is illustrated in his many sermons about martyrdom and suffering that were deftly discussed by Polen, Schweid, Diamond, Seeman, Hershkovitz, Abramson, and Leib, among others. These sermons about martyrdom are nothing less than learning how to die with dignity; how to understand that, although beyond comprehension, they are part of some divine drama and serve as its cadre of heroes. One gets a sense in these sermons that Shapira knew he was speaking to individuals who would likely not be alive the following year. To read these sermons with that in mind is heartbreaking. In the final period, ending abruptly in July, 1942, with the crucial addendum in November, 1942, Shapira emerges as a radical theologian, implicitly rejecting, or certainly contesting, some of his earlier sermons by suggesting that this moment does not fit into any paradigm, that what he and his constituents were experiencing was "unprecedented" and "unparalleled." These two words separate Shapira from his ultra-Orthodox colleagues and, as Leib notes, plants the seeds of what would become post-Holocaust theology a few decades later. Paradigmatic thinking cannot absorb a true *novum*.

The paradigm that enabled Jews to withstand disbelief throughout Jewish history simply would no longer carry the burden of this historical moment even as it was not historicism that broke the back of "paradigmatic thinking" but rather witnessing the pure and bizarre evil that erased a covenantal God. By this time, more than in the previous two sermons, one gets the sense that Shapira is preaching largely to himself or, perhaps with that final note, writing for posterity, to those who may read these sermons if any Jews survived at all. Shapira seems left alone to process the brokenness of his inner world as the world around him collapsed.

As to the theological, or historical, question, "Is the Holocaust a *novum*?" I think that question was utterly irrelevant for Shapira because that question is an act of historical, or historicist, explanation one way or the other. It is significant that Shapira is not advocating silence in the moment where the paradigm, and faith, reaches its limit, where God seems to absent Godself from history, such as we see in other ultra-Orthodox thinkers writing during the war, examined in Barbara Krawcowicz's work.[55] Shapira realizes that he will die with a God who has abandoned his people, a faith that is shattered, a belief in a God who is broken, a God who cannot save or will not save. To believe in God becomes as absurd and as blasphemous as not to believe in God. Braiterman uses the term "anti-theodicy" to describe post-Holocaust theology as that which refuses to view catastrophe as instrumental in the divine covenant. Shapira was not anti-theodic in that sense; and here I disagree slightly with Leib. Shapira's view might more accurately be described as a "broken theodicy." His final flourish, "God should have mercy on us and save us from their hands in the blink of an eye" was not only rhetorical. Yet I submit that this formulaic liturgical flourish was no longer coming from the faith that had existed before. Of course, we can never know what he, or anyone, believed, especially in such a traumatic moment, but his use of "unprecedented" was not in my view written without an understanding of its theological implications. Perhaps in that breach, between pure rhetoric and uttering something that he no longer believed but also could not put to rest, opened the door for the anti-theodicy that was to come a few decades later.

In the final section I want to explore a little more deeply what may have been the nature of Shapira's "broken faith." I do so by comparing my reading of Shapira with two fictitious characters from the Warsaw Ghetto, Yosl Rakover, the creation of Zvi Kolitz, and the Holy Hunchback, the creation of Shlomo Carlebach.

V

When the story "Yossel Rakover Speaks to God" first appeared in a Yiddish newspaper in Buenos Aires in 1946 it was thought to be an authentic document of one of the last Jews in the Warsaw Ghetto in April, 1943 discovered in the rubble of the ghetto. It was then edited by the great poet Abraham

---

55 Barbara Krawcowicz, "Covenantal Theodicy among Haredi and Modern Jewish Thinkers During and After the Holocaust."

Sutzkver for the Yiddish press in Israel and appeared in French in 1955. It soon came to be known that it was a fictitious story written by Zvi Kolitz, a Jew from Lithuania living in Israel who was visiting Argentina on an assignment for the Zionist Revisionist Movement. The fictitious nature of the story did not diminish its power, or its influence, and this story quickly became iconic and inspired commentaries by the likes of Emmanuel Levinas among others.[56]

Briefly, the story is about a Jew, a *ḥasid* from the ḥasidic court of Ger, trapped in a building as the ghetto collapses, preparing for one last assault on the Germans below (he has a few jerry cans of gasoline he will use to drop on the Nazis and gleefully watch them burn) before he succumbs to inevitable death.[57] The story is often cited as one Jew's defiant belief in God. "You may torture me to death—I will always believe in You. I will love you always and forever—*even despite You*" (my emphasis). He remains a "believer but not a supplicant, a lover of God but not His blind Amen-sayer."[58] He says, "I cannot say after all I lived through, that my relation to God is unchanged. But with absolute certainly I can say that my faith in Him has not altered a hair's-breath."[59] This takes us back to Wiesel's comment at the outset: can it really be that someone experiences what Yosl experienced and his faith has not changed one bit? That is precisely what Wiesel fails to comprehend. And yet this appears to be what Yosl is saying.

In his short rendering of the French version of the so-called essay published in the Zionist Parisian paper *La terre retrouvee*, Emmanuel Levinas offers an indirect response to Wiesel's question. Levinas writes, "On the road that leads to the one and only God, there must be a way station without God. True monotheism must frame answers to the legitimate demands of atheism. An adult's God reveals Himself precisely in the emptiness of the child's heaven."[60] For Levinas the lynchpin in Kolitz's testimony (real or fabricated) is the rabbinic citation, "I love God, but I love God's Torah

56 See, for example, Franz Josef Van Beeck, *Loving the Torah More than God: Towards a Catholic Appreciation of Judaism* (Chicago: Loyola Press, 1989). Cf. Leon Wieseltier's Introduction to *Yosl Rakover Talks to God*; and Marvin Fox, "Yossel Rakover," in *Yossel Rakover Speaks to God.*

57 The only place where I have seen the ḥasidic identity of Yosl as playing a central role in the story is in Marvin Fox's "Holocaust Challenges to Religious Faith: The Case of Yossele Rakover, Hersh Rasseyner, and Chaim Vilner," in *Yossel Rakover Speaks to God*, 73–100.

58 All citations are from Carol Brown Janeway's translation of *Yosl Rakover Talks to God*, 9.

59 Kolitz, *Yosl Rakover Talks to God*, 3.

60 Levinas, "To Love the Torah More than God," reprinted in *Yossel Rakover Speaks to God*, 29.

even more … and even if I have been deceived by Him and, as it were, disenchanted, I would nonetheless observe the precepts of God's Torah." This was one of Levinas's early essays on Judaism, and Tamra Wright argues that the idea that for Judaism love of Torah precedes love of God, certainly of a God who reveals Godself to humans, becomes a fundamental principle for Levinas's later work.[61] For Levinas, teaching as opposed to experience becomes the very contribution Judaism has to answer the legitimate questions of the atheist. For our purposes, Levinas suggests that Yosl frames his final "belief" on a protest that becomes the transition from the "emptiness of the child's heaven" to the one who stands ready to die, not necessarily for God, but for Torah. And so Levinas ends his brief commentary, "To love the Torah more than God—this means precisely to find a personal God against whom it is possible to revolt, that is to say, one for whom one can die."

Levinas does not mention that Yosl was a *ḥasid*, but perhaps it is relevant to his rendering. The God Yosl believes in at the end, at least according to Levinas, is no longer the ḥasidic God. It is not a God with whom one can experience *deveikut*; it is a God who has abandoned Israel but left the Torah behind. "The emptiness of the child's heaven" is the great and legitimate question of the atheist, especially after the Holocaust, a question Levinas claims monotheism must answer. For the believer without Torah, Levinas implies, citing Simone Weil, there is no real answer to atheism, surely not after the Holocaust, which is why Levinas says to Weil, "you do not understand anything about the Torah!"[62] What does Yosl love? An absent God? An "empty heaven"? No, Yosl loves a God who gave Torah because that is the only thing from God that remains, even though, or precisely because, God cannot.[63]

To clarify, I do not think there is an exact symmetry between Yosl and Shapira. But there is a resemblance worth noting. Shapira's final note to us, one he never shared with his congregants, exhibited the following: "The God of the covenant, the God who saves, the God to whom prayer is efficacious, that God is no longer. That God cannot survive the death of theodicy, the 'unparalleled' and 'unprecedented.' But there is still the God who created the world, even as that very God is now destroying

61 See Tamra Wright, *The Twilight of Jewish Philosophy: Levinas' Ethical Hermeneutics* (London and New York: Routledge, 2013), 99, 100.

62 Ibid., 30.

63 In some way this can be seen as following the rabbinic teaching in Pesikta de Rav Kahane 15:5, "R. Huna, R. Jeremiah said in the name of R. Hiyya bar Abba, *Me they have abandoned?* (Jeremiah 16:11). Is it possible that they have kept My Torah? Would that they would have abandoned me and kept My Torah!"

it." And Shapira can still believe in and love that God. But in relation to what existed before, that faith is not whole; that faith is broken.[64] Yosl professes love for God but in that rabbinic quote there is a protest. "I love you despite the fact that you have abandoned me. Why? Because you left us Torah. That's all. It's not what I had hoped, but I guess it will have to be enough." Levinas calls it "mature" faith. I call it broken faith, a faith without theodicy, in some way, a faith without covenant. Whether Levinas would agree with that formulation, we will never know. The difference between theodic faith and anti- or post-theodic faith is that anti- or post-theodic faith can never claim superiority over non-faith. It can never fully answer the atheist because it is faith in a God who is not there. It is faith in a God who has torn the covenant.

"The greatest thing in the world," said the Holy Hunchback, quoting his rebbe, Kalonymus Kalman Shapira of Piaseczno, to Shlomo Carlebach on the Yarkon in Tel Aviv, "is to do someone else a favor." In the story of the Holy Hunchback, Shlomo meets an elderly Jew, a street cleaner in Tel Aviv who reveals himself as one of Shapira's students in his *yeshivah* for children. When asked to repeat any Torah he learned from Shapira, the Holy Hunchback can only remember what the rebbe used to repeat at the Shabbat table. "My children, listen, the greatest thing in the world is to do someone else a favor." It is with these words, and with the story of the Holy Hunchback, that Shapira and his work *Eish Kodesh* became known to the non-ḥasidic world.

Here, the Holy Hunchback enters through the portal of Shlomo Carlebach. "Can you tell me please," asks Carlebach, "tell me something you learned from him [Shapira]?" The Holy Hunchback puts down his broom. He washes his hands, puts on his jacket and hat, straightens his tie. "From my years in Auschwitz, I have long forgotten his Torah," he says in a heavy Polish Yiddish, "but I remember that during the Friday night Shabbos meal, between every course, between the soup and the fish and the fish and the chicken, he used to say to us, 'Children, take heed, the greatest thing in the world is to do someone else a favor.'" And then Carlebach added, "Do you know how many favors you can do in Auschwitz?"

The Holy Hunchback's recollection—if it happened at all—happened before the ghetto, when Shapira had a *yeshivah*, *Da'at Moshe*, for children in Warsaw. But perhaps there is some foresight here as to what would happen some years later, a response to Shapira's own realization that the covenant is fractured beyond repair, that we are left to take care of ourselves. In

64 Here Seeman seems to concur, although he maintains that even the covenant remains, whereas I do not. See his "Ritual Efficacy."

that world where God will not save, where history will not conform to the confines of tradition, where we are left alone in the thralls of radical evil; in that place of utter despair, "unprecedented" and "unparalleled," there is nothing better than doing someone else a favor. *That* becomes the covenant. Perhaps Shapira's message is that after the Holocaust, the only thing left is the ethical. And a new Torah, if it will be constructed at all, will be constructed on that foundation. And any new Torah without that foundation is not worth having. What is a belief in God without a covenant? Doing someone else a favor.

Some months later Carlebach returned to the Yarkon in Tel Aviv to find the Holy Hunchback. He looked everywhere, to no avail. He asked a passerby, "Have you seen the Holy Hunchback?" only to realize that he had left the world. But he had passed on his torah of broken faith.

Tragically, Shapira did not live long enough to offer any resolution to what I take to be his crisis of faith. He never had the opportunity to explain to us what he meant in that last addendum from November, 1942. But in any case, he also did not fool those who would read his words after the war into believing that the covenant could carry the burden or could survive what transpired in the summer of 1942. It could not. The pastoral vocation in the first period of his work had become, for him, obsolete. He taught his congregation how to die; many of them had already died. And now he was left to his own devices, quite different and yet also oddly similar to Yosl Rakover. It is better to die facing the truth of the moment, even if it tears the fabric of tradition, than to defend a paradigm that has already become obsolete. Shapira famously says in numerous places in *Eish Kodesh*, "Since God does this, that is the way it is supposed to be." But from the perspective of paradigmatic thinking, or covenantal theology, if something is unparalleled, that is precisely *not* the way it is supposed to be. Shlomo Zalman Unsdorfer and Shlomo Zalman Ehrenreich could respond to the Holocaust only with silence. But Shapira was not silent. He added that note in November, 1942 to say something to his future reader. In my view, that note was not written by a man of faith; it was written by a man of broken faith. Faith may have remained, but it was not like before. It could not be. And so what we are left with is a ḥasidic master who was not able to finish his theological work, a ḥasidic master who in the privacy of his dilapidated home, in the months before he too would succumb to the Nazi evil, wrote the ostensibly blasphemous final words that this catastrophe was not like all the others. That it was unprecedented. It was a tear in, or rupture of, the covenant. All (of Jewish history) is *not* one. With that stroke of his pen, post-Holocaust theology truly begins.

Chapter 10

American Jewish Fundamentalism: Ḥabad, Satmar, ArtScroll

I

Introduction: The Context of American Jewish Fundamentalism

Fundamentalism is arguably one of the most widely used and least understood terms in the popular discourse about religion. We find it applied to all kinds of groups, religions, communities, even societies. The formal term applies to a very defined group of American Protestants in the beginning of the twentieth century who viewed themselves as part of a particular spiritual trajectory that extended back to at least the 1740s in America and likely the seventeenth century in England.[1] In its modern context it usually refers to Protestant communities who strictly adhere to five basic principles: (1) biblical inerrancy or scripturalism; (2) virgin birth; (3) substitutionary atonement; (4) bodily resurrection; and (5) Christ's divinity.[2]

---

1 See George Marsden, *Fundamentalism and American Culture* (New York: Oxford University Press, 2006), 221–28. There he argues, "In many respects fundamentalist Christianity was not unique to America" (221). Yet he acknowledges that the term "fundamentalist" was coined in America around 1920 and thus has a certain American resonance (250).

2 For a brief discussion see *The Oxford Companion to Christian Thought*, ed. A Hastings, A. Mason, and H. Pyper (Oxford: Oxford University Press, 2000), 255–57. On the complex nature of the principle of scriptural inerrancy see Richard Antoun, "The Complexity of Scripturalism," in *Understanding Fundamentalism: Christian, Islamic, and Jewish Movements*, 2nd ed. (Lanham, MD: Rowman and Littlefield, 2008), 37–54. Jay Harris

Despite the specificity of the term, "fundamentalism" is often loosely deployed to demarcate the present phenomenon of religious revivalism outside the confines of Protestant Christianity. In the past three decades, and especially after 9/11, scholars of religion have charted the rise of religious radicalism and suggest that we may be witnessing a seismic shift in religious history unlike anything since the "Great Separation" of the Enlightenment.[3] In 1999 Peter Berger coined the term "desecularization" to describe the rise of religious extremism in the Muslim world, America, on the Indian subcontinent, in Asia, Israel/Palestine, and in the West.[4]

Fundamentalism has more specifically been applied to various branches of Judaism both in Israel and the Diaspora. It largely applies to three distinct movements: (1) Ḥasidism, (2) non-ḥasidic ultra-Orthodoxy, and (3) religious ultra-nationalism (i.e., the settler movement in Israel).[5] One and two have coalesced into an umbrella group that has become known as *ḥaredi* Judaism.[6] A portion of the ultra-nationalist camp has also taken on a *ḥaredi* persona under the term *ḥardal* (*ḥaredi dati le'umi* or *ḥaredi* national religious). These fundamentalist Jewish communities do not view themselves as partners. In fact, many vehemently oppose one another. For example, the Satmar branch of Ḥasidism is at war with the ultra-nationalist Zionist "fundamentalists" in Israel.[7] And the Ḥabad branch of Ḥasidism has been in an ideological war with Satmar for decades. Non-ḥasidic ultra-Orthodoxy (sometimes known as Yeshivah Orthodoxy, represented

---

delineates a slightly different set of characteristics. See Harris, "'Fundamentalism': Objections from a Modern Jewish Historian," in *Fundamentalism and Gender*, ed. John Stratton Hawley (New York/Oxford: Oxford University Press, 1994), 137.

3 On the Great Separation, see Mark Lilla, *The Stillborn God: Religion, Politics, and the Modern West* (New York: Alfred Knopf, 2007), 53–106.

4 Peter Berger, "The Desecularization of the World: A Global Overview," in *The Desecularization of the World: Resurgent Religion and World Politics*, ed. Peter Berger (Grand Rapids, MI: Eerdmans, 1999), 1–18. The quote is on p. 4. Cf. Gilles Kepel, *The Revenge of God* (University Park, PA: Penn State Press, 1995), 1–12.

5 These are the Jewish communities examined in the multi-volume *Fundamentalism Project* (1992–95) published by the University of Chicago Press, as well as *Jewish Fundamentalism in Comparative Perspective*, ed. Laurence Silberstein (New York: NYU Press, 1993).

6 It is important to note that ḥasidic and non-ḥasidic ultra-Orthodoxy now includes a large contingent of Mizraḥi Jews who come from the Maghreb, the Levant, and Yemen.

7 For the seminal description of ultra-Orthodoxy as it developed in Eastern Europe, see Michael Silber, "The Emergence of Ultra-Orthodoxy: The Invention of a Tradition," in *The Uses of Tradition: Jewish Continuity since Emancipation*, ed. Jack Wertheimer (New York-Jerusalem: JTS, distributed by Harvard University Press, 1992), 23–84. For the history of Gush Emunim and the settler movement, see Ehud Sprinzak, *The Ascendance of the Israeli Right* (New York: Oxford University Press, 1991).

here by ArtScroll) that dominates Israeli cities such as Bnei Brak (near Tel Aviv) and small pockets in America, such as Lakewood, New Jersey, has little sympathy for ḥasidic ultra-Orthodoxy. While they often share resources and, from the outside, seem to live similar religious lives, especially in the Diaspora, they maintain very different worldviews in matters of religious custom, ideology, and even theology. Jay Harris is surely correct that "fundamentalism" is a subjective term, used as a pejorative, whose definition depends on where the accuser stands in the trajectory of tradition. Hence the old Jewish adage, "everyone to the left of me is a heretic and everyone to the right of me is crazy." Yet I feel it is too dismissive to simply abandon the term as describing certain contemporary Jewish movements, especially in America.[8]

Almost all the studies on Jewish fundamentalism focus on postwar communities, suggesting, by implication, that ultra-Orthodoxy in prewar Europe, while similar in tenor and even in substance to its postwar progeny, cannot properly be called fundamentalist. This is curious for a number of reasons. First, it raises the question as to whether Jewish fundamentalism is a post-Holocaust phenomenon. Second, given that postwar Jewry has two main centers, Israel and North America (smaller *ḥaredi* communities exist in other parts of the Jewish Diaspora, particularly England), it raises the question as to whether Jewish fundamentalism can only exist in (1) a society where Jews comprise the dominant culture (Israel) or (2) a society where religious freedom and disestablishment are the societal norms (America)?[9] That is, does the activism necessary to constitute contemporary Jewish fundamentalism require a level of freedom of expression that only exists for Jews in Israel and North America?[10] Moreover, while Israel and America both offer conditions conducive to Jewish fundamentalism,

8 See Harris, "Fundamentalism," 142, 143.

9 Here I respectfully disagree with Jay Harris when he writes, "The modernity that prevailed among the Orthodox of the nineteenth century and prevails today among the 'fundamentalists' of our time." Harris, "Fundamentalism," 150. I would argue that in many ways our "modernity" is quite different, especially in regard to the Jews' place in society, opportunities, and religious freedoms, all of which affect how these ultra-traditional communities fashion themselves today.

10 I would include here other democratic countries that respect religious freedom such as Canada, Australia, countries in Western and Central Europe, Argentina, etc. Jay Harris bases his criticism of the use of the term "fundamentalism" for Jewish groups largely on the fact that they are based on older European precedents. While acknowledging those precedents I argue here that, in fact, the American instantiation of these communities differs enough from their European forbearers (largely due to the new context in which they live) that their differences may efface their similarities, at least when it comes to defining them under the term "fundamentalist."

each has distinctive qualities. Thus, it would be necessary to view American and Israeli ultra-Orthodoxy as different not only in context but also in substance. One of the deficiencies of the many excellent studies on Jewish fundamentalism thus far is that they generally do not distinguish between Jewish fundamentalism in Israel and in America.

In this chapter I focus on three Jewish fundamentalist groups in America, two ḥasidic and one non-ḥasidic: Ḥabad, Satmar, and ArtScroll (a term representing Yeshivah Orthodoxy). I argue that their fundamentalist agenda, while originating in prewar Europe, are products of the United States and thus particular to the American context. Here I respectfully disagree with those who argue that "fundamentalism" is not applicable to Judaism.[11] In part this is because my assumption is that the "American" nature of Jewish fundamentalism is as much sociological as it is theological. That is, I believe it is a mistake to look only at the theological premises of Christian fundamentalism and then determine whether they cohere with a Jewish case. Under such criteria, Judaism would certainly not reach the fundamentalist bar. But this is unfair because the theological premises of Judaism—excluding perhaps biblical inerrancy—differ enough from Christianity that any comparison purely on theological grounds is unhelpful. Religious communities are not simply products of their theological convictions as much as they would like us to

11 See, for example, Harris "Fundamentalism," 137–73; Leon Wieseltier, "The Jewish Face of Fundamentalism," in *The Fundamentalist Phenomenon*, ed. Norman Cohen (Grand Rapids, MI: Eerdmans, 1990), 194; and Charles Liebman, *Deceptive Images* (New Brunswick, NJ: Transaction Books, 1988), 43–60. Wieseltier erroneously, in my view, collapses the term "fundamentalism" to refer to a few precepts: (1) the inerrancy of Scripture and (2) the rejection of historical progress. He notes that "Judaism is based on the authority of commentary," which is surely true, but he does not address the position of the *inerrancy* of commentary, which is not prevalent but surely exists in some of the circles we are discussing. Moreover, he simplifies the notion of the inerrancy of Scripture and scripturalism, which is much more nuanced. See, for example, Antoun, "The Complexity of Scripturalism," 37–54. Or, in the case of Ḥabad, the inerrancy of the Rebbe himself! In terms of historical progress, I think Wieseltier ignores many ultra-Orthodox texts, ḥasidic and non-ḥasidic, that make such claims about history. Teitelbaum of Satmar surely did not believe in historical progress, and one could argue that Menahem Mendel Schneerson's assertions against evolution and against the scientific fact of the Earth revolving around the sun (because it ostensibly contradicts talmudic teaching) comes fairly close to a rejection of historical progress, if such progressive ideas contradict traditional teaching. In the end Wieseltier defines for himself "normative Judaism" (based on his reading of Maimonides), and then asserts that fundamentalism is not part of it. But isn't normativity, at least to some degree, in the eyes of the beholder? And today, given the prevalence of ultra-Orthodox Judaism, can we really say that Maimonides, the rational theologian, is the template of normative Judaism? See, for example, the argument in Menahem Kellner, *Maimonides' Confrontation with Mysticism* (Oxford: Littman Library of Jewish Civilization, 2006).

believe they are. They are also responding and adapting to societal conditions and are in a constant state of absorbing and reframing the ethos of the world in which they live, sometimes consciously, sometimes not. Thus, while ostensibly remaining true to their theological principles inherited from a very different societal context, religious communities can often be quite innovative, even radical, in the name of continuity and tradition. The question is thus not whether insiders in these communities think they are absorbing American fundamentalist positions. Surely they do not. It is, rather, whether we on the outside can ascertain if the communities' "lived religiosity" reflects an ethos in concert with external forms of belief.

I suggest Jewish fundamentalism in America is a postwar phenomenon generated in response to at last three issues: (1) the destruction of European Jewry in the Holocaust; (2) the coalescence of Zionism around a Jewish state; and (3) the so-called corruption of tradition via the predominance of Reform and other progressive Judaisms on American soil. Each one of these issues resonates in very particular ways in America, which served as the tolerant new home for most of world Jewry that chose not to immigrate to Mandate Palestine/Israel.

While I do maintain, against others, that the term "fundamentalism" can apply to Judaism, particularly in America, I also acknowledge that its particular context within a minority community in a free society gives it distinctive qualities. While the issues confronting Christian and Jewish fundamentalisms in America may seem similar, these fundamentalisms are also confronting very different challenges. The Jewish challenges focus on being a minority group ostensibly threatened by at least two things: (1) the erasure of Jewish identity; and (2) the irreparable distortion of Judaism as it was previously known and practiced through the teachings and influence of progressive Jewish communities (Conservative, Reform, Reconstructionist). The major nemesis of Jewish fundamentalisms in America is therefore not secular America but progressive American Judaism. Making full use of the secular American landscape, the rise of Jewish fundamentalism in America has become an internal battle for the soul of American Judaism. While assimilation and the transformation of tradition are not unique to America, the battle lines were different in prewar Europe and contemporary Israel, where traditional Judaism had, and has, a stronger foothold in society's civil religion.

Therefore, while the fundamentalist groups examined here are not exclusive to America, I argue their existence in America is an integral part of their project. The adjective "American" is a description of substance and not merely geography. America presents a religious, cultural, and legal context that enables these groups to express themselves in particular ways. These expressions, while certainly a manifestation of their own religious traditions, are also a specific articulation of American religion, in this case, American fundamentalism.

II

Millennialism and Messianism: "Premillennialist," "Postmillennialist," and "Nonmillennialist" Judaism

Scholars of non-Protestant fundamentalisms often list the basic principles of Protestant fundamentalism to show how their tradition can or cannot cohere with many of those principles. Hence, some argue, there can be *no* Jewish fundamentalism. Others suggest that while Jews cannot abide by some of the specifics of Protestant fundamentalism there are some broader paradigms indicative of fundamentalist movements that accurately describe some maximalist Jewish perspectives. Here Gabriel Almond, Scott Appleby, and Emmanuel Sivan's broad definition of fundamentalism might suffice: "Fundamentalism, in this usage, refers to a discernible pattern of religious militance by which self-styled 'true believers' attempt to arrest the erosion of religious identity, fortify the borders of the religious community, and create viable alternatives to secular institutions and behaviors."[12] Many of those who write about fundamentalism stress that it is not only situated in modernity but is, in fact, a product of modernity.[13] In this sense, fundamentalism is a particular construction of "tradition" that is uniquely equipped to confront modernity and offer an alternative template for human civilization. Almost all fundamentalisms in contemporary America are committed to some form of activism to oppose either secularism, liberal religion, or both.[14]

Millennialism is one of Protestant fundamentalism's founding principles.[15] Millennialism is a belief in society's close proximity to the end-time

12 Introduction to *Strong Religion: The Rise of Fundamentalism around the World*, ed. Almond, Appleby, and Sivan (Chicago: University of Chicago Press, 2003), 17.

13 Peter Berger, *Homeless Mind* (New York: Vintage Books, 1974). Jacob Katz makes similar comments about the "modernity" of ultra-Orthodox Judaism. See his discussion in "Orthodoxy in Historical Perspective," *Studies in Contemporary Jewry* 2 (1986): 3–17. Cf. Katz, *A House Divided: Orthodoxy and Schism in Nineteenth-Century Central European Jewry* (Hanover, NH: Brandeis University Press, 2007).

14 Marsden, *Fundamentalism and American Culture*, postscript.

15 Ibid., 5, 232.

and invites either political activism to create conditions for the immanent redemption or cultivates a separatist mentality that builds walls against the impure influence of decadent society. Both of these options exhibit a highly charged sense of urgency. Dispensationalist millennialism has been influential in millennial communities. Many contemporary Protestant fundamentalists and evangelicals (a similar but not identical group) view themselves as either living immediately before the new, and final, dispensation or already part of a new dispensation.[16] George Marsden offers a succinct definition of dispensational premillennialism.

> According to dispensationalists' scheme of world history, the current dispensation, or "church age," was marked by the regressive corruption of so-called Christian civilization and the apostasy of its large churches. Only a remnant of its true believers would remain pure. The Kingdom of Christ would not be brought in by united Christian effort, as the Social Gospel had promised, but only by the dramatic return of Jesus to set up his millennial kingdom in Jerusalem. Dispensationalism thus suggested that Christian political efforts were largely futile. Believers should give up on the illusion of "Christian civilization."[17]

While there are substantive differences between dispensational millennialists and non-dispensational millennialists, for our limited purposes these distinctions are not relevant.[18] The relevant point here is whether these terms can be adapted to Jewish fundamentalism in America. For most Jewish fundamentalists, messianism is an operative and often a central tenet of their religious worldview. The messianist stances of the two American fundamentalisms under examination, Ḥabad and Satmar, loosely cohere with the pre- and postmillennialist perspectives of Christian fundamentalism, albeit each refracts their view through their respective theological lenses.[19] ArtScroll embodies a nonmillennialist stance less common in

---

16 Ibid., 233–35. Cf. Glenn QW. Shuck, *Marks of the Beast: The Left behind Novels and the Struggle for Evangelical Identity* (New York and London: NYU Press, 2005), 29–52.

17 Marsden, *Understanding Fundamentalism and Evangelicalism* (Grand Rapids, MI: Eerdmans, 1990), 101.

18 For some of differences between dispensational and non-dispensational premillennialists, see Marsden, *Fundamentalism and American Culture*, 51, 52. Cf. David Harrington Watt, "The Private Hopes of American Fundamentalist and Evangelicals, 1925–1975," in *Religion and American Culture* 1, no. 2 (Summer, 1991): 155–75.

19 On messianism in Menahem Mendel Schneerson, see Max Kohanzad, "The Messianic Doctrine of the Lubavitcher Rebbe, Rabbi Menahem Mendel Schneerson (1902–1994)"

Protestant fundamentalist circles. While ArtScroll surely espouses belief in the Messiah, it does not place messianism at the center of its ideology. Its focus, rather, is on Torah study, ritual performance, and promoting Judaism as a lifestyle that contains a moral core, an answer to divine command, and perhaps the best assurance for Jewish continuity.

Many premillennialists claim to live "outside" history, viewing society's state of irreligion as irredeemable and even a necessary part of the divine plan to bring the end-time. Postmillennialists, on the other hand, adapt a spiritual return to Christ, leaving open the possibility of viewing history in a progressive state toward the final end-time.[20] The premillennialist belief in redemption solely by divine fiat, including the advent and ultimate destruction of the anti-Christ, promotes a religious perspective that no human agency *in the world* is possible to bring about the end-time.

Postmillennialists have a more optimistic view of history, including in some cases even relegating the secular/political spheres as having a redemptive role, believing the contemporary moment represents the first stages of the end-time.[21] More traditional postmillennialism is expressed in various evangelical movements today, in the "family values" movement in the early 1990s, and even arguably among some Tea Party activists who have entered the halls of Congress to stem the tide of post-Christian secularism in favor of an American society more deeply rooted in Christianity and its values. This, they believe, will create the necessary conditions for the continued unfolding of redemption.

Fundamentalist postmillennialist messianists, such as American Ḥabad, have very specific and complex views about tradition in juxtaposition to—and in symbiosis with—the secular, and exhibit moderate separatist tendencies even as they engage in evangelism and political action. While Ḥabad views itself as antithetical to and, to some extent, at war with American

(PhD thesis, University of Manchester, 2006), and Elliot Wolfson, *Open Secret* (New York: Columbia University Press, 2009).

20 See the discussion in Ernest Lee Tuveson, *Redeemer Nation: The Idea of America's Millennial Role* (Chicago and London: University of Chicago Press, 1968), 26–39. Marsden argues that this attitude became common after the Civil War partly as a response to the bloody war and partly influenced by Darwin's challenge to religious doctrine, the growing emergence of urban life in America, and the rise of biblical criticism. Timothy Weber offers the opposite assessment when he writes, "Postmillennialism lost credibility after the Civil War because in the eyes of most people things were getting worse, not better." See Weber, *On the Road to Armageddon: How Evangelicals Became Israel's Best Friend* (Grand Rapids, MI: Baker Publishing, 2004), 42.

21 In Judaism, the great Jewish postmillennialist might be Rabbi Abraham Isaac Kook (d. 1935), the first chief rabbi of Palestine.

Reform Judaism, both share a concerted effort to transform society through Jewish values. Reform adapted many secular principles as part of it religious ideology. Ḥabad rejects secularism in principle yet readily engages with and utilizes the fruits of secularism (e.g., technology, free speech, and the freedom of religious expression, language, and nomenclature) to further its postmillennial agenda.[22] What separates them is what each views as the essential character of Judaism and what a transformed society would look like.

Another important component for our purposes is how American Jewish fundamentalists view America. Many Jewish premillennialists (e.g., American Satmar) view America as not significantly different than other diasporic venues except that American freedom is more spiritually dangerous than previous host cultures where Jews may have been physically threatened but spiritually safe. That is, America requires Jewish premillennialists to be more steadfast in protecting the values they hold dear. As we will see with Satmar, in America separatism becomes sacrosanct, and legal stringencies become more operative. Many Jewish postmillennialists (e.g., American Ḥabad) explicitly hold America to be different, the place God has chosen to complete his mission. Ḥabad often refers to America (and Canada) as a "country of kindness" (*medinah shel ḥesed*), indicating a substantive difference from all other Jewish diasporas. This difference becomes a central tenet of Ḥabad's postmillennialism. Yet, as I will argue below, while Satmar proclaims (in line with the sixth Lubavitcher rebbe R. Yosef Yizhak Schneersohn) that "America is no different," its history in America, including its post-1967 stance on Zionism and the establishment of its rural enclave in upstate New York, Kiryas Joel, points to the fact that even for those who proclaim that America is *not* different in principle, in practice, America *is* different.[23] The nonmillennialists (e.g., ArtScroll) seem to have a less charged relationship to the secular. Their agenda is more about survival and less about apocalypticism. In many ways, as a publishing house ArtScroll owes it very existence to the secular realm of capitalist consumerism even as its books often espouse a rejection of those very ideas. Yeshivah Orthodoxy is quite comfortable in America, makes ample use of

---

22 See, for example, Jan Feldman, *Lubavitchers as Citizens* (Ithaca and London: Cornell University Press, 2006). This is also true to some extent with Jewish premillennialists like Satmar especially regarding Kiryas Joel and church-state matters, but Ḥabad is much more open to the secular world as a tool to foster redemption than Satmar.

23 On this see the forthcoming work on the Satmar enclave of Kiryas Yoel by David N. Myers and Naomi Stolzenberg.

its resources, and, unlike Ḥabad, Satmar or even Modern Orthodoxy, does not place much intrinsic value on the secular realm.

In order to analyze Jewish fundamentalism in America these movements must be situated within the larger culture in which they live and not only the traditions they draw from. Jewish movements take part in the general millennial spirit even though some specifics of Christian millennialism are foreign to them. For example, the notion of dispensations is largely based on an interpretation of a series of opaque verses in the ninth chapter of The Book of Daniel that has attracted the attention of many Jewish scholars throughout the ages. As mentioned earlier, the Babylonian Talmud provides us with its own rendering of the ninth chapter of the Book of Daniel.[24] The notion that the Messiah will rule for one thousand years before the world will be fully transformed is a talmudic teaching and has been interpreted creatively by post-rabbinic Jews.[25] In short, there are many Jewish ideas of redemption that underlie the Jewish fundamentalisms examined below, some of which are cosmological and astrological, and some of which are more conventionally historical.[26]

I do not argue that any of these groups are overtly influenced by American Christian fundamentalists, although Ḥabad and ArtScroll are certainly aware of tactics used by other fundamentalists and freely borrow from them.[27] Grand Rabbi Menahem Mendel Schneerson of Ḥabad was actively involved with the public school prayer issue in

---

24 BT Sanhedrin 97a.

25 See, for example, Gershom Scholem, *Origins of the Kabbalah* (New York: JPS, 1987), 460–75; Haviva Pedaya's *Nahmanides, Cyclical Time and Holy Text* [Hebrew] (Tel Aviv, 2003); and Moshe Idel, "The Jubilee in Jewish Mysticism," in *Fin de Siecle—End of Ages* [Hebrew], ed. J. Kaplan (Jerusalem, 2005), 67–98. On the astrological aspects of Jewish messianism, see Idel, "Saturn and Sabbatai Tsevi: A New Approach to the Study of Sabbateanism," in *Toward the Millennium: Messianic Expectations from the Bible to Waco*, ed. P. Schafer and M. Cohen (Leiden: Brill, 1998), 173–202.

26 For example, see the long essay by the thirteenth-century rabbinic leader Moses Nahmanides, "The Book of Redemption" [Hebrew], in *Kitvei Ramban* (Jerusalem: Mosad ha-Rav Kook, 1963), 1:261–95, available in English as *Ramban: The Book of Redemption*, trans. and ann., Charles Chavel (New York: Shilo Publishing House, 1978). Cf. "Essay on Redemption," by the eighteenth-century Italian kabbalist Moses Hayyim Luzatto, in *Sifrei Ramḥal: Ḥoker ha-Mekubal be-Milḥamot Moshe* (Jerusalem, n.d.). These are two of many such essays in post-rabbinic Judaism. Menahem Mendel Schneerson claimed the First Gulf War was part of the apocalyptic wars of Gog and Magog, and the anti-Zionist R. Hayyim Elazar Shapira of Munkacz (the Satmar Rebbe's teacher), among many others, perhaps including the Zionist R. Abraham Isaac Kook, thought the First World War was the beginning of the messianic wars of redemption.

27 See, for example, in Maya Katz, *The Visual Culture of Chabad* (Cambridge, UK: Cambridge University Press, 2010), 144–73.

1964 and openly supported the position of Jerry Falwell in favor of a moment of silence in public schools.[28] He also challenged church-state law in the Supreme Court in 1989 with his construction of a menorah in public squares in Philadelphia, San Francisco, and other American cities and towns. It was a highly symbolic and, to my mind, intentional, choice to erect the first public menorah at the foot of the Liberty Bell in Philadelphia in 1974.[29]

I situate these groups around the question, "Is America different?" That is, does American provide a diasporic context unique in Jewish history that would enable, or require, traditional Jews to respond to the challenges of Jewish survival in new ways? If America is not different for the Jews than, say, Germany, Poland, or Hungary, how does this impact the way the group lives "in" America? Alternatively, for the premillennial Satmar *ḥasidim*, it seems America is *not* different, but I suggest that while proclaiming America as no different, this group acts differently in America, and its position even vis-à-vis Israel and Zionism is partially a response to its American context.[30] Thus in America even this extreme branch of Ḥasidism, with its ideological separatism and premillennial tendencies, does not fully disengage from its external environment.

III

American Ḥabad as a Jewish Postmillennial Fundamentalism

The ḥasidic sect known as Ḥabad or Lubavitch (from the Belarus town where it was founded) had very humble beginnings.[31] Its founder, R. Shneur Zalman of Liady (d. 1812), was a disciple of Dov Baer, the Maggid (Preacher) of Mezritch (d. 1772), a disciple of the founder of Ḥasidism,

28 Jerry Falwell's "Moral Majority" was considered perhaps the most popular fundamentalist group in the postwar period in America. When *Time* magazine devoted its September, 1985 edition to "Fundamentalism in the U.S." they chose to put Falwell on the cover.

29 See Katz, *Visual Culture*, 204–24. It is also significant that many of the groups that contested the legality of the public menorah lightening were Jewish, such as the American Jewish Congress.

30 On the social life of Satmar more generally, see Israel Rubin, *Satmar: Two Generations of an Urban Island*, 2nd ed. (Peter Lang, 1997); and Jerome Mintz, *Ḥasidic People: A Place in the New World* (Cambridge, MA: Harvard University Press, 1992), 309–27.

31 Ḥabad in Hebrew is an acronym for wisdom (*ḥokhmah*), understanding (*binah*), and knowledge (*da'at*), in kabbalistic nomenclature.

R. Israel Ba'al Shem Tov (d. 1760).[32] After Dov Baer's death his disciples slowly dispersed to various parts of Eastern Europe and began to establish ḥasidic courts. While many courts were established in Poland, Galicia, and Hungary, Shneur Zalman and later his son Dov Baer (no relation to the Maggid of Mezritch) established a court in Belarus, an area largely cut off from ḥasidic activity.[33] Coupled with its geographical isolation and Ḥabad's claim that it was the sole carrier, or the best representative, of the authentic teachings of Ḥasidism's founder, Ḥabad developed its own mystical system and customs, even publishing a Ḥabad prayer book with its own liturgical variants. Its independent self-fashioning contributed to its autonomy and unique messianic ideology, first in the region of White Russia and later in the U.S.[34]

During its early years Ḥabad developed an ideology of outreach to Jews living in more isolated parts of Russia. This program was not only practical but also part of a larger messianic agenda, an ideology much less developed than it would become in America. In line with kabbalistic sources, it believed that the power of Jewish observance held the potential to bring about redemption. Maximizing that power by encouraging otherwise "fallen" Jews to engage in these acts and behaviors was fostered through various means. While active in certain parts of Eastern Europe, as a movement Ḥabad remained quite small yet grew exponentially in America after World War II. This was largely the result of the innovative and courageous leadership of its seventh grand rabbi, Menahem Mendel Schneerson (1902–1994) who became the movement's leader in 1951 one year after the passing of his father-in-law, the sixth grand rabbi, Yosef Yizhak Schneersohn (the younger Schneerson dropped the second "h" in his last name after immigrating to America).

---

32 On the Ba'al Shem Tov as the founder of Ḥasidism, see Moshe Rosman, *Founder of Ḥasidism: A Quest for the Historical Ba'al Shem Tov* (Los Angeles and Berkeley: University of California Press, 1996); and Immanuel Etkes, *The Besht: Magician, Mystic, and Leader* (Waltham, MA: Brandeis University Press, 2005).

33 The ascendance of Dov Baer to become the second rebbe of Lubavitch was a hotly contested episode in the history of Ḥasidism. Shneur Zalman's eldest son Moshe was passed over and eventually converted to Christianity. See David Assaf, *Untold Tales of the Ḥasidim* (Waltham, MA: Brandeis University Press, 2010), 29–96.

34 Its founder, Shneur Zalman, composed and published his own *Shulḥan Arukh* (Code of Jewish Law) that incorporated his interpretation of the standard *Shulḥan Arukh* and his customs that became Ḥabad practice. This work is the halakhic compendium of Ḥabad Ḥasidism. See *Shulḥan Arukh ha-Rav*, 6 vols. (Brooklyn, NY: Kehot, n.d). On Shneur Zalman, see Roman Foxbrunner, *Habad: The Hasidism of R. Shneur Zalman of Lyady* (Tuscaloosa: University of Alabama Press, 1992).

While Ḥabad historiographers like to emphasize the continuity between Ḥabad's European roots and R. Menahem Mendel's agenda in America, the picture is more complex. While it is true that the campaign mission that became the signature of Ḥabad in America had roots in Europe, the difference between the European model and its American counterpart is more than situational.[35] The fifth Lubavitcher rebbe, Shalom Dov Baer Schneersohn (1860–1920), assumed the role of rebbe in 1893 when he was thirty-three years old and reigned during the heyday of the Jewish Enlightenment in Eastern Europe, including the advent of Zionism. He was the last Ḥabad rebbe to live and die in Europe and witnessed first-hand the secularization of European Jewry and the struggles of traditional societies to stem the tide of modernity.

Like many Christian millennialists and Jewish messianists, R. Shalom Dov Baer viewed the degradation of society as the "birth pangs of the Messiah," the beginning of the end of civilization as we know it.[36] He understood his times according to the (premillennial) talmudic teaching that the world will descend (perhaps *needs* to descend) into chaos immediately before the advent of the Messiah.[37] He addressed his students, whom he referred to as "pure ones" (*temimim*), in the military language common among later fundamentalists, language that would be deployed somewhat differently by Menahem Mendel Schneerson in America. Shalom Dov Baer charged his disciples to "wage war" against the Enlightenment, including Zionism. His was a classical premillennial charge, not a call to transform the world through kindness but to wage war against those who are creating darkness. His weapon of choice was the proliferation of Torah, *miẓvot*, and *frumkeit* (a Yiddish term referring to religious practice and behavior). R. Shalom Dov Baer's approach was not dissimilar from the one adopted by Hungarian Ḥasidism in the late nineteenth century that became the signature of Satmar in America.

Shalom Dov Baer's war was not expressed as quietist piety or absolutist separation. As mentioned above, he initiated "missions" to the far-flung parts of Russia and Siberia to provide Jews there with basic resources and religious materials. The sixth rebbe of Ḥabad, Yosef Yizhak Schneersohn (1880–1950), continued these activities in Russia, secretly thwarting authorities and organizing clandestine missions that landed him in a Russian

35 See, for example, Yitzchak Krauss, *The Seventh: Messianism in the Last Generation of Ḥabad* [Hebrew] (Tel Aviv: Yediot Ahronot and Chemed Books, 2007).

36 See BT Ketubot 111a. On Menahem Mendel Schneerson's rendering of this idea in English, see *From Exile to Redemption* (Brooklyn, NY: Kehot, 1992), 1:53–66.

37 See BT Sanhedrin 97a.

prison. With the intervention of world leaders, including American statesmen, R. Yosef Yizhak was released from prison in 1927, migrated for a time to Warsaw and then to America in 1940.

These Ḥabad "missions" would continue in an attempt to counter Jewish assimilation in America and would reach new heights with the seventh rebbe, Menahem Mendel, who transformed the Ḥabad mission program from a premillennial Manichean battle of light against darkness to a postmillennial attempt to transform the world, including reaching out to gentiles, something unprecedented in Ḥasidism in general and Lubavitch in particular.

Ḥabad in America was the brainchild of Yosef Yizhak, father-in-law of Menahem Mendel. Their visions, however, were not identical. Upon his arrival to the U.S., Yosef Yizhak proclaimed "America is no different," a call that remained operative for Ḥabad until his death in 1950. This proclamation insinuated that the Ḥabad program in Europe, including the battle against secularism and Zionism, would continue on American soil.[38] The very proclamation "America is no different" suggests an anxiety about the new challenges America posed to ultra-Orthodoxy. The dominance of non-Orthodox Judaism, religious freedom, the absence of systemic anti-Semitism, and the economic and educational opportunities in America all suggested America was indeed different. Yet Yosef Yizhak, even though he had strong messianic inclinations, viewed America as the next phase of exile and did not believe that America required a new ḥasidic agenda. The insular premillennial inclinations that drove his prewar agenda largely remained intact even as Yosef Yizhak instructed certain *ḥasidim* to reach out to the assimilated Jews on college campuses in the winter of 1948.[39]

Menahem Mendel did not lead the cloistered life of his father-in-law or his predecessors.[40] Growing up in the court of Ḥabad in Russia, he later lived in Berlin and Paris, studied in universities in both cities, and worked as an engineer in the U.S. Navy Yard upon his arrival to the U.S., all unusual for

38 See Menahem Friedman, "Habad as Messianic Fundamentalism: From Local Particularism to Universal Jewish Mission," in *Accounting for Fundamentalism*, ed. M. Marty and S. Appleby (Chicago: University of Chicago Press, 1994), 340.

39 See Mintz, *Ḥasidic People*, 29: "The shared mission of Ḥasidic Jewry in New York City was to recreate the world that had existed in prewar Europe. In part this was a debt that they owed to a generation that had been destroyed. It was a way too of affirming victory over those who had tried to annihilate them."

40 Most recently see Samuel Heilman and Menahem Friedman, *The Rebbe* (Princeton, NJ: Princeton University Press, 2010), 65–89; and Moshe Miller, *Turning Judaism Outward: A Biography of the rebbe, Menachem Mendel Schneerson* (Brooklyn, NY: KOL Menachem, 2014).

someone being cultivated to become the leader of a ḥasidic dynasty. While there is considerable debate between those inside Ḥabad and scholars who study them as to the extent and nature of his engagement with liberalism and secularism, there is little doubt that, as opposed to his father-in-law, for Menahem Mendel America *was,* in fact, different, although the specific nature of that difference is never explicitly developed.[41]

For Menahem Mendel, America was an important conduit for his vision of messianism. He often invoked the national American slogan "*e pluribus unum*" (from many, one) as both a justification for his engagement with American society and as a metaphysical principle that was in concert with Ḥabad's acosmic worldview.[42] Unlike previous Ḥabad rebbes, whose interest was solely with their constituents and other Jews in need, Menahem Mendel entered the political arena on such issues as public school prayer (almost none of his disciples attended public school) and was responsible for a Supreme Court case on the issue of church-state matters when he directed his disciples to erect large Hanukkah menorahs in town squares to foster Jewish pride. He had influence in the halls of Congress, appointing a close disciple, Lev Shemtov, as a permanent emissary to the Hill, and he was awarded the Congressional Gold Medal, one of the highest honors for an American citizen, in 1994. American Ḥabad's attitude toward its host culture was decidedly different than other ḥasidic communities that engaged in government matters only as they related to their communities. American Ḥabad is an example of a Jewish fundamentalism that navigates between a firm commitment to "fundamental" doctrinal beliefs yet proactively engages in the larger to world in order to transform it and thus achieve its goals.

Menahem Mendel's "Army of God" (*Ẓivos ha-Shem*), Ḥabad's youth movement, was not constructed as warriors of light against darkness like his predecessors but rather as representatives of Judaism to an assimilated Jewish public as well as a *gentile public* that had little exposure to traditional Judaism.[43] For example, in 1988 *Ẓivos ha-Shem* sponsored a musical and cultural arts fair in New York City and in 2004 opened a Jewish Children's Museum in Brooklyn's "Museum Row," a very different tack than the polemics against Zionism and the Jewish Enlightenment (*Haskalah*)

41 See, for example, in Feldman, *Lubavitchers as Citizens*, 38–59; 111–34. Cf. Friedman, "Habad as Messianic Fundamentalism," 340–45.

42 See his use of that term as a justification for his public menorah campaign in *Chabad Magazine* (November, 1994): 49, cited in Katz, *Visual Culture*, 211. On the acosmism of Ḥabad and its political ramifications see Wolfson, *Open Secret*, 27–65.

43 See Susan Fishkoff, *The Rebbe's Army* (New York: Schocken, 2003), 46–65; 339–60.

in prewar Ḥabad and other postwar ḥasidic groups.[44] While he advocated strict adherence to Jewish law and practice, he instructed his disciples to be tolerant of non-practicing Jews and offer them a taste of Judaism (or *yiddishkeit*) that may, or may not, take root later. He advocated using traditional religion as a source of identity and pride even for those who did not practice. In some way this is a novel attempt to use tradition as a tool of Jewish secularism. Moreover, in addition to his advocacy of Jewish ritual as central to Jewish survival, he also stressed matters of Jewish doctrinal belief (focusing on Maimonides' Thirteen Principles of Faith), a campaign that touched many who would not adopt the rigorous life of ultra-Orthodoxy.[45] While surely not pluralistic in any formal sense, the American Ḥabad program was one of tolerance and flexibility. The Manichean premillennial tenor of Ḥabad's previous agenda seems to have all but disappeared.

Three examples will serve to illustrate the ways in which American Ḥabad moved from the Jewish premillennial posture of Shalom Dov Baer and Yosef Yizhak to the Jewish postmillennialism of Menahem Mendel. The first is the Ḥabad Noahide Law campaign. The second is Ḥabad's anti-Zionist engagement with the Jewish State. And third is the peculiar nature of Ḥabad's rejection of Jewish secularism as an operative category.

Throughout his career Menahem Mendel broadened the missions of his predecessors with what became known as *mivẓoyim*, expansive missionary activities to bring Torah and *miẓvot* to unaffiliated Jews around the world.[46] In 1992, when the messianic fervor of Ḥabad was sharply on the rise largely due to Menahem Mendel's failing health, he instituted what was an unprecedented program in the annals of ultra-Orthodox, or even Orthodox, Judaism. As a way of preparing the non-Jewish population of the U.S. for the impending redemption, R. Menahem Mendel initiated a massive educational campaign about the Noahide Laws, the seven laws instituted by the rabbinic sages that gentiles are required to fulfill to be considered "righteous gentiles" in the messianic era.[47] While the initial impetus for this

44 Katz, *Visual Culture*, 197, 198.

45 On the Thirteen Principles of Faith see Marc B. Shapiro, *The Limits of Orthodox Theology: Maimonides' Thirteen Principles Reappraised* (Oxford, UK: The Littman Library of Jewish Civilization, 2004).

46 The *mivẓoyim* campaigns started after 1967 when Menahem Mendel announced his *tefillin* campaign following the Six-Day War. See Katz, *Visual Culture*, 174, 180n12.

47 See, Ravitzky, "The Contemporary Lubavitch Ḥasidic Movement," 309–13; and Wolfson, *Open Secret*, 229, 230. On the Noahide Laws more generally see David Novak, *The Image of the Non-Jew in Judaism* (New York: Edwin Mellen Press, 1983); and Novak, "Noahide Law: A Foundation for Jewish Philosophy," in *Tradition in the Public Square: A David Novak Reader*, ed. R. Rashkover and M. Kavka (Grand Rapids, MI: Eerdmans,

move was with his immediate predecessor, Yosef Yizhak, upon his release from prison in 1927, Menahem Mendel's sustained campaign was perhaps the first time traditional Jewish outreach devoted considerable resources toward influencing the non-Jewish world about Jewish ideas of messianism and the role of the gentile in that end-time vision.[48] Pamphlets were printed and distributed widely, Menahem Mendel spoke publicly about the importance of the Noahide Laws, and Ḥabad emissaries across the country (and beyond) began exposing their gentile neighbors to this idea.[49] In some way this culminated in the turn toward a Jewish postmillennialism focused on transforming the world while maintaining allegiance to its own strict doctrinal principles. Instead of hunkering down and "waging war" against the forces of darkness, Menahem Mendel positively engaged the larger world in an attempt to prepare them for the redemptive era that he believed *had already begun.*

The second example is contemporary Ḥabad's engagement with Zionism and the Jewish State. From Shalom Dov Baer onward, Ḥabad Ḥasidism was anti-Zionist. Yosef Yizhak actively opposed the establishment of a Jewish state and sided with some of the most vehement anti-Zionists of his era, even though he did initiate Kefar Ḥabad, the first ḥasidic agricultural community in Israel. Both Shalom Dov Baer and Yosef Yizhak exhibited what could be viewed as premillennial attitudes that the state was apostasy, a corruption of true Jewish messianic ideals, and, in fact, anti-messianic.

Unlike his Ḥabad predecessors and many of his ultra-Orthodox rabbinic contemporaries Menahem Mendel actively engaged with secular

2008), 113–44. Cf. Michael Broyde, "The Obligation of Jews to Seek Observance of Noahide Laws by Gentiles: A Theoretical Review," *Tikkun Olam* (1998): 103–43. See Martin Katchen, "Who Wants Moshiah Now?," *Australian Journal of Jewish Studies* 5, no. 1 (1991): 70–72.

48 Wolfson, *Open Secret*, 229. The only comparable campaign to my knowledge was the Reform rabbi Isaac Mayer Wise's attempt in the mid-nineteenth century to make American Christians "denationalized" Jews. See Isaac Mayer Wise, *The American Israelite*, May 14, 1875, cited in Dena Wilansky, *Sinai to Cincinnati* (New York, 1937) and Benny Kraut, "Judaism Triumphant: Isaac Mayer Wise on Unitarianism and Liberal Christianity," *AJS Review* 7 (1982): 194n46.

49 Books began to appear written by Jews about the concept of the righteous gentile. See, for example, Michael Shelomo Bar Ron, *Guide for the Noahide: A Complete Manual for Living by the Noahide Laws* (Lightcatcher Books, 2010); and Michael Ellias Dallen, *The Rainbow Covenant: Torah and the Seven Universal Laws* (Lightcatcher Books, 2003). This is an instance of two works written by traditional Jews published by a Christian press to encourage gentiles to live by the Noahide Laws. Moreover, the U.S. Congress passed a resolution in 1991 designating "Education Day" in honor of Menahem Mendel. Part of this resolution proclaimed the Noahide Laws the basis of human civilization. See H. J. Res. 104, Public Law 102–14, passed on March 26, 1991.

Israeli prime ministers and parliamentarians, evincing a hawkish stance of territorial compromise founded on his understanding of Jewish law in regard to preparation for the coming of the Messiah. He openly supported political parties in the Israel Parliament and urged his constituents to vote in Israeli elections. In an Israeli election in 1988 a picture of Menahem Mendel Schneerson appeared on Israeli voting cards encouraging voters to vote for Agudat Israel, his party of choice.[50] Here anti-Zionism (which often refuses to engage in the politics of a *treife medinah*, i.e., a non-kosher state) is combined with messianic activism. Menahem Mendel's rejection of any land-for-peace initiative is not founded on the argument of security but rather his messianic vision that the era of redemption has begun and Jewish sovereignty in the entire Land of Israel is a requirement for its continued unfolding, an idea that has parallels among many Christian Zionist fundamentalists in America.[51]

Whereas most *ḥaredi* anti-Zionists reflect premillennial tendencies, arguing that we can do nothing other than perform *miẓvot* and wait for the Messiah, Menahem Mendel's postmillennial turn offers a different approach. His argument against Zionism was not so much that we must wait patiently in the Diaspora for Messiah to come but that we must contest the Zionist's secular narrative of redemption. As Maya Katz argues regarding Ḥabad's decision to place a Hanukkah menorah in the pubic square (in the first instance in Liberty Bell Park in Philadelphia), Menahem Mendel wanted to embrace the rich cultural life of Diaspora Judaism as a form of messianism in and of itself.[52] His problem with Zionism was less political (the existence of a Jewish state) and more cultural (rejecting the secular narrative of Zionist cultural revolution). He offered what he deemed was a religious and authentic cultural paradigm as the foundation of his messianic vision. In this sense, Ḥabad's anti-Zionism was a postmillennial response to Zionism as a secular form of, or substitution for, traditional Judaism.

The final example requires us to touch briefly on Ḥabad's metaphysical worldview. In accordance with kabbalistic teaching, Ḥabad believes that the Jewish soul contains a dimension of divinity that is absent in the non-Jewish soul. The *Tanya*, a book written by R. Shneur Zalman of Liady, is Ḥabad's major source for its metaphysical system. This

---

50 See Ari Goldman, "Israelis Vote, and the Lubavitchers Rejoice," *The New York Times*, November 14, 1988.

51 See, for example, in Timothy Weber's *On the Road to Armageddon*. It should be noted that most of the Christians who shared the Ḥabad rebbe's view were dispensationalist premillennialists.

52 Katz, *Visual Culture*, 202.

book makes a categorical distinction between the divinity of the Jewish soul (*neshamah elohit*) in contrast to the pure corporeality (*neshamah behamit*) of the gentile soul (the Jewish soul has *both* a divine and corporeal component while the gentile soul has *only* a corporeal component). While Ḥabad has often been accused that its doctrine constitutes a form of spiritual racism, Elliot Wolfson has shown that this doctrine is not exclusive to Ḥabad Ḥasidism or Ḥasidism more generally but permeates much of kabbalistic literature upon which the *Tanya* is based.[53] In any case, Ḥabad in America has done something quite ingenious with this doctrine. As mentioned above, the war against secularism in general and Jewish secularism in particular was paramount in the Ḥabad teachings of Shalom Dov Baer and Yosef Yizhak. In the postwar period, especially in America, there appears to be a shift in emphasis that may point to a change in orientation. Ḥabad's belief that all Jews, secular or religious, contain the divine spark of a Jewish soul (in Yiddish it is called the *pintele yid*, or the Jewish spark) leads them to the conclusion that "secularism," expressed as a deep rejection of religious belief and practice, is simply impossible for the Jew.[54] Espousing an acosmic worldview that all but erases the distinction between the sacred and the profane, Ḥabad in general and American Ḥabad in particular denude secularism for the Jew by claiming it does not exist.[55] On this Aviezer Ravitzky notes, "[For Ḥabad] Jewish religious identity is a matter of essence and substance; it is a given objective fact. It is not based on ethnic, cultural, mental or historical factors, or even on the actual relationship of the individual to

53 This doctrine has creeped into more mainstream Jewish life in the depiction of the fictitious Ladover ḥasidic sect (obviously taken from Ḥabad) in Chaim Potok's national bestseller *My Name is Asher Lev* (New York: Random House, 1972). See 187–89. On the more widespread history of this doctrine, see Elliot Wolfson, *Venturing Beyond: Law and Morality in Kabbalistic Ethics* (New York: Oxford University Press, 2006), 17–128. Cf. Wolfson, *Open Secret*, 239f.

54 Jonathan Sarna succinctly describes a *pintele yid* as "a dormant Jewish homunculus waiting to burst forth." See Sarna, "Ethnicity and Beyond," in *Ethnicity and Beyond*, ed. Eli Lederhendler (New York: Oxford University Press, 2011), 108. This idea is quite common in ḥasidic literature, including Ḥabad. See, for example, in the celebrated "*Bati le-Gani*" essay, Menahem Mendel's inaugural sermon as rebbe of Ḥabad in 1951. See in *Torat Menaḥem: Sefer Ma'amarim Bati le-Gani* (Brooklyn, NY: Lahak Hanochos, 2008), 1:9.

55 The idea that the "Jewish spark" is "asleep" in "exile" appears in the first master of Ḥabad, Shneur Zalman of Liady. See, for example in his *Torah Or* (Brooklyn: Kehot, 1991), 28 c/d. Cf. Elliot Wolfson, *A Dream Interpreted in a Dream* (New York: Zone Books, 2011), 202–208. Thus secularism, like exile, is a kind of dream state where the dreamer does not even know she is dreaming.

the Torah and to halakha (Jewish law), but rather the divine nature of the Jewish soul."[56]

On this reading "secular" Jews should not be rejected or marginalized. Rather, they should be given access to their "inner-souls," to their "Jewish spark," after which they will, on their own accord, come to see the truth of traditional Judaism. The divisiveness and rancor of prewar Ḥabad against the "secularists" and Zionists has been transformed into a campaign to get American Jews to "know themselves."[57] While spiritual "self-knowledge" has its roots in prewar Jewish pietism and is expressed in similar ways in earlier Ḥasidism, this idea has arguably undergone a transformation in American Ḥabad, not only in rhetoric but also in substance.[58] Cultural, ideological, or historical factors melt away when the "Jewish soul" is able to breathe. The way back to tradition for the Jew is not to be convinced of Judaism's truth but to be reintroduced to his or her own self.[59] The gentile may have to be convinced that the Noahide laws are true. The Jew, however, only has to know who they are. In Ḥabad, the gentile must be convinced via rational means; the Jew must be "woken up" up emotionally and spiritually.

As much as this is all founded on metaphysical grounds, some of which are quite jarring to the modern ear, I suggest this is a novel way to confront secularity. This older idea, of the divine nature of the Jewish soul, is applied in a new way that results in tolerance, patience, and the erasure of the siege mentality that dominated Ḥabad before its arrival in America. This new way is not a *novum* theologically, i.e., the notion that the Jewish

---

56 Ravitzky, "The Contemporary Lubavitch Ḥasidic Movement," 311. This idea is rooted in earlier kabbalistic literature that argues that Jews really cannot sin. See, for example, in Zohar 3.16a. More precisely, that only the lower dimension of the Jewish soul can sin (*nefesh*) but not the higher divine element (*neshamah*). This becomes a central theme in Ḥabad as expressed in Menahem Mendel's essay "*Bati le-Gani*" cited above.

57 The whole notion of "knowing oneself" as a religious precept is very much a part of contemporary American spirituality that matured with New Age religion in the 1980s. While American Ḥabad draws from ḥasidic literature that similarly emphasizes self-knowledge as a spiritual precept (drawing from earlier sources), Ḥabad's utilization of this idea is in concert with contemporary spiritual trends in America.

58 See, for example, in Simon Jacobson's *Toward a Meaningful Life: The Wisdom of the Rebbe Menahem Mendel Schneerson* (New York: William Morrow and Co., 1995).

59 The idea of sin as being a severance of the individual Jew from his or her true "divine" self is a common theme in later spiritual Jewish theologies. See, for example, a similar locution defining repentance in R. Abraham Isaac Kook's *Orot ha-Teshuvah* 15:10 (Jerusalem: Gar Or Press, 1977), 143, 144. Another example can be found in the little known early twentieth-century ḥasidic writer R. Menahem Mendel Eckstein. See his *Ta'anei ha-Nefesh le-Hasagat ha-Ḥasidut*, 46, cited in Daniel Reiser, "To Fly Like Angels: Imagery or Waking Dream in Ḥasidic Mysticism in the First Half of the Twentieth Century" [Hebrew] (PhD thesis, The Hebrew University, Jerusalem, 2011), 233, 234.

soul speaks even unconsciously has precedent in classical Kabbalah, but it takes on practical newness in that Ḥabad becomes more provisionally open to secularism in a way it was not in Europe, believing it will draw those distanced from tradition closer. This is another example that illustrates an "America is different" sensibility and where Menahem Mendel's revision of his predecessor's thinking embodies an American form of postmillennial fundamentalism committed to the transformation of a society already in the early stages of redemption. Jewish secularism need not be the object of consternation and confrontation; it must be massaged until it disappears, since it is, for the Jew, only an illusion.

IV

"Come to my Garden": "Holy Folly" as Jewish Postmillennialism

Below I briefly illustrate how these attitudes can be drawn from one seminal essay in Menahem Mendel's writings. His writings, both in Hebrew and Yiddish, are voluminous. One of his most celebrated essays is the inaugural lecture he delivered when becoming rebbe of Ḥabad in the winter of 1951.[60] Entitled "*Bati le-Gani*" (known in Ḥabad circles using the Ashkenazi pronunciation "*Basi le-Gani*," "Come to my Garden," Song of Songs 5:1), it is a kind of blueprint for his entire institutional and spiritual career. Below I offer a brief reading of "*Bati le-Gani*" to illustrate how this captures American Ḥabad's postmillennial agenda.

This lecture is a metaphysical reflection on the kabbalistic idea of the divine presence descending into the material world. Much has been made of the fact that Menahem Mendel refers to the *shekhinah* (divine presence) as the seventh realm of divine emanation as he is becoming the seventh rebbe of Ḥabad.[61] This is often viewed as an early, albeit esoteric, proclamation of his messianic status. Most of the lecture is based on the kabbalistic idea of "turning inside out" (*itkafya ve-itkafya*), in Menahem Mendel's language, transforming darkness into light. Darkness is depicted as the concealment of divine light from the upper worlds, and the job of the Jew is to disclose that light in the most material realms. This activity is not accomplished

60 It should be noted that every year Menahem Mendel would give additional "*Bati le-Gani*" lectures to commemorate the *yahrzeit* of his father-in-law, the sixth rebbe of Ḥabad. These are collected in *Torat Menaḥem: Sefer Ma'amarim Bati le-Gani*, 2 vols. (Brooklyn, NY: Lahak Hanochos, 2008).

61 See, for example, in Wolfson, *Open Secret*, 11, 18, 41.

solely by means of personal worship (e.g., *miẓvot* and prayer) but by an active engagement with the world and, in particular, with other Jews.

The orientation is made clear but never quite explicit in the second part of "*Bati le-Gani*." After the first metaphysical section, Menahem Mendel turns to a notion of "profane folly" and "holy folly."[62] Although he never says so explicitly, I think it is plausible to suggest that "profane folly" is a thin veil for the "secularism" practiced by the Jew. He argues that "profane folly" conceals divinity. Thus when Jews who are engaged in "profane folly" (which could just as easily be intellectual as materialistic) commit a sin, they don't feel that they are separating themselves from godliness because their folly has already concealed it. Secularism makes religious experience impossible. The way out of sin, or to transcend secularism, is to recognize what it does, which requires someone else to disclose the divine nature of the individuals' Jewish soul. There is, of course, a circular logic at play. If the Jew sees the sin for what it is, it is a sign he is experiencing things from his "divine" spark. If he does not, it is a sign that his "divine" spark remains concealed.

Menahem Mendel then proceeds in the final section of the lecture to talk about "holy folly," tying it back to an earlier discussion of how sacrifices bring divine light into the world. This "holy folly" is described as part of the prophetic vocation. Harkening back to the beginning of the lecture, he states, "And this is what it means, *make me a sanctuary and I will dwell among you* (Exodus 25:8), among each one of you."[63] He continues, "By means of divine worship one enacts the reversal of darkness to light, that is, one turns (*lehafokh*) that which is below consciousness (*da'at*) in this world to a state *of* consciousness." Here he interjects the Yiddish *fun velt* in addition to the Hebrew *olam* (world) to suggest, I think, that he is now talking practically about *this very world* and not a kabbalistic hypostasis of it. In other words, the vocation of the *ḥasid* is to engage in the world and disclose its divinity, including engaging with non-religious Jews (enactors of "profane folly") and showing them the divinity of their own soul. This can only be done by interactive worship or "holy folly," with the belief that darkness can be dispelled through engagement rather than confrontation. And so officially began postmillennial Ḥabad fundamentalism.

This charge was accompanied by a growing belief over time that Menahem Mendel was himself the Messiah and that his directives were a

62 On the rabbinic distinction upon which this is based, see BT Ketubot 17a.

63 This is a common midrashic reading of the verse. An early ḥasidic rendering can be found in *Keter Shem Tov*, collected teachings of the Ba'al Shem Tov (Brooklyn, NY: Kehot), #319, 186–89.

secret message to the "pure ones" (*temimim*) of what needed to be accomplished before he could reveal himself as such. This belief reached a crescendo in the 1990s and then came crashing down after his death in the summer of 1994. Ḥabad is still reeling from this tragedy, some believing he did not die, others continuing his work and remaining agnostic about his messianic status.

Ḥabad did not change its daily routine of religious life (*halakhah*) after Menahem Mendel's proclamation in 1991 that the Gulf War was the beginning of Armageddon. And his death in the summer of 1994 did not result in sweeping practical changes to coincide with the claim of his postmortem messianic status. I argue that the transformation from Ḥabad's prewar premillennialism to an American postmillennialism is the trademark of American Ḥabad and is an integral part of their messianic program.[64] Martin Katchen argues just the opposite when he writes, "Lubavitch has remained faithful to its premillennial belief system. It will not be stampeded by events into declaring a premature entry into the Messianic Age in the absence of a messianic faith to accomplish it. In this, Lubavitch remains faithful to the best traditions of Judaism."[65] My disagreement with this assessment is based on two points: First, the extent to which "America is different" (as a postmillennial position) runs through R. Menahem Mendel's entire American career and Ḥabad's continued adherence to *halakhah* is no proof that substantive, even radical, changes have not taken place. Second, in the postwar period in America, Christian premillennialism adopted postmillennial positions or activism or at least made gestures toward postmillennial positions. On my reading, American Ḥabad, under the tutelage of their leader and for both similar and different reasons, followed suit.

V

Satmar Ḥasidism and American Jewish Premillennialism

When Hillary Clinton was campaigning for a New York State Senate seat in 2000 she met with a group of ḥasidic women from the town of New Square in Rockland County, north of New York City. New Square is an incorporated village made up almost exclusively of ḥasidic Jews, mostly

64 On the changes that took place in the movement following his death in 1994 see Yori Yanover and Nadav Ish-Shalom, *Dancing and Singing: The Truth about the Ḥabad Movement* [Hebrew] (New York: Meshy Publishing, Inc., 1994).

65 Katchen, "Who Wants Moshiah Now?," 74, 75.

descendants from the ḥasidic town of Skver and its environs in present-day Ukraine. She began her talk by noting what a pleasure it was to address a group of *American* Jewish women. I wonder how these ḥasidic women, who live in a separatist religious enclave, primarily speak Yiddish, and are mostly unaware of the basic elements of American culture, music, and fashion, felt about being referred to as *American* Jews. Formally, of course, they are American Jews: most hold American passports, pay taxes, and vote in American elections. However, their Americanness and, more specifically, being part of American Jewry, is a much more complicated story. The ḥasidic Jews of New Square, and their counterparts in the Satmar communities in Williamsburg, Brooklyn, and Kiryas Joel, a short distance from New Square, have little interaction with American Jews and even less with American Judaism. And yet, they are a part of American Judaism even against their will. Below I argue that this identification is more than circumstantial. Satmar Ḥasidism in America is what it is because of and in response to the American landscape in which it lives, and its distinctive brand of separatist fundamentalism shares some substantive components with Christian premillennial fundamentalism in America.

Satmar Ḥasidism is probably the second most recognizable ḥasidic community in postwar America, largely as a consequence of its radical separatist and vehemently anti-Zionist ideology. The name "Satmar" comes from the town Satu Mare (also spelled Szatmar) in present-day Romania, thirteen kilometers from the Hungarian border, where the young scion of a rabbinic and ḥasidic family, R. Yoel (Joel) Teitelbaum (1887–1979), first attracted a following in the interwar period. Teitelbaum was a child prodigy from a family of rabbis and ḥasidic masters that extends back to R. Moshe Teitelbaum of Satorakja-Ujhel (1759–1841)—better known by the name of his book *Yismakh Moshe*—one of the great masters in the first generations of Ḥasidism.[66]

---

66 For more on his background see Allan Nadler, "Politics and Piety: The Satmar Rebbe," *Judaism* (1982): 135–52. More recently see the hagiography culled from the eight-volume Hebrew *Moshian shel Yisrael*, by Yaakov Shlomo Gelbman (Monroe, NY: published privately, 1980–present); Dovid Meisels, *The Rebbe: The Extraordinary Life and Worldview of Rabbeinu Yoel Teitelbaum*, trans. Y. Green (published privately by Dovid Meisels, 2010), Menachem Keren-Kratz, "Marmaros – The Cradle of Extreme Orthodoxy," *Modern Judaism* 25 92): 147-174, and idem. *Marmaros-Sziget: 'Extreme Orthodoxy' and Secular Culture at the Foothills of the Carpathian Mountains* (Jerusalem: Carmel, 2013) The most extensive study of Teitelbaum is Keren-Krantz, "Rabbi Yoel Teitelbaum – The Satmar Rebbe (1887-1979)," PhD dissertation Tel Aviv University, 2013 (Hebrew).

Given his ḥasidic lineage it is somewhat surprising that the young Teitelbaum did not function as a ḥasidic rebbe in Satmar but as a rabbinic authority and spiritual leader of a relatively small community in a town whose Jewish community consisted of a mix of ḥasidic, non-ḥasidic, Zionist, and non-religious Jews. Teitelbaum's radical separatist and anti-Zionist ideology, for which he later became famous, was not new—nor was it limited to Ḥasidic Judaism —but was an extension of Hungarian ultra-traditionalism from the middle decades of the nineteenth century.[67]

Hungarian Jews were exposed to the Jewish Enlightenment earlier than most of Eastern European Jewry. The reformist community in Hungary, known as the Neologs, were quite influential and challenged the hegemony of traditional Judaism before similar communities arose in Poland and Galicia. This, in part, sparked a vehement rejection of religious innovation known as the *Austrittsgemeinde*, led by, among others, R. Moshe Schreiber, better known as the Hatam Sofer (1762–1839), perhaps the most influential leader of Hungarian Jewry in the modern period.[68] Sofer's adage, "innovation [*ḥadash*] is prohibited in the Torah"—a clever wordplay on Leviticus 23:14 prohibiting the consumption of new grain before Passover—served as the banner of the traditionalist camp. The spiritual progeny of the Hatam Sofer developed a separatist mentality and waged war against modernity that by the late nineteenth century included Zionism.[69] Teitelbaum was very much a part of this non-ḥasidic Hungarian traditionalist tradition, and the Satmar dynasty he built in postwar America remained committed to the principles he learned in prewar Hungary. In fact, Teitelbaum arguably became the most well-known carrier of this Jewish separatist mentality in the twentieth century, making separatism into a devotional doctrine.[70]

As opposed to Menahem Mendel Schneerson of Ḥabad, Teitelbaum did not represent a long ḥasidic tradition, even as he was part of a long line of ḥasidic leaders. Satmar Ḥasidism is solely the product of Teitelbaum's

67 See Silber, "The Emergence of Ultra-Orthodoxy," 23–84.

68 See Jacob Katz, "Toward a Biography of the Hatam Sofer," in *Profiles in Diversity*, ed. Frances Malino and David Sorkin (Detroit, MI: Wayne State University Press, 1998), 223–66.

69 On Sofer and his thought in relation to Jewish fundamentalism, see Harris, "Fundamentalism," 151–55.

70 This separatist mentality was forged in Mandate Palestine/Israel by R. Asher Zelig Margoliot whose community still exists today as the "Edah Ḥaredit" in Jerusalem and other pockets in Israel. Yehudah Liebes analyzed the separatist nature of this group, comparing them to the Dead Sea Scroll sect of late Antiquity. See Liebes, "The Ultra-Orthodox Community and the Dead Sea Scroll Sect," [Hebrew] *Jerusalem Studies in Jewish Thought* 3 (1982): 137–52.

learning, leadership, and charisma. Satmar may be one of the only ḥasidic dynasties that has no distinctive *ḥasidic* ideology and even harbors a disdain for mysticism more generally. In fact, Teitelbaum was alleged to have said that the tradition of the Ba'al Shem Tov, the founder of Ḥasidism, is no longer operative. In this sense Satmar Ḥasidism is a kind of anti-ḥasidic Ḥasidism, anomalous among other ḥasidic sects, especially Ḥabad, which claims to have a direct line to the mystical ideology of Ḥasidism's founder. What makes Satmar ḥasidic is their lineage and customs and lifestyle and less their fidelity to the tradition of the Ba'al Shem Tov, which Teitelbaum claimed was lost.

Many of Teitelbaum's followers in Satmar were murdered in the Holocaust, where over one million Hungarian and Romanian Jews were exterminated in the last years of the war. The dynasty Teitelbaum built in America consisted largely of Hungarian and Romanian Holocaust survivors who were members of other ḥasidic sects or traditional communities that were destroyed.[71] In America many survivors who had lost their communal affiliation coalesced around him, as he was arguably the most charismatic ultra-Orthodox Hungarian figure to survive the war.

In this sense, Satmar Ḥasidism as we know it today is a postwar American phenomenon, even as it embodies an ideology that stretches back to prewar Hungarian ultra-Orthodoxy. As I argue below, the Americanism of Satmar is more than situational. Satmar's unrelenting war against Zionism—a battle that only increased after the Six-Day War in 1967, when many ultra-Orthodox Jews reconciled with the existence of the Jewish State—its increased focus on punctilious observance and extreme modesty, and its separatist ideology that resulted in the emergence of Kiryas Joel, a rural Satmar enclave in Rockland County, New York, are all products of a Jewish premillennialist sentiment that has roots in prewar Europe but is made possible by living in America.

While much has been written on the socio-political and spiritual dimensions of Satmar Ḥasidism, mostly concerning their unrelenting anti-Zionism, my interest in this chapter is quite narrow. I will briefly address three elements that illustrate Satmar as a premillennialist Jewish fundamentalism whose continued separatist and anti-Zionist ideology is made possible by living in America's liberal democracy. I will also suggest that the radical nature of Satmar's separatist ideology has become more pronounced than it was in prewar Europe due in part to its home in a society where religious freedom and practice are legally protected. The three

71 See Mintz, *Ḥasidic People*, 7–43.

issues I focus on are: (1) Satmar's relationship to Jews who do not agree with their separatist and anti-Zionist principles, whether they are Orthodox or non-Orthodox; (2) Teitelbaum's desire to create an "American *shtetle*" or enclave community in rural upstate New York; and (3) Teitelbaum's unwavering critique of Zionism that became more vociferous as Israel became more accepted by ultra-Orthodox communities, American Jews, and the West after 1967. Rather than soften his position on Zionism, the "triumph" of the Six-Day War made him more resolute that Zionism was the most egregious error committed by the Jewish people in its long history.

As discussed briefly in the previous chapter on Ḥabad, premillennialism, specifically post–Civil War dispensationalist premillennialism, was founded on the Augustinian principle that "Christ's kingdom, far from being realized in this age or in the natural development of humanity, lay wholly in the future, was totally supernatural in origin, and discontinuous with the history of this era … For the [premillennial] dispensationalists the prophecies concerning the kingdom referred wholly to the future. This present era, the 'church age,' therefore could not be dignified as a time of the advance of God's kingdom."[72] It is not only that this age *cannot* be a part of the unfolding redemption; it is that this age represents the *necessary* decline of civilization that will be radically reversed when the Messiah arrives (or in Christianity, returns). Teitelbaum was quoted as saying, "The Rambam [Moses Maimonides, the twelfth-century legalist and philosopher] says that we do not know how messiah will come until he comes, so let us wait patiently *without taking any action* toward the redemption, and let us have faith that God will fulfill the promises of the prophets at the time he sees fit."[73] It is significant to note that Maimonides does not explicitly say we should *not take any action*, only that we should "wait each day for him to arrive." Elsewhere Teitelbaum writes, "the future redemption will come solely on the merit of the Great Avenger, [we must] wait until the coming of the messiah and should not turn to [or be seduced by] any other redemption, heaven forbid, before the coming of the Messiah."[74] This premillennial passivity does not yield pacifism. As a premillennialist, R. Teitelbaum is at war with the world, particularly the Jewish world, because his ideology is founded on the biblical idea in the Book of Daniel of the false prophet or, in Christianity, the anti-Christ that appears in the Book of Revelations.[75]

72 Marsden, *Fundamentalism and American Culture*, 51.
73 Gelbman, *Moshian shel Yisrael*, 7:141–42.
74 Teitelbaum, *Al ha-Ge'ulah ve-al ha-Temurah*, new ed. (Brooklyn, NY, 2001), 20.
75 On the "great tribulation" so prominent in Revelations, see also Matthew 24:2, "Nothing will escape destruction. No stone upon a stone will not be thrown down."

This satanic figure impersonates and even acts like a messenger from God but is an evil force intended to draw society to its doom. As we will see, for Teitelbaum, the Jewish "anti-Christ" is secularism and, more importantly, Zionism. This idea is very much in concert with many premillennial Protestants in America who deemed the Pope and the Catholic Church more broadly as the anti-Christ. The circularity of this premillennial logic is that success in this world is a sign that such success is the result of demonic forces that must be resisted. The exile is for suffering and maintaining allegiance to the tradition until which time God will intervene. The messianic ideology, with roots in rabbinic literature, that the world must come to the very precipice of destruction before it will be redeemed, lies at the center of Satmar's separatism.

VI

Satmar: Separatism as Devotion

This spiritual separatism, largely adopted from his great-grandfather R. Moshe Teitelbaum and the Hatam Sofer, is not only a practical way to avoid foreign influence. It becomes a spiritual value in and of itself.[76] It is a devotional posture that enables one to be in constant awareness of the illusory nature of social progress. And it is not by any means limited to separating from the gentile world. Jewish unity is not a pre-messianic goal for Satmar but a consequence of "false prophecy" that precedes redemption. The satanic force can appear inside Judaism as easily as outside it, perhaps even more so. According to this demonological view of history, hatred is the only proper response to the forces of evil that pervade the world.[77] "The Rebbe [R. Teitelbaum] often repeated the words of R. Yehoshuah of Belz: Separatism was of such importance that if a city had no wicked Jews, it would be worthwhile to pay some wicked Jews to come and live there so that the good Jews would have something to separate from. The very act

---

76 This was true of certain strains of Hungarian ultra-Orthodoxy before Satmar, but Satmar should be credited with taking this ideology to a new level in the postwar period, both in Israel and in the Diaspora.

77 Satmar's worldview as "demonological" is discussed in Norman Lamm's "The Ideology of Neturei Karta: According to the Satmarer Version," *Tradition* 13 (1971): 38–53. In his ḥasidic teachings, R. Moshe Teitelbaum describes how hatred between the righteous and the sinners is natural and a good thing as it keeps them apart. See Moshe Teitelbaum, *Yismakh Moshe* (Jerusalem: Gross Brothers, 1989), 2:72c.

of declaring separateness from the wicked strengthens the commitment of the righteous."[78] Citing a talmudic passage (BT Sotah 49b), "just before the Messiah comes truth will be divided into flocks [*ne'ederet*]," Teitelbaum wrote, "In these years as falsehood spreads, those who practice the truth will grow fewer and fewer. The flock of truth must separate again and again from those who go astray. Every time a part of the small group of the faithful takes a step in the wrong direction, those who remain faithful must once again separate from them."[79] This suggests an infinite regress of separation until evil is destroyed by divine fiat. The postmillennial spirit of Ḥabad resulted in spreading its message of *yiddishkeit* (Jewishness) to Jews and the Noahide Laws to non-Jews as a prelude and even pre-requisite for the final redemption. This is countered by Satmar's premillennial ideology of separation as a spiritual discipline. The world is dominated by the forces of evil. God does not want us to erase them by engaging or transforming them. He wants us to separate ourselves to prevent contamination. Only separation can save the dwindling remnant. Concerning extreme separatists in various religions Emmanuel Sivan writes, "There is no concern for the klal or umma of the so-called believers, for one is faced with an 'infidel society', and 'evil kingdom'. Doomed to damnation it can be saved, if at all, either by messianic intervention or by imposing the divine law upon one and all once the elect take power by force."[80]

Teitelbaum spoke and wrote with great passion about worldly matters and engaged with the New York State and U.S. governments to assure the rights and safety of his community. He did not advocate living "off the grid" in a desolate area independent of governmental influence like David Koresh's Branch Davidians in Waco, Texas. Quite the opposite, as we will see with regard to Kiryas Joel, his separatism was quite activist. He was very engaged with government agencies. American liberal democracy was very much a tool of Satmar's ḥasidic separatism. Absolute separatism was only

78 Gelbman, *Moshian shel Yisrael*, 3:247. This reflects the attitude initially proposed by the Hatam Sofer regarding separating from religious innovators (reformers). See Sofer, *Kan Sofer* #39, 38, cited in Allan Nadler, "The War on Modernity of T. Hayyim Elazar Shapira of Munkacz," *Modern Judaism* 14 (1994): 234. "The general principle is to distance oneself from the innovators; we must form a strong fortress to assure that the community is divided into two camps, so that the separation between the Jews and the innovators will be as great as the distance between heaven and earth. Only in this way shall we succeed..."

79 Teitelbaum, *Kuntres Ḥiddushei Torah*, 5 vols. (Brooklyn, NY, 1962–1969), *parashat eikev* 5717, cited in Meisels, *The Rebbe*, 159.

80 Sivan, "The Enclave Culture," in *Strong Religion*, 44.

relegated to the Zionist entity, as he felt Zionism was the great sin of modern Jewry, the very root of modernity's false prophecy. For example, it was said that when he visited Israel to bring much needed financial resources to his community there, he refused to handle Israeli money or make use of Israel's buses or other public services. While Teitelbaum viewed American democracy in purely utilitarian terms, he viewed Zionism in absolutist terms.

It is significant to note that while Satmar is not overtly messianic like Ḥabad, and in some ways can even be construed as anti-messianic, in other ways it is no *less* messianic than Ḥabad. The difference between their messianisms is very much a product of their respective postmillennial and premillennial dispositions. Menahem Mendel believed that we are living on the cusp, or even inside, the messianic era and *we* (Jews *and* gentiles) must do the final work to complete the process. This position argues that the beginning of the age of redemption precedes the coming of the Messiah. Many of Menahem Mendel's disciples considered him the Messiah (many even after his death) and toward the end of his life he appeared to be in agreement with that assessment. Teitelbaum held that any belief that humans can do anything to erase evil and bring Messiah is blasphemy, even idolatry. The Messiah will usher in redemption by destroying the illusion of historical progress.[81] Only the Messiah can finally erase the stain of satanic temptation. Thus religious Jews, even ultra-Orthodox ones, who capitulate to Zionism (for Teitelbaum the satanic "other"), whether ideologically or practically, are implicated in this idolatrous act. He eschewed all rebbe worship and would have thought it absurd for anyone to consider him Messiah. Speaking against the belief in the miraculous nature of the Six-Day War, Teitelbaum warned against being impressed with miracles, whether they come from holy men or men of unknown reputation.[82]

For Teitelbaum evil will reign and even increase until it will be eradicated in the end-time. Jews must separate themselves from all manner of

---

81 Richard Hofstadter notes in reference to certain forms of premillennialist fundamentalists in America that for them "history is a conspiracy, set in motion by demonic forces of almost transcendent power." See Hofstadter, *The Paranoid Style in American Politics, and Other Essays*, r.p. (Cambridge, MA: Harvard University Press 1996), 29.

82 See *Al ha-Geulah*, 13. He often cited a teaching by R. Kalonymus Kalman Epstein of Cracow (1754–1823) to Deuteronomy 13:2 about the signs of a false prophet. R. Epstein warned of the weakness of those who pursue a man simply because he ostensibly performed miraculous deeds. See Epstein, *Me'or ve-Shemesh* (Jerusalem, 1986), 2:162d.

evil, mourn the destruction, and await the redemption.[83] In many ways what separates Ḥabad and Satmar on this point is that Ḥabad is committed to the kabbalistic idea of eradicating evil by transforming it and Satmar is committed to a Manichean worldview that humans cannot eradicate evil. In this sense Satmar is perhaps the *least* mystical sect of Ḥasidism. It is worth noting that this anti-mystical worldview is also common among certain branches of Christian fundamentalism in America. While Kabbalah plays a role in Teitelbaum's teachings it does not do so as a template of his worldview but simply as part of the canon of classical Jewish literature. The Ḥatam Sofer, whose influence is pervasive in Satmar's ideology, was not a mystic, and Teitelbaum's sermons, collected in the multi-volume *Divrei Yoel*, do not exhibit strong mystical tendencies. Alternatively, Menahem Mendel's teachings are saturated with Ḥabad's distinctive acosmic mystical worldview, and one cannot adequately understand Ḥabad's social program without understanding its kabbalistic foundation.[84]

One of the most overt expressions of Satmar's separatism in America was Teitelbaum's dream of establishing a Satmar enclave in a rural community in close proximity to Brooklyn. This would enable his *ḥasidim* and their families to escape the secular temptations of the city while remaining close enough to New York's commercial center where many had businesses. Established in 1974 in Monroe Township, Kiryas Joel is about fifty-five miles north of New York City.[85] In one sense Teitelbaum wanted to establish an "American *shtetl*." However, as Nomi Stolzenberg astutely notes, this *shtetl* is perhaps more a product of his imagination than any real prewar *shtetl* in Europe. "Kiryas Yoel is, in many respects, more insular, more homogenous, more exclusive than the European *shtetl*. It is stricter in its observance and, symptomatically, the rates of yeshiva learning and life-long Torah study are far higher in Kiryas Yoel than they were in Europe." It is precisely the American context of this *shtetl* that makes it possible. The ability for this American fundamentalist community to realize this vision of separation is "in part because the American welfare system alleviates the pressure to find *parnasa* [a livelihood] that weighed on most European Jews. All of

83 The belief that we are living in the "birth pangs of Messiah" was very much as part of R. Teitelbaum's teacher R. Hayyim Elazar Shapira of Munkacz. See Nadler, "The War on Modernity," 237 and 260n26. See Teitelbaum, *Al ha-Geulah*, 3.

84 This is argued quite convincingly in Wolfson's *Open Secret*, and I think points to a weakness in Samuel Heilman and Menahem Friedman's biography of Menahem Mendel entitled *The Rebbe* (Princeton, NJ: Princeton University Press, 2010). American Ḥabad is perhaps the most notable case of applied mysticism in Judaism since the Sabbatean heresy in the seventeenth century.

85 See Mintz, *Ḥasidic People*, 198–215.

these features that distinguish the 'American *shtetl*' from the European one are clearly signs of the community's success in resisting assimilation and Americanization (even as the community avails itself of the American system's largess)."[86]

While Teitelbaum fanatically advocated against reaping any benefit from the Zionist State, he was fully open to participating in the commercial life of America's liberal democracy. This was not hypocritical because he was in full agreement with the divine decree of exile and Jeremiah's call for the Jewish exiles to make homes in the Diaspora until the coming of the Messiah (Jeremiah 29:4–7). Alternatively, his attitude toward the State of Israel was purely ideological and uncompromising. For him the Zionist State was an act of heresy that not only "forced the end" (the rabbinic category that deemed premature messianism to be blasphemy) but was an embodiment of the demonic force that was testing the Jewish people's resolve to resist the temptation of premature redemption.[87] To reap benefit from Israel was to participate in an egregious act and, from his perspective, the most serious anti-messianic endeavor imaginable. In this sense, his protest against any redemptive quality of the Jewish State is an expression of his premillennial messianism.

Kiryas Joel was a party in a Supreme Court case in 1994 (Kiryas Joel v. Grumet) regarding the establishment of a public school district for this American town made up solely of Satmar Ḥasidim.[88] Among other things, this would give the Kiryas Joel school district access to state funds for certain school programs, such as assistance for special needs children. The particulars of this case are beyond the scope of this chapter. Nomi Stolzenberg notes that Kiryas Joel was able to establish itself as a "public" community, which enabled it to be *more* separatist than its European predecessors. By internalizing "American liberal and cultural norms" Kiryas Joel established a self-segregated community that is as "deeply rooted in fundamental principles of liberalism and individual rights and the free market as it is opposed

86 David Myers and Nomi Stolzenberg, "What Does Kiryas Joel Tell us about Liberalism in America?," *The 2006 Dr. Fritz Bamberger Memorial Lecture 2008*, 52, 53.

87 See Teitelbaum, *Va-yoel Moshe* (Brooklyn, NY, 1961), "Essay on the Three Oaths." Cf. Aviezer Ravitzky, "Forcing the End: Radical Anti-Zionism," in his *Messianism, Zionism, and Religious Radicalism*, trans. Jonathan Chipman (Chicago: University of Chicago Press, 1996), 40–78.

88 See Mintz, *Ḥasidic People*, 309–27 and Louis Grumet *The Curious Case of Kiryas Joel: The Rise of a Village Theocracy and the Battle to Defend the Separation of Church and State* (Chicago" Chicago Review Press, 2016).

to them."[89] While the ideal of Satmar separatism is rooted in Hungarian ultra-Orthodoxy, its success in America is in part due to America's commitment to religious freedom and the ways in which closed communities like Satmar can use that to their advantage. Thus, like Ḥabad's missionary program, the "American" in Satmar's "American *shtetl*" is more than a geographical adjective.

VII

Satmar's Anti-Zionism and its American Articulation: Al ha-Ge'ulah ve-al ha-Temurah

Satmar is perhaps most well known for its vehement position against Zionism. Much has been written about Satmar's anti-Zionism and its roots in prewar European Orthodoxy, and I will not rehearse those observations here.[90] While Orthodox anti-Zionism was very popular before the Holocaust and even after the establishment of Israel in 1948, the Six-Day War in 1967 softened many of the remaining anti-Zionist Jews, both Orthodox and Reform. While many remained less than enthusiastic about the Jewish State, the anti-Zionist rhetoric diminished precipitously by the early 1970s. The exception to this rule was Teitelbaum.

After the Six-Day War in 1967 Jews worldwide celebrated Israel's victory over its Arab neighbors, including sovereignty over East Jerusalem and many "biblical" lands in what became known as the West Bank. This included an increased sense of security many Jews felt about the fledgling Jewish State. In light of, and in spite of, this new triumphalist spirit Teitelbaum, by then quite frail, set out to write an anti-Zionist manifesto that sought to prove that the Zionist victory was yet another illustration of

89 Myers and Stolzenberg, "What Does Kiryas Joel Tell Us," 53. On Teitelbaum's relationship to America, Allan Nadler notes, "At all his political rallies, a huge American flag covered the wall behind Teitelbaum's podium. He constantly urged his Ḥasidim to be upright citizens faithful to the statutes of American law." Nadler, "Politics and Piety," 147.

90 For some examples in English, see Ravitzky, "Forcing the End"; Nadler, "Politics and Piety"; Lamm, "The Ideology of Neturei Karta"; and Kaplan, "Rabbi Joel Teitelbaum, Zionism, and Hungarian Ultra-Orthodoxy," *Modern Judaism* 24, no. 2 (2004): 165–78. Cf. David Sorotzkin, "Building the Earthy and Destroying the Heavenly: The Satmar Rebbe and the Radical Orthodox School of Thought" [Hebrew], in *The Land of Israel in Twentieth-Century Jewish Thought*, ed. A. Ravitzky (Jerusalem, 2004): 133–67.

Zionism as the "anti-Christ." This work, "On Redemption and on Exchange" (*Al ha-Ge'ulah ve-al ha-Temurah*), is based on a midrashic reading of the Book of Ruth 4:7. The Book of Ruth has often been accorded messianic import, as it ends with a genealogy leading to King David, the messianic symbol in classical Judaism. The midrash links the illusion of "redemption" (*ge'ulah*) to "exchange" (*temurah*, its opposite)—in the midrashic case, the sin of the golden calf in Exodus 32. Teitelbaum makes his case that Zionism is a contemporary golden calf, and all who participate in it, even if they outwardly do not support it, are guilty of the gravest sin in Jewish history.

The initial reviews of this book were predictably negative, although some praise came from the ultra-Orthodox circles in Jerusalem and other pockets in the Diaspora.[91] Most Jews were understandably at a loss for how to understand Teitelbaum's sustained anti-Zionism in the wake of what many viewed as a miraculous victory for Israel and the Jews. While many ultra-Orthodox Jews understood and sympathized with Teitelbaum's misgivings about the establishment of a secular state, the Six-Day War resulted in free access to the Wailing Wall and other holy sites, including Rachel's tomb in Bethlehem, Joseph's tomb in Nablus, the Tomb of the Patriarchs in Hebron, and the Temple Mount in Jerusalem (even though many ultra-Orthodox Jews do not visit the Temple Mount because of a prohibition against setting foot on its sacred ground). Thus, while many in the ultra-Orthodox camp still refused to celebrate Israel's Independence Day, many recognized Jerusalem Day (commemorating the "unification" of Jerusalem in 1967) as a day of thanksgiving. For many this was not about the secular state but divine intervention. Below I will offer a brief synopsis of the introduction to *Al ha-Ge'ulah* and make a number of suggestions as to what is really at stake in this book. It is in this late work that I argue his most pungent version of anti-Zionism, and its American context, emerges.[92]

In his introduction to *Al ha-Ge'ulah ve-al ha-Temurah*, Teitelbaum makes a series of audacious claims that, given its charged rhetoric, makes one wonder what is really at stake. He claims that Zionism is not only a contemporary embodiment of the golden calf, "it is thousands of times worse than the golden calf" (19), worse than the Sabbatean heresy that racked

---

91 After a careful study of the work, the chief judge in the ultra-Orthodox rabbinical court, P. Pinhas Epstein, said, "*Vayoel Moshe* is something that I think I could have written. But *Al ha-Geulah*, where the Rebbe exposes the falsifications of the religious Zionists, is a feat that no one could duplicate." Cited in Meisels, *The Rebbe*, 516.

92 I choose to limit myself to the twenty-six-page introduction because this is the only part of the book he wrote himself. The remainder of the book contains collected oral teachings that were edited by his students.

world Jewry in the seventeenth century (22), an instance of Jewish idolatry that requires martyrdom (10), and the work of Satan himself (7, 17).[93] He believed this was the final test of the messianic generation to overcome (6, 10). Like a lone wolf in the wilderness after 1967 he watched as Zionism engulfed the entire Western world. For him the fundamental premillennial framework of waiting patiently for redemption was shattered by the "satanic miracle" (7, 17) that he claimed is founded on a talmudic teaching that suggests Satan is given dominion to test humanity. Zionism and its acceptance resulted in the fate of the Jews delivered to satanic powers (18). "It is known from writers and books that any time there is an arousal of redemption from above … Satan cleverly intervenes to transform it into a false redemption" (20). This satanic dominion, Teitelbaum argues, is strengthened by Torah-observing Jews who support the Zionist project. "Religious Jews with their leaders who are drawn after them [the Zionists] give strength and power to the heretics [*apikorsim*] in a powerful way" (19). While many of these themes exist earlier in *Va-yoel Moshe*, written in the late 1950s, the language here is much sharper and the stakes are much higher. Teitelbaum knew that the events of 1967 made it more difficult for sympathizers to maintain their resolve in the face of what so many viewed as a miraculous moment in Jewish history.

While we cannot know for certain what precipitated this escalation of rhetoric, I will suggest three possibilities. First, Teitelbaum witnessed how the "religious" consequences of the Six-Day War (i.e., the "unification of Jerusalem," access to holy places, etc.) softened the attitudes of many who were sympathetic to his absolutist ideology before 1967. Viewing the events of '67 as another manifestation of "false redemption" facilitated by the dominion of evil, he needed to reiterate his position to an ultra-Orthodox community vulnerable to succumbing to the illusion of historical progress.[94] In classic premillennial fashion, Teitelbaum held that the illusion of historical progress is the most useful tool of Satan to do his work.

93 See Nadler, "Politics and Piety," 138. Nadler notes that Teitelbaum took this so seriously that he said, "A Jew ought to give his children up to Christian missionaries rather than entrust them to the Zionist authorities." Satmar was also accused of stealing Yemenite children from Israel and bringing them to be raised in the Satmar community in America. Stories of Yemenite children being taken from their religious parents upon arrival in Israel in 1948 and raised in youth villages is a tragic part of early Zionist history and has lately received new attention as some of the children, now aging, have been telling their stories.

94 See Nadler, "Politics and Piety," 136 and 137, where he makes a similar albeit not identical suggestion. On the analogy with Sabbateanism see Nadler, "Politics and Piety," 142.

Second, his call to dismantle the Jewish State may have in part been a consequence of the reality of Jewish life in America. That is, when Jews were in danger in prewar Europe he spoke out against the establishment of a Jewish state as an act of heresy. And even though he finally wrote *Va-yoel Moshe* in the late 1950s, the trauma of the Holocaust and instability of world Jewry were still quite palpable. But by the late 1960s ultra-Orthodox Jewish life (which was his focus) had re-established itself in the safe haven of America. Whatever negative things he may have said about America, like Menahem Mendel, Teitelbaum knew America was a place where Jews could practice their religion in relative safety. Hence, the dismantling of the Jewish State would not by definition put the Jewish people in grave danger. This of course assumes many things that could not be taken for granted (i.e., open immigration to democratic countries such as America), but it may have enabled him, coupled with his belief in the impending redemption, to invoke the absolutist rhetoric prominent in *Al ha-Geulah*. For Teitelbaum the only "safe haven" for Jews was the life of *miẓvot* and separation from the forces that seek to undermine the religious life. The notion that Jews could be safe by having an army was anathema in his premillennialist perspective.

Unlike Menahem Mendel, whose anti-Zionism was really about the cultural project of secular nationalism, Teitelbaum's anti-Zionism was primarily political. By that I mean the heretical imperative for Teitelbaum was the exercise of political sovereignty in Ereẓ Israel before the apportioned time. Secularism was not the issue for him because secularism was anathema in any form and he did not have to convince his readers of that. The issue was the heretical use of political power as an insurance of Jewish survival that undermined his premillennial ideology. As a postmillennialist, Menahem Mendel held that the political could be used as a tool to procure redemption's unfolding, as long as it adhered to traditional theological principles. Hence, he strongly advocated against relinquishing even "one inch" of territory, as a theological precept and not a matter of security, and supported the secular government of Israel as a means to achieve that theological end. For Menahem Mendel the state only functioned to maximize the security of Jews and the protection of the sanctity of Ereẓ Israel. Zionism had no intrinsic value for him viz. Jewishness or Judaism. For Teitelbaum, the very existence of the Jewish State was an ideological impossibility, a manifestation of pure evil.

Finally, it seems *Al ha-Ge'ulah* is a new and increasingly desperate articulation of Teitelbaum's theology of separatism that he adopted from his prewar Hungarian predecessors. It is not distinct from his activity in creating Kiryas Joel and, like Kiryas Joel, is made possible by his American context.[95] As Nomi Stolzenberg notes in her analysis of Kiryas Joel, liberal America made Kiryas Joel as an "American *shtetl*" more relevant—and more possible—than anything that could have been created in Europe. Before 1967 Zionism did not have the same cache among secular American Jews or among Americans more generally. For many American Jews, Israel was barely on their radar before 1967. While President Truman supported the establishment of Israel (after much heated discussion in his cabinet) subsequent American administrations before 1967 were more tepid in their support.

The Six-Day War changed that for American Jews and most of the Western world.[96] As noted above, for Teitelbaum, separatism was more than pragmatic; it was devotional. Each new moment in history introduced another opportunity to separate from evil. After 1967 Zionism was not only an ideology of "some" Jews, it became the default ideology of most Jews, and many ultra-Orthodox Jews in America who were not Zionists could not retain their ideological commitment to wage war against it. For Teitelbaum, the disease that infected modern Judaism now had become a pandemic infecting most of the world. *Al ha-Ge'ulah* was thus his final act of separatism, a message not only to Jews but to the world. While Teitelbaum remained primarily concerned with his community and supporters, after 1967 he viewed the world as increasingly hypnotized by the successes of the Zionist State. Hence, he widened his lens to include not only the ultra-Orthodox community but the larger world and its shift in political policy toward what he deemed was the antithesis of his vision of redemption. Not enough attention has been paid to the extent to which *Al ha-Ge'ulah*, written in the dense style of rabbinic prose, is actually a book that has as much to say to the gentile world as to the audience that can read and understand it. I would argue this is not the case with his earlier *Va-yoel Moshe*, which is more limited in its scope and, in many ways, more similar to a prewar European mindset.

If I am correct in my assessment, Teitelbaum's ideology, especially as expressed in *Al ha-Ge'ulah*, is very much an American Jewish fundamentalism. The reality of non-Orthodox Judaism as the template of American

95 It is certainly true that this theology of separatism remained operative in his community in Israel. But *Al ha-Ge'ulah* was written in America and was part of a much larger ideological project undertaken by Satmar there. I am not aware of any analysis of the American context of this work or any attempt to view it in light of Teitelbaum's American program.

96 France's loaning its fighter jets to the Israeli army in 1967 greatly helped the war effort. Ironically, it was the occupation, the consequence of the Six-Day War, that turned many of those same countries against Israel.

Judaism that supported his theology of separatism, his use of American goods and resources in the establishment of Kiryas Joel, and his belief that Zionism's universal acceptance after 1967 required a more radical act of separatism than before all point to the fact that Teitelbaum, consciously or not, viewed his new home in America as a platform to develop and even radicalize an ideology born in prewar Europe.

VII

ArtScroll's "Torah-True Judaism" as a Nonmillennial American Jewish Fundamentalism

As opposed to Ḥabad or Satmar, ArtScroll is not a ḥasidic court, it is not a religious sect, it is arguably not even a religious movement. It is, rather, a publishing house run by rabbis Nosson Sherman and Meir Zlotowitz that began publishing translations of the Hebrew Bible into English in the late 1970s with extensive notes and annotations from traditional sources and commentaries. ArtScroll began with one modest volume consisting of a translation of and commentary on the Book of Esther (*Megillat Esther*) in 1976. The occasion was to honor a recently deceased teacher and mentor of one of the editors. No other volumes were planned.[97] The reception to *Megillat Esther* was overwhelming. In consultation with their teachers, some of the leading Torah sages in America, Sherman and Zlotowitz decided to embark on subsequent volumes. Within a span of a little more than three decades ArtScroll has revolutionized Jewish print media in English with hundreds of translations, including a fully annotated translation of the Babylonian Talmud (the Jerusalem Talmud is now being translated), the completion of which was celebrated at the Library of Congress in Washington, and hundreds of volumes on history, biography, self-help, cookbooks, children's books, and more. One reviewer coined this print-culture explosion in American Judaism "the ArtScroll revolution."[98] Whether or not it is a

---

97 See Nosson Sherman and Nessanel Kasnett, "The Schottenstein Edition of the Babylonian Talmud: The Next Stage in Talmudic Elucidation," in *Printing the Talmud: From Bomberg to Schottenstein*, ed. S. Mintz and G. Goldstein (New York: Yeshiva University Press, 2005), 155.

98 Nelson Barber, "The ArtScroll Revolution," *Judaica Book News* 19 (1989): 15–16. The only full-length book to date on ArtScroll is Jeremy Stolow's *Orthodox by Design: Judaism, Print Politics, and the ArtScroll Revolution* (Berkeley and Los Angeles:

revolution—a term its traditionalist leaders might even find offensive—it has certainly changed the landscape of American Orthodoxy and given voice to a traditional alternative to Modern Orthodoxy. Below I examine this phenomenon, its ideological, perhaps even "revolutionary," program, and how it represents a third instance of Jewish fundamentalism in postwar America.[99]

While most forms of fundamentalism in America contain millennial elements, presenting their position as the proper, often exclusive, way to procure redemption or wait for its immanent unfolding, there are various instances of fundamentalism where millennialism appears to be absent or, at best, dormant. I thus deploy the term "nonmillennial" Jewish fundamentalism to describe ArtScroll. By nonmillennial I mean a fundamentalist position that does not view the end-time as its primary focus. It may believe in the end-time, as ArtScroll surely does, but its program is not founded on that precept.

What, then, makes ArtScroll fundamentalist? To return again to the definition of fundamentalism suggested by Emmanuel Sivan and Scott Appleby cited in the beginning of this chapter, "Fundamentalism, in this usage, refers to a discernible pattern of religious militance by which self-styled 'true believers' attempt to arrest the erosion of religious identity, fortify the borders of the religious community, and create viable alternatives to secular institutions and behaviors."[100] I would add a more recent definition by Peter Berger: "Fundamentalism is the attempt to restore or create anew a taken-for-granted body of beliefs and values. In other words, fundamentalism is always reactive, and what it reacts against is precisely the aforementioned relativization process."[101] I argue that both of these definitions hold true for

---

University of California Press, 2010). Cf. my review essay, "ArtScroll and the Bourgeois Revolution of American Orthodoxy: A Review of Jeremy Stolow's *Orthodox by Design*," *Zeek Magazine*, July 22, 2010, available at www.zeek.forward.com. A valuable critique of ArtScroll's Bible translations can be found in B. Barry Levy, "Our Torah, Your Torah, Their Torah: An Evaluation of the ArtScroll Phenomenon," in *Truth and Compassion: Essays on Judaism and Religion in Memory of Rabbi Dr. Solomon Frank*, ed. H. Joseph, J. Lightstone, and M. Oppenheim (Canada: Wilfrid Laurier University Press, 1983), 137–90.

99 On ArtScroll as an indication of the "slide to the right" toward Jewish fundamentalism in America, see Stolow, *Orthodoxy by Design*, 180.

100 Introduction to *Strong Religion*, 17.

101 Peter Berger, "Introduction: Between Relativism and Fundamentalism," in *Between Relativism and Fundamentalism* (Grand Rapids, MI: Eerdmans, 2010), 7. It is interesting that Berger's definition of "fundamentalism" is precisely the definition Wieseltier uses to define why ultra-Orthodox Judaism is *not* fundamentalist. Wieseltier writes, "The Jewish fundamentalists today might be more properly called restorationists. They seem

ArtScroll and many of its traditional readers, albeit ArtScroll's approach is not militant in the formal sense but expresses a strident polemical program against the corruption of Judaism in the English-speaking world. By defining itself as representing "Torah-true" Judaism it excludes any form of Judaism that does not align itself with its precepts and doctrines, e.g., any form of non-Orthodoxy or secular Judaism and perhaps some progressive forms of Modern Orthodoxy.

Like Ḥabad and Satmar, ArtScroll is rooted in prewar European Judaism. It embodies the religious sensibilities of the central and eastern European Mussar tradition that in America has largely melded with the high-minded talmudism of Lithuanian Jewry (sometimes known as the *mitnaggedim*) to constitute Yeshiva Orthodoxy.[102]

The Mussar figure R. Nosson Zvi Finkel, known as the Elder of Slobodka (1849–1927), looms quite large in the ArtScroll canon of heroes as does R. Aaron Kotler (1891–1962) and his son R. Shneur Kotler (1918–1982), both of the Lakewood Yeshiva in Lakewood, New Jersey, as well as R. Moshe Feinstein (1895–1986) and R. Ya'akov Kamenetsky (1891–1986), two of the leading Lithuanian *yeshivah* deans in America. I mention these names because they constitute the patriarchs of Yeshiva Orthodoxy in America, a brand of Jewish fundamentalism that offered a non- and even anti-ḥasidic and non-messianic Judaism that coalesced around the ArtScroll phenomenon. As stated by its editors, ArtScroll proceeded with its project *only* with the blessings of some of these men.[103]

Many of ArtScroll's writers, translators, and editors herald from this spiritual lineage. It is thus my contention that ArtScroll serves as the "Americanization" of Yeshiva Orthodoxy and represents an important transformation of nonmillennial traditionalism whose influence was often overshadowed by Ḥasidism and Modern Orthodoxy in postwar America. The inward world of Yeshiva Orthodoxy, whose focus was the proliferation of kollels and expanding Torah study to as wide an audience as possible, largely existed under the radar screen of most American Jews outside

to be agitating for a return, either to a text or to a time." Wieseltier, "The Jewish Face of Fundamentalism," 194.

102 On the *mitnaggedim* see Allan Nadler, *The Faith of the Mithnagdim* (Baltimore, MD: Johns Hopkins University Press, 1999). For a study of this phenomenon in Israel, which is very different than its American cousin, see Nurit Stadler, *Yeshiva Orthodoxy: Piety, Gender, and Resistance in the Ultra-Orthodox World* (New York: NYU Press, 2009).

103 For example, they began their massive Talmud project only after being asked to do so by R. Kamenetsky. See Sherman and Kasnett, "The Schottenstein Edition," 156. They also asked for, and received, approbations from many contemporary American sages, such as Moshe Feinstein.

Orthodoxy. With the inception and subsequent success of ArtScroll in the late 1970s, this community has become a major player in American Jewish religiosity.

The existence of American Jewish fundamentalism takes three distinct forms, representing three strains of prewar ultra-Orthodoxy in Europe: one from the distinctive ḥasidic line of Ḥabad (postmillennial), one from the separatist *cum* ḥasidic world of Hungarian ultra-Orthodoxy (Satmar, premillennial), and one from the Mussar tradition and Lithuanian Orthodoxy (ArtScroll, nonmillennial). All three have transformed American Judaism in different ways, giving life not only to Orthodoxy but to Jewish fundamentalism, and, by extension, each has transformed their prewar (and thus pre-fundamentalist) predecessors, accommodating to the American religious landscape.

Upon examining such a large translation project such as ArtScroll one could justifiably ask "why this, why now?" That is, publishing books assumes a readership. And publishing translations of texts already translated assumes the need to address deficiencies in previous translations. In short, such an enterprise is, by definition, reactive and arguably even polemical. In answer to the first question, the editors of ArtScroll offer the following:

> Why has *Megillat Esther* [The Book of Esther] earned such unexpected reception? In retrospect, the reason was obvious; it was an illustration of an old cliché, "an idea whose time has come." At that point in time, there were two generations of Jews who had received a yeshiva or day school education … However, their *mama lashon* (mother tongue) was English. They might have been able to "study" the classic Hebrew texts and commentary but they could not curl up in a recliner and read Hebrew. And, of course, the vast majority of English-speaking Jews were totally unequipped to deal with a Hebrew text at all. If such people were to deal with a Torah work, it would have to be presented in their own idiom … The Torah belongs to every Jew; it should not be locked behind a language barrier.[104]

In a 2007 interview Sherman tweaks this assessment to include *ba'alei teshuvah*, newly religious Jews with no previous training.[105] As we will presently see, while this assessment may be true, it is hardly the whole story. The Americanness of the project is made explicit in numerous instances. For example, the editors call their Schottenstein Talmud translation project an

104 Sherman and Kasnett, "The Schottenstein Edition," 156.

105 "An Interview with Artscroll's Rabbi Nosson Sherman," *Mainline*, June, 10, 2007.

"American" Talmud. In his address at the Library of Congress on February 9, 2005, celebrating the completion of the Talmud translation, Sherman said, "And now, after more than 200 years, that edition, the Latin edition of Baba Kama [owned by Thomas Jefferson] is being joined by a full edition of the Talmud is our language. And it's an *American* contribution. And it's no exaggeration to say that [in] 350 years of Jews in America, in this blessed country, there has not yet been a literary, religious, cultural publishing effort of this magnitude."[106] This definition may be exaggerated but hardly revolutionary. Who would contest maximizing one's access to Torah for both Jew and non-Jew alike? And why would we call that an example of fundamentalism?

Most of the classical Jewish texts produced by ArtScroll were already available in English translation. Thus Sherman's claim that ArtScroll is merely making classical Jewish texts available to readers unable to read the original conceals more than it reveals. Regarding Ḥabad above I suggested that the Jewish fundamentalist war in America is not against secularism *per se* but against non-Orthodox Judaism.[107] Reform Judaism was the template of American Judaism until mid-century, after which it shared that role with Conservative Judaism. Many ultra-Orthodox Jews who immigrated to America after the Second World War held that they did not only arrive in a *treife medinah* (a non-kosher land), they landed in a country dominated by *treife yiddishkeit* (a non-kosher Judaism). There is a story told of the Satmar Rebbe, Teitelbaum, soon after his arrival in New York. He was in a car that passed by a kosher restaurant in the Lower East Side of Manhattan that had a flashing neon sign that read: "Kosher." Teitelbaum turned to his companion and said, "You see, this is *yiddishkeit* in America. Kosher, not kosher, kosher, not kosher." Even though parts of prewar Europe were populated by assimilated Jews, secular Jews, Zionists, and Reform Jews, Orthodoxy was never too far away and still wielded considerable control over Jewish life. This was not the case in America.

Upon their arrival in America, each ultra-Orthodox group responded to non-Orthodox Jews and their institutions in particular ways, yielding the three different forms of American Jewish fundamentalism examined here.

---

106 Nosson Sherman's speech at the Library of Congress, February 9, 2005, cited in Stolow, *Orthodox by Design*, 34. It is unclear from Sherman's speech if he is referring to a "Jewish" literary project of this magnitude or any literary project in America.

107 This would arguably include, by the way, Modern Orthodoxy, if not in principle than surely in practice. On Orthodoxy in America more generally see Jeffrey Gurock, *Orthodox Jews in America* (Bloomington: Indiana University Press, 2009), esp. 48–83, 256–73, 312–25. Cf. my "Is There an Orthodox War against Modern Orthodoxy?" *The New Vilna Review*, July, 2008.

Ḥabad began a missionizing enterprise to expose irreligious (i.e., non-Orthodox) Jews to *yiddishkeit* and *miẓvot*, brilliantly utilizing the magnetism of religious nostalgia and the search for authenticity in postwar multicultural America. Part of that project was making messianism palatable and relevant to American Jews. Satmar exercised its devotion of separation from the satanic claws of Jewish heresy. ArtScroll countered Jewish heresy in America (i.e., non-Orthodox Judaism) though translation and commentary with which they hoped to re-educate American Jews about the true nature of Torah. It is in this sense that ArtScroll is "reactive" and even revolutionary.

In the preface to *Megillat Esther*, ArtScroll's first publication, we read, "Most of us have become indoctrinated with a non-Jewish, anti-Torah version of history."[108] In an essay on ArtScroll Barry Levy remarks, "The prefaces of the various volumes (particularly early ones) and occasional commentaries scattered throughout the work leave no doubt that one of the major interests of the ArtScroll effort is the replacement of certain unacceptable Jewish commentaries."[109] Can we say that according to ArtScroll these ostensibly "Jewish" commentaries are the product of "non-Jewish" version(s) of history? We can see from these as well as other comments that Sherman's assertion that ArtScroll is merely making Hebrew texts available to the non-Hebrew reader is somewhat disingenuous. ArtScroll is attempting to reshape American Jewish thinking about Judaism—to subvert the non-Orthodox ideologies that permeate previous translations—using all the tools and resources at its disposal in the free-market and advertising-obsessed culture of the American marketplace. As Jeremy Stolow shows, through savvy marketing ArtScroll presents its product as non-parochial and integrated into the American "mainstream."[110] Its message, however, is hardly mainstream. Rather, it is an expression of genteel militancy, a slow process of passive coercion through literacy. Is this un-American? Quite the opposite. As Nomi Stolzenberg argues regarding the American context of Satmar separatism, it is liberal democracy that makes such fundamentalism possible, as long as it is presented in a way that is not openly, and legally, coercive.[111] The ArtScroll correlate to Ḥabad's Mitzvah Tank is the Jewish book, very much in accordance with the prewar division between Ḥasidism and Mitnaggedism. The difference, however, is that while Ḥabad's program is driven by its postmillennial messianism, ArtScroll's Jewish book is more about correcting non-Orthodoxy's

108 *Megillat Esther*, xx.
109 Levy, "Our Torah," 167.
110 Stotlow, *Orthodox by Design*, 145–75.
111 Myers and Stolzenberg, "What Does Kiryas Joel Tell Us," 52, 53.

educational program and promoting "Torah-true" Judaism in the Diaspora. It is not driven by any kind of messianic politics.

One more example of this phenomenon, even more explicit than ArtScroll itself, is the multi-volume work on Jewish history by the ultra-Orthodox rabbi from Monsey, New York, Berel Wein. Published by Shaar Press and distributed by Mesorah Press, the original press of ArtScroll, these works offer a history of the Jews fully in accord with ultra-Orthodox doctrine.[112] This is a curious phenomenon. As is well known, ultra-Orthodox Jews traditionally showed little interest in history as a vehicle for religious truth. In many ways, ultra-Orthodoxy, like many other fundamentalisms, rejects history as a legitimate discipline when it comes to understanding its tradition.[113] Yosef Hayim Yerushalmi argues that the interest in Jewish history and historiography represents a rupture in tradition and one sign of the onset of Jewish modernity. While history and historiography were often used by "enlightened" scholars to complicate traditional claims founded on Jewish memory, Wein uses it to defend traditional renderings of Judaism against the professional historians.[114] In this way, Wein uses history to de-historicize Judaism the way ArtScroll uses translation and commentary to counter the modern/heretical approach to the Jewish textual tradition.

Yerushalmi was largely correct when he asserted, "In this sense, if for no other, history becomes what it had never been before—the faith of fallen Jews. For the first time history, not a sacred text, becomes the arbiter of Judaism."[115] It is therefore significant that Wein, an Orthodox rabbi and not a professional historian, undertakes a grand rewriting of the entire trajectory of Jewish history according to the "sacred texts."[116] This squares nicely with ArtScroll's retranslating "sacred texts" according to what they determine is their Torah-true interpretation. Both appear to adhere to Rabbi Mordechai

---

112 This project includes four volumes, *Triumph and Survival 1650–1900*, *Herald of Destiny 750–1650*, *Echoes of Glory 350 BCE–750 CE*, and *Faith and Fate: The Story of the Jewish People in the Twentieth Century*. ArtScroll editors Nosson Sherman and Meir Zlotowitz are mentioned in the acknowledgements to *Herald of Destiny* as having "revolutionized Jewish scholarship through the ArtScroll series."

113 On this see Marc B. Shapiro, *Changing the Immutable: How Orthodox Judaism Rewrites its History* (London: Littman library of Jewish Civilization, 2015).

114 Yosef Hayim Yerushalmi, *Zakhor* (Seattle: University of Washington Press), 90–97.

115 Yerushalmi, *Zakhor*, 86. Yerushalmi notes, "Modern Jewish historiography cannot address itself to those who have never fallen" (98). What would that say about Wein (and ArtScroll's) traditional readership?

116 It is significant to note that the grand narrative of writing history is no longer taken seriously by historians more generally and Jewish historians in particular.

Gifter's comment in his preface to ArtScroll's *Bereshis I* (the first volume of Genesis), "God's Torah may be explained only by the light of Torah."[117] Both ArtScroll and Wein set out to correct the "heretical" rendering of sacred texts sullied by the historical consciousness modernity provided.

One should wonder how much the spirit of Gifter's comment is in accord with the texts of tradition. Speaking only about ArtScroll's Bible translations Barry Levy notes, "In closing off the doors to innovation and sealing them in the face of all external ideas and information, we see an expression of the most revolutionary concept in the entire history of traditional Jewish biblical interpretation."[118] On this reading ArtScroll is a classic example of the *novum* of fundamentalism dressed in the sacred garments of tradition. As others have noted about fundamentalism more generally, the imaginative program of restoration is, in essence, a creative, sometimes radical, project of innovation, even deviance. In addition, the fact that Wein uses "history" and ArtScroll translation as the method of subverting the *treife* Judaism of America, both of which were previously ignored by ultra-Orthodoxy, points to another aspect of the innovativeness of Jewish fundamentalism in America.

ArtScroll flourishes in the pluralistic culture of the American marketplace. But does it present its rendering of tradition as part of that pluralistic universe? Its self-description as "Torah-true" Judaism would seem to suggest that it does not. ArtScroll's "Torah-true" self-fashioning suggests that its presentation of Judaism is both exclusive and ostensibly "authentic" and leaves little room for alternative interpretations, surely not those that depart from Gifter's directive above. Admittedly, this exclusivist mentality is not overt in many of the works (the prefaces to the early works are good places to look for more explicit statements) and remains largely unspoken in the many interviews with its editors. But Sherman's comment that "Jews needed an *authentic* Torah literature in their own language, a literature that was proud and *faithful* to its origins," is quite suggestive (my emphasis).[119] One can assume that the *need* for an authentic literature is a response to a body of literature deemed *inauthentic*. And one can argue that translation is, by definition, inauthentic. Yet translation and commentary are ArtScroll's primary vehicles for the erasure of *inauthenticity*, in other words, its literary war against Jewish heresy. ArtScroll does not exhibit the desperateness or

117 Rabbi Mordechai Gifter (1915–2001) was perhaps the most renowned American-born sage in the Lithuanian school and *rosh yeshivah* of the Telz Yeshivah in Cleveland, Ohio.

118 Levy, "Our Torah," 186.

119 Sherman and Kasnett, "The Schottenstein Edition," 156.

passion of Ḥabad nor the dark ominous quality of Satmar. It does not view itself as standing on the precipice of the messianic era. ArtScroll is engaged in a slow process of re-education. It is trying to save Jews in America from *treife* Judaism, that is, from American Judaism, and replace it with "Torah-true" Judaism, an American Judaism created in its own image. It is concerned with the proliferation of Torah-true values. What that will produce only time will tell.

Sherman suggested in an interview that ArtScroll came "at the right time." This is true but not for the reasons he might have intended. The nostalgic spirit and search for authenticity common among many Americans from the 1960s onward, that gave us everything from the New Thought movement in the early 20th century to the Jesus Freak movement to the Human Potentiality movement to New Age religion to evangelicalism, also created the opportunity for the success of Jewish fundamentalism. America's liberal democracy made this all possible, and the ostensible failure of postwar secularism and liberal religion to offer sufficient solutions to some of the basic individual and collective problems of human existence arguably created the space that ArtScroll and many other groups filled.

Conclusion: How Ḥabad, Satmar, and ArtScroll Contributed to Jewish Americanization

When we think of "Americanization" as the American Jewish project, we often think of progressive Judaism's acculturation and assimilation. This often takes the form of amelioration and accommodation to the ethos of liberal (Protestant) religion and secular culture that is perhaps most prominent in classical Reform Judaism. Here I argued that the turn to multiculturalism and the celebration of diversity beginning in earnest in the late 1970s has created space for a new form of Americanization: the return to tradition. American Jewish fundamentalism is part of that story.

This return to tradition grew out of the counterculture of the 1960s, resulting in the *ba'al teshuvah* movement in the 1970s and 1980s, the return to religious practice in Reform Judaism, and the growth of religious nostalgia in the rise of Ḥabad. A renewed sense of Jewish "difference" was promulgated by radical movements such as Meir Kahane's Jewish Defense League in the late 1960s and very different kinds of inclusive programs such as Birthright Israel in the 2000s.[120] The fundamentalism of Ḥabad, Satmar, and

120 For an insider's view of the Jewish Defense League, see Meir Kahane, *The Story of the Jewish Defense League* (New York: Chilton Books, 1975) Cf. my "Anti-Semitism as

ArtScroll are part of this phenomenon. This is most apparent, and arguably successful, in American Ḥabad and ArtScroll. Ḥabad's programs offer secular Jews a taste of authentic *yiddishkeit* (Jewishness) that has reinvigorated the search for identity among many American Jews. ArtScroll's new Jewish library has provided interested Jews an entryway to tradition, one that does not support their liberal Jewish inclinations but challenges them to use diversity as a vehicle to reaffirm traditional particularity and even chauvinism. It does so by adeptly utilizing every facet of American consumer culture. The ways in which ArtScroll's use of this culture has unwittingly changed its worldview is a topic for another essay.[121]

While many who are touched by Ḥabad or ArtScroll do not become a part of their communities or adopt their fundamentalist ideology, many are given a new sense of Jewish identity through its unapologetic approach that serves as a counter to accomodationalist Jewish alternatives. Satmar is certainly less successful with those outside its closed circle, but they have grown both in size and influence in the past few decades. For example, their strident anti-gay agenda has resonated with some of the Jewish neocons as an "authentic" Jewish response to homosexuality. Most American Jews who are convinced the State of Israel is a positive development are not receptive to Satmar's absolutist anti-Zionist ideology. Yet Satmar's uncompromising practices, devotion to old-world traditionalism, and willingness to confront America's democratic process to achieve their goals of separation have gained moderate respect among some American Jews who have a nostalgic sense of the old-world Judaism they have abandoned.

This new phase of multicultural "Americanization" arguably puts groups such as Ḥabad, Satmar, and ArtScroll in proximity to Christian fundamentalists, surely not in basic beliefs and practices but more subtly in orientation and a commitment to using the secular government and the advantages of religious freedom for the benefit of promulgating their religious ideologies. Ḥabad's *miẓvah* campaign, Menahem Mendel's advocacy of public school prayer (in support of Jerry Falwell), and their claim to the legality of erecting Hanukkah menorahs in the public square; Satmar's claim to the right of state funding in Kiryas Joel; and ArtScroll's re-education of American Jews from an ultra-Orthodox perspective are some examples of how each in their own way are both functioning within the parameters

Colonialism: Meir Kahane's 'Ethics of Violence'" *Journal of Jewish Ethics* 1.2 (Summer, 2015): 231-261.On Birthright Israel, see Shaul Kelner, *Tours that Bind: Diaspora, Pilgrimage, and Israeli Birthright Tourism* (New York: NYU Press, 2010).

121 I discuss this in chapter 7 of my book *American Post-Judaism: Identity and Renewal in a Postethnic Society* (Bloomington: Indianan University Press, 2012).

of the disestablishment clause and challenging its legitimacy in regard to free public worship and support. In the case of Ḥabad and Satmar, their respective views and visions of redemption inform their larger programs not unlike the various kinds of Christian fundamentalisms. Ḥabad, Satmar, and ArtScroll, whether they openly acknowledge it or not, seem to work under the assumption that America is a political and cultural environment traditional Jews have never quite confronted, presenting unprecedented opportunities and unexplored challenges. For each, the nature of America's difference informs the core of their fundamentalist program.

Index of Sources

Index of Names

www.ingramcontent.com/pod-product-compliance
Lightning Source LLC
LaVergne TN
LVHW020504100826
845148LV00003B/697

* 9 7 8 1 6 4 4 6 9 1 1 5 1 *